T0305291

THE POLITICS OF
MIGRANT LABOUR

Understanding Work and Employment Relations

Series Editors: **Andy Hodder**, University of Birmingham and **Stephen Mustchin**, University of Manchester

---

Published in association with the British Universities Industrial Relations Association (BUIRA), books in this series critically engage with issues of work and employment in their wider socio-economic context.

Also available in the series:

The Value of Industrial Relations
Edited by **Andy Hodder** and **Stephen Mustchin**

Labour Conflicts in the Digital Age
A Comparative Perspective
Donatella della Porta, Riccardo Emilio Chesta and **Lorenzo Cini**

Organizing Women:
Gender Equality Policies in French and British Trade Unions
Cécile Guillaume

Forthcoming in the series:

Crises at Work
Economy, Climate and Pandemic
Harriet Bradley, Mark Erickson and **Steve Williams**

Find out more at

bristoluniversitypress.co.uk/
understanding-work-and-employment-relations

THE POLITICS OF MIGRANT LABOUR

Exit, Voice, and Social Reproduction

Gabriella Alberti and Devi Sacchetto

BRISTOL
UNIVERSITY
PRESS

First published in Great Britain in 2024 by

Bristol University Press
University of Bristol
1–9 Old Park Hill
Bristol
BS2 8BB
UK
t: +44 (0)117 374 6645
e: bup-info@bristol.ac.uk

Details of international sales and distribution partners are available at bristoluniversitypress.co.uk

© Bristol University Press 2024

British Library Cataloguing in Publication Data
A catalogue record for this book is available from the British Library

ISBN 978-1-5292-2773-4 hardcover
ISBN 978-1-5292-2775-8 ePub
ISBN 978-1-5292-2776-5 ePdf

The right of Gabriella Alberti and Devi Sacchetto to be identified as authors of this work has been asserted by them in accordance with the Copyright, Designs and Patents Act 1988.

Cover design: Nicky Borowiec
Front cover image: Josue Isai Ramos Figueroa/Unsplash
Bristol University Press uses environmentally responsible print partners.
Printed and bound in Great Britain by CPI Group (UK) Ltd, Croydon, CR0 4YY

FSC
www.fsc.org
MIX
Paper | Supporting
responsible forestry
FSC® C013604

Contents

Series Editors' Preface

We are very pleased to introduce the next volume in this book series, Understanding Work and Employment Relations. *The Politics of Migrant Labour: Exit, Voice, and Social Reproduction* by Gabriella Alberti and Devi Sacchetto is the third text to be published in the series.

This series has been designed as a space for both monographs and edited volumes to highlight the latest research and commentary in the academic field of employment relations. The series is associated with the British Universities Industrial Relations Association (BUIRA), which marked 70 years of existence in 2020. The series seeks to draw on the expertise of the membership of BUIRA and contributions to its annual conference, as well as employment relations academics from around the world. Employment relations is a mature field of study and continues to be of relevance to academic and practitioner audiences alike. BUIRA recognises the broad nature of the field of employment relations, and acknowledges that the field of study is constantly developing and evolving. BUIRA regards employment relations to be the study of the relation, control and governance of work and the employment relationship. It is the study of rules (both formal and informal) regarding job regulation and the 'reward-effort bargain'. These issues remain relevant today, in an era where the standard employment relationship has become increasingly fragmented due to employers' pursuit of labour flexibility, and we see the continued expansion of the gig or platform economy. Employment relations (and adjacent research areas including human resource management and the sociology of work) is taught widely in universities around the world, most commonly in business and management schools and departments. The field of study is multidisciplinary, encompassing law, politics, history, geography, sociology and economics. HRM has a tendency to focus uncritically on management objectives, without exploring issues of work and employment in their wider socio-economic context, and has its disciplinary roots in psychology, whereas employment relations retains a strong critical social science tradition. As scholars in this area we feel that there is a need for regular, up-to-date, research focused books that reflect current work in the field and go further than standard introductory texts. Through this book series, we aim to take an inter-disciplinary approach to understanding work and employment relations, and we welcome proposals from academics across this range of disciplines. We also welcome ideas and proposals from a broad range of international and comparative perspectives in order to reflect the increasingly diverse and internationalised nature of the field both in the UK and globally.

This monograph makes a major contribution to our knowledge of labour mobility and work, adopting an innovative historical and multi-locational perspective that goes beyond the temporally and spatially fixed methodologies seen more frequently. The theoretical themes of the book, in relation to debates on migrant labour, labour turnover, enclaves of differentiated labour, social reproduction and worker power, are drawn out in relation to four 'vignettes' of migration regimes in different parts of the world and different time periods, including the contemporary kafala system in the Persian Gulf, internal migration in China, Ford in the 1910s and migrant women in 1970s Germany.

We hope you enjoy reading this book. If you would like to discuss a proposal of your own, then email the series editors. We look forward to hearing from you.

Andy Hodder and Stephen Mustchin

List of Tables

Acknowledgements

This volume is the outcome of a long-standing collaboration and intellectual exchange. Although we have never conducted fieldwork together, our common passion for investigating contemporary and historical forms of migrant labour and its politics have put us in continuous dialogue on the basis of our results and reflections, finding several points of contact.

Our empirical research, mostly developed in Europe, has certainly helped us to understand the 'bastard place' (Bourdieu, 2004) in which migrant workers find themselves, but with this volume we wish to go beyond a Eurocentric approach to the question of migrant labour, looking at both labour and industrial relations transnationally and across world regions. This book brings together at least a couple of decades of research on migrant workers' experiences as they confront exploitation, precarity, and the effects of state policies across their workplaces and communities. Gabriella Alberti spent four months during the academic year 2016–17 as visiting scholar at the University of Padova (Department of Philosophy, Sociology, Education, and Applied Psychology), where she further developed her research on migrant hospitality work, unions' engagement with migration, and the politics of intersectionality with Devi Sacchetto and his doctoral students. The visit provided a unique opportunity to expand our theoretical debate on the effects of migrant labour turnover as relatively problematic for management, which both of us had already explored in separate papers (Alberti, 2014; Gambino and Sacchetto, 2014).

A critical step for our collaborative research for this volume took place at the International Institute of Social History (IISH) in Amsterdam in February 2020, just a few weeks before the COVID-19 pandemic forced us to withdraw to our homes and work remotely during the subsequent lockdowns. We thank librarians at IISH for their help with accessing the archives, as well as librarians at the Ettore Anchieri Library at the University of Padova, and the Leeds University libraries. We are grateful to Marcel van der Linden, whose encounter at the IISH helped illuminate critical aspects of our reflections, especially regarding our theoretical chapter and the relationship between migration and the welfare state.

A first paper, 'Theorizing Labour Mobility Power Through the Lenses of Migration' was presented in 2019 at the Global Labor Migration: Past and

Present Conference in Amsterdam (20–2 June). Subsequently, we presented our work at the symposium Giornata di Studi sul lavoro imbrigliato, about the legacy of the work of Moulier-Boutang on the continuum of free and unfree labour in capitalism, held at the University of Bologna in dialogue with Sandro Mezzadra, Irene Peano, Martino Sacchi, and others (April 2022). Devi Sacchetto has also presented some of our book chapters at the Labour Transfer Summer School: 'Establishing links between research and labour activism', held in Buggerru, Sardinia, in June 2022 organized by Maurizio Atzeni and Sabrina Perra. We thank all participants at these events for their comments that stimulated deep reflections.

Ongoing discussions with colleagues at the International Labour Process Conference (ILPC), that we both attend every year, have critically contributed to developing our thinking around the everyday practices of control and resistance of migrant workers inside and outside the transnational labour process and dormitory regimes. We are particularly grateful to Chris Smith for being an ongoing source of inspiration and critical reflection in and beyond the ILPC annual conferences.

For the important contributions to our intellectual journey that led to this book we would like to thank Ferruccio Gambino, Valeria Piro, Maurizio Ricciardi, and Francesca Alice Vianello, who have also carefully read some of our draft chapters and provided critical and helpful suggestions. The Labour Mobility in Transition (LIMITS) project team at the Centre for Employment Relations, Innovation and Change (CERIC), University of Leeds, who are working with Gabriella Alberti on the effects of the end of free movement of workers post-Brexit, have also provided critical food for thought on the limits and potential of migrant worker agency vis-à-vis management and state practices. Special thanks go to Chris Forde, who provided earlier comments to the book proposal and introduction, Marketa Dolezalova, Zyama Ciupijus, and Jo Cutter for their ongoing input and support during the making of this book. Thanks to Simon Joyce who has provided helpful and critical feedback to our conceptual tables.

Marek Čaněk has been an ever-helpful interlocutor and in-depth expert on migrant workers, in particular, but not exclusively, in Eastern Europe. Ongoing discussions with Marek about what is happening on a daily basis in critical regions of Europe and his long-standing knowledge were invaluable in the writing of various parts of this volume. Ĺubica Kobová participated in and sometimes endured our discussions and time spent into the research field of Eastern Europe. The many practitioners in the trade union movement and anti-racist campaigners who we met in these past 20 years have given an immense contribution to our thinking for this book.

We are deeply grateful for inspiring us to new ideas in our conversations during these years to our colleagues: Rutvica Andrijasevic; Maurizio Atzeni; Francesco Bagnardi; Carlotta Benvegnù; Mark Bergfeld; Vando

Borghi; Davide Bubbico; Bruno Cartosio; Antonella Ceccagno; Jenny Chan; Sandro Chignola; Sonila Danaj; Alisa Del Re; Neda Deneva; Olena Fedyuk; Costanza Galanti; Giorgio Grappi; Bue Hansen; Jane Holgate; Francesco Eugenio Iannuzzi; Mariya Ivancheva; Ľubica Kobová; Gwyneth Lonergan; Robert MacKenzie; Stefania Marino; Miguel Martínez Lucio; Guglielmo Meardi; Graziano Merotto; Alessandra Mezzadri; Mohammad Morad; Claudio Morrison; Pun Ngai; Dimitris Papadopoulos; Davide Però; Domenico Perrotta; Al Amin Rabby; Maurizio Rasera; Veronica Redini; Lisa Riedner; Anne-Iris Romens; Ru Gao; Maite Tapia; Xanthe Whittaker; Steve Wright; Manuela Zechner; and Yu Zheng.

We have certainly forgotten someone and remain indebted to anyone who has contributed to our decade-long reflections on the politics of migrant labour, and especially those who in the trade unions and other social movements work tirelessly to improve the working lives of our fellow workers by fighting everyday racism, xenophobia, and precariousness.

Finally, we want to thank the reviewers and the team at BUP for bearing with us during the different phases of our work and for the smooth and helpful editorial process they facilitated. We are grateful, of course, to our families who help us keep a sense of place, including baby Etna, who did not kick too hard during the drafting of the final chapter.

Introduction: Migration and Labour Turnover

The question of labour turnover has been variously examined across labour and organization studies but it has not been studied systematically in relation to international migration. In this book we tackle the question of labour turnover (the churning of workers in and out of workplace organizations) from the perspective of migrant labour. Here we build on the critical strands of labour and migration studies to shift our gaze to the social composition of labour (Wright, 2002), focusing on the specific drivers and subjective and social dynamics that link the phenomenon of labour instability to international migration. We consider the relationship between labour migration and turnover as emblematic of the wider effects of the intersectional differentiation of work and employment on workers' lives and action for change in capitalist societies.

Since the pioneering work of Hirschman (1970), the act of workers quitting their job, described as labour mobility or exit, has been countered to worker voice and presented as an individualistic, opportunistic behaviour taken autonomously by workers as opposed to engaging in labour collective voice over effort bargaining (usually expressed through trade union representation). The tendency to see turnover as a primarily individualistic behaviour can be found especially in the field of industrial relations, which privileges collective forms of action in the workplace, whether or not institutionally mediated by trade unions (see Smith, 2006; Beynon, 1973). In the field of organization and management studies, scholars have tended to favour a functionalist approach both to the question of turnover and the role of migration in flexible labour markets revolving around costs and efficiency issues for employers, while employment studies have concentrated on the impact of labour mobility on collective bargaining in the workplace.

Looking at turnover in relation to the transnational movement of workers is of paramount importance today. While the COVID-19 pandemic has left its mark on 2020 as an unprecedented time of low mobility, in 2019 there were 169 million international migrant workers globally (IOM, 2021). Migrant workers are differently distributed geographically, with the US and Europe constituting the largest share among destination countries, and with the Arab

States[1] representing the subregion with the largest quota of migrant workers as a proportion of the entire working population (about 41.4 per cent as compared to 20 per cent in North America) in 2019. Alongside migration for work, family migration should be considered directly or indirectly linked to labour migration, constituting one third of overall permanent flows. Still, among the migrant workers who entered Organization for Economic Cooperation and Development (OECD) countries in 2018 more than 5.1 million were temporary, which represents a continuous upward trend from 2018 into 2019.[2] Temporary migrants are also among those often suffering poorer and relatively more insecure employment conditions as compared to the indigenous counterparts, working the longest hours and earning poverty wages in non-unionized jobs (Castles, 2011; ILO, 2004; OECD, 2019; Pun, 2016; and Strauss and McGrath, 2017).

Migrant working conditions must indeed be analysed in the context of market creation as well as wider regulatory frameworks. As scholars based in Europe, we cannot avoid noticing that the so-called free movement of labour for EU citizens, as well as migration from outside the borders of the European Union (Fiedler et al, 2017), have been and will remain at the core of the ongoing crisis of integration of the EU single market. The response to the recent pandemic has yet again seen nation-states reasserting their sovereign power to shut entry into their territory, even excluding European Union citizens from member countries within the Schengen area (Favell and Recchi, 2020), and yet certain types of mobilities have been allowed, and considered essential, in Europe and internationally, even during lockdowns (for example, Xiang, 2020). Initially, across the world, state governments made a momentous and brutal return to the scene of border controls to respond to the health crisis. Tens of thousands of migrant workers in the Gulf countries lost their jobs and have been either stranded and locked in overcrowded accommodations, detained, or deported back to their countries (IOM, 2021). Meanwhile, in response to the Indian government's enforced national lockdown in March 2020, 7.5 million internal migrants rushed back to their home in the space of two months, with many undertaking their journey on foot, dying on the way due to lack of transport and poor travelling conditions (The Tribune, 2020). In contrast to these forced return migrations and the immobilization of labour, special programmes for the just-in-time supply of seasonal workers deemed essential for the reproduction of the population, such as in farming and fruit picking, were quickly introduced to respond to labour shortages during the peaks of the COVID-19 crisis (Nikolova and Balhorn, 2020; Tagliacozzo et al, 2021; Creţan and Light, 2020).

Against a backdrop of growing tensions or struggles around the question of human mobility and the politics surrounding it, we refocus the debate by wearing the lenses of *labour mobility* and *worker power*. Our aim is to unpack, through a historical and multilocational perspective, the relationship between the movement of people across geographical borders in search of work, their strategies of reproduction and survival as they do so, and the impact of their ongoing movement across labour markets, workplaces, unions, areas of residence, and origins. Far from pretending to offer a comprehensive reconstruction of the history of labour turnover and migration from the 20th century, throughout the book we present particularly illustrative events or moments (what we call vignettes) in the development of labour mobility regimes and in relation to the emergence of 'turnover as an organizational problem' to be managed by employers (March and Simon, 1958), but also: states, and unions.

The OECD has recorded data on labour turnover since the 1970s, looking at the 'distribution of workers by job tenure intervals which is measured by the length of time workers have been in their current or main job or with their current employer'.[3] The Employment Outlook by OECD (1996: 162) distinguishes between job and labour turnover: while job turnover occurs at 'the level of an individual establishment or firm' and corresponds to 'the total number of jobs created less the number of jobs which have disappeared' between two points in time, labour turnover is a more comprehensive figure which comprises 'the movements of individuals into jobs (hirings) and out of jobs (separations) over a particular period'. In this sense labour turnover encompasses job turnover (OECD, 1996: 165). This comprehensive notion of labour turnover is more critical because it recognizes the nature of workers' decisions to leave firms as being independent from firms growing or declining, and in turn being independent from employers' decisions on whether and how to replace workers. Still, there are various limitations to the ways in which official bodies and statistical agencies understand and track labour mobility. Moreover, they do not consider migrant status in relation to labour turnover rate or job tenure. In addition, official measurements of labour turnover take the firm or the economic sector as units of analysis, collecting the data by country, whereby a harmonized dataset allowing for cross-national comparisons of labour turnover rates is still lacking.

Besides national datasets, some limited regional and international level analyses exist. An OECD study from 2009 included statistics on labour turnover for 22 countries, using harmonized data. The annual average labour turnover rate was found to be 33 per cent of total employment between 2000 and 2005 (European Commission, 2010). Differences between countries are usually explained with reference to the degree of employment protection legislation and unemployment insurance (OECD, 1996; EC, 2010). The analysis of the EU Labour Force Survey (LFS) by the EU Commission in 2010 also shows that labour turnover rates change, critically, according to the group demographics, whereby young people tend to experience significantly more 'transitions both in and out of the labour force and between jobs than an average worker',[4] which is interpreted also as the result of the extensive use of temporary contracts for this group. Beyond OECD countries, labour turnover data from the Global South are scarce or irregularly collected, and this omission may be also explained by the strong link between high turnover level and incidence of precarious work in those countries: as Professor Akua Britwum, a Ghanian scholar, responded to an International Labour Organization presentation on precarious employment, at the 2011 Global Labour University Conference, 'What you are calling precarious work [in the Global North] sounds like what we in Ghana call work' (cit. in Mosoetsa et al, 2016: 8).[5]

Knowledge of statistical and institutional definitions is certainly important to identify organizational monitoring processes and institutional responses to the labour turnover. Considering the official national and international statistics, we can identify at least three definitions of labour turnover: as the movement of a single worker between jobs in the labour market; as the churning of workers in a single workplace or industry; and, more generally, as the overall rotation of the workforce in global production processes (as international labour mobility). Besides government and internal bodies, different academic disciplines tend to refer to some of these three aspects or levels neglecting the others. However, in what follows, we move beyond these quantitative measurements of labour mobility as they are mostly concerned with labour market or cost/efficiency measures. In this book, we take into consideration these three different definitions or aspects of turnover in their connection with international labour migration, problematizing the question of labour turnover historically.[6]

One of the central arguments of the book is that the relation between migration and turnover is critical to understand worker struggle over mobility: migrant labour may be used by employers to access docile labour and reduce high turnover, but under different conditions it can also increase voluntary or worker–led turnover, as in the case of migrants who gained mobility rights through freedom of movement and are able to quit their job without losing residence rights or welfare entitlements.

It is indeed because of the differentiation of labour on the one hand (through state regulations of migration, citizenship, or residence status) and on the other, the precariousness generated by intense work and the differential access to welfare and labour protections, that turnover becomes a terrain of social contestation. In other words, we argue that labour turnover constitutes for migrants a first, rough response, not only to degrading and unacceptable working conditions, but also to the forms of racialized and gendered segregation that they are subject to inside and outside their workplaces. These forms of segregation are put in place by management but are sometimes also (directly or indirectly) reproduced by trade unions when they are bargaining and representing the 'vested interests' of their members in the workplace. In fact, labour unions are a source of worker power but in some cases they are also imbricated in racial politics and can be considered themselves as racialized formations (Lee and Tapia, 2021). In other words: the more migrants find hostility in the workplace, and are unable to count on the support of local unions or other political groups, the more they will express their dissatisfaction and seek alternative strategies in the form of labour turnover. Selecting particular cases where tensions around labour mobility are predominantly stark, we show that labour turnover and migration have been historically related: either when employers have used racialized immigrant labour to tame high turnover (at Ford in the early 20th century), or because immigrant labour has caused high levels of turnover and required a substitution of local workers with new groups or with new groups of migrants (from the Gastarbeiter in Germany and the post–World War 2 Bracero programmes in the US, to the kafala system in the Gulf countries).

The shifting maelstrom

The problem of turnover has existed since employment itself, but it has only been explored academically in the last hundred years[7] when excessive labour instability appeared as the result of 'the heavy loss of employees to competitors whose labour policies are more enlightened, who pay higher wages, and who provide more attractive working conditions' (Brissenden and Frankel, 1922: 4).

Since the early 20th century, from the perspective of management studies, labour turnover has been understood 'strictly in reference to the extent of shift and replacement necessary for the maintenance of the workforce' (Brissenden and Frankel, 1922: 7), that is, from the point of view of management-led turnover or retention needs. In the field of management and human resources research, Bolt et al (2022), based on a systematic review of 1,375 articles on voluntary turnover (the largest to date), have called for a holistic theory of turnover to develop a finer understanding of what still remains 'an enigma'. Bolt et al (2022: 569) propose a framework that is 'strategically differentiated, multi-level, and longitudinal', able to overcome important limitations such as the lack of application of existing turnover theories to qualitative case studies, the emphasis on individual rather than contextual factors, and the lack of attention to sector and occupational differences influencing the behaviours of different groups of workers. While remaining primarily concerned with the relative (dis)functionality of voluntary turnover and costs for the firm, this recent review makes the important point of integrating different theories from the social sciences as well as considering more carefully the macro and meso levels: the labour market and more specifically 'the context of changing employment relationships and flexible careers that render loyalty and commitment largely redundant' (Bolt et al, 2022: 571), and the organizational and occupational level respectively. While we do not aim to contribute to management theories, we build on these suggestions by bringing the interdisciplinary insights of migration and sociological research into the study of the labour process and worker mobility as turnover/exit.

From a labour studies perspective, turnover can indeed be measured concretely as the circulation of labour as variable capital in the process of production. In this sense, labour turnover concretely refers not to quantities of variable capital that have completed their churns within a certain period of time, but to the modes and effects of the use of that labour force vis-à-vis capital accumulation (Marx, 1993). While labour scholars have observed these dynamics of labour mobility within the workplace, we extend our gaze to include cross-border mobility.

What does history tell us about the interrelationship between labour turnover and migration? Our review of the literature shows that governments and employers are constantly attempting to coordinate a joint state–capital response to the ongoing uncertainties around labour mobility, whether across borders or workplaces, uncertainties that are expressed by the increase of labour turnover. These efforts have been carried through policies to manage migrant labour across borders and occupations, including contemporary point-based and temporary schemes.

Indeed, if the primary objective of capital is to speed up the churning of labour so that the extraction of surplus is maximized and the cost of labour reproduction minimized (Burawoy, 1976), then the labour force in its concrete form adopts a relatively constant behaviour: that of refusing the intense pace of work tentatively dictated by management. Such individual, and sometimes collective, action of refusal only *appears* as the turnover of labour force (Gambino and Sacchetto, 2014), while in fact it represents the immediate form of protest and resistance against the command of capital over labour and life. Indeed, vis-à-vis the mobility of capital, labour is not merely following or remaining inert. As argued by Guglielmo Meardi (2012b: 105) in his ground-breaking analysis of both the social consequences of EU enlargements to incorporate new Eastern European member states, and the power imbalances between capital and labour's differential mobilities, 'the common assumption that mobility is a prerogative of capital but not labour has been shown to be inaccurate, and this has not failed to impact on power relations between capital and labour'.

The analysis of the churning/rotation of the labour force brings to light the need for a continuous mobility of living labour in order to sustain the labour process. This mobility has often been subject to a variety of controls by a range of private and public actors: states, local authorities, recruitment agencies, formal and informal brokers, employers, migrants' communities, and networks. The ways in which capital has historically attempted to entrap or bridle wage labour is certainly instructive of such relationships, an aspect that is considered throughout the book as we look at the actions of multiple agents and their infrastructures in the management of migration (Xiang and Lindquist, 2014).

Historically, the endless processes of primitive accumulation and rapid industrialization have often generated high labour mobility to support the needs of enterprises (Fisher, 1917; Douglas, 1959). Since the 16th century, capital has sought to continuously access and replenish sources of labour, both mobilizing workers and/or expanding across differentiated geographies of production and starting new processes of accumulation (Harvey, 1989). We may understand these processes in terms of options or strategies available to capital, whereby the first option to access labour is precisely by obtaining workers through migration, as labour mobilization under capitalism is intimately connected to the movement of workers across borders for the sake of capital (Hofmeester and van der Linden, 2018; van Rossum and Kamp, 2016; Linebaugh and Rediker, 2000). In the fascinating reconstruction by Bridget Anderson (2013), the disciplining of the vagrant population and of the poor, the codification of the slavery of Amerindians and African Americans, and the reintroduction of forms of servitude in Eastern Europe were all mechanisms that allowed for a better surveillance and confinement of the labour force between 1600 and 1700. And yet this history was not the only one of forced migration and subjugated racialized people.

One of the first and most significant examples of labour mobilization can be found in the forced labour of African migrants in the transatlantic slave trade from the 16th century.[8] The slave trade from about 1500 to the mid-19th century encompassed about 12 million people, mainly from western Africa to the Americas, and developed particularly to expand the availability of the necessary workforce and to substitute Amerindian and indentured European workers.[9] The turnover for Amerindians and indentured European workers had higher costs than mobilizing African slaves, because the former held power to quit thanks to their good knowledge of the surrounding environment which facilitated escape, while European indentured labourers enjoyed greater freedom and rights than slaves (Moulier-Boutang, 1998). However, also for the slaves, the first and foremost form of resistance, organized 'from sundown to sunup' (Rawick, 1972), were runaways, individually or in groups, although for them the chances of successful escape were lower. Planters gradually learned about the importance of the composition of the labour force to manage their plantations since workers' common socio-economic conditions provided a source of elemental unity among them – at a time when forms of racialization were not yet refined to maintain rigid internal hierarchies (Breen, 1973). Thus, the strong institutionalization of slavery at the end of the 17th century in the so-called New World may be seen as a response to the forms of labour resistance and turnover of the Amerindians and later of the European indentured workers and African American slaves. The resistance and revolts of African American slaves expanded the demand for Asian indentured labour as well as for European migrants, indentured or not.[10] After the abolition of the slave trade by Great Britain (1807), this request increases, and gets stronger after the abolition of slavery in the British colonies (1833) and in the United States (1865). Labour turnover represents, in this sense, the possibility of escape from the lynch law, flee from exploitation or social oppression, and even the struggle for a better life. Against the multiple labour regimes built around the world, workers put in place forms of mobility by building maroon communities, moving to other countries, or turning to other identities and jobs. Sooner or later capitalists and governments learn that workers, even in the more coercive situations, resist and organize themselves.

It was the pioneering work of Moulier-Boutang (1998) that highlighted that as soon as waged labour was created from the 16th century, it immediately appears in its form with a Janus face, that is, half free, half constrained. In fact, 'free' wage labour is channelled from its birth through the legal mechanisms enforced by colonial powers (and capital) to govern the mobility of the labour force. This oscillation points to the historically blurred boundary between free and unfree labour (Steinfeld and Engerman, 1997). The ambivalent nature of wage labour in this context is articulated by Moulier-Boutang in his understanding of labour as a continuum from the slave labour of the modern era, through the indentured labour of the colonies, to the free waged labour of the industrial era until today. According to this interpretation of the history of the commodification of human labour, indentured labour should not be considered as a form of pre-capitalist labour as compared to the contemporary form of waged employment, but as both being part of the same continuum, of the same process of exploitation.

If free labour nowadays represents the prevalent form of migration, various systems of coercion and segregation continue to debase the conditions of migrant workers, through temporary recruitment schemes, postings, and other migration regimes as state-managed circulatory labour migration (Buckley, 1995; Lillie and Greer, 2007; Pun, 2005; Morrison et al, 2020; Parreñas, 2022). Institutional controls on the right of free residence are still a primary factor in lowering the conditions of migrant workers across all countries. And yet, long distance recruitment remains the main device to compensate for high turnover in generally low-appeal sectors, such as agriculture, construction, and in-person services, that cannot be relocated overseas (Stalker, 2000).

Together with the mobilization of labour, a second option or strategy for capital to access (cheap) labour is through the relocation of production (or spatial fix, see Harvey, 1989; Silver, 2003).[11] Although indirectly linked to migration, this strategy of capital accumulation has been widespread in particular since the 1950s, when US investments started to aim towards less unionized areas within the country, such as Indiana and Tennessee, and later towards Asian and Latin American countries (Cowie, 1999), where a young and low-wage workforce, low taxation, and freedom from pollution controls could breathe life into capital. The *maquiladora* system based on cross-border foreign direct investment (FDI) in Mexico provided a case in point (Sklair, 1989; Hutchinson et al, 1997). Work in outsourced plants did not deter migration; on the contrary, it stimulated it by disrupting traditional local economies while imposing at best modest pay and working conditions, and thus familiarizing workers with the motivational and economic structures of the US (Williams and Passe-Smith, 1989; Sassen, 1996). Since the 1990s, a similar process of relocation has developed in Europe; it was characterized by the dislocation of distinctive economic activities from Western to Eastern Europe and a corresponding segmentation of labour market conditions (Ellingstad, 1997). As has emerged in the first thirty years of political and economic freedoms in Eastern Europe, workers have elected exit as their primary form of resistance to the post-1989 restructuring (Meardi, 2007), prompting employers to design tighter forms of control, such as subcontracting and new migration policies. At the beginning of November 2022, the Romanian government, for example, approved new legislation restricting the rights of non-EU workers, including the obligation for migrants to obtain the written consent of their first employer in order to change jobs during the first year of their labour contract (Dumitrescu, 2022). And yet, as in the past, migrant workers are unlikely to accept the place assigned to them by employers and destination country authorities (Castles, 2006).

The two options for capital are interrelated, since relocation of production also necessitates the mobilization of new labour, making the process far from smooth for the state and for corporations. These relations of mobility do not correspond with unidirectional or regular patterns. As also argued by Harvey (2018: 385) there is an irregularity springing from the intrinsic contradiction between and within capital and labour as opposite forces in capitalist social relations, as they are rather 'forced into curious patterns of struggle and compromise over the geographical mobility of labour'. Rather than clear directionalities, it is the fluctuating and mutually influencing movement of workers and capital that seem to characterize the past decades of globalization of both labour and investment flows (Alberti, 2019).

However, we suggest that in addition to the institutions that manage these mobilities, attention should be drawn to workers' ways of life and struggles that tend to constitute themselves as social spheres on the basis of which they renegotiate their conditions of existence. In the public arena one still notices the political and social response by those who resist *this vortex* (the 'maelstrom' of capital), that is, the process where capital tends to reduce the workforce to a simple bearer of labour to be consumed: from the fugitive slave in the Americas to those who still migrate against the dictates of capitalist accumulation. As in the past for fugitive slaves, 'the strongest expression of individuality coincides with the most powerful manifestation of collective action. It is within this nexus that the possibility of overthrowing the barriers of discrimination is situated.' (Gambino and Sacchetto, 2014: 118–19).

Contradicting the simplistic binary view between individual and collective action, Lucassen and van Voss (2019) stress that between 1600 and 1850, not only deserters ran away in groups, but individual runways also depended on collective networks. Furthermore, the experience of one person could support others 'to vote with their feet', because every worker running away represents someone who was able to break dominant constraints, while directly or indirectly supporting the spread of radical ideas (Linebaugh and Rediker, 2000). In this way we stress how mobility may be considered itself as a form of protest: in the words of Marcel van der Linden (2008: 179), 'the transition between 'running away' and 'fighting for better working conditions' is in reality rather fluid'. Following this approach, we are interested in exploring the continuum of mobility and worker power through the lenses of international migration.

Beyond nationalistic perspectives

This book tackles the question of labour mobility and engages with theoretical debates across different fields of the social sciences, with sociologists of work and labour researchers as primary interlocutors. The starting point of this book is that understanding the struggles around labour mobility and immobility today is a necessary endeavor for scholars of work and migration alike. In our effort to bridge labour and migration studies, one of the key insights that a labour approach to international migration may adopt is the critique of methodological nationalism. Far from indicating simply nationally-based research, we follow   Çağlar and Glick Schiller's definition of methodological nationalism, understood as:

> an intellectual orientation that approaches the study of social and historical processes as if they were contained within the borders of individual nation-states. … [M]ethological nationalists confine the concept of society within the boundaries of nation-states and assume that the members of these states share a common history and set of values, norms, social customs, and institutions. (Çağlar and Glick Schiller, 2018: 3)

As we will show, moving from methodological nationalism to an approach that takes into consideration how specific localities and local labour regimes (Baglioni et al, 2022) intersect with global dynamics is an essential step to move away from many of the biases and myopia of the social sciences and employment and labour studies, specifically vis-à-vis international migration. The studies of human geographers Wimmer and Glick-Schiller (2003), and more recently Glick Schiller and Çağlar (2011), have been path-breaking in illuminating the persistence of the ethnic lens and of the privileging of transnational communities, rather than transnational social fields, as fundamental categories in migration studies.[12] Indeed, the point of view of the destination country and the nation-state has remained dominant in Western migration studies, constraining research in the field and attention to processes of social change (see also Castles, 2010).

As we illustrate in the book, if migration studies have reproduced the ethnic lens, this is even more the case for industrial relations scholarship, which has maintained a national prejudice in terms of selecting the boundary of the nation-state. In this way, the nation-state remains both a primary terrain of joint-regulation with national-level actors, and a key player in social dialogue on work and employment (Giles, 2000; Meardi, 2012a). Paradoxically, even the more enlightened and migration-sensitive literature in industrial relations has remained concerned with the questions of governments, employers, and union control over the borders of national labour markets, and the 'impact' of migration *on* national markets and national union strategies (Penninx, 2017; Marino et al, 2017a). More broadly, most of comparative industrial sociology and global political economy (see Afonso and Devitt, 2016) maintain the nation-state, its institutional system of employment relations, and the national welfare state (Alesina et al, 2004) as the main unit of analysis, whether or not they are considered victim or under threat from the effects of international migration flows on local workers and citizens.[13] Further, methodological nationalism in migration research widely intertwines with Eurocentric or Westernized approaches to migration and labour research, whereby empirical studies appear largely concentrated in the Global North (King et al, 2011). Denaturalizing the categories of 'nation' and 'space', we support an approach that 'considers the simultaneity of the transnational practices of individuals, organizations and institutions taking place in multiple localities' (Amelina and Faist, 2012: 2).

Whether or not a country's government represents its own national borders as more or less porous according to the needs of the time, we argue that their labour market has never been purely national, in the sense that at least since the origin of the capitalist era, any market has been structured by the possibility for employers to meet their labour demand by mobilizing workers worldwide. As Tilly and Tilly (1998) argue, labour markets are not homogeneous or defined entities, but open systems that can be affected by various factors, and particularly by mobility.

Labour markets today are certainly less prone to slavery and serfdom than their predecessors in the 18th and 19th centuries and up to 1920 when high rates of labour mobility were the norm (Jacoby, 1983: 261). It is no coincidence that the first explicit treatment of the question of labour turnover is found at the beginning of the 20th century, when large enterprises in the US were confronted by exponential growth (over 300 per cent) in the rates of turnover (Alexander, 1917; Slichter, 1919), but also by increasing levels of cross-border migration.[14] In response, they started developing new personnel strategies to counter such movements, and retained or attracted new labour forces in a context of increasing inter-firm competition over labour supply.

In contrast to methodological nationalism, we believe that any treatment of the topic of migration demands a global perspective (Hofmeester and van der Linden, 2018), for the simple reason that the migrant workers move from and to an extremely wide range of countries according to historically accumulated differences and inequalities (Federici, 2004). In short, they operate in highly differentiated local contexts, bringing with them a multiplicity of experiences not only of the different working regimes, but also of the strategies of their mobility (exit), of resistance (voice), *and* of self-organization in the terrain of social reproduction.

Migration studies have developed a critical research agenda on human mobility by looking at the variety of subjective and objective factors moving people across the globe, and at the socio-economic and cultural implications of such inter/transnational movements in terms of policy, identities, everyday practices of reproduction, family, and ethnic relations (Miller and Castles, 2009; King et al, 2010; Hoang and Yeoh, 2015; De Genova, 2017). However, the field of labour studies has only recently appreciated the importance of studying migration as a distinctive topic. In the words of McGovern (2007), it is quite ironic if not paradoxical that Western industrial relations have remained disinterested in migration for many decades, if we consider that one of the primary reasons for people to move is linked to work. In other words, the implications of migration concern all workers, regardless of their citizenship.

The contribution of migration studies has been essential to throw some light on the complex factors shaping the interlocking of mobility and immobility (for example, Xiang, 2020). Differently from migration scholars, however, we privilege the point of view of labour mobility rather than human mobility, qualifying our field in terms of our interest in the history of worker struggles (Silver, 2003; van der Linden, 2008) and the question of labour indeterminacy (Edwards, 1990; Smith, 2006). We distance ourselves from 'classless studies' of migration and transnationalism, particularly those that assume a falsely universal 'middle-classness' of all individuals on the move (Conradson and Latham, 2005a; Favell, 2008), problematizing the relations between class and migration historically (van der Linden, 2008; Papadopoulos et al, 2008).

Furthermore, we take a critical stance towards the labour and political economy scholarship that reproduces a structuralist or functionalist approach towards migration, whereby migrant workers tend to be depicted as merely economically driven and self-interested individuals, 'greasing the wheels' of the labour markets of destination countries (Ruhs, 2006a; McCollum and Findlay, 2015); or unilaterally moved by sending states as sources of remittances to benefit the economy of the home country; or as 'hopping' from country to country with the aim of financial maximization, as atomized individuals detached from their wider communities and households, 'dancing on the tune of the wage differentials' (Rogers, 2009: 45).

Overall, in terms of the relationship between labour turnover and migration, it is without doubt that the very nature of work and the specific working conditions experienced by the workers – whether repetitive, precarious, with low wages, and highly disciplined, are key factors in explaining why workers decide to quit their jobs across different historical periods and degrees of labour market fluidity. However, in what follows, we endorse Jacoby's (1983) approach highlighting the importance of the compositional analysis of the workforce, by paying attention to the specific race, legal, and gender differentiation of workers at a certain time and place. Our aim is to understand the dynamics of labour mobility today and how it interacts with historically specific forms of 'race management' of different groups of workers (Roediger and Esch, 2012), as well as with its gendered dimensions, hitherto seldom considered (Chapman and Prior, 1986; Theodossiou, 2002). Indeed, the history of controls over the movement of populations is a long one, because mobility modifies the composition of the workforce and critically impacts on the management of workplaces and on the forms of worker agency. This emphasis on the labour composition of turnover across jobs, industrial sectors, and global production processes allows us to explore the specific relationship between the recruitment and management of migrant labour, the control of labour mobility, and worker struggles.

Four lenses to understand the turnover of migrant labour

Our approach to the question of labour turnover moves away from mainstream economic and management/human relations approaches, mostly concerned in measuring the flows of the individual movement of workers in and out of workplaces and industries, and their costs for organizations. We rather adopt a holistic and critical approach that considers the mobility of workers multi-dimensionally (in terms of individual job changes, churn within an industry, and the rotation of labour in global production processes), which takes into account both the wider social factors and subjective drivers of such mobilities. In particular, starting from a wider consideration of the structural constraints that capitalist accumulation imposes on labour mobility, we privilege four crucial lenses across migration and labour studies to understand the dynamics and effects of the turnover of migrant labour, namely rising from the labour process theory (LPT), the autonomy of migration, social reproduction theory(s), and industrial relations. Such an interdisciplinary framework is necessary, we believe, to investigate the question of labour mobility across the cited dimensions, and to explore the workplace, national borders, the community, and the institutional spheres of mobility negotiations respectively.

The first lens follows the assumption of LPT that acknowledges the existence of 'structured' antagonism as constitutive of the capital–labour relation (Edwards, 1990; Thompson and Smith, 2001; Elger and Smith, 2005). As Chris Smith (2006: 392) put it: 'labour power has two elements, the power over work effort and the power to move between firms'. In his work, Smith (2010) developed a flow approach to labour power that understands it in relation to wider issues of labour mobility and its management by states and other actors. The flow approach emphasizes the importance of the impact of free wage labour on capital controls and the freedom of movement of individual workers in and out of work (see also, Smith, 2015; Pun and Smith, 2007). We think this approach should consider not only free wage, but also unfree or semi-free labour (slavery, indentured, and tied to temporary work permit; see Sarkar, 2017) since workers developed agency and were able to open spaces of negotiability even in harsh situations (Strauss and McGrath, 2017; Coe and Jordhus-Lier, 2011).

The second lens builds on Chris Smith's theorization of labour mobility power grappling with the problem of the transformation of living labour power into expendable labour effort (Deutschmann, 2002), from the point of view of migrant labour strategies of mobility as an instance of freedom and rebellion from capital controls (for example, Alberti, 2014; Andrijasevic and Sacchetto, 2016; Morrison et al, 2013). These latest approaches have drawn from a view of migration as a social force that is larger than mere economic motivation and that follows an autonomous logic beyond capital needs, by nodding to the autonomy of migration perspective (Mezzadra, 2004; Bojadžjev et al, 2007; Papadopulos et al, 2008). Our study shows how labour turnover can therefore be understood as a manifestation of this antagonistic and unequal relationship, where the subjectivity of migrants alongside capitalist dynamics of production and reproduction plays a critical role.

Throughout history, the work considered outside the parameters of production has often been associated with marginalized and oppressed subjects, such as slaves, children, colonial and postcolonial migrants, and women. Instead, our third perspective pays attention to social reproduction, namely all the activities that facilitate the maintenance and reproduction of a labour force (Picchio, 1992), and capitalist society and life as a whole (Katz, 2001), as strictly connected with every worker experience. In so doing, we emphasize that social reproduction is not just another way of conceptualizing domestic or care work. All these activities are interlinked with labour processes, both when they are shaped by the system of production in a specific location, and when they in turn shape workplace relations. As the different welfare regimes highlight, class relations are developed in the double dimension of the labour and reproduction processes. Capitalists are aware that the localization of their investments have to take into account the practices related both to work processes and to social reproduction, alongside global supply chains (Tsing, 2009). Reproductive practices can in fact constitute a crucial element in the forms of organization and worker mobilization as they develop at a political and economic level (Laslett and Brenner, 1989).

Finally, with regard to the industrial relations lens, in the past decade we have noticed a growing interest in the question of labour mobility and international migration across industrial sociology and employment relations (Pun, 2016; Bal, 2016; Martínez Lucio and Connolly, 2010; MacKenzie and Forde, 2009), including the working experiences of asylum seekers and refugees (Bakker et al, 2017; Tören, 2018), trade unions' efforts to integrate migrant workers (Adler et al, 2014; Tapia and Turner, 2013; Marino et al, 2017a; Ford, 2019), diversity and equality strategies in organizing workers (Holgate, 2005), and emerging theorizations on how labour systems of regulation are related to international migration (MacKenzie and Martínez Lucio, 2019). Despite this renewed interest in migration, however, very few have looked at the different dimensions of migrant labour regimes worldwide and at their implications for employment relations. We deem it necessary to span the fields of production and social reproduction as criss-crossed by tensions and struggles (Cravey, 2004). Furthermore, some fundamental biases and erasures remain in the field of industrial relations that create opacity in fully understanding migrant labour and migrants' constraints to access voice in the workplaces, as well as to articulate their multifarious forms of resistance. This erasure needs to be traced back to the ways in which turnover has been negatively associated with migration and variously racialized (Roediger and Esch, 2012). Even within the more radical tradition of industrial sociology, while turnover and quitting have been recognized as valid expressions of conflict over the 'frontier of control', of capital over labour (Edwards and Scullion, 1982), there is a tendency to stigmatize all forms of mobility as individualistic behaviour primarily responsible for a race to the bottom in working conditions (Cremers et al, 2007; Krings, 2009). Such mobility power has also recently been considered in contrast with the experiences of indigenous workers, who are rather deemed lacking such capacity (Thompson et al, 2013).

While the effects of immigration controls on dividing workers and making migrants more vulnerable are increasingly recognized by national union confederations (for example, Crawford, 2020), the emphasis of the trade union literature remains on the negative effects that mobility, turnover, and immigration policies have on 'unionizing potential' in the workplace. Fixated on the role of unions in controlling demand and supply in the labour market and monitoring state borders, or in integrating by servicing migrants according to their specific issues, labour scholars do not seem to pay enough attention to the hindering effects of immigration controls on worker voice and on their opportunities to resist in the workplace. The extensive research by Anderson (2010), as well as Fudge and Strauss (2014), have clearly shown how statutory and regulatory systems of labour mobility and citizenship produce 'institutionalized uncertainty' for migrant workers, where the temporariness of the work permit, and dependency on the employers, limit migrant labour chances of unionization or any other form of collective and individual voice (see also, Novitz, 2009; Rigo, 2005). The issues of migration, worker mobility, and quitting practices by workers continue therefore to represent a contested terrain and a somewhat unresolved issue, especially in the sociology of work and industrial relations, which are specific areas of our research. We believe that labour scholars can profit from research in migration studies and human/labour geography. We illustrate below how we tackle these distinctive issues in the book and the specific arguments we develop across five chapters and the conclusion.

Structure of the book

In Chapter 1 we explore the theoretical debate, reviewing the primary approaches to the study of labour mobility across migration and employment studies. Alongside the critical review of wider theory of capital and labour mobility, the aim of this chapter is to reinterpret labour mobility through the lenses of migration research. We show how underpinning most of the debates on migrant labour in both the political economy and labour studies literature is a tendency to reproduce methodologically nationalist frameworks, that tend to ostracize migrants and their mobility as the external and dangerous outsider, from which to protect a romanticized and sedentaristic view of the working class. In contrast, we point out the contributions of both critical migration and feminist studies in human geography, and the autonomy of migration (Mezzadra and Neilson, 2013; Karakayali and Bojadžijev, 2007; De Genova, 2017; Papadopoulos and Tsianos, 2013), to overcome the functionalist framing of migration labour, as well as homogenizing views of worker identities and solidarity. Rather than seeing the migrant as 'the other', we embrace mobility as foundational for both migrant and non-migrant workers (Çağlar, 2016). In this chapter we show the ambivalence of turnover in terms of the relative advantage for either workers or employers according to the state of the labour market, the sector, or other circumstances. We also show that, contrary to mainstream readings, voluntary turnover as worker escape from poor conditions can be understood as an expression of conflict, as well as and in particular by migrant workers, moving beyond binary views of individual vs collective forms of resistance (compare Hirschman, 1970; Edwards and Scullion, 1982).

As we highlight in the logistics of living labour (Chapter 2), labour turnover may assume a relatively orderly or disorderly character under different economic and social circumstances, since the relation between migration and turnover may be variable as they highlight different interests for the management and exercise of mobility by multiple actors. Migration controls and the state regulation of mobility have in fact often been aimed at limiting migrants' mobility across jobs and occupations – and ideally, forcing them go back to their countries when they are no longer needed: from the temporary migration programmes of the 1970s in Europe and their reappearance in contemporary migration policy in the Global North (Ruhs, 2006b), to the spread of temporary programmes in East Asia and the Gulf today (Liu-Farrer and Yeoh, 2018; Bal, 2016). Since the 2000s, the debate on international migration has stressed how employers, labour brokers, and intermediaries move workers 'from above' (Xiang and Lindquist, 2014), thanks also to the support of states that enforce migration controls (Castles, 2011) through visa and residency regulations. However, labour mobility cannot be considered only from the point of view of the constraints, as migrants build their own infrastructures to gain and sustain their mobility (Ciupijus et al, 2020). Similarly, the mobility practices of migrants need to be understood in relation to their experiences of the labour process and the nature of work (Alberti, 2014).

Labour scholars have tended to highlight how it is often the intense nature of the labour process (Chapter 3) and poor working conditions that cause high labour turnover, and how such situations require the 'expansion' of the labour market through the import of foreign labour or labour from a different location in the same country. High salaries and welfare policies may be alternative strategies to retain the labour force at the enterprise level, and yet such strategies may be limited to a certain period and can be practiced only when an enterprise has a monopoly of a certain technology or skills.[15] Moreover, past research has shown that is it difficult to identify a certain level of wages by which it is possible to make up for repetitive and demanding work. Peña (1997: 57) argues as well that the employer may not be interested in improving working conditions in the first place, whether because technological levels may be difficult to improve in that particular sector, or because the costs of machinery outweigh that of higher wages for workers. Etienne Balibar (1974)[16] highlights how technological innovation, the 'parcelling out' and intensification of labour, are strictly linked with labour mobility, influencing each other, because they are part of the same process. As other historical sources have shown (Gambino and Sacchetto, 2014), the spatial fix (Silver 2003; Harvey 1989; 2018), operated by multinationals through the developing of long supply chains sometimes located in Export Processing Zones (EPZs), employs migrant workers in repetitive, routine, and simplified labour processes that require a constant daily renewal of the workforce. Scholars stress how young unmarried women in the Global South are often preferred because they are cheap, docile, and come with a low level of labour turnover (Fernández-Kelly, 1983; Elson and Pearson, 1981). However, as we argue, migrant and (often) women workers, employed in what we call enclaves of differentiated labour (EDL) dotted along global supply chains and concentrated in the Global South, put in place 'oppositional tactics' (Ong, 1997) and struggles that emerge through a multi-sited form of collective and individual resistance (Pun, 2005). With the notion of EDL, we therefore contribute to a labour-centered approach to the functioning of Global Production Networks (Newsome et al, 2015) by introducing an intersectional analysis of the migrant workforce put to work in these 'free' zones, and by providing a deeper understanding of how a differentiated regulation of labour mobility shapes the unique character of these areas in the Global South and their control regimes, and partly in the precarizing migrant sectors of the North, as well as workers' resistant practices.

In Chapter 4, we argue that the realm of social reproduction (Katz, 2001) is a necessary field of analysis of migrant practices if we want to understand the tensions of migrant labour and labour turnover, but that it has been overlooked by labour scholars. Our overview of cases shows a tendency whereby the lower the cost of social reproduction for the individual worker (for example, a migrant worker without a family to support in loco, or without the need to send remittances back home), the higher the labour turnover. The other side of this argumentation is indeed the one developed by the labour sociologist Michael Burawoy, who as early as 1976, while researching the system of migrant labour in South Africa and at the Mexican frontier with the US, showed how the geographical separation of reproduction and maintenance of labour produces a reduction of the costs for employers. In other words, the family of the migrant back in the country/area of origin was responsible for reproducing the life of the worker and future workers. While these insights have been path-breaking in understanding the continuous exploitation of workers across the two spheres, our perspective moves beyond structuralist approaches to social reproduction that have hitherto concentrated on the role of migration in saving employers' labour reproduction costs. We point to the frictions that migrant labour can create on the terrain of social reproduction, that is both within and beyond the labour process. Social reproduction indeed needs to be understood transnationally through the everyday practices of migrants. The control of reproduction emerges again in the way migration policies prevent migrant families from reuniting or exclude migrants from access to welfare benefits.[17] By bridging the spheres of production and reproduction, our historical and multilocational analysis shows that migrant mobility practices and their political potential should be understood beyond a narrow focus on the workplace and the point of production as the only one shaping worker action.

On migrant organizing (Chapter 5) we show how the 'problem of turnover' has influenced the ways in which temporary migration has been variously stigmatized, including within the labour movement, through processes of racialization and gendering, with migrants often left at the margins or outside of union structures, or at best incorporated in special committees while unions ignored any appeal to an in-depth understanding of migration and racial issues. Our starting point is that because of the persistence of nationalist frameworks of integration and the ideology of the universalism of working-class unity, trade unions in Western countries, but also in other world regions, have reproduced the marginality of migrant labour. Despite some initiatives by traditional unions to support migrant workers' empowerment, migrant and precarious workers have organized to create new forms of representation inside and outside union structures by exposing major cracks in the system of labour representation, already in crisis. Migrants have developed industrial action or have organized their own resistance both in collective and individual forms, despite their temporary status as casual workers, through either union internal structures, or via NGOs, or by setting up their own unions (Alberti, 2016; Iannuzzi and Sacchetto, 2020; Però, 2020; Peano, 2017; Weghmann, 2022). With increasing mobility across borders in different world regions, some local unions as well as global confederations have become more sensitive to migration, by accepting the need to tackle the realities of mobility and transnationalism, and by carrying out more or less successful attempts at creating migrant branches (Rogalewski, 2018) or transnational union networks (for example, Meardi, 2012a). Non-union actors in these efforts appear to have played a critical role particularly in the Asian regions, where migrants experience extreme forms of precariousness (Ford, 2019), opening up industrial relations to a multiple- and hybrid-actors perspective, with the potential to radically renew labour organizing. Their attention has gone to bottom-up approaches, highlighting democratic participation rather than mere greenfield recruitment (McAlevey, 2016; Holgate et al, 2018). Overall, recent grass-roots initiatives across Europe, the US, and beyond, in poorly unionized and fragmented sectors, show new patterns of the autonomous self-organization of migrants within and outside traditional union structures, indicating the rise of migrant-led radical unions (Moyer-Lee and Lopez,

2017; Cillo and Pradella, 2018) amidst the wider crisis of institutional unionism and the decline of collective bargaining. We note that despite the theoretical developments with the incorporation of mobility into the labour process framework, and despite the increasing interest of industrial relations in migration, the consideration of the concrete effects of migration controls over the working lives of migrant workers remains limited for both industrial relations scholars and union practitioners. It is time for industrial relations scholarship and practice, we suggest, to take the issue of labour mobility fully into account, analysing more carefully migrant worker organizing.

Our theoretical argument that is developed in the final chapter (Conclusion) suggests that the critique of the trade union approach to migrant workers needs not only focus on migrant collective action or agency (Arnholtz and Refslund, 2019; Milkman, 2020), but on a broader rethinking of our understanding of worker power (van der Linden, 2008) through the lens of migration. With this aim, in our concluding chapter we reinterpret Wright's (2000) forms of power, including new insight on mobility bargaining power, and discuss it in relation to the question of migrant labour turnover. Considering the relevance of migrants' own mobility bargaining power (Strauss and McGrath, 2017: 203) as one form of labour market power (Silver, 2003), we renew Erik Olin Wright's traditional framework showing how, in the context of the complex logistic of migrations, the ongoing crisis of social reproduction (Mezzadri, 2019), and the tightening of racialized and gendered (im)mobility regimes across an increasingly uncertain world, turnover emerges again as a critical practice of escape and resistance for workers. As immigration controls and growing precariousness critically hinder migrant voice and autonomy in the workplace, the 'power' of turnover, and what we identify as *social labour mobility power* transcending individualistic views of migrant mobility practices, may encourage unions to fully confront the question of temporariness and mobility of the workforce by building multiple and hybrid forms of solidarities also involving the reproductive sphere. We therefore present our theorization of labour turnover through the lenses of migration by looking at the *continuum* of migrants' mobility struggles, encompassing both the individual and the collective realms, as well as the fields of production and social reproduction. The question of unions' organizational renewal to strengthen internal democracy, sustain their dynamic aggregation with other forms of worker organizations, and truly open up industrial relations to the realities of transnational mobilities, constitutes the pragmatic horizon of our inquiry.

1

Theorizing Labour
Mobility Power

Introduction: migration and labour turnover as contested terrains

In this chapter we take a journey across different literature streams to review the origins of the study of labour turnover in the nascent modern factory of the early 20th century, to then move on to approaches to turnover and mobility power (Smith, 2006), and that of migrant workers in particular, across labour process theory (LPT), comparative political economy (CPE), and critical migration scholarship (CMS). We explore the parallel (and ambivalent) efforts of capital at both facilitating and constraining mobility in the history of 'labour capture' (Smith, 2006: 397), and in relation to the mobilities of capital (Harvey, 2018; Sassen, 1990; Brenner, 1998). The relatively unfree nature of labour in capitalism, showing elements of continuity with pre-capitalist forms of labour control (van der Linden, 2008; Moulier-Boutang, 1998), helps in understanding why workers have always engaged with mobility strategies in the forms of desertion, migration, and quitting to counter or diminish exploitation (van Rossum, 2018).

While the following chapters will focus on specific cases and locations of labour migration and the management of labour flows in different world regions, we need to first grapple with the theoretical debates that have emerged from the study of the relationship between labour mobility (as labour turnover) and international migration, looking at theorizations of the mobility and fixity of labour in relation with those of capital. Here we thus set the theoretical core of our argument, which aims to move beyond the ongoing 'suspicion' towards labour migration held by industrial relations, political economy, and employment studies. While we illuminate the ways in which labour studies can learn from migration scholarship and the autonomy of migration perspectives (Karakayali and Bojadžijev, 2007), we add to both by proposing ways to overcome the limitations of both labour and migration studies which tend to reproduce either functionalist or individualized notions of migrant mobility. We contend that both dualist segmentation theories of the migrant labour function in capitalist markets and integrationist approaches to migrant workers fail to grasp the mobility power of migrants. To overcome deterministic readings of cross–border migration in capitalist economies, we rather suggest a compositional approach (Gray and Clare, 2022) to mobility practices. Therefore, we propose a re-theorization of mobility power through the lenses of migration that overcomes the binary views of collective and individual resistance – especially among precarious workers experiencing restricted mobility, emphasizing the historical continuity and relationality between exit and voice.

The origins of turnover as a problem

The notion of turnover as a problem to be managed and minimized was first developed in early management and organization studies, reflecting the concerns of employers and supervisors on the shop floor. In the first years of the 20th century, employers started to commission studies to understand how to predict and reduce voluntary turnover, or, in the words of a US government official, to deal with 'the individualistic strike' (Jacoby, 1985: 32). From the early 20th century, firm-hired practitioners or consultants started to produce detailed analyses and assessments of labour turnover and its costs to devise reduction strategies (Fisher, 1917), while scholars began to assess and generate hypotheses, theories, and modelling of why employees leave their jobs and organizations (Douglas, 1918).

The work of Slichter (1919) and Brissenden and Frankel (1922) represent the first studies on turnover during the first decades of the 20th century, which saw the emergence of the modern factory. Perhaps surprisingly, their apparently 'less theoretical' (Hom et al, 2017) research appears more sociologically nuanced, context sensitive, and less functionalistic than the successive organization studies. These very early studies developed in the context of the nascent Fordist factory, and expressed a greater sensitivity to the questions of the specific (migrant/racialized) composition of the workforce in relation to the problem of turnover. Brissenden and Frankel (1922) define the problem of 'workers-led mobility' as primarily occurring in labour markets with abundant alternatives and, critically, caused or entrenched by inadequate management and working conditions. It is fascinating to observe how already in these first rudimentary theorizations, there was a high sensitivity to the social problems pushing workers to quit their jobs (insanitary environments, and inferior or inadequate housing and transportation facilities) that are not always strictly related to the place of work, but rather consider the wider community/social environment. This is in contrast to those who argue that sensitivity to the environment was only a later discovery, and that the embeddedness theory of turnover (Mitchell et al, 2001; Hom et al, 2017) was a radical departure from original approaches.

For our purpose, it is important to highlight how in the first set of studies, turnover has been explicitly considered a measure of the extent of labour unrest and therefore explicitly associated with conflict in the workplace, to which suitable management responses must be developed. Indirectly supporting our view that turnover as labour mobility expresses a form of conflict in the workplace, Brissenden and Frankel (1922: 7) argued that labour turnover is a narrower and more helpful term than labour mobility because 'it deals chiefly with the shifting and replacement involved in force maintenance', hence putting the emphasis on management's need for control over worker voluntary mobility and the sourcing of alternative labour, rather than on worker perspectives (the reasons for leaving).[1] In other words, who measures turnover and for what purpose matters substantially in its political and sociological definition and when considering the relatively disruptive effects of labour turnover on the firm. In this regard, already from the work of Brissenden and Frankel (1922), the management of the problem of turnover is presented as an element of competitive advantage with other organizations, at a time in which the notion of employment policies and personnel management was just emerging. Similarly, Slichter (1919) highlighted the coincidence of the birth of turnover with the dawns of personnel policies and human resource strategies. Its groundbreaking work on the modern organization shows how 'the necessity of "handling manpower" and turnover were at the very origins of HRM' (Alberti, 2011: 201). It was no coincidence that his work emerged at this unique point in the history of the US large firm, when companies responding to the growth of the direct-employment relationship, away from putting-out systems and 'gang bosses', realized that it was inconvenient for them when workers started to move because of personal mobility choices. His study of turnover conducted between 1912 and 1915 reported unprecedented rates, with nearly half of his survey companies having rates in excess of 100 per cent annual labour turnover (Slichter, 1919: 343). Such figures were a clear expression of workforce dissatisfaction.

Similarly, the intuition of Brissenden and Frankel (1922) remains valuable because they show the inextricable links between labour effort and labour mobility, and the actual concern underpinning employer struggles at measuring and monitoring turnover. The figures emerging from their analysis are striking: labour mobility in US manufacturing in the years 1910–19 (measured in terms of 'rate of replacement') amount to no less than 63 per cent of the work force, and even during a more stable year like 1915 were completely overturned, meaning that there were at least as many accessions and at least as many separations as there were workers on the force. In the war period 1917–18 this pattern became more striking, with more than four labour changes for each full-year worker in the aggregate work force (Brissenden and Frankel, 1922: 38; Douglas, 1959: 710).

The huge efforts of production during the First World War and the mass mobilization of labour, including new supplies, at a time of mass conscription were so substantial as to require an enormous number of workers, although it was noticed how these were not as malleable as the patriotic rhetoric required, and workers continued to leave the factory and strike.[2] Indeed, high fluidity and turnover in the labour market far from coincided with a period of social acquiescence, anticipating a pattern by which turnover and collective unrest need to be considered in relation rather than in opposition to each other.

During the first two decades of the 20th century, labour turnover appears high and is characterized by the relative freedom of workers to leave their workplace, but also by the lack of social protection and loose regulation. This is the time when the labour movement in the US starts organizing more extensively and also brings into its ranks migrant and African American workers. It is in particular from 1910 that employers start being more concerned about working conditions because of their negative impact on turnover, decrease in labour productivity, and the spread of unionism (Fishback, 1997: 10). Indeed, these high rates reflected the fact that the labour market was extremely fluid and workers had plenty of opportunities to find jobs in different firms, developing a pattern of 'job shopping' increased by the limited opportunities of occupational mobility inside the firm (Brissenden and Frankel, 1922: 17). The low rate of unemployment (1–2 per cent) in 1917–18 created a situation where workers were allowed to accept up to seven jobs in one day (Montgomery, 1979: 96). Critically, the same author reports that these high turnover rates were actually accompanied by intense and ongoing collective disputes, both self-organized and supported by the trade unions.

It is without doubt that the very nature of work and the specific working conditions experienced by the workers – whether repetitive, with low wages, or highly controlled and disciplined – are key in explaining why workers decided to quit (Smith et al, 2004: 377).[3] Sanford M. Jacoby (1983: 261) later argued that the decline of turnover after 1920 was actually not related to the new personnel management policies, or the threat represented by the unionization of workers, nor the desire of management to obtain economic benefits through purposefully reducing turnover levels. For Jacoby, the different composition of the workforce was rather the key factor that explains changes in labour mobility at that time. A compositional analysis of the workforce helps to pay attention to the specific racial, ethnic, legal, and gender status of the workers in a certain time and place, and in particular to explore the specific relationship between the recruitment of migrant labour and the control of labour turnover (see Chapter 3).

Economic historians Sanford Jacoby and Sunil Sharma (1992) focus on the specificity of the composition of labour, providing a long-term review of labour mobility patterns in industry within two centuries (1880–1980). Contrary to Carter and Savoca (1990), through a comprehensive account of subjective and macro factors, they show that the great majority of jobs before the First World War were short-term and only a few sectors had longer term employment, whereas since the war there was 'a sharp shift in the relative size and importance of the short and long term job sectors' (Jacoby and Sharma, 1992: 161). This point goes back to the importance of examining the general state of the labour market and its fluidity in different historical contexts to understand the relative turnover as labour market power by workers. Further, Jacoby and Sharma (1992) show a corresponding pattern between migration and turnover, confirmed for a big chunk of the 20th century. Such heightened turnover tendency in migrant-rich sectors is explained by the fact that migrants were taking jobs in the least protected and poorly unionized industries. They conclude that it is unmanageable to count and measure the patterns of constantly floating populations, indicating the impossibility of definitely measuring or predicting labour turnover.

In summary, while economic historians have later illuminated the wider socio-economic context that influenced turnover, migration, and unionization during the first part of the 20th century, early scholars of turnover, like their contemporaries in the nascent disciplines of organization studies and human relations, struggled to come to a conclusion on how to define and *measure* labour turnover. The historical attempts at measuring the turnover of labour since the beginning of the modern organization indicate how it remains a strongly ambivalent terrain, even simply because it does not differentiate between the voluntary or non-voluntary nature of separations, for example, between discharge, layoff, or voluntary turnover by workers. Turnover as such can indeed be either positive or negative for management or the workers, according to a variety of contextual, organizational, political, and social factors that influence power in the employment relationship.

From management studies to the labour process perspective

The organizational and management literature is important to understand how and why turnover starts to be considered troublesome from a management and social perspective, and what kind of solutions were proposed. The first studies in this field tended to be published in journals with an individualistic/cognitivist approach to social relations, such as organizational behaviours and applied psychology. Among them, organizational psychologists like March and Simon (1958) and Price (1977) were primarily interested in advancing a human relations approach to the science of labour management. They criticized the classical theory of cognitive rationality by economic actors, highlighting the complexity of behavioural choices by individuals and their importance for organizations. Still, theirs remains primarily a management-oriented agenda, since their objective is to understand the problem of turnover in order to develop strategies to 'tame' this worker behaviour and predict how organizations can survive at their best despite workers quitting, and low levels of satisfaction, productivity and participation among the workforce. The hundreds of studies published in the first years of the 20th century were conducted to solve the concrete problems experienced by firms: hiring and replacement expenses (Fisher, 1917); disruption of productivity related outcomes; and other financial disadvantages for the company (Hom et al, 2017: 530). From the more descriptive studies of the 1930s, research developed into a complex examination of turnover demographics and psychological traits, into the development of models of turnover such as that by March and Simon (1958).

Hom et al (2017) attempted to identify different phases in the history of turnover research: the first phase was the association of turnover with individual, community, and family factors (embedded behaviour); then the more recent psychological turn; and finally the human resource management (HRM) turn, where it is recognized that turnover may have effects and drivers that go beyond the individual (collective turnover). However, despite the consideration of how the demographics of different social groups affect turnover behaviours, mainstream organization and management studies tend to rely on generalizing social categories, such as expats, to identify patterns of behaviour by those who decide to stay when they integrate in the new country; or women who decide to quit because they have already planned to stay with their child if they got pregnant. In this way their approach leaves underexplored the multiplicity of social profiles that workers may hold at one time.

Only more recently have management and organization studies tackled the question of migrant workers' turnover intentions as compared to that of natives. Studies in specific sectors with high flexibility and labour shortages have introduced the idea that migrants may acquire higher 'professional mobility' according to macro-economic factors, such as increasing demand for migrant labour and the relatively global nature of the industry they work in. In sectors like hospitality, the presence of occupational communities that expose migrants to the social norms of the country of destination are deemed to reduce the gap with natives' behaviours, facilitating voluntary turnover of migrants, who show similar patterns to natives in terms of their quitting (Choi et al, 2017). This recent research is critical to the extent that it challenges the assumptions common to earlier studies that migrants necessarily suffer greater constraints and dependency on work and therefore would rather 'not quit that work due to low job satisfaction or a lack of fit with an organization because that person sees work as a way to survive' (Blustein, 2006, cited in Choi et al, 2017: 55). Rather, focusing on how structural conditions may provide greater opportunities for mobility, so that 'individual workers will act and engage in turnover more frequently' (Hall, 2004), Choi et al (2017: 55) de-essentialize migrant intrinsic *in*capacity to engage in turnover in circumstances where 'a labor shortage may allow migrant workers more opportunities to move between companies'. This approach signals a less essentialist way of looking at turnover and migration even within organization studies.

Notwithstanding the renewed emphasis on the importance of context (for example, Hom et al, 2017), as well as sector and macroeconomic factors (Hall, 2004) to understand turnover behaviours by specific categories of workers such as migrants (Choi et al, 2017), there is still little attention paid to the wider social dynamics, and especially workplace power dynamics that underpin voluntary labour turnover. Besides some consideration of collective aspects, most of the theories appear embedded in an understanding of turnover as fundamentally driven by individual psychological expectations and economic calculations ('subjective expected utility'), and oriented to problem-solving for the firm.[4]

Instead, since the late 1970s the sociology of work and LPT have introduced the point of view of the employment relation to consider the different meanings of turnover for employers and workers as immersed in an intrinsically unstable and indeterminate relationship subject to unequal power dynamics (Edwards, 1990). Considering the ambivalent meaning of labour mobility in the workplace, employers may be in favour of a system with a relatively high and constant level of turnover when these better serve industries with high fluctuation in demand or high seasonality of the service/product (for example, in the hospitality sector, see Lai et al, 2008). Employers may favour turnover when the management of the workforce does not require loyalty and permanence, when the costs of recruitment are relatively low, when the supply of labour is large, and when training is not required (Brown and McIntosh, 2000).[5] A different reason for employers to promote turnover may be understood in relation to the cost of maintenance and reproduction of certain groups of workers, such as women (see also Chapter 4). The decision to hire women only temporarily to avoid covering the costs of their maternity leave, or avoid their retention after return from leave, are classic examples of how turnover may be purposely encouraged by employers of female workers; and it is also a way to avoid the possible reduction of productivity in the case of workers with parental duties (Caraway, 2007).

Managers may also explicitly support a higher turnover rate as it removes 'the discontented and more vociferous workers from the workplace, eliminating potential leadership from trade unionism or collective workplace organization, which was positively ranked above exit' (Smith, 2006: 393). Processes of socialization and politicization among workers in the same workplace, which usually require time and a certain employment continuity under the same employer, are considered essential to develop bonds of strong solidarity that can give rise to collective action. Here key industrial sociologists (Beynon, 1973; Burawoy, 1979; Nichols and Beynon, 1977) have celebrated the importance of shop floor mutual action to maintain a level of conflict with management, and exposed them as more effective than individual strategies of dispute resolution based upon labour market competition, such as workers' decisions to quit, which have in contrast been seen as disruptive of collectivism. This idea has been used as the conceptual ground for morally ranking unionism and worker organization above exit (Smith, 2006). This was because of the alleged implications of exit for voice, rather than solely for the individualism associated to exiting behaviours in the firm. In fact, some scholars stress how high levels of turnover are linked to the absence or low levels of union density or of independent unions representing workers' grievances in a particular production unit: a high turnover may contribute to hinder the level of solidarity, impede collective action, and foster fragmentation in working conditions (Smith et al, 2004). In contrast, a powerful trade union will be able to improve working conditions, carry out progressive bargaining with management, and reduce or eliminate high turnover.

The ambivalent meaning of turnover, however, does not only lie in the different meanings that the two main parties in the employment relation attribute to it. Under different circumstances from those described earlier, employers may also have good reasons to try and limit the high turnover of workers. There are plenty of examples of employers finding ways to stop workers from moving at will, for example, by establishing length of service and notice periods of separation on the contract of employment, and other procedures for constraining labour supply and mobility (Jacoby, 1991). Mann (1973) talks about a 'mutual dependency obligation' whereby internal promotion may be used by the employer to disincentivize an employee from seeking alternatives jobs elsewhere, and where employers are then expected to favour internal to external labour markets according to a paternalistic approach based on workers' loyalty.[6]

More broadly, the question of worker retention vs turnover appears critical in situations of either scarce skills or high labour shortages. Skill retention, or the reproduction of abilities that are deemed critical for the profitability of a particular production process, lead employers to be concerned about workers moving away, possibly to competitors, especially if they have made substantial investments in training and employees are difficult to replace (Campbell, 1993; Smith et al, 2004). The relationship between skills and turnover has long been recognized both in labour studies and CPE precisely because it brings to the fore the relative dependency of employers on skill supplies, as 'any investment by an employer in an employee in the form of training runs a high risk of being lost as an *employee moves elsewhere*' (Bickerton, 2019: 237).[7]

The question of skills as well as worker autonomy was indeed at the very core of the LPT and Braverman's theory of monopoly capitalism (1974) at its origin. For Braverman, the autonomy of the worker lies primarily in the skills owned by the latter. One of his main concerns with the development of capitalism was the fact that the new processes of Taylorization were depriving workers of their knowledge about the process of production and their craft, leading to an overall trend of skills degradation, which fundamentally diminishes worker autonomy and bargaining power at the point of production. This idea that worker autonomy is a function of their skills lies in turn in the Marxian distinction between labour and labour power, whereby the employer may buy the availability of the worker to deliver effort power, but not labour power itself, which remains indeterminate and requires a specific system of management control in the labour process.

Moving to the point of view of the workers, Edwards and Scullion (1982) draw from the notion that the extraction of labour power by capital is always contested and subject to power struggles between capital and labour, whereby the 'threat' of turnover is always present and constitutive of the double indeterminacy of both effort and mobility power of labour (Smith, 2006). Labour mobility indeterminacy refers to the uncertainty over 'the disposal of labor power to the individual worker who has the burden and freedom (constraint and choice) as to *where and to which* employer the individual sells his or her labor services' (Smith, 2015: 231).

The flow perspective to labour power must therefore be considered in light of the historical tradition of labour process studies, which put at the centre 'the constant need for capital to obtain consent from workers because of the unspecified magnitude of work effort' (Alberti, 2014: 868). At the centre of the research by the pioneer of industrial sociology and LPT lies indeed the fragile balance between management interest in the ongoing circulation and supply of labour on the one hand, and its capture or immobilization on the other, which also gives rise to the possibility of overcoming capitalist social relations. In this sense, the work of Chris Smith (2006) also moves away from the attention that Braverman (1974) has put on skills and production under monopoly capitalism, rather focusing on the ability of workers to quit certain employment relations, which may or may not depend on the type and level of skills they possess and how scarce they are in the wider labour market. Highlighting the other face of the indeterminacy of labour power, we shift the attention to other capacities that may or may not be measurable according to a classic understanding of crafts and skills owned by workers and passed on from generation to generation in occupational groups. We will show in Chapter 4 how there may be different types of allegiances and kinships that shape the relative market power and transnational mobility power of migrants, however entrenched in the skills regimes regulating cross-border migration (Collins, 2021).

Migration and the segmentation of labour markets

We have considered previously how the debate over labour mobility has developed in direct connection with that on the control over the reproduction of skills by capital and the state, and how CPE have tended to understand migration as a way for employers to substitute scarce skills given their dependency on skill supplies (Thelen, 2014; Bickerton, 2019). In turn, from the point of view of trade unions, it has been historically important to draw some boundaries and introduce forms of protectionism in the area of skills formation and occupations (Cobble, 1991), arguably as a way to control labour mobility.

Within political economy, scholars have shown the historical work of unions in protecting skilled labour market segments (for example, through occupational guilds excluding newcomers from certain occupations), and how certain types of unions have excluded 'outsiders' from certain professions. Comparing Europe and the US in the early year of industrialization, Thelen (2004) problematically blames open borders and migration for the loss of craft and the burgeoning mechanization of jobs in the US: it was the wider availability of low-skilled migrant labour that allegedly weakened the importance of skilled labour and countered the emergence of a coordinated market economy in the US as compared to Europe, where unions more successfully protected skills and jobs of local workers and their regulatory power in the labour market (Afonso and Devitt, 2016: 600).

More recently, higher levels of labour mobility such as those in the EU common market are believed to have coincided with higher constraints on worker bargaining power as a result of employer-led flexibility, labour turnover, and exploitation (Krings, 2009; Cremers et al, 2007). According to this reading, freedom of movement of labour in the EU context has often been held responsible for a race to the bottom in working terms and conditions (Berntsen, 2016). One of the reasons why mobility and turnover have been associated with individualistic and detrimental forms of conflict has to do with the ways in which labour studies and CPE rather see the wider phenomenon of labour migration as disruptive or fragmenting forces in relatively protected or regulated national labour markets. In particular, we may identify two main approaches to the study of labour mobility in the political economy and employment relations literature: a neoclassical approach and an institutional one (Bickerton, 2019).

The neoclassical approach tends to see labour mobility as a mere competitive market response to existing mismatches between labour supply and demand. According to this viewpoint, labour mobility reflects wage differentials across countries, but contributes to erasing them and producing equalizing effects by naturally following market rules. On the opposite side, the institutionalist turn is represented by scholars studying the interaction between labour mobility and national Varieties of Capitalism (VOC) (for example, Wright, 2012; Devitt, 2011). In broad terms, the VOC perspective (Hall and Soskice, 2001) distinguishes different economic models across countries in liberal capitalist economies, primarily liberal and coordinated market economies (LMEs and CMEs). While the former are mostly regulated by market mechanisms, characterized by low wages, flexible labour markets, lower protections, and lack of sector collective bargaining, the latter presents a higher level of coordinated wage bargaining, education skills, and training policies, usually managed by the state providing for the reproduction of the workforce and its skills, and cooperative industrial relations systems. Some labour migration scholars have also used this framework to understand different management systems of labour mobility, arguing that: 'Compared to coordinated market economies with relatively regulated labour markets, liberal market economies with flexible labour markets and relatively large low wage labour markets can be expected to generate greater employers' demand for migrants, especially but not only for employment in low-waged jobs' (Ruhs and Palme, 2018: 1488–9).

In our view the point here is not to argue against the neoclassical model of labour migration by showing that migration has no effect on wages or terms and conditions. The problem with institutionalist and VOC approaches lies instead in the simplistic language of competition that pervades the relation between indigenous and migrant workers and focuses on the effects of migration on the national labour market and on the local workforce, as if these were bounded and naturally counterposed entities with no social and historical relationship between each other. These approaches tend to naturalize the existence of national borders, clearly defining who belongs to the national workforce and who does not (another way of reproducing methodological nationalism), and imagining a mechanic competition between them. Adopting a more nuanced view of how segmented markets operate, including informally and 'from the bottom up' (Peck and Theodore, 2010), means to look at migrant workers in their subjectivity and migrant labour in its complex relations with local markets and citizens (Anderson, 2017). In this way we may start seeing how migrants are not simply subjugated to what employers may expect from them as a unique type of human resource, and that they may rather be considered as more than a mere factor of production or an economic variable in capitalist systems.

Overall, the recent engagement of CPE with international migration, a long overdue endeavour, has contributed to highlight a more dynamic interaction between migration and capitalist institutions, representing an important break away from the tendency of labour and employment research to look at migration as a static factor, either victim of bad employers or faulty of race to the bottom in the labour market. However, the economic disposition of migrant workers (rather than the range of their wider motives and household dynamics) continues to be taken for granted in most VOC and CPE approaches. Emphasis on the functions of substitution or complementarity, used to describe the role played by migration in relation to existing institutions such as industrial relations systems or training and skills formation, tends to still treat migrant labour as a variable in capitalist markets (Afonso and Devitt, 2016). Migration in political economy jargon remains fundamentally a pawn of labour market and institutional dynamics led by the state and employers, or pushed by mainly individual economic drivers. While it is important to take into account the regulatory and economic context at the country level, contrary to institutionalist readings we cannot simply extrapolate worker mobility behaviours from political economic conditions in the state and labour markets (compare Afonso and Devitt, 2016), nor as simply reflecting already formed employer or government strategies (Ruhs and Palme, 2018).

Operating within the VOC perspective, Afonso and Devitt (2016) are interested in understanding how migration influences changes and continuity in institutional forms given the diversity of capitalist systems. They bring a more nuanced view of actors and social processes in relatively regulated markets, considering that migration is not merely a tool of liberalization of political economy but may rather allow for segmentation, for example between stable and unstable employment markets characterized by different behaviours and patterns. Drawing from Piore (1979) and Thelen (2004) the notion of labour market dualization, Afonso and Devitt (2016: 595) argue that migration may be used to shield rather than merely challenge or liberalize existing CMEs. In this sense, migration allows for coexisting processes of flexibilization (where migrants would allegedly benefit LMEs) and protection requirements for society (indeed, for natives; see also Erne and Imboden, 2015). A key concern of Polanyi in *The Great Transformation* (1957) was indeed the re-embedding of social relations under pressure of neoliberal market economies, and Afonso and Devitt (2016) argue that migration can be understood as a way to reconcile these two movements. This reconciliation is paradoxically possible only through a kind of protectionist segmentation of the labour market, which creates separate niches that impede or moderate downward competition on wages. Afonso (2017), in particular, has shown how in the case of Switzerland, such fragmentation and dualization have allowed employers and unions to compromise over certain levels of free movement of labour from the EU. Similarly, Erne and Imboden (2015) showed how in the same country, trade unions managed to compromise over the free movement of labour agreement by using Swiss capitalists' interest to access the EU common market as a lever to force employers to accept stronger labour rights for EU nationals (comparably stronger than the equal pay for equal work between Swiss women and Swiss men), hence forming two unequal pay policy regimes in the same country.

However, a problem with these approaches within CPE is that unions and employer associations remain the ultimate representative actors negotiating the regulation of the labour market, and do so uniquely at the national level, according to an analytical framework that overlooks the direct representation of migrant interests (see Chapter 5) and the multiplicity of regulatory actors shaping international and cross-border labour markets. It is no coincidence that the considered 'cross–class coalitions' compromising around migration and free movement only partially address the ongoing inequalities between natives and migrants, taking for granted the national boundaries of the state and the economy according to what we can consider a residual methodological nationalism of CPE, employment studies and union practice.

Shire (2020) recently discussed the 'social order' of transnational labour markets, arguing that the very segmentation of labour markets between primary and secondary allows for a sort of tolerance of migrant labour, which is however accepted to the extent that it guarantees the continuation of segmented markets with better conditions and pay for the citizens, and poorer and more precarious terms for the foreigners. While inserting a more critical view of the drivers of such social ordering, including a variety of actors (see Chapter 2), what is still problematic in these understandings of migration in the capitalist economy is that they maintain a form of essentialization (Romens, 2022) or fetishization of migrant labour, as if migrants would only benefit from labour market flexibility (incorporating the wild spirit of capitalism and free mobility), while the social security aspects would only be wanted and reserved for the natives.

Research on the contrary demonstrates how even in highly segmented markets with niches of degraded migrant labour, the effects of precarization may become *pervasive* for hitherto protected sections of the workforce (Alberti et al, 2018) and that not only those at the bottom of the labour market but all workers may see their conditions degraded when informal labour markets and unregulated sections continue to expand. In other words, indigenous workers also appear to suffer the consequences of the overall processes of precarization, of which migrant labour is just a paradigmatic exemplar. Thinking more systematically about not only 'how the other half works' (Waldinger and Lichter, 2003) but how the core and the margins of the labour markets are related, employment studies and CPE have underestimated such interdependencies. On the contrary, the history of the 'standard employment relation' shows that secure employment with social benefits has been limited to some sections of the workforce in Western countries and at a particular time of economic growth, but to the costs of coexisting with the unpaid, lower paid, and temporary work of many other (women) precarious workers (Vosko, 2006, 2010).[8] These readings show how we need to be suspicious of any understanding of what is the employment 'norm' and what are the 'exceptions' in more or less regulated or segmented employment markets.

Returning to Shire's (2020) idea that migration can contribute to a socially ordered system where segmentation allows for the continuation of differentiated labour markets certainly helps explain why, in some contexts, trade unions have been more accepting of labour migration (Afonso, 2016; Erne and Imboden, 2015). However, this over-emphasis on the impermeability of segmented markets is in contrast with the notion of precarization as a process, whereby migrant labour is rather understood as anticipating general trends that sooner or later will affect all workers, and is paradigmatic or anticipatory of what happens in the labour market more broadly (Mometti and Ricciardi, 2011). We can rather say that both the fragmentation of employment relations and workers' ongoing practices for the recomposition of work (Jordhus-Lier, 2014; Gray and Claire, 2022; Coe and Jordhus-Lier, 2011), along with pervasive precarization, are at play at different speeds and with different outcomes across regulatory contexts.

The good, the bad, and the intractable (migrant) worker

While industrial relations, the sociology of work, and even political economy have increasingly taken into consideration the role of international migration in the labour market and in the labour movement specifically, we have shown the tendency for this to occur within a framework that privileges the nation state as a unit of analysis and that tends to overlook migration in its social aspect (Bauder, 2006). The step forward in labour process studies has been to finally recognize 'the dynamic tensions in the patterns of advantage and uncertainty that accompany the use of migrant labour power' (Thompson et al, 2013: 134), challenging an uncontested and victimizing view of the migrant as the 'good worker' (Dench et al, 2006), or of migration as simply fulfilling the 'function' of sustaining and extending flexible labour market structures (McCollum and Findlay, 2015). Thompson et al (2013) have indeed criticized a victimizing approach to the analysis of the role of free-moving Eastern European workers in the UK, as they rather highlighted the problems that employers found in managing this relatively unruly migrant workforce, because of their relatively instrumental approach to work and earnings and their tendency to adopt 'local's attitude and behaviours' as they became familiarized with their present environment (see also MacKenzie and Forde, 2009; Baxter-Reid, 2016).

Looking at the patterns of migrant labour over time in the same factory, Forde and MacKenzie (2009), pointed out that as soon as migrants became more integrated in the local labour market they started to refuse the expectations of long and irregular working hours and were soon replaced by the new generation of 'less-settled' migrant workers. The substitution process has been stressed in the case of agriculture in the south of Italy (Caruso, 2016; Corrado, 2017), where circulation of different groups of migrant workers has been observed. Similarly, McCollum and Findlay (2015), studying the role of Eastern European migrants in the flexible British labour market across a variety of sectors (from agriculture to hospitality), noticed the patterns of substitution of labour in employers' recruitment practices before employers claimed they would have rather hired post-colonial Commonwealth (Asian) migrants if the system based on visa sponsorship had been less cumbersome.

More recently, Thompson et al (2013), studying migrant labour in the food packaging and processing sector in Scotland, further developed the critique of the 'good worker', showing how migrants themselves decide 'when and how to be good', or rather 'misbehave'. While Thompson and colleagues' research is important in foregrounding the agency of migrant workers rather than solely focusing on employers' instrumental use of migrant labour in food retail supply chains, alongside other labour scholars their focus remains on the opportunism of migrants' behavior and the mutual interest of both migrants and employers in perpetuating temporary and casual employment relations (see also Janta et al, 2011 on migrants' and employers' 'matching goals' in the hotel and restaurant industry). Migrants' primary intention 'to send money home, to pick up language and other skills' are rather cited as drivers of their instrumental approach to low-paid casual work (Thompson et al, 2013: 132). While these external drivers and non-wage related motives for migrants to pick up employment (often below their skills level) has been critically emphasized in the migration literature (for example, Currie, 2007; Bauder, 2006), the risk is to reproduce the view of migrants as rational cost-benefit calculators and exemplars of *homo economicus*. Such a view was criticized by early labour sociologists that originally interrogated the biases of industrial relations towards migration and its historical dismissal (McGovern, 2007). While the question of wage differentials across countries has been and always will be critical in shaping the macro patterns of international migration in capitalism, reducing migrants' labour market behaviour to economic or individual aspects is particularly problematic in that it shadows the myriad of objective and subjective, individual and household related factors that shape the complex intentions, directionalities, and temporalities of migration.

As noted by Thompson et al (2013: 142), it is revealing that in sectors like the supermarket supply chain, local workers usually located in semi-rural areas show greater patterns of labour market and social immobility as compared to migrant workers, for example, preferring unemployment benefits over 'harsh and unrewarding jobs in supplier companies'. Migrants, in contrast, are more successful at 'moving on from initial jobs and navigate the labour market in search of better rewards' (Thompson et al, 2013: 142s). However, highlighting such mobility differentials between migrants and indigenous workers should not lead to associating migrants with a higher instrumentalism/opportunism, but simply realizing the difference in the structures and social differences that shape their strategies and behaviours. Alberti (2014) has applied this notion of mobility differentials to describe different degrees of precariousness and 'stuckness' in insecure employment within the migrant workforce in London, overcoming this false dichotomy between locals and migrants and showing instead how migrants also have different opportunities according to their immigration status, legal entitlements to benefits, their social networks, but also the barriers they encounter because of their class, gender, race, age, and education (see also Samaluk, 2016). In other words, it is not just about the economic resources available to the individual in a particular labour market that shape opportunity structures, but also the overall sense of security provided by more or less tangible assets, such as family, friendship networks, and institutional or political support, that offer migrants the prospects to flourish in a particular context.

The tendency in labour studies is to associate self-interested and market-focused behaviours with highly mobile foreign workers as the ultimate incarnation of neoliberal capitalism, in contrast with the relatively immobile, marginalized, and unskilled local labour presented as the victims of such market forces, corroborating the (often racialized) sense of divisions between different segments of the workforce. Such narratives risk pushing migrants again to the end of the spectrum of collective vs individual forms of resistance/conflict, where their practices are described as weak expressions of discontent and poor work ethics/misbehaviour. Another risk is to indirectly justify the racializing tones of divisions between migrants and the local workers, whereby managers and unions tend to blame the unethical, self-interested behaviour of temporary migrants quitting their jobs and expecting to return to them after a few months, or lowering productivity to cope with tiring and monotonous labour processes such as in food manufacturing and warehousing. Such 'opportunistic behaviour' may rather be considered the inevitable response to hard HRM strategies dominating those low-skilled labour intensive sectors, and a fair response that most workers, rather than migrants in particular, are likely to adopt as they became aware of the devaluation of their labour and the low pay beyond their initial frame of reference: migrants are therefore rather 'good when they *can* be' in the words of Baxter-Reid (2016).

Economistic approaches to migrant behaviours, as well as the underpinning methodological nationalism of industrial relations research, concur to limit the ability of our field of study to deeply understand migration and its social and political significance in a transnational perspective. We argue, instead, that a radical view of labour mobility power involves questioning the very assumptions between migrants vs non-migrants, individual and collective forms of resistance, rather acknowledging the material benefits of migrant mobility power beyond the mere realm of production (see Chapters 3 and 4). Furthermore, our approach to migration tries to go beyond the institutional lens, constantly interrogating not only the differential implications of the operation of institutions (including trade unions) on natives and migrants, but also the fact that migrants' own behaviours or dispositions (for example, earnings maximization) cannot be taken for granted as they interact with those institutions, and that an economic rationale may not always shape theirs and their family's mobility practices as it is the case with any other worker.

Individual exit vs collective voice: a hierarchy of resistance?

Migrant workers' conflicting practices in the workplace have been rarely addressed or acknowledged in the sociology of work and employment relations. One of the reasons for this lies in the wider tendency of labour studies to categorize migrants' strategies as individual 'coping' rather than 'true resistance'. More broadly, the emphasis on migrants' individualized market behavior points to the deep-seated distinction between individual and collective action that permeates studies of worker resistance in the sociology of work and in the labour process tradition.

The individual vs collective binary has underpinned the labour studies debate on worker forms of resistance at least since the discussion was inaugurated by Hirschman in the 1970s. In 'Exit, Voice and Loyalty' (1970), Hirschman was the first to theorize the foundational difference between exit as a market-type behaviour – celebrated by the economists to indicate an individualistic way of expressing discontent – and voice as a more constructive way to engage with one's organization to improve matters while continuing to be members or customers.

However, going back to the origin of the debate, rather than treating it in purely sociological or categorical ways, the original argument by Hirschman must be considered in its own historical context. Hirschman indeed developed a nuanced critique of the ideological argument by economists, who elevated exit as a more efficient way of 'voting with one's feet' and who explicitly disregarded the contribution of voice, political participation, and protest at a time when neoclassical economics and market-driven (individualist) approaches to organizational life were penetrating the mainstream debate and shaping early neoliberal economic discourses (Friedman, 1964). In a later article, Hirschman (1978) would actually acknowledge how differently distributed 'voice capacity' may be, and the relative easier access to forms of exit for certain groups of workers, critically referring to differences in wealth and income among individuals, hence relativizing the superiority of voice over exit.[9] Noticeably, Hirschman (1978: 96) highlighted the limited resources of racialized minorities in making use of voice: 'In the United States, where the problem is compounded because of race discrimination, inequality in access to exit has had some appalling consequences, such as the 'ghettoization' and partial ruin of our big cities'.

Contrary to the view common to organizational psychology that quitting may be an emotive and immature response of workers to unsatisfactory conditions (March and Simon, 1958), Edwards and Scullion (1982) explicitly acknowledged the possibility that turnover became a rational and collective expression of conflict, for example when quitting was used as a response to common problems and reflected previously shared 'pride in collective control'. According to this interpretation, if we take the term control in simple terms, quitting is likely to be an important form of escape in situations where 'managerial control is relatively intense'. The material benefits of quitting at the individual level should also not be discounted or degraded on a moral level: even when 'quitting was unable to resolve collective grievances, and it was therefore not necessarily a strategy that furthered workers' interests as a whole (…) it did of course permit individual workers to escape to a preferred job' (Edwards and Scullion, 1982: 92).

Early LPT scholars are therefore helpful to illuminate how difficult it is to draw a definite line between individual exiting behaviours and the more or less individual/collective gains accrued by such behaviours. Are these individual decisions to quit only impacting on the individual? What about their coworker, their bosses, their family members? Smith's (2006: 394) conclusion is a balanced and convincing one in this regard, suggesting that rather than dwelling on the debate as to whether exit is superior to voice or vice versa, we rather 'need more research to investigate the disruptive, conflictual and destabilizing effects workers can exert by using the labour market for dispute resolution'. This would also help in forming a better understanding of how management is forced to change or develop specific practices to manage high labour turnover and experiment with alternative ones, 'especially within competitive labour markets'.

Turnover as labour mobility power is important for us, not only in so far as it uses the threat of quitting to improve conditions in the workplace, but also as a way to enact the freedom to move within the labour market to a completely different job. Scholars have highlighted how such labour market power may be constrained in the case of migrants subject to immigration controls by the state, that bonds their residence to a contract of employment with a particular sponsor. Elaborating on the notion of mobility bargaining power as a mix of marketplace mobility and associational power, Strauss and McGrath (2017), from within labour geography, have studied the forms of agency that migrant in precarious work use *in the context of relatively unfree labour relations*. Drawing from E.O. Wright's (2000) distinction between structural and associational forms of working-class power, as well as from Silver's (2003: 13) notion of 'marketplace bargaining power', Strauss and McGrath (2017: 204) summarize the latter as 'marketplace or mobility bargaining power' and describe it as the 'form of power exerted by workers in relation to their ability to exit employment relations in a tight labour market' (2017: 204) These labour geographers thus critically add to the debate on the significance of labour mobility for migrant workers constrained by temporary visas.

While the 'flow-like approach' in LPT has identified the unique trait of labour power as a commodity in its movement through space and time, it has only partially discussed the importance of international migration and state policies to control the movement of workers across borders. The consequences of such policies for the sake of 'the segmentation of employment and weakening of unionizing potential' (Smith, 2010: 276) has indeed remained the focus of attention within LPT, perhaps reflecting the long-standing primacy of collective forms of agency in industrial relations, rather than focusing on the micro and macro level effects that constraints on migrants' mobility, and their precariousness specifically, imply in terms of management and labour control/autonomy dynamics. Human and labour geographers (for example, Rogaly, 2009) have rather helped to reconsider how workers have developed spatial mobility strategies, including quitting, alongside traditional forms of associational power to set themselves free from highly exploitative situations and challenge their subjugated position. The importance of migrant spatial practices of mobility has been noted especially in the context of the absence of collective bargaining rights (Reid-Musson, 2014: 163), but in our view grasping them requires a more radical departure from dualistic views of worker power or resistance. We will further develop our conceptual proposals about forms of worker power through the migration lens (see tables in Chapters 3 and 6).

Table 1.1 summarizes the forms of worker power and bargaining power as traditionally represented in the sociological and employment literature, which tends to distinguish between forms of worker power according to whether they are individual or collective (*organizational form*), where they are exerted (the *realm* where they manifest, workplace or marketplace), and whether their *resources* are associational or structural – dependent on the position of the worker at the point of production (Wright, 2000). The 'resource approach' to worker power, recently popular in the field of labour and industrial relations research (for example, Schmalz et al, 2018) highlights the extent to which these forms are based on the individual's strategic position in the production process or on the ability of workers to cooperate and leverage pressure from outside the workplace, in the labour market and local community. Beverly Silver's (2003) distinction of structural power between the workplace and marketplace realms clarifies that workers can develop their bargaining power either internally (within the workplace, for example by reducing or withdrawing their work effort to obtain improved conditions) or externally (in the labour market, by quitting or threatening to quit). Silver also highlights under what circumstances workers tend to develop their associational power outside the workplace, building wider alliances with social movements and community groups; for example, if workers have limited bargaining power but their labour needs to be delivered in place, such as in services. Smith (2006) has further developed this distinction by elaborating on the two aspects of labour power, defining them as work-effort and mobility-effort bargaining. The latter can be either exerted individually or as a group and be more or less a concerted effort to negotiate change in management practice.

Drawing from both Wright's (2000) original typology of worker associational and structural power, and combining it with Smith's (2006) work on the Marxian notion of the double indeterminacy of labour power, which emphasizes labour mobility-effort bargaining alongside work-effort bargaining, Table 1.1 illustrates our understanding of the intersecting nature of labour mobility power, bringing together both collective and individual organizational forms, and associational and structural power resources. We maintain the distinction between the power of the worker as such (for example, ability to withdraw one's labour) and the bargaining leverage arising from such power in relation to other workers and employers (for example, collective bargaining).[10]

Table 1.1: Forms of worker power and bargaining

	Workplace	Marketplace
Individual	Structural power	Marketplace mobility power (ability to exit a job)
Resource approach	Structural *and* associational ⟶	Mobility effort bargaining (threat of exit)
Collective	Associational power	Coordinated mobility effort bargaining

Note: See 'Forms of worker power' in Glossary

One of Smith's (2006: 394) main points is that 'the simple threat of exit, whether latent or manifest can also facilitate change to internal regimes and interact with effort bargaining'.[11] While Smith does not develop this aspect further, we build on his first intuition to further emphasize the hybrid nature of mobility power (as exercised in particular by migrant workers) as able to take both an individual and collective organizational form (see Chapter 3).

Looking at the debate on exit and voice in relation to labour migration specifically, Meardi (2007) has looked at migrants' exit strategies in the context of migration from Eastern Europe, thus somewhat considering migration itself as a form of mobility power. Meardi explored the implications of mass exits of post-enlargement emigration from countries like Poland, Slovakia, and the Baltic countries (most moving to richer countries such as Germany, the UK, and Sweden), highlighting how these impacted on the balance of power in employment relations in the home country. In our view, Meardi allows us in this way to move towards a transnational understanding of mobility power by measuring the wage gains that exit as bargaining power has accrued for those back home, while contributing to smooth the binary between exit and voice.

Although the correlation between outmigration and wage increase is not the only element relevant to understand salary patterns in the new EU member states, it is certainly important to understand the transnational outcomes of labour mobility beyond a destination-focussed approach, as well as one looking only at financial gains in terms of remittances (compare Kelly, 2009, Datta et al, 2007). Another strength of Meardi's (2007) work is showing how exit can be used in combination with voice and/or how both follow a cyclical pattern. His work vindicates Hirschman's original approach as more nuanced than the official narrative opposing exit and voice. Industrial relations views on exit have tended to follow a 'cyclical logic' whereby voice would appear strengthened according to long-term economic cycles (for example, Kelly, 1998), or according to an endogenous explanation where 'movement and counter-movements' (Polanyi, 1957), in the form of social paternalism and commodification tendencies intrinsic to capital, would follow each other in waves, alongside different intensities of voice and social protest to 're-embed' social relations. Differently from these approaches, argues Meardi, Hirschman (1982) provided the grounds for a more dynamic theorization of the relationship between these forms of social conflict. By highlighting the 'rebound effect of disappointment', Hirschman shows how '*both* the pursuit of private concerns (manifest in individual exit) and that of public concerns (manifest in collective voice) are shown to be inherently dissatisfactory' (Meardi, 2007: 518). Such dissatisfaction explains the continuous movement between the two forms of worker agency in ways that are far from mutually excluding:

> At a given moment in time, the two options are alternative, although *their combined intensity is not fixed*: it will depend on the amount of discontent and of 'labour problems', and on the available options. However, in a dynamic perspective, they are complementary or mutually re-enforcing: strong exit at t0 will lead to strong voice at t1, and vice versa. (Meardi, 2007: 518; author's emphasis)

Applying this theory to the analysis of mass exit in the post–enlargement EU, Meardi concludes that strong exit at a given time prepares strong voice at a later one. This also means that exit behaviours have consequences not only in terms of macro trends in wages but also vis-à-vis management in the workplace. In their study of management of turnover in transnational corporations' (TNCs) manufacturing in England, Smith et al (2004: 374) similarly highlighted how, through high mobility, 'workers encounter workers from other factories and can thus compare and perhaps overestimate the quality of alternatives, producing an over propensity to quit'.

In other words, exit and voice can be generative of each other rather than being alternative solutions available to workers, or that workers select from a range of more or less ethical practices. It is out of contention that transnational migration as exit may therefore represent problems to both governments, in terms of their wider social impact, and management, in terms of economic effects on shortages and wages in the origin country, showing how there are not simple 'market solutions' to these issues. We will consider later how such approaches contrast with neoliberal accounts of the function of migration in capitalist markets.

In summary, with the help of labour and industrial relations scholars we start grasping the interdependencies of voice and exit as two forms of worker power as they developed beyond the individual vs collective moral hierarchy of resistance. More broadly, the use of quitting by workers subject to more or less constraining employment conditions across different phases of capitalist development, and of the continuum of freedom and unfreedom into the wage relation, shows how mobility power rather constitutes an irreducible social force with critical implications for individuals and their communities.

Runaways, desertion, and migration as historical forms of resistance

However, to further uncover the relationship between individual and collective action, we need to examine briefly some valued contributions made by social historians. Recent developments in global labour history (van der Linden, 2008) provide tremendous insights into the relationship between workers' exit practices, such as desertion and runaways, and their collective action to free themselves from exploitative working conditions, further illuminating the continuity that exists between exit and voice. These insights are in our view important to shake entrenched biases in our disciplines and to overcome false dichotomies between individual and collective acts of resistance in both pre-capitalist and capitalist labour markets. In particular, a new wave of studies on worker escape practices has emerged in the past few years, highlighting how runaways (that is, deserting, absconding, being absent) need to be considered a workers' strategy 'in and of itself' that can be studied as an independent historical phenomenon (Hofmeester and van der Linden, 2018). Different from Scott's (1985) interpretation of desertion as an unintentional act of everyday resistance or reluctant compliance, as well as from Hardt and Negri's (2000) romantic view of desertion as the paradigmatic form of resistance opposed to sabotage in the era of 'imperial control', the social historian van Rossum (2018: 506) argues that workers', slaves' and prisoners' practices of running away, desertion, or quitting are 'active form of *conscious* non-compliance' rather than acts of defiance. In this regard, van Rossum (2018: 507) criticizes the notion that running away was a negative act by workers in harsh circumstances. On the contrary, it 'appears as an attempt to gain or regain some control over one's living and working conditions. And, as such, desertion was very clearly marked by ideas of justice and by aspirations of creating a better life'.

Under this account, everyday forms of resistance are not merely the response to institutional forms of control from above, but fundamentally shape and influence them. Certainly, employers and states applied hard measures to curb such acts of desertion, from using cruel to more lenient punishments, but also developed 'seemingly limitless inventiveness in their endeavours to confine and control their workers' (van Rossum 2018: 507). An earlier historical overview of different forms of desertion by van Rossum (2018: 508) showed that while forms of desertion were brutally punished, especially across the 16th century, 'in many places in the world withdrawing oneself from the work process was a punishable offence well into the twentieth century'. This is testament to the continuing importance of formal and informal mechanisms to constrain labour mobility, and the continuities across enslaved, 'free', and salaried labour encompassing different phases of pre- and capitalist social formations (Moulier-Boutang, 1998; Steinfeld and Engerman, 1997; van der Linden, 2008; Silverstein, 2005).

According to van Rossum's (2018: 509) newly elaborated framework of exit and voice, desertion is no longer merely contrasted to forms of collective action, rebellion, and protest, but part of a bundle of strategies that could be deployed both individually and collectively.[12] In this sense, Hirschman's options of voice and loyalty (or acquiescence in later formulations), are presented in a *continuum* rather than in opposing ways, occupying a dynamic space between individual and collective strategies that express wider forms of contestation, from temporary absence (as individual desertion) to mass escape and revolt (as mutiny). Solutions included finding a better job, but also more broadly expanding the opportunities for social mobility for the wider family/community. Hence, rather than being presented as a strategy by which workers, either individually or collectively, simply reject working conditions and power relations, *exit* variously intertwines with negotiation, forming alliances with others, and sometimes developing shared practices such as petitions, all aimed at the betterment of either collective or individual situations. Further historical examples of exit practices used in collective forms or as direct ways of negotiating/bargaining with the employers emerged in the form of taking time off (van Rossum, 2018: 515). Rethinking the notion of absenteeism is indeed critical to note how practices such as Saint Monday and also Saint Tuesday were carried out by European and Americans artisans and workers in the 18th century and also during the 19th century in a more or less collective fashion (Thompson, 1967; Gutman, 1973). While absenteeism has been a classic subject of labour studies, including labour process research, it has often been relegated to forms of 'organizational misbehaviour' (see for instance Ackroyd and Thompson, 1999) or as 'deviant' in management studies (Everton et al, 2007), rather than been considered a legitimate or creative form of social conflict to take back 'our time'.

Differently from past literature that has focused on particular categories (for example, rural workers, peasants) to analyse desertion and escape and other everyday forms of resistance, the novelty of van Rossum's (2018: 511) approach also lies in highlighting the universality and transversality of these practices across a range of differently constrained types of labour and employment relations. Critically, rather than solely in the formal cases of forced labour, the type of employment relations that gave rise to acts of desertion included also free wage labour characterized by specific forms of control and where exit or movement were restricted. Among these categories the authors include sailors, contract workers, *and migrants* (van Rossum, 2018: 510–11).[13] The relative use of this form of resistance depended however on the actual working experience of the worker and the alternative options available. In our words, mobility power depends on what we may call the affordability of turnover and exit (see Conclusion).

Moving forward from the early modern world, it is critical to understand how the margins of workers' exit strategies were gradually restricted under pressure of wider processes, where increasing discipline and surveillance (Foucault, 1975) and global regulation made runaways more difficult and more politicized. As we will further explore in Chapter 4, the ongoing restriction of mobility was therefore 'transferred' into the field of social and welfare controls (Anderson and Hughes, 2015), whereby the compulsion to work became more and more prevalent and part and parcel of welfare regimes: 'The criminalization of withdrawal from the work process was slowly transformed into criminalization of the act of not working, or the state of not being employed' (van Rossum, 2018: 518). The forms of sanctioning for unemployed workers and the compulsion to work as a condition to obtain benefits are characteristic of so-called workfare regimes in many Western countries today (Cohen et al, 2002; Dwyer, 2016), and are illustrative of the continuing forms of control over workers' mobility and exit from the labour market.[14] These are still a major concern for employers and the state, who develop inventive strategies to put people to work or tie them to particular workplaces, including in regimes of apparently free wage labour.

This long and more comprehensive view on workers' exit practices shows how these *were part and parcel of collective forms of refusal* or chosen as the only alternative in the absence of access to large organizations and power. The latter is often the case for disaffected migrants today, similarly to how it was for racialized minorities in the US at the time of the Hirschman study, who rarely find opportunities for engagement in existing trade unions (see Chapter 5).

The autonomist gaze

One way of overcoming deep-seated biases against mobility and the tendency of reproducing essentialized divisions between individual and collective actions as well as migrant and indigenous workers is to recentre mobility as a foundational aspect of society rather than as the exception, while criticizing the methodological nationalism that characterized not only labour but also mainstream migration studies. Human geographers of migration, as well as those belonging to the so-called autonomy of migration perspective, have in this regard criticized essentialist notions of ethnicity, whereby migrants are considered inherently different from the indigenous population, the paradigmatic bearers of 'culture', the expression of internally homogeneous and 'ancestral' ethnic identities, and of religious/cultural practices (Romens, 2022). Mainstream migration scholarship also considers these attributes as distinctive to migrants, migration, and settlement process, thus reinforcing 'the culturalising and racialising logic of methodological nationalism' (Çağlar, 2016: 953).

Recently, Çağlar (2016) has made an important theoretical intervention in human geography that recentres mobility understood as the ordinary and common experience rather than the exception. The notion of foundational mobility highlights the experiences of those who remain migrants despite several years of 'emplacement' in the country of immigration. The key argument of Çağlar (2016) is that methodological nationalism equates society and culture with one nation and prioritizes national and ethnic identities, inscribing indigenous and migrants into distinct temporal frameworks whereas indigenous people never arrived but were always already here. Hence, rather than being concerned about mobility per se, we need to reconceptualize migrants' sociabilities and agency more broadly in a way that does not limit them to the national scale, so that their transborder practices and social relations can be best captured.

The critique of methodological nationalism in migration studies has been accompanied by a radical critique of notions of migrant integration in the country of destination. In this regard, the temporal sensitivity of Çağlar's (2016) analysis towards the chronotopes of migration allows us to put under scrutiny also mainstream labour market studies' approaches to migrant integration, whereby migrants are assumed to incrementally increase their labour market power as they integrate in the society of arrival. While it is intuitive that anyone who settles in a place for a certain amount of time is more likely to acquire the needed language skills, social ties, and local knowledge to better navigate the local environment (for an excellent example of how this creates problems for employers, see Forde and McKenzie, 2009), it is still important to question the alleged linearity of such 'integration pathways'.

Deconstructing the linear temporal line underpinning notions of migrants' integration, whereby migrants 'are meant to uproot themselves from their home countries in time and integrate themselves in the country of settlement', Çağlar's (2016: 958) notion of foundational mobility as preceding notions of original settlement by natives effectively overcomes such narratives. Denaturalizing the assumed 'integration pathways' typical of migrants as compared to citizens, Çağlar rather emphasizes the 'coevalness' of migrant and non-migrants, which rather helps identifying the commonalities, shared norms, experiences, and values as migrants and natives are embedded in the same social and economic processes (of a city/a locality/a country). Similarly, the notion of liminality developed by Underthun (2014) in the case of young migrant transnationals working in the hospitality sector describes the ways in which these migrants were far from following an integration or settlement process with a start and an end, but were in constant transition and never completely 'arrived' in the country of destination nor in their workplace. Their precarious labour trajectories embody a kind of flexible subjectivity where the boundaries between arrival, stay, and departure are blurred by an extending phase of 'in-betweenness', accentuated by the precarious nature of their jobs, but also by their subjective existence as transnational migrants.

Authors like Nicholas De Genova (2005) have targeted the nationalist assumptions around integration behind other established migration studies approaches such as the 'new economics of migration' (Massey et al, 1993; Portes, 1997). Such strands of labour economics had usefully revealed the importance of community and household practices in sustaining migration, thus overcoming individualistic views of the migrant as a disembedded individual, alongside networks and chain migration studies (see Schrover, 2018). This emphasis on migrant ethnic ties and networks, or ethnic enterprises, while apparently shifting attention to the agency of migrants, tend to reflect yet again the native point of view as it turns successful migrants into the best representatives of the ideology of meritocratic systems of social mobility promised by the free market economy and its liberal state. Those 'who make it', especially if they are migrants, demonstrate the 'reality' of social mobility and incorporate the notion of 'deservingness' by succeeding under competitive economic systems and labour markets (see also Chauvin et al, 2013). Such an approach has been criticized by authors such as De Genova (2005) and Mezzadra (2011a) for reproducing at the same time the fixed and internally homogenous notions of ethnic communities (Glick Schiller and Çağlar, 2011), and the idea that social mobility (as well as migrant-self-exploitation) occurs mostly along the line of ethnic succession (compare Bloch, 2013).

Mezzadra (2011a: 128) is particularly critical of the notions of migrant integration reproduced by the new economics of migration, in that they are far from questioning the very 'integrative code' of capitalist or commercial models of citizenship (see also Honig, 2001) and individual success. In the new economics of migration, the processes of exclusion, stigmatization, and discrimination that migrants and minority Black and ethnic people continue to be subject to are presented as mere 'side effects' of a capitalism (and citizenship), in turn reinforced by migration as victims. In contrast, the autonomy of migration approach starts from highlighting the power of the tensions that migration generates (Papastergiadis, 2000). These tensions are primarily identified in the historical conflict between the politics of labour controls and the politics of migration, including migrants' own collective practices of resistance despite their lack of citizenship and despite their precarity in the workplace.

Further criticising integrationist approaches with the term 'differential inclusion', Mezzadra and Neilson (2013) indicated the current attempts by states and capitalists to manage the mobility of migrants in a differential manner: rather than merely by excluding or expelling undocumented migrant workers, or simply segregating them to the margins or the secondary segment of the labour market, migrant labour appears as partially included in the local labour market through migration regime, sexist racialization, and subordination. In turn, such forms of differentiation are made possible by a multiplication of 'subject statuses', through the production of a variety of legal and contractual figures that differently exploit migrants through differentiated categories of dependency, constrained mobility, and efforts at controlling their intractable political subjectivities (Neilson, 2009). Critically, these differences are also used by management to actively fragment instances of solidarity in the workforce (Jordhus-Lier, 2014). Similarly, the threat of deportability and the illegalization of undocumented migrants (De Genova, 2002) show how, far from merely expelling paperless migrants from the labour market, the border functions as a disciplining tool to keep wages low and make migrant workers disposable. The fact that mobility is differentially accessed also indicates its relationality: mobility for some maybe means immobility for others (migrant and non).[15]

State migration policies appear, therefore, critical to sustaining regimes of labour valorization and segmentation, adding to the mix of labour market de- and re-regulation, welfare reforms, and new transnational migrations and migrant division of labour in the global cities of the North (Ehrenreich and Hochschild, 2003; Wills et al, 2009), as well as in emerging capitalist economies and global production sites (Chan and Selden, 2017; Chan et al, 2020). And yet, such 'bordering technologies' are constantly challenged and put under pressure by migrant mobility practices, which are far from simply reacting to strategies of control and governmentality in contemporary migration regimes (Mezzadra and Neilson, 2013). Therefore, state and supranational borders should not be seen as rigid entities established once and for all and impenetrable, but as continuously criss-crossed and made porous by migrants' own mobility practices (Papadopoulos and Tsianos, 2013), as well as by the states' and capital's own interest at differentially including rather than merely excluding migrants and foreigners.

Understanding the relative autonomous nature of migratory movement is part and parcel of the same epistemological effort at overcoming methodological nationalism and recentering mobility as a form of social conflict in capitalism that we have considered previously in our critique to segmentation theories. The stream of interdisciplinary research known as the autonomy of migration perspective has made a critical contribution in this regard. Drawing from research on the historical mobility of workers across borders and across the Atlantic (see Moulier-Boutang, 1998; Steinfeld and Engerman, 1997; van der Linden, 2008), members of this current argue that the historical accumulation of capital has been marked by 'a *structural tension* between the ensemble of subjective practices in which the mobility of labour expresses itself' (Mezzadra 2011a: 121). In this sense, the autonomy of migration perspective transcends the nation state and understands migration as a social movement, 'in the literal sense of the words, not as a mere response to economic and social malaise ... but as a creative force within these structures' (Papadopoulos et al, 2008: 202).

Scheel (2013b) has recently summarized the different components of the autonomy of migration perspective as follows: the emphasis of the socio-subjective dimension of migration (beyond economistic readings of migrants' drivers to move); the fact that migration is a constituent force 'from below' rather than simply driven by macro dynamics inherent to capitalist social systems 'from above'; that the movement of people across borders precedes rather than reacts to the attempt at controlling and valorizing it; and that borders constitute critical sites of contestation and social conflict. Hence, borders as a capital strategy of valorization are a response to migrants' autonomous mobility practices in the same guise as capital control functions are a response to the autonomous practices of workers. Migration can be interpreted as a form of refusal that destabilizes and questions the omnipotence of the state in controlling people's movements (Gray and Clare, 2022: 1193, but also state assumptions about social integration.

Against the accusation that this autonomist perspective romanticizes individual escape practice as intrinsically rebellious (Hastings, 2016; Scheel, 2013b), there have been attempts at redefining the concept by emphasizing the embodied and relational aspects of migrants' mobility practices, as practices of appropriation that always need to interact and always incorporate the effects of regimes of controls or government (that is, they cannot be considered in themselves as pure practices of self-determination or self-legislation):

> If autonomy is understood as the institution of a conflict between migration and the attempts to regulate it, then the analysis of people's embodied encounters with the means and methods of mobility control unravels the diversity of the practices through which people willing to move try to appropriate mobility, thereby initiating that conflict. (Scheel, 2013b: 283)

These remarks by the new generation of autonomy of migration scholars may help in understanding how we study the forms of conflict that mobility generates (including the labour turnover of migrants), without elevating them to paradigmatic forms of resistance, but as incorporations of differentially accessed forms of power that migrants may use to free themselves from exploitative labour relations. Gray and Clare (2022: 1187), from within human geography, have similarly highlighted how the strength of an autonomist approach to migration, and the question of labour mobility, lies precisely in its ability to avoid idealizing concepts whereby they rather succeed at developing 'agency oriented approaches that neither forsake determinate analysis nor romanticize resistance'. Using the language of the dialectic relationship between modes of production and modes of contestation, Gray and Clare (2022) emphasize the relationality of processes of de- and recomposition of labour and working class struggles.

Overall, recentering mobility and building this language of commonality is extremely important in an era of sharpened divisions between migrants and citizens, and even more now with the deepening inequalities in mobility and immobility that the global pandemic, energy crises, and new austerity politics has brought severely in evidence. Highlighting the commonalities between the migrant and the native is also an imperative for Anderson (2017) as she argues for bridging the discursive and material divisions between the citizen worker and the migrant worker: the relations between the two must not follow the logics of a zero-sum game where one must compete or 'take the job' of the other, even when the migrant worker may be preferred to the citizen because they are subject to immigration controls and therefore more exploitable (see also Vickers, 2020). 'Everyday bordering' (Yuval-Davis et al, 2019), where the state controls and maintains borders not only at the outside edge territory of the nation but also internally across local domains such as schools, hospitals, and workplaces, becomes therefore a process that impacts on society as a whole: while those formally excluded from access to social citizenship because of their immigration status suffer most, the experiences of migrants become exemplary and anticipatory of wider patterns of inequalities and of the denial of the 'right to belong' that affects working people and minorities more broadly. A deeper analysis of working-class divisions and the 'moulding' of employment relations through immigration controls demonstrates that 'what is bad for migrants is not necessarily good for the citizens and regulations that work to marginalize and exclude migrants do not necessarily centralize or include citizens' (Anderson, 2017: 1532).

On the contrary, the two (socially-constructed categories) seem to have more in common than it first appears. Applying this foundational mobility and notion of commonality between migrants and non-migrants, we consider that the tensions that mobility of labour produces vis-à-vis management are relatively universal and constitute in themselves a practice of resistance for all workers. Applied to the field of migration, this means considering migrant mobility power and everyday practices as embedded in particular processes of labour control and state borders' regimes, while also considering how these practices exceed them (Papadopoulos and Tsianos, 2013). Still, with its emphasis on the non-economic and subjective levers of migration as a broader social movement, what the autonomy of migration could not do was to look more carefully at the dynamics of the politics of mobility in the labour process and at the subjectivities of migrants embedded in the capitalist employment relations. This is where we believe that combining LPT and the autonomy of migration, together with insights from labour and human geographies, yields major advantages to better grasp the contemporary expression of migrant mobility power.

Concluding remarks: migrant mobility power

In summary, while labour turnover can be interpreted as an agentic form or everyday practice of mobility if voluntarily enacted by the worker (for example, to move to a better job), a compositional approach to labour migration and its autonomy highlights the ongoing efforts at the entrapment of such mobility and how this has been historically central to capitalist accumulation (Harvey, 2006; Moulier-Boutang, 1998). In particular, we have attempted deconstructing mainstream theories of labour segmentation that relegate migrants to the secondary segment of the labour market. Criticizing the deterministic approach prevalent in employment studies and CPE to the function of migration in segmenting national labour markets, we rather recentre mobility as a form of social conflict and class struggle in and beyond the labour process and in a transnational perspective. Drawing from the autonomy of migration but also geographical accounts of foundational mobility as overcoming an essentializing distinction between the migrant and the citizen, the foreign and the indigenous worker, we have rather disputed the residual nativism or nation–centrist approach to migration in industrial relations and parts of political economy.

Still, we also believe that the conceptual tools offered by critical approaches within the labour process tradition and in particular the notion of labour mobility power are necessary to understand the everyday dynamics of resistance and contestation by migrant workers in the workplace and the labour market. Our review of the theoretical literature surrounding labour migration has shown how we need to promote interdisciplinary dialogue to unpack the moments of tensions that mobility engenders for management, and the opportunities it opens for workers to build forms of resistance both individually and collectively.

Connecting the discussion on migrant labour mobility power with early studies of labour turnover, we have also highlighted that there are always elements of constraints underpinning this choice of movement, and vice-versa there are always subjective drivers that shape employers' strategies of churning labour in the organization (March and Simon, 1958). What migration studies illuminates in different ways than organizational studies do, is that the two aspects are differently entangled according to who the mover is – and how mobility is differentially managed.

The relationality between different levels and forms of mobility must therefore be considered when analysing migrant mobility practices and capacities (compare Collins, 2021) as well as the important relationship between mobility and its opposite, fixity (Brown, 2019), to reveal old and new forms of worker struggle under different compositional configurations across the Global North and South.

In the following chapters we discuss some recent studies that have indeed detected the relative turbulent nature of migrant labour in the workplace either through explicit forms of workers' resistance/cooperation, or through triggering the introduction of new forms of management and capture of migrant labour along networks of global production. We explore the links between labour mobility and labour turnover, against the tendency of industrial relations studies to see turnover as merely employer-led strategy to reduce costs and allow flexibility, or as a disruptive force individualizing worker strategies and weakening collective power on the shopfloor. Rather, we look at *labour mobility power through the lenses of transnational migration* as not solely economically driven, but a wider social force that attempts to reappropriate forms of livelihood across fields of production and social reproduction. The next chapter applies this perspective to understand the mechanics of the management of migration by multiple actors.

2

The Logistics of Living Labour

The kafala system in the Persian Gulf

On 4 August 2019, hundreds of workers in Al Shahaniya, Qatar, went on strike to get their overdue wages and to demand the abolition of the kafala sponsorship system that forces workers to obtain permission from their employer if they want to work for another company.[1] Although strikes are illegal in many of the Gulf Cooperation Council (GCC) countries, and migrants are not allowed to join a union, workers in this region have a long history of informal or unauthorized strikes as well as forms of desertion (Hammer and Adham, 2022).[2] More often than not, protests end with the imprisonment and deportation of migrant workers to the country of origin and the importing of new and possibly less conflictual workforces. Qatar and Kuwait have the worst reputations in terms of treatment of workers, and migrants often prefer to move to Saudi Arabia and the UAE in search of better working and life conditions (Babar, 2021). In 2021, the Guardian estimated, based on government sources, that about 6,500 people died in Qatar for the construction of the infrastructure for the football World Cup of 2022.[3]

Starting in 1960–70s, thanks to the development of oil production and its export, labour migrations to the GCC countries came mainly from neighbouring Arab countries, such as Egypt, Palestine, and Yemen, but they have gradually been replaced by Asian workers and, recently, by migrants from Africa. The substitution of Arabs accelerated after the invasion of Kuwait and the Iraq War, when many Arab migrants (particularly Palestinians and Yemenis) were repatriated or expelled for both political and distrust reasons: if in 1975 Arabs accounted for 72 per cent of migrant workers in the GCC, by 1985 this had decreased to 56 per cent, and dropped to 23 per cent by 2009 (Babar, 2017). Critically, the substitution of Arab with Asian migrants is linked both to lower labour costs for employers and the greater difficulty for Asians to settle in the country permanently. For the local population, Asians represent a smaller demographic, and a smaller cultural and political 'threat' than Arab migrants who cannot be easily segregated into specific areas or repatriated. Moreover, the Persian Gulf countries have been active in avoiding too-large flows from a smaller number of countries, preferring a diversification strategy whereby a variety of groups is employed. These include Indians, Pakistanis, Filipinos, Bangladeshi, Yemenis, Egyptians, Indonesians, Burmese, Sinhalese, Nepalese, Lebanese, and Sudanese migrants, who constitute the backbone of the economy.[4]

The migrant labour regime operating in the Persian Gulf shows some similarities with the indentured labour system of the 19th and early 20th centuries used in the colonies of Western countries, as well as with the guest worker programme in Europe (1955–73) and the Bracero programme in the US (1942–64). One of the differences is that in the Gulf countries today, it is also the state of the country of emigration that guarantees the controllability of workers in the workplace abroad. Moreover, the strong dependence on migrant labour of Gulf countries pushes these governments to tighten state control with police repression and the co-option of trade unions. In the construction, trade, and service sectors, as well as in the education and health sectors, millions of migrants arrive to work often after having paid a fee to recruitment agencies, which play a key role in the functioning of the kafala migrant labour regime.[5] The six GCC countries account for over 10 per cent of all migrants worldwide, hence representing the third-largest hub of international labour migration. Migrant workers account for a large part of the active population, rotating constantly (IOM, 2021). As part of this programmed rotation system, with labour contracts lasting a few years, no rights to family reunion and settlement included, and with no strong unions present, migrants are left alone to face the ongoing threat of deportation.

Overall, the characteristic of the migrant labour regime in GCC countries lies in the mix of tight monitoring and the constant mobility and temporariness of migrant workers, thanks to a network of recruitment agencies and contracting companies who rely on labour camps which are sex-segregated and located in remote areas, under the daily threat of being fired if any kind of complaint is made. Further, migrant women working as domestic workers are also secluded and unable to exit their place of work unless under authorization. Crucially, workers have been long deprived of the right to freedom of movement and the right to change employment and employer, being separated from the local community (Damir-Geilsdorf and Pelican, 2018; Fernandez, 2021; Parreñas, 2022).

Private agencies in the GCC and in the countries of origin use extensive social networks in their day-to-day operations in order to obtain employment contracts and reproduce a constant supply of labour. Agencies and potential employers do not have particular face-to-face contacts, but rather rely on means such as email and online interviews. Some agencies specialize in only recruiting people for certain job positions, such as nurses, domestic workers, carpenters, or unskilled construction workers, or focus on specific destinations (Bal, 2016). These specialization niches tend to segment the employment system by gender and race, showing how what we call the logistics of living labour is also stratified according to the social characteristics of the workers (see Chapter 3). The process of evaluating individuals for a job involves a number of aspects that go beyond their work capacity strictly understood. In the case of domestic work, for instance, reliability, creativity, sociability, deference to authority, adaptability; as well as embodied and socially constructed attributes such as race, skin colour, religion, nationality, language spoken; and social characteristics such as level of education, marital status, age, and weight are all important factors that indicate that the workforce is not a commodity among others but has specific and variable attributes (Peck, 1996: 34; Parreñas, 2022). The selection and recruitment process is largely based on the demands of employers and on the professional category of labour the employer is looking for, so that stereotypes and international workforce management tend to segment specific types of workers into specific occupations. This could also be viewed as a minimization of risk due to the need to survive in a particularly competitive market (Tyner, 1998: 334–6). This unique labour regime shows how the concerted action of multiple agents, including the state and its immigration controls, employers with their geographical containment and segmentation strategies, migrant networks, and, crucially, temporary placement agencies and labour brokers, shapes the complex architecture that regulates and valorizes the mobility of labour across borders.

Making borders, making states, entrapping labour

As the case of the Gulf countries highlights, the availability of labour in places where it can be mobilized to enhance capital assets and investments has not always been extensive and cannot be taken for granted. Capital's endless search for new locations to find the best options for profit (Silver, 2003) constantly meets the problem of finding the required workforce. As highlighted by Rogaly (2009: 1975), 'capital sought its own "spatial fix", but so did labour'. For labour, moving is not an easy choice because it is embedded in particular social contexts, networks, family relations, and speaks a specific language. For this reason, a variety of national and international systems to make labour available (and transport workers to the places where they are needed), have emerged historically: from different forms of organized slavery and indentured labour (Anderson and Davidson, 2004; Moulier-Boutang, 1998), to bilateral agreements between states, through nationally coordinated recruitment schemes by state-controlled employment offices (Castles and Kosack, 1973), to the expansion of private recruitment agencies globally 'assembling' local workforces (McDowell et al, 2009; Peck and Theodore, 2007; Lindquist et al, 2012; Ward, 2004).

The management of labour mobility has varied greatly over the centuries both in terms of the scale of labour needs and the complexity of activities. In this regard, the application of one system rather than another is linked to the political situation and to the power relations between both states and classes at local and international level. On the one hand, some areas have been deliberately kept poor by international forces in order to increase the emigration of labour and guarantee labour availability elsewhere (Cohen, 1987). On the other hand, there is no doubt that workers have resorted to even spontaneous movements, helped in this by kinship and friendship networks (Andrikopoulos and Duyvendak, 2020; Choldin, 1973; Ciupijus et al, 2020; Gold, 2005).

As Schrover (2018) notes, a rigid distinction has often been drawn between forced migration and labour migration, whereby the former always means compulsion and the latter means choice. In contrast, he argues that it is only in recent discussion that intermediaries and brokers (largely studied in the 19th century) are now seen in a negative light as increasing the exploitation of migrants, because they circumvent state regulation of migration. Going strongly against such a dichotomy, Schrover (2018: 444) argues that we must find in the 'dominance of the traditional push-and-pull paradigm, with its emphasis on choice' the overlooking of the fact that slavery as forced migration was a form of labour migration.[6]

Schematically, the debate on the regulation or government of migration may be divided into two camps, between scholars that support the idea that migration is driven from above and those who argue that it is a self-governing movement from below, but recently more nuanced middle-ground solutions have also been developed. In the first camp, scholars underline how the state, or other international institutions like the European Union (Castles and Kosack, 1973; Mantu and Guild, 2013; Castles, 2006), or indeed individual employers, act as 'gatekeepers' (Rodriguez, 2004) of migration and critically shape its pace and patterns, primarily according to labour and economic demand. This literature notes that the control of migration flows is governed and 'paced' primarily by state policies, employers, and international labour intermediaries, reducing access to housing, constraining migrant workers' opportunities in the labour market, and making them vulnerable through the borders of citizenship. When capital must stay in place, like in the service sector, or because there are international rules and institutional constraints that do not allow its flow, migrants are assembled to meet production needs in the different locations (for example, McDowell et al, 2009). In fact, labour migration is not only the movement of individuals, but it is a means to support the needs of capital's (relative) immobility (see Chapter 1). Analysing the situation of Chinese migrants in Japan, Korea, and Singapore, Xiang Biao (2012) underlines that migrants move on the basis of their employer's (or agency's) needs, and they are moved to the exact places where they are expected to start working immediately. This 'labour transplant' therefore seeks not only 'just-in-time migration' but also to bring labour 'to the point of allocation' to satisfy the demand of an immobile capital (Xiang, 2012).

In the opposite camp to the governance from above, moving away from institutionalist approaches, researchers from the autonomy of migration perspective understand labour migration as a collective form of exit from environments where capital and the state control labour movement (Mezzadra, 2011b; Papadopoulos and Tsianos, 2013). As Moulier-Boutang (1998) underlines, the control of labour mobility explains, at least in part, the formalization of the employment relationship, and more generally the emergence of wage labour as the historical expression of capital's interest to entrap labour in place. In his book 'De l'esclavage au salariat: économie historique du salariat bridé' [From Slavery to Wage Labour: historical economy of restricted wage labour], Moulier-Boutang (1998) argues that there is a continuity in the form of labour exploitation from slavery into capitalism, and that the tightening of labour in place through migration controls is one of the mechanisms that allows for the reduction of workers' ability to escape from the subjugation of wage and pre-capitalist forms of subjugation, whether through slavery, indenture mechanisms, serfdom, and others forms of spatial mobility constrictions, punishment, and discipline (see also Anderson, 2013; van Rossum and Kamp, 2016). On similar lines, and from within critical and postcolonial theory, Mezzadra (2011b: 159) has argued that a variety of social science disciplines have long taken for granted the 'normality' of the wage labour relation in capitalism, and rather indicated in the growing heterogeneity of semi-free labour and employment relations that featured both in colonial societies and reappear in postcolonial ones, a more suitable form to understand labour in global capitalism vis-à-vis the relative decline of the so-called standard employment relation (see also Vosko, 2010).

In the middle camp, the mobility infrastructure perspective (Lindquist et al, 2012; Xiang, 2007) has provided a critical framework to understand the operation of migration infrastructures from below (including migrants' own networks, migrant private brokers and state agencies, employers, and international bodies) as still directed by the state and capitalist market, encapsulating a form of 'delegation of state authority to private actors as part of a process of deregulation and neoliberal globalization' (see also MacKenzie and Martínez Lucio, 2019; MacKenzie, Forde and Ciupijus, 2012). Indeed, in the words of Schrover (2018: 452), one of the benefits of the concept of migration infrastructure developed by Xiang and Lindquist (2014: 122) is that it explains the ambivalent patterns of migration today as the outcome of such infrastructures, whereby for instance in the case of Asia, labour migration is made at the same time 'more accessible and more cumbersome'.

As critically discussed by Schrover (2018), a profusion of categories and definitions of migration have emerged in the past few years without however advancing comparisons and dialogue between different strands of research. For instance, migration system, chain migration, and network migration all pointed to the self-perpetuating nature of migration beside original factors that trigger labour flow in the first instance (employer demand at a particular time and in a particular sector), as the migrant community becomes the main source of new migratory movements (Lucassen and Bloch, 1987).

From our perspective, we are witnessing the involvement of a wider range of actors in the management of labour migration, and some sharper forms of labour constrictions and immobilization of migrant labour. It is no coincidence that a variety of temporary migrant labour regimes have sprung up across the world, including in Global South countries. In this regard, Charanpal S. Bal (2016) has emphasized the notion of migrant regimes specifically from the point of view of capitalist social relations in contexts where the role of the state in managing migration is of greater importance. Comparing migrant labour struggles in Asia and in the GCC, Bal (2016) observes a wider shift towards both more flexible labour relations as well as temporary arrangements for the recruitment and residence of migrant workers. While such common trends emerge, the comparisons across different Asian and Gulf countries confirms the general argument that 'while migrant labour regimes are highly suppressive of workers agitation, they nonetheless generate a range of contextually specific workplace tensions which either forward or limit civil society pressures for reform' (Bal, 2016: 209). As emerged from Bal's study, even in the same country, such as in Singapore, there are differences in the ways migration controls operate for construction workers from China and Bangladesh. While the latter's major risk is connected to early repatriation and indebtedness, the former are confronted with difficulties in quitting their jobs before the completion of their contracts, as the penalty of leaving is particular high (their 'deposits', three months withheld wages, and further financial fines) (Bal, 2016: 212). Bal (2016: 7) critically emphasizes that: 'a migrant labour regime is a more specific mode of macro-level labour control based on the construction of migrant worker powerlessness as a means to inhibit the political contestation of labour'. What the notion of migrant labour regime offers as compared to, for example, migration systems is precisely its emphasis on the hegemonic and power dynamics built into these systems of control/regulation. In this sense, agencies as intermediaries are not 'simply selling opportunities for migrating, but are also dealing with various components of infrastructure—such as collecting documents, organizing medical tests, or conducting pre-departure training—which have far-reaching regulatory effects' (Schrover, 2018: 452). We note that these components of infrastructure can be understood as critical aspects in the renewal of labour. Hence, labour intermediaries enter in the largest affair of the reproduction and sustainability of labour mobility. Bal's definition of migrant labour regimes, while still state-centered, is important for our analysis because it brings together the question of labour controls, the regulation of immigration, and worker voice. Therefore, although different migrant labour regimes can follow a similar logic, the different social compositions and spatial configurations of the workforces create unique power dynamics and situations in each location.[7]

Each regime also expresses unique tensions and characteristics which are specific to the particular place and time in which they develop, illustrating the different roles played by migrant networks and migrant mobility practices in reproducing or challenging the stability of such systems. In our final section we will return to the strengths of migration studies which have lain in their capacity to bring together a sharper analysis of the policy dimension of migration (Castles, 2004), and the focus on the everyday lived experiences of key actors in the making of different migration systems. They have thus combined the analysis of subjective and regulatory forces shaping migration (compare Sassen, 1996), but perhaps fail to include the critical perspective of labour-capital conflict in the logistics of living labour.

Taking into account the debates on migration, this chapter analyses what we understand as the logistics of living labour from the perspective of relatively (in)formal actors: state policies, employers, agencies/intermediaries, migrants, and their social networks and families.[8] Overall, we suggest that *labour turnover is a receptive sensor of migrants' behaviour* that builds on, but also partly challenges, Bal's (2016) emphasis on the creation of migrant powerlessness in his definition of the migrant labour regime. In spite of the several mechanisms put in place by employers, states, and agencies to limit the mobility and opportunities for protest and organizing of migrant workers, we show how migrants' mobility defies or at least questions capital and state efforts to maintain a continuous recruitment flow, to dispose of migrant workers at will, and smoothly substitute them with new groups of workers.

The politics of mobility and everyday practices

As part of the 'mobility turn' in migration studies during the 2000s, Cresswell (2010) defined mobility as encompassing a range of cases, 'from the micro-movements of the body to the politics of global travel', to then develop the notion of the politics of mobility to capture the various elements of mobility that make it a political act. He developed a meso theoretical approach that can in turn inform theorizations of gender, ethnicity, or any other form of social relations. This author criticized past migration studies for having focused more on place, and push and pull factors moving people from one place to another, and rather highlighted how 'pervading constellations of mobility' exist at any one time historically, consisting of 'particular patterns of movement, representations of movement, and ways of practising movement that make sense together' (Cresswell, 2010: 18).

Such a holistic approach to mobility is helpful to understand the historically specific representation of turnover as a form of both labour and human mobility, while looking at workers' mobility practices on the ground to overcome or survive their precariousness (see also Hansen and Zechner, 2017; Zechner and Hansen, 2015). In this regard, we found particularly helpful Yuval-Davis's (2013) notion of everyday practice, as developed in her study of 'everyday bordering': rather than reducing mundane practices of individuals and groups to mere survival, habit, and repetition, as individuals search for stability in their social reproduction, or constraining them to the realm of the domestic and the private, Yuval-Davis (2013) posits the everyday as also constituting:

> An arena of conflict and struggle. A struggle aimed at maintaining continuity, accommodating the constant disruption of tradition and the production of the new, struggles between classes, genders, ethnicities etc, between producer and consumers, human desire and obdurate and exhaustible worlds. It points to the material actuality of living through conflict and change. It's often the site of the invisible hurt of discrimination, of constant negotiation of a changing world, of our attempt to live. (Yuval-Davis, 2013: 10)

In turn, the study of everyday bordering must be located within this construction of the everyday life and practice. 'Borderwork' is understood by Yuval-Davis (2013: 14–16) as not simply the outcome of high politics, visa regimes, and media debates on national identities, but as continuously made and remade by everyday cultural, economic and social practices. These include the involvement of private agencies in enforcing borders and controlling people's mobility, such as employers, and health and educational institutions, which have, we would argue, important effects in terms of increasing precarity in the employment relationships. In this sense, 'bordering practices and social divisions affect one another, are constantly changing and can include as well as exclude'.

Further unveiling the politics of mobility, De Genova (2013: 253) argues that 'if there were no borders, there would be no migrants—only mobility'. Conversely, borders and migration create each other, and 'are brought into being in and through the daily encounters between people on the move and those charged with controlling their mobility' (Scheel, 2013a: 285). This scholarship illuminate the politicization of migration as a problematic field, because it is embedded in a network of often conflicting interests and power dynamics in the global economy.

In this context, it is also important to point out the relative limitations of migration studies that tend to homogenize the migrant subject under a false universalism, erasing the labour question (ironically in a way mirroring employment studies' treatment of the worker as a universal category of subjectivity/consciousness). While labour studies may lack sensitivity for the subjective aspects of migration, presenting an over-institutionalist view (see

Chapter 1), on their part migration studies have tended to reproduce another form of functionalism, where emphasis is put on the increasing transnational mobility of people as an unavoidable effect of wider social, technological, and cultural processes of globalization, including the democratization of travel with low cost opportunities for long-distance mobility (see for instance Vertovec, 2009). Recent research on the mobility practices and survival strategies of 'middling transnationals' (Conradson and Latham, 2005b), for instance, highlights the multiplicity of subjective drives and reasons to move (against the crystallized notion of the 'economic migrant'), developing more nuanced notions of social class as also transformed through migration (see also McDowell et al, 2007). However, the same research also again risks depoliticizing the issue of migrant labour and its exploitation, and reproduces the mistaken image of a deregulated and permissive labour market where free-floating migrants exercise their mobility, acting as free individuals, or economically or self-development driven market actors (Conradson and Latham, 2005b: 228). In other words, by emphasizing mobility as the major factor shaping migrants' experiences, mainstream approaches to transnationalism risk building a 'class-neutral' view of transmigrants and transform their mobility into a fetish. This is a risk that an interdisciplinary approach to the politics of mobility and the labour power implications of migrant mobility might help us overcome.

Against the risk of remaining trapped by a 'fetishizing' view of mobility, romanticizing it as a radical act of liberation or demonizing it as disruptive of orderly labour and social relations (see Chapter 1), we refer to labour mobility as a mundane fact of many workers' lives around the world, and to their practices of mobility as politically meaningful not because they represent a superior form of agency, but because they appear as historically embedded in power dynamics, and because workers use mobility as a source of liberation against oppression and exploitation.

Understanding the everyday politics of mobility requires one also to question the nationalistic approaches pervading the field of migration studies. In a recent article, Paul and Yeoh (2021) have developed the notion of multinational migration as an umbrella term trying to bring together other concepts proliferated in the past decade to highlight the transient, irregular, multidirectional, and stone-stepping nature of migration. Their notion differs from early definitions of transnational migration which, while including a third or more countries in their theorization (Glick Schiller et al, 1995; Faist, 2006), still maintained as a focus of analysis the transnationalism of already settled migrants. Authors like Glick Schiller et al (1995: 48) focused on how transmigrants create transnational ties mostly between 'societies of origin and settlement', maintaining an emphasis on the different degrees or type of attachment that migrants still maintain to 'their' countries.[9] For instance, Engbersen et al (2017: 340), while trying to identify new patterns of migration, maintain the nation state and social integration as the main lenses. From our point of view, the question today is that even if nationalism is growing in many countries, the attachment of migrants to the nation (and to a single workplace) appears very feeble, providing a further ground for the critique of integrationist approaches to migration based on methodological nationalism (see Chapter 1).

The unique perspective offered by Paul and Yeoh's (2021) theorization of multinational migration in this regard is to emphasize the different nature or directionality of these movements, not always upwards in terms of the preferred destination, but also backwards and 'lateral', when for instance a state's strict immigration controls push migrants to move away from the preferred country when the contract of employment has expired. Critically, what makes these multinational migrations possible is precisely the embeddedness of mobilities in infrastructures that 'enable (and sometimes requires) such movements between countries' (Paul and Yeoh, 2021: 7).

But what migration theories help to do vis-à-vis this past labour literature it to bring to the fore the cracks and tensions that may emerge from this fragile architecture of mobility and fixity. While Yeoh and Paul emphasize the importance of the embeddedness of such mobility infrastructures into existing regulatory systems, markets, and opportunity structures, Andrijasevic and Sacchetto (2016) have developed an understanding of the multinational migrant worker as disrupting the very assumptions about mobility and fixity that capital project onto migrants. This figure of the multinational worker (see also Serafini, 1974) is considered the most effective to illustrate 'the practices of an emergent workforce' engaged in monotonous, low paying, and intense work, such as those involved in the factory work of the electronics plants in Eastern Europe. And yet, rather than as a mere response to employers' strategies of stratifying the workforce, or merely the temporary arrangements of labour management to satisfy fluctuating demands and high labour turnover, this notion of the multinational worker recentres mobility focusing on migrant 'desire to improve their lives and create better opportunities for themselves and their families' (Andrijasevic and Sacchetto 2016: 222). Rather than limiting mobility practices to an individual workplace or country, the multinational worker shows how migrants share knowledge about job searches and strategize around their opportunities to find employment across different labour markets, comparing wages, terms and conditions, and life in different sites. In doing so, they defy both employers' expectations about their availability to work irregular and insecure jobs (for meagre remuneration), as well as trade unions' strategies that tend to exclude migrant agency workers and reduce them to the role of a disposable reserve army of labour. The multinational migrant worker is therefore a critical figure of how both economic and non-economic drivers of labour mobility intersects, how they involve a multi/transnational perspective, but also how they contribute from below to the regulation of labour and mobility both within and across states (Bauder, 2006; see also Morrison et al, 2020).

Drawing from the mobility turn in migration studies, the autonomy of migration, and the notion of mobility practices, and retaining the notion of migrant labour regime, we further develop theories of migration and mobility infrastructures, emphasizing labour capital dynamics. In addition we highlight migrant non-economic drivers of mobility through a multi-agents' understanding of the contemporary mobility assemblages underpinning the logistics of migrant labour as living labour transnationally.

Migration infrastructures: states, intermediaries, and migrant networks

According to Xiang and Lindquist's (2014: 124) original formulation in the context of East Asia, migration infrastructures are defined as 'the systematically interlinked technologies, institutions, and actors that facilitate and condition mobility'. Migration infrastructures can be distinguished along five distinct dimensions: "the commercial (recruitment intermediaries), the regulatory (state apparatus and procedures for documentation, licensing, training and other purposes), the technological (communication and transport), the humanitarian (NGOs and international organizations), and the social (migrant networks)' (Xiang and Lindquist, 2014: 124). From the point of view of cross-border mobility, other researchers argue that the role of infrastructures need to be seen as encompassing the whole trajectory of migrant movement, whereby a proper migration industry has emerged as an organized transnational business (with connections to different parts of the world), and where a variety of actors such as recruiters, brokers, coyotes, travel agents, missionaries, transportation providers, lawyers, and money lenders play a critical role aimed at enabling and managing migration (for example, Schrover, 2018).

Considering the political regulation of migration, while migrant labour has historically been seen in the Global North as a supplement to the domestic workforce (as in the tradition of the post-war 'guest worker programmes'), today's reorganization of the labour market rather takes the shape of a 'porous' and differential border regime (Bojadžijev et al, 2004), reflecting the need for an increasingly flexible and just-in-time supply of labour structural to the current modes of production. In the past decade, points-based systems for immigration have spread across countries as different as Australia, Britain, Canada, Czech Republic, Germany and Singapore, indicating an effort by governments to facilitate highly skilled migration in the 'global race for talent' (Ruhs, 2013), while formally curtailing the channels for medium- and low-skilled workers.[10] In reality, employers and states continue to eagerly look for relatively low-skilled labour, whereby behind the rhetoric of the 'global race for talents', or hostile systems to 'illegal immigrants' guaranteeing sovereign control, ongoing adaptation of national and international migration policies allow for the entry of different categories of exploitable migrants 'through the back door' or/and indirectly favour the formation of informal labour market niches for undocumented migrants (De Genova, 2002; Anderson, 2013).

In recent years, there have been a proliferation of circular migration programmes as new versions of guest workers schemes (Castles, 2006; Ruhs and Martin, 2008), reflected in initiatives by supranational institutions adopting developmental narratives about 'win-win-win' solutions for both country of origin and destination *and* individual migrant workers, achieved through temporary migration programmes such as between the EU and Africa (Vertovec, 2009; Castles and Ozkul, 2014). In Europe, bilateral labour agreements between states flourished in the first part of the 20th century when they became the principal tool to organize and regulate the temporary mobility of workers.[11] Bilateral agreements have reflected the power relations between states, and have been put in place as a way to cage, discipline, and regulate the mobility of workers, establishing also the rights and duty of this rotating workforce. This form of regulation of the labour market had strong social and political effects. On their side, under bilateral agreements, one of the aims of receiving countries was to obtain almost 'a workforce on loan', avoiding the permanent settlement of migrants. The purpose of migrants' highly controlled, temporary status under these state-managed rotation regimes is not limited to the aim of avoiding migrants' longer term settlement, but also to shape their employment relations in the country of destination (Fudge, 2012).

If bilateral agreements fluidify the flow of migrant workers, sometimes countries of origin and countries of destination struggle to exert control over the labour force. On 16 October 1948, a group of about a thousand men gathered on the Mexican side of the river that separates Ciudad Juarez from El Paso. The scene had been repeated for three days; at a signal, they moved, crossing the shallow river and, despite some timid attempts by Mexican soldiers to stop them, arriving on the opposite bank. Here, dozens of US farmers were waiting for them in large trucks used to transport cattle. After quickly negotiating wages and working conditions, the farmers went to the immigration office to declare how many men they had recruited, promising to deliver the list of names shortly. As they left the office, they realized that some of the newly recruited Mexicans had already changed employers, enticed by the offer of slightly higher wages from other farmers (Salinas, 2018: 139–40). This episode, known as the El Paso Incident, grew from the tension between Mexico and the US on the bargaining of workforces within the so-called Bracero programme (1942–64) that brought about four to five million people from Mexico into the US. In fact, the

Bracero programme, while born out of pressure from the US growers' lobby to provide an available and temporary labour supply, and reduce its costs of maintenance and reproduction, must be considered also as the result of a negotiation between two countries and as including some new 'rights' and 'benefits' for these workers, while showing the important role played by intermediaries and gangmasters in this process (Salinas, 2018). However, now it is well evident that Mexican migrant workers were able to bargain for themselves without waiting for the protection of their state.

The recent migration literature has illuminated how circular migrations are not always induced/programmed by the state, multi-state agencies, or employers' needs, but they are more an outcome of the effects of restrictions on migrant workers' mobility and their own strategies in dealing with them. The in-depth ethnography on the global 'trade' of Indian IT workers as 'body shopping' across Australia, the US, and Canada, conducted by Xiang (2007), is a masterful illustration of the role of third parties in the ongoing reproduction and circulation of migrant labour. Serving the larger IT multinationals in the US and Australia, these 'body shops' constitute the bones and the blood of the logistics of the global information technology industry, and the secret and invisible infrastructures allowing for the success of venture capitalists and entrepreneurs in innovation hot spots like Silicon Valley in California. However, moving to the terrain of worker resistance, the account of Xiang does not leave much space for freedom or agency. While the author acknowledges practices of exit as the most significant in the temporal system of labour management in global body shopping, he also constructs a relatively totalizing image of a system that atomizes, fragments, and carefully controls a workforce made of fundamentally compliant bodies. Critically for our study, Xiang (2007) himself makes reference to Hirschman's distinction between exit, voice, and loyalty, but maintains a rigid distinction across these concepts and types of acts among workers, rather than acknowledging some levels of fluidity among them.

Despite these limitations, Xiang's contribution to the debate on the logistics of living labour is absolutely critical. In particular, the proposed notion of 'benched labour' as one of the key functions of the logistics of body shopping in the 'Indian triangle' is particularly relevant for our analysis, since it highlights the important role of the temporal aspect of labour management operated by these intermediaries as they manage labour across borders and provide ready-made skilled workers to the market on demand; hiring but then leaving workers on the bench was a practice considered profitable by the body shops because it provided a pool of labour on-site and produced a labour reservoir 'to recruit workers whenever they needed without having to maintain a relationship with any particular small agent' (Xiang, 2007: 72). The larger firms were favoured not only by state regulation, attributing them special entitlements as business sponsors of overseas workers, but they also developed their own 'specialised immigration personelle' to sort visa applications, liaise with the government, and keep up to date with policy reform. Such specialization by agencies in the field of migration and visa management is certainly an aspect that few scholars have studied (Alberti, 2014; Samaluk, 2016), and that we consider central to understanding the reshaping of migration management in terms of the multiplication of actors (not only borders) that sustain the ongoing mobility of labour transnationally. It is also crucial to achieve the temporal arrangements that allow the holding of potential labour in reserve, the externalization of socially reproductive costs, and the artificial reduction/increase of the migrant wage while on the bench, and to 'regulate' the time of work and non-work, formal and informal work, and indeed the reproduction of the entire system of global body shopping. This system of global body shopping is therefore key to understanding migration management today, as it illustrates not only the spatial (national labour regimes), but also the temporal role that borders perform in the differential inclusion of labour (Rigo, 2005) whereby the subjecting of migrants to programmed delays to raise the price of their labour also functions to reproduce the need and demand for transnational labour mobility (and therefore the sustenance of the business that facilitates it).

In recent years, and particularly under the global economic crisis, beginning in 2007–8, we have witnessed a growing differentiation of 'recruitment schemes and types of visa, aiming at encoding the position of individual migrants according to their presumed 'skills' as well as to nationality, language, cultural and religious criteria' (Mezzadra, 2015: 36). Such points systems allegedly predict a series of capabilities according to migrants' prospects to integrate in the destination country's society, which increasingly include language skills, age, financial resources, and endorsement of national values (Mezzadra and Neilson, 2013: 139). In a nutshell, the migrant that does not comply with such complex criteria or simply does not own the right assets is either relegated to a highly temporary status (often tied to particular sectors or occupation) or simply denied legal access. These mechanisms have critical implications for the employment relation, producing high degrees of insecurity and precariousness in the areas of work, mobility, and social rights. The central device of the temporary work–residence permit of many migration regimes in Global North countries (Miller and Castles, 2019) is, in fact, the dependency of migrants upon the employer-sponsored contract which directly produces migrant precariousness in the context of their employment relations (Anderson, 2010).

It is worth noting that research stressing the role of states and intermediaries in the management of migration are often based in Asian countries, where governments systematically encourage the circulatory transnational mobility of migrants through different systems, from new visa categories to extending special rights to emigrants. At the same time, the role of migration industries in managing borders is particularly crucial when migration policies are restrictive and the controls at the point of entry are strengthened. Xiang (2012: 735) highlights how the regulation of migration 'remains a jealously guarded prerogative of state sovereignties, and its operation has become even more centralized, precisely because of increasing public concerns about migration and perceived national vulnerability in the face of globalization'.

From the point of view of the workplace and social reproduction, we may therefore add further actors operating migration infrastructures to those mentioned earlier, such as supervisors, managers, trade unions, housing and benefits agents, and other agents and brokers that intermediate and shape migrants' employment relations. Indeed, who exactly is intervening in such precarious relations also needs including in our understanding of migration infrastructures if we are interested in the shadow that the border projects onto the workplace.

The mobility of individuals and their opportunities to find jobs are indeed becoming more and more subject to formal and informal restraints as repressive and selective mobility control techniques operate both directly at the frontier and at a distance (Bigo and Guild, 2005). This regimentation of mobility has to undergo special contractual arrangements through private recruitment agencies supported or enforced by specific state legislations. In the EU, for example, a specific legislation on labour mobility has been adopted under the free movement of service, the so-called posted workers directive. In this way, labour mobility is institutionalized to immediately fulfill employers' needs and regulate the local labour market (Lillie, 2012), as we will further explore in Chapter 3.

Migrants and their networks are a daily challenge for state and employers as it is precisely the ability and will of migrants to move, with their social networks, which makes them a subject to be closely monitored through widespread social control practices. The creation of a specific legislation makes the state (or as in the case of posted workers, a supranational institution, the EU) formally a 'monopolist' in the management of migrant workers (Moulier-Boutang, 1998: 45), attempting to keep track of the sudden movements and 'whereabouts' of migrants, but also pursuing the externalization of migration controls to private actors (Dajani, 2021; Yuval-Davis et al, 2019), and deepening migrant socio-labour vulnerability through exclusion from public services for different categories of illegalized or precarious subjects (for example, Schweitzer, 2015; Hodkinson et al, 2021).

In summary, while acknowledging the complex interactions of formal and informal agents of migration from above and below, and their mutual political interest in shaping relatively unpredictable cross-border migration (Shire, 2020), it is helpful to maintain a degree of analytical distinction of the different forces and actors that concur to shape labour mobility, including *the state, intermediaries, and migrant networks*. Still, we find some limitations in defining a neat distinction between: a) the state as the principal regulator and controller of the mobility; b) intermediaries as operators that manage mobility driven by profit; and c) migrant social networks as developing a system of self-help and support for compatriots, friends, and parents (compare McCollum and Findlay, 2018: 571).[12] On the contrary, we believe that the actions of these different actors are often intermeshed and mutually constituting. As it will become apparent throughout this and the following chapters, the former two are substantially reliant on, or embedded in, migrant networks, while workers use their knowledge and the freedom of movement, when it is there, to their advantage for work opportunities in different markets that suit them best. Contrary to the victimization scenario, migrant workers through their mobility practices and social ties can utilize mobility and temporariness to exit unfavourable working and living conditions, and set themselves free from constraining labour regimes imposed by employers on the low-paid temporary workforce (see also Azmeh, 2014).

The transnational state management of migration

Certainly one of the main contributions of migration studies since the classics (Castles and Kosack, 1973; Castles et al, 2003) has been to show the relevant role of the state in managing labour mobility. Historically, it is possible to detect the action of governments, including during colonial times, in moving cohorts of workers and residents across their dominions, but also in building infrastructures themselves for the facilitation of human mobility. As highlighted by Schrover (2018: 446), the role of governments to stimulate migration has been historically significant by 'improving transport infrastructures, subsidizing travel, initiating liberal migration regulations, and establishing indentured labour regimes.' When states and employers coordinate their needs for migrant labour, their collaboration shapes recruitment chains in which labour intermediaries play a fundamental role, acting as gatekeepers (Rodriguez, 2004) of labour migration. The state, therefore, plays a central role in the social construction of the process of commodification of migrant labour by both encouraging the proliferation of private employment agencies specializing in overseas job placement, and involving employer associations and other actors in the management of migration, since they are invited regularly to take part in government consultations to regulate immigration flows (Axelsson et al, 2022). However, if the enlargement of worldwide supply chains requires more labour mobility, at the same time it increases mobility power, pushing governments and employers to strengthen controls on migration. In fact, the receiving state formulates policy to manage foreign workers through visa regimes, allowing employers to have additional control over migrant lives as the residence permit is often linked to the labour contract (Anderson, 2010). One of the more striking episodes that exemplify how the 'states have the authority to decide who is who and differentiate rights accordingly' (Schrover, 2018: 434) come from the US–Mexico border. In April 1947, for the first time in history, Mexican workers without documents could legalize themselves through the Bracero programme. A.L. Cramers was the first US farmer to arrive in the public immigration offices with his hundred or so employees. For regularization, migrants had undergone an interview and other examinations both north of the border, that is, in the US, and south of the border, that is, in Mexico, by crossing the Hidalgo Bridge. At the end of this wandering back and forth over the border, those who were illegal workers become legal, highlighting how the state defines the status of each individual (Salinas, 2018: 132–3). The role of the state in differentiating rights is also evident in the cases of China and Russia (and before the USSR), where internal migrant workers are confronted with compulsory residence systems, respectively, the hukou and propiska systems (Andrijasevic et al, 2020; Morrison et al, 2020).

Throughout history, the management of mobility within the state or within an empire has, in fact, often been regulated by governments. With the higher immigration rate worldwide in the period 1881–1939 (Huff and Caggiano, 2008), Malaya could be considered an interesting historical case study of the transnational control of migrant workers by the state and its multiple agents: 'All the necessary arrangements for their sojourn abroad – recruitment, transportation, and employment – were made by a mix of state and private apparatuses including four parties: the sub-imperial Indian government (or India Office); the Colonial Office in London; the Malayan (Straits Settlements and FMS) government; and Western entrepreneurs' (Kaur, 2012: 232). After the British state extended their control on the Malay Peninsula at the end of the 19th century, they used the imperial connections to mobilize a labour supply chain involving, in particular, India and China as sending countries and Malayan states as receiving (Breman, 1990).[13] Migrant workers relied on labour brokers who were supported by the Malayan government, that in turn regulated the legal mobility of labour including the indentured labour regime and the *kangani system*.[14] These labour brokers and the indentured labour system represents historical examples of what we may call today a 'migration infrastructure', highlighting both elements of constraint and enablement of mobility. Under the indentured system (widespread between 1844 and 1910[15]), employers had to pay for transport and recruitment expenses, while wages were fixed at the point of enrolment when workers signed a contract for three to five years. Migrant workers were de facto treated as unfree and were 'bounded' to employers (Kaur, 2012: 233). The hierarchy structure of Malaya's plantation system was supported by racialized and ethnic characteristics: Europeans worked as managers, educated Asians from Kerala and Ceylon were employed in clerical and supervisory roles, while Tamils constituted the larger part of mass labourers (Ramasamy, 1992: 100). Despite the strong control inside and outside the workplaces, Indian and Chinese workers in Malaya contrasted this plantation system, both deserting in the first years of the 20th century, and progressively, from the mid-1930s, putting in place an unprecedented wave of labour actions for the improvement of working conditions (Ramasamy, 1992: 100).[16] After independence in 1957, the Malayan state introduced new legislations to manage migration, maintaining a strong continuity with the colonial migration policies, developing more links with migration-sending countries such as the Philippines, Bangladesh, and Thailand, and allowing private labour brokers and agencies to manage the recruitment of migrant workers to particular employers and localities (Kaur, 2010: 393).

Like Malaya, Germany has also been depicted as an example of the continuity of the centrality of the state in managing migrant labour regimes from the end of the 19th century till the mid-1970s (Rhoades, 1978), even if in this case the gradually growing importance of social networks of chain and family migration, that arguably made the system relatively autonomous in the longer term, should be stressed.[17] The role of the state was strengthened during the 1920s when Germany and some other European governments began to act themselves as intermediaries, including through the use of specific recruitment commissions to select migrant workers (Rass, 2012). From the 1930s and until the end of the Second World War, migration to Germany moved progressively from a voluntary to a forced system of labour control, with restrictions on the workers' free mobility (Hachtmann, 2010: 488):[18] between 1939 and 1945, foreign forced labourers amounted to 13.5 million, of whom 12 million were coerced to move (Schrover, 2018: 448).[19] The deployment of foreign workers was based on the race's hierarchy set by the Nazis: 'Workers from Scandinavia, the Netherlands, and Flanders were placed at the top, and Poles, Soviet citizens, 'Gypsies', and Jews were at the bottom of the hierarchy' (Schrover, 2018: 448; Hachtmann, 2010: 495).

Following the highly coercive and racial labour control system under the Nazi regime after the Second World War, Germany moved to a *Gastarbeiterprogramm* (1955–73). The fear of permanent settlement by migrants pushed the state at local and federal level to approve laws to support the rotation of migrants, discouraging family reunification, establishing national quotas, and imposing a recruitment term for a maximum of two years (see Chapter 5). This was the essence of the *Gastarbeiter* system: foreign workers were presented as a temporary solution for labour shortages. As in Germany, many other north-western European countries developed specific migration programmes to satisfy the needs of employers: between 1960 and 1973, more than 30 million migrant workers from the south of Europe, as well as from Africa, Asia, and Latin American countries, moved voluntary into north-western Europe (Fielding, 1993).[20]

It was the pioneering work of Castles and Kosack (1973) and Piore (1979; 1983) in migration scholarship that first spoke of a large buffer of migrant labour supply with precarious contracts and residence permits, used by industrialized nations to compromise between the need to protect and provide a certain level of security to the native workforce, and the demands for flexibility of the capitalist system. Through the rotation of migrant workers, capital and the state could save money for the reproduction of workers and get a continuous renewal of the labour force. Employers received a young, healthy, and ready-made workforce without paying the costs because reproduction was outsourced to the country of origin and migrants were accommodated in barracks, dormitories, and apartments, allowing the employer to often get an additional gain (Rhoades, 1978: 565). Indeed, the guest worker regime was attractive for capital, and not just for governments, because of the control it could exercise on the political expression and unionization of migrant workers. While Black immigrants from the Commonwealth (from the Caribbean to the Indian subcontinent) had the right to freely migrate to the UK until 1962,[21] the racialized forms of segregation and open discrimination against post-colonial migrants in the labour market acted as a force of marginalization and precarization that the temporariness of work permits similarly produced in continental Europe (Sivanandan, 1981).

However, according to Leo Lucassen's (2019) reconstruction of the post-war 'European Migration Regime', the decolonization process had a double effect on these segregation dynamics, introducing an 'ideology of equality' that led to a multiculturalism rhetoric by the state in certain contexts. Critically though, Lucassen highlights the ongoing restrictions towards Asian and African immigration by many European countries under the argument that full integration of immigrants and refugees was possible only when numbers remained limited and controlled (compare similar discourses in contemporary migration debates: Ruhs, 2013). If Lucassen illuminates the wider post-war political processes in terms of migration rhetorics and the interlinks with the growing welfare state, Castles and Kosack (1973) remain among the first to adopt an approach to migration that focuses on the labour/capital dynamics, while recognizing the importance of the ethnic segmentation of the labour market. They still emphasize the wider function of migrant labour in capitalism to explain why migrant workers fill a socio-economically disadvantaged position in the labour market and society of the destination country: having the worst jobs and social conditions are the real causes leading migrants to develop a high labour turnover (Castles and Kosack, 1973: 118).[22]

While researches on the role of destination countries have been plentiful, the migration policies of the countries of origin have not been taken as much into consideration, or have been considered passive actors due to a persisting Western-centric approach to the power of receiving countries to attract, constrain, and force these flows (Castles et al, 2003).[23] In contrast, sending countries have developed historically different and increasingly sophisticated migrant labour regimes to manage and take advantage of the economic benefits of outward migration. Lee (2017: 1457) underlines how sending countries can use three general state regime types: accommodating through *ex post* policies of diaspora management; facilitating thanks to policy aims to enable and regulate the migration flow; and, finally, directing through the intervention to reshape or build new migration channels. Further, as emerged from the case of the Philippines, some states support the construction of a 'migrant nationality', highly racialized through training programmes based on the needs of potential employers, but at least formally offering to migrants a set of rights which they can also benefit from while they are abroad (Rodriguez, 2010). In this way, workers become migrants even before they leave home (Rodriguez and Schwenken, 2013; Hoang, 2016). The Philippines can therefore be defined as a 'Migrant Export Zone', taking upon itself 'the role of national body hire agent' (Gibson and Graham, 1986: 141–2).[24] In this case, the state manages migration by authorizing private agencies and firms to export the workforce abroad. As shown by studies of migrant Filipina domestic workers in Asian countries like Taiwan, states also tend to manage a global propaganda about the ability of its migrant workforce to deliver and specialize in certain services, which also involves the formation of a sense of belonging to the country; this is not necessarily with a view to reincorporating returnees, but to keep them connected to the country of origin, and maintain a secure flow of remittances (Lan, 2006). In fact, the export of workers is one of the means by which governments deal with unemployment and foreign debt, treating labour like any other export commodity (Gibson and Graham, 1986: 131). The transnational bureaucratic apparatus of the Philippines shapes and assembles this particular commodity, labour for export, and seeks to sell it on the world labour market through bilateral agreements with other states. While for some countries this is only a temporary ploy, for others this business has become central to sustaining the national economy through remittances.[25]

In this section we have illustrated some of the different historical forms of the 'transnational state' in the management of migration, from the colonial government's restrictive policies in the case of Malaya, to the temporary migration programmes of post Second World War Europe in the case of Germany, to the role played by the country of origin in 'exporting migrants'. We have also shown how the state is imbricated with the action of multiple actors in the everyday management of labour mobility, and how government policies do not solely shape but are also reacting to the enactment and organization of migrant mobility from below.

In summary, we argue that migration cannot be understood as a fully regulated process, nor a linear movement between two places or sites, but a complex assemblage, where many actors, including the state, employers, migrants, expatriates, and residents, and their political claims, are involved and shape mobility and citizenship. Observing migrations through the prism of their various interrelated assemblages of agents and agencies, as well its intricate infrastructures, becomes necessary to fully understand the mobility of labour and the interactions of the different actors shaping the logistics of living labour from above and below.

Recruitment agencies, brokers, and gangmasters

Even in highly regimented systems of migration management, such as the case of colonial Malaya considered earlier, it is worth noticing that the employment and work of migrants were managed by the state apparatus through reliance on gangmasters, intermediaries, merchants, *kangani,* and other brokers: colonial states 'gave legal status to labour contracts issued by official recruiters and imposed penal sanctions on employees leaving work without their employers' consent' (Bosma et al, 2012: 6).[26] The use of *kangani* appears central in the Malay case, where especially Tamil and Telugu workers were initially recruited mainly under indenture contracts (1840–1910) and then, from the late 1860s (but particularly after 1910), were engaged through the *kangani* system. A *kangani,* an employer's trusted worker, moved back and forth to his village to recruit migrants among relatives, friends, and neighbours, developing a chain migration and occupying an intermediary position between the European planters and the labourer as agent of capital.[27] This system helped to decrease the costs of recruitment because the fees paid by workers to recruitment agencies were higher, making it difficult to abscond (Kaur, 2012). In contrast, the recruitment of Chinese migrants was mostly arranged by labour brokers and Chinese migrants tended to enjoy a higher degree of freedom as compared to their Indian counterparts: they could change their job easily, also moving away from the mines to urban centres.[28]

Contractors, private employment agencies, or more generally labour intermediaries, have a long history of intermediating and handling various aspects of labour flows (Piore, 1979), contributing to shape the movement of migrants worldwide since the 19th century (Lin et al, 2017).[29] In moving migrants inside a colonial empire, from country to country or from one region to another region, intermediaries facilitate mobility and insert themselves in existing migrant networks. In some cases, as underlined by Lincoln (2009: 138) for the case of Mauritius, the contractual labour migration has been 'foreshadowed by the indentured labour system'. However, to understand the role of labour intermediaries we need to 'complicate and interrogate the static view of them as profit-oriented middle-men engaged in exploitation, unethical, and criminal practices' (Babar, 2021: 70).

Generally, a labour intermediary is considered to be one point in the triangular employment relationship, the others being the direct employer (or client) and the worker (Andrijasevic and Sacchetto, 2017). Groutsis et al (2015: 1559) describe migration intermediaries 'as agents that intervene at various critical junctures to connect the migrant to the destination country labour market'. In so doing, they have to cope with the labour market of both countries, through the mobilization of labour, attracting potential migrants in the country of origin, and allocating (and managing) them (Groutsis et al, 2015). However, in some cases labour intermediaries can manage only the flow of labour, in others they (also) control workers in the workplaces, with very different relationships with the 'real' employer and the worker: we can find legal and illegal situations with exploitative gangmasters; community intermediaries as worker-agents; large recruitment agencies; subcontracting; and, as we saw, *kangany* systems. Adopting a labour migration analysis, we highlight the ways in which labour intermediaries shape the management of (mobility of) migrant workers, but at the same time how they are shaped by migrant workers' behavior (Andrijasevic and Sacchetto, 2017). In fact, the idea that labour intermediaries (and migration networks) build migration corridors within which the mobility of migrants can flow as in a kind of assembly line is misleading if it implies the annihilation of the subjectivity of migrants. What we are interested in is to emphasize two aspects of this channelling process: first, that it requires infrastructures from above and below; and second, that this system shapes racialized labour niches.

Migration industries can be described as an outsourcing of state functions to external actors, such as private firms/structures, with the aim of externalizing costs and rationalizing the flow of labour migration (Cranston et al, 2018: 546; Menz, 2013). At the end of the 1990s, about 80 per cent of all migrant workers from Asian to Arab countries – one of the major migration flows worldwide – went through private recruitment agencies (ILO, 1997). In the following years, the role of private agencies in this area continued to dominate for the vast majority of movements (Wickramasekara and Baruah, 2017: 28).[30] In the European context, it is in the 1990s that EU countries encouraged private recruitment agencies to operate. In the process of EU accession, the EU Commission required Eastern European countries to introduce agency employment into the Labour Code and set out the rules for temporary work (Hála, 2007). A strong support to the development of private agencies has been the ILO Convention no. 181/1997 (ILO) as it considers agencies important actors in job placement. This was a turnaround from ILO's recommendation of 1919 that prohibited 'the establishment of employment agencies that charged fees or carried on their business for profit' (Wadauer et al, 2012: 176).[31] In particular after 1945, governments involved unions and employer organizations in administering public employment centres, also because these centres were charged with the management of unemployment benefits. Public labour intermediation became a crucial point for European states as a way to organize, manage, and shape labour markets and to institutionalize a new labour regime controlling job placement and labour mobility (Wadauer et al, 2012).[32] However, public job centres in Western countries also remained only one of the many ways to find a job, because workers, in particular migrants, relied on social networks or walked from factory to factory looking for jobs (to be discussed later).

Labour intermediaries may act on the basis of licences, as mediators in the labour market according to the idea that there is a need to broaden the possibility of matching demand and supply of labour. This is a way of bypassing public placement offices, that are basically competitors, who are invited to deal mainly with unemployment benefits, vocational training, and the most vulnerable workforce. Beyond employment contracts, intermediaries can manage different services: training, transport, housing, loans, repatriation, support with the administrative burden of documents (Coe and Jordhus-Lier, 2011).

One of the questions about the ability of intermediaries to control workers is connected to the fees charged to migrants, because high fees are a powerful deterrent to changing jobs, by disciplining migrant workers' behaviour, and controlling their mobility (Rodriguez, 2010). In particular, in Asian countries, getting a new job through an agent means in fact having to pay fees (Woodward, 1988: 77). Intermediaries are often paid by both the employer and the worker, but this depends often on the skills of the worker: usually lower skilled migrants have higher fees to pay for the services they get.[33] This means that migrants with significant financial resources can be supported by large and trustworthy service intermediaries, and to a certain degree they can bargain both about the destination country and the type of job abroad. On the contrary, poor migrants hired by temporary agencies are more vulnerable because they have to rely on low-cost intermediaries and cannot bargain any elements of the labour contract or the country of destination.[34] Therefore, labour intermediaries can produce and propagate power asymmetries (Faist, 2014), supporting different experiences of mobility and immobility among migrants.

Employers can prefer to rely on intermediaries, avoiding hiring workers directly and getting a continuous flexible and docile flow of workforce to maintain a large pool of labour supply (Mavrakis, 2015; Meszmann and Fedyuk, 2019). How Forde et al (2015: 369) underline, 'agencies can serve not only as an institutionalization of flexible labour but also crucially they may act as a means of socializing workers into a certain regime of work'. Indeed, agencies can be useful to handle the costs of hiring and firing, and some of the hidden costs of the reproduction of the migrant labour supply.

Further, intermediaries can be the only instrument for migrants to have access to the labour market of some countries, facilitating illegal repatriation or early termination of the contract in order to keep migrants indebted (Lindio-McGovern, 2004: 223). In southern Italy, migrants often rely on *caporali* (that is, gangmasters) that control agriculture's labour market and the condition of social reproduction in the ghettos, even if the slave-driving gangmaster is an exception (Perrotta and Sacchetto, 2014: 81). These social brokers usually do not base their power on violence, but rather building a sense of community by maintaining an oligopolistic power on some small labour markets. *Caporali* are often other migrants who have been living in Italy for a long time, and with good social networks that provide a 'communication channel' between migrant farmworkers and local farmers as they draw their profit from the isolation of the workforce (Perrotta and Sacchetto, 2014). Where this seclusion has been broken and migrant workers were supported by solidaristic NGOs, as in Nardò (Apulia) in 2011, migrant workers self-organized and put in place a 15 days' strike against the *caporalato* system and to get higher wages (Perrotta and Sacchetto, 2014). However, the relation between labour intermediation and unionization is often critical, as Coe and Jordhus-Lier (2011: 226) put it: 'While the impact of labour intermediaries on individual workers is variegated, their effect on trade unionism is unequivocally destructive'.

Social networks and migrant labour regimes

In order to better understand the role played by migrant networks in the logistics of living labour and migration regimes, it is important to return to the theoretical discussion across migration and labour studies, about the ways in which we understand migrant everyday practices and how they are more or less structured or embedded in larger households or community-based dynamics, as well as constrained or facilitated by state regulation and markets. Shire (2020) brings a perspective of coordination and negotiation among lay actors from below in understanding cross-border labour migration, starting from the assumption that these actors may benefit from coordinating and negotiating each other's interests and power struggles in setting the rules of the game in transnational markets. The politics of regulation of labour migration therefore remains central to such exchanges. This view is certainly less conflict-oriented than those developed in labour process literature (Edwards, 1990) and critical labour migration studies (MacKenzie and Martínez Lucio, 2019), as they question the positive role of regulation among institutional industrial actors in the context of neoliberal markets. Still, Shire's (2020: 447) approach is worthy of attention to the extent that it recentres the question of migrant agency alongside that of their networks and other 'meso–actors', suggesting that the interests of intermediaries and sending states may at times overlap with those of migrants. There is leverage in her argument that new research is needed on the ways contractual status and rights are made available and constrained, focusing on the role of multiple actors in regulating the migrant work situation at the point of arrival and how they negotiate the cross-border labour market. In fact, demand and supply can be structured more or less autonomously thanks also to informal actors who recruit workers through social networks.

From an historical point of view, migrant networks have played a crucial role in migrant labour regimes thanks to a dynamic multiplicity of activities in the relationship between workers, intermediaries, and employers. Goss and Lindquist (1995: 329) note that social networks are 'webs of interpersonal interactions' involving relatives, friends, or other individuals that can channel information and resources through different countries. However, as Wierzbicki (2004) has argued, migrants do not simply slip into networks that provide them with good information on how to insert themselves into the 'new' society, finding a job, house, and financial and emotional support. In fact, migrants can not only prefer to access some specific networks, and also create new ties, but also to transform networks on the basis of their different life and work experiences.

Migrants can move within social networks that represent their connections with the communities of both origin and destination countries, build bridges between distances, collect information to estimate the consequences of voluntary mobility, find the right answer to bureaucratic hurdles, and negotiate acculturation. Networks produce migratory chains that influence the continuity and expansion, but, critically, also the contraction of particular migratory flows. Social networks can provide potential migrants with valuable information and support about mobility and inclusion in the different societies: visas, brokers, destinations, money, accommodation, employment, sociality (Ambrosini, 2018; Goss and Lindquist, 1995). While in some cases kinship networks are the most important, as in the case of Bangladeshi migrants in Italy (Morad and Sacchetto, 2020) in other cases, friendship or acquaintance ties can be important as well (Seferiadis et al, 2015). In particular, friendship and weak ties could be more important for migrants when they undertake an onward or multiple migration (Tsujimoto, 2016; Della Puppa et al, 2021).

Hernández-León (2013) argues that when a migration system becomes mature the importance of intermediaries decreases because migrant social networks will replace them. The shift of economic and political contexts can weaken the role of intermediaries: in some Indian tea plantations, professional contractors have been replaced by the figure of worker-agent, based on social networks from below resulting in 'democratisation of the relation between the recruiter and the recruited' (Raj and Axelby, 2019: 290). As Massey (1990) underlined, migrant networks can affect the migration choice, making migration a self-perpetuating phenomenon. In the last years of the *Gastarbeiterprogramm*, migrants started to arrive via chain migration as employers preferred to recruit new employees by relying on the more trusted of their (migrant) workers. By doing so, they could also save some 'money that they would spend on mediation' (Schrover, 2018: 461). After a few years, in 1973, Germany decided to bring the *Gastarbeiter* system to an end. Among the reasons for the so-called *Anwerbestopp*, Lucassen (2019) identifies two main factors: the role of unions, who put pressure on the state to prevent unequal competition and wage reduction, and employers themselves, interested in lengthening the stay of workers opposing the rotation system. While we may disagree with Lucassen in terms of his misrecognition of the initial benefits that the rotation system of labour may accrue for employers, it appears to us that the *Answerbestopp* must be understood in relation both to the struggle of migrant workers during the 1960s and 1970s, and to the effects that the informal processes of chain migration and family migration practiced by migrants had on the German economy and society. These processes somewhat contributed to causing a purely labour regime, such as the *Gastarbeiter*, partly fail in its initial intentions (Castles, 2004). These processes also show the importance of considering the interactions of different actors and agents, including migrant networks, in shaping state-managed migration regimes, and in the 'spilling over' or *exceeding* of the initial logics of highly functional temporary schemes of migrant recruitment.

Social networks operate according to internal and invisible logics, often rooted in specific social norms and cultures, so that the destination societies struggle to manage and control them. In research on the construction sector comparing Moldovans' and Ukrainians' mobility to Russia and to Italy, Morrison et al (2013) underline how, while in their emigration to Russia, migrants' coping strategies rely on transnational informal networks as well as on recruitment supported by intermediaries (under the brigade system), in Italy, migration is based on family reunification or irregular paths (at least until 2014) perceived as a long-term experience, and remains dependent on obtaining work permits. Further, and more important for us, they underline that in Russia, agencies recruit migrants from central Asia instead of from Moldova and the Ukraine on the basis of informal networks that offered greater bargaining chances vis-à-vis agencies (Morrison et al, 2013; on transnational coping strategies of Albanians in Southern Europe see Dimitriadis, 2023).

Migrant workers may also become recruiters in order to satisfy the need of the employer where they are working (for example, Schling, 2014; Ciupijus et al, 2020). From our and others' research we learned that sometimes employers can also reward monetarily these recruiter migrants if they find good workers. The recruitment through migrant social networks often means that the new migrants recruited will be under a double control: that of the employers and that of the migrants that help them to find the job (Rabby, 2022). While the first one is connected with the workplace, the second kind of control can easily also extend its power outside the workplace.

In research on sugarcane in Brazil, Menezes et al (2012) underlined how employers use internal migrant workers' kinship and friendship networks to recruit and select workforce coming from north-eastern areas. The recruitment of north-eastern migrants has been a way to enlarge the labour market, avoiding local workers who since the 1980s started a process of organization and unionization. Recruitment and selection are based on labour intermediaries that act on the basis both of ability and on trustworthy social networks. Therefore, these social networks are permitted to manage and control migrant workers, but are also a cultural resource and support for forms of resistance, as the strike at Bertoglio Mill in 2011 highlights (Menezes et al, 2012). The ambivalence of social networks is evident also in the Italian logistics sector, where migrants, in a first phase since the 1990s, used community ties to enter the industry and were subjected to a dual control of labour, in the workplace and community of origin. Since 2010, warehouse migrant workers have strategically used their community networks inside the warehouses of the Po Valley region for coordination and mutual support during the strikes (Benvegnù et al, 2018). Social networks, in fact, can be used by management as an instrument for work organization, but are also a tool of workers' organization. From this point of view, social networks are a web of micro-power and dependency that cross borders and workplaces involving different individuals. Migrant social networks not only influence the decision to migrate, but also where to migrate to and how to insert oneself in the country of destination. Analysing the migration of professional Indians to New York and London, Poros (2001) shed light on how local labour markets and networks can be strictly intertwined at transnational level. Migrants' social networks can in fact dominate some labour niches through historical ties.

In addition, migrant social networks are strongly gendered and can be a tool to control behavior, in particular for women. In research on Vietnamese migrants in Taiwan, Hoang (2016) notes that migrant networks functioned as an informational channel not only to support women's intimate relationships, but also to control their behavior at transnational level, that is, in the country of destination as well as in the country of origin. Patriarchal relations can force migrant women to move only inside social networks, based on ties to close family, as in the case of Mexican migrants studied by Lindstrom (1996). However, as highlighted by Hondagneu-Sotelo (1994) in her in-depth ethnography with undocumented Latina migrants in the US, women are also able to build their own networks, renegotiating gender relations and transforming patterns of family authority. Migration processes can transform relations in more egalitarian ways inside families and develop new social networks where women can find different kinds of support. In Italy, Eastern European migrant women, often first-generation migrants, while they are constrained by a dense network of obligations to their relatives in the country of origin (maternal responsibilities, remittances), build new and larger social networks in the country of destination that often weaken relatives' ties and strengthen paths of emancipation (Vianello, 2009; 2014). Further, Cristina Mazzacurati (2005) notes how among Moldovan and Ukrainian migrant women in Italy, the Soviet practice of *blat* has been losing its original function as a friendly exchange of favours: as there is no guarantee that a 'service' offered to someone would later be reciprocated with another favour, the exchange has to close immediately with a payment. In fact, in the informal Italian labour market of care, migrant women from Eastern Europe often paid a fee to other conationals that found them a job on the basis of different elements, such as the health of the elderly person needing care and the possibility of getting a permit to stay.

Table 2.1 summarizes the different types of actors, terrains and workplace effects, including the turnover of migrant labour involved in the migrant labour regime that we have discussed in this chapter.

Concluding remarks: rethinking the migrant labour regime

The different historical and contemporary cases analysed across this chapter illustrate the functioning of the logistics of migrant labour regimes. By critically reviewing such geographically situated cases in dialogue with the literature we have shown that a multitude of actors, not simply national governments and individual migrants, contribute to shape the temporality, patterns, and power dynamics of migrant labour regimes; infrastructures that both facilitate and constrain labour mobility across borders and the extraction and valorization of living (migrant) labour.

The logic of temporariness and a certain level of coercion imposed on people's mobility by states and other supranational institutions is a constant trait that has cut across historical phases since the introduction of migration controls, whether under the shape of state-managed systems (often based on bilateral or multilateral agreements), or by completely commodified systems of cross-border exchanges. In either case, both relatively structured migrant networks, migrant kinship and families, or more atomized mobility practices by individual migrants contribute to both regulate (Bauder, 2006) but also unsettle capital expectations of mobility and fixity towards living labour. This point is critical for our discussion on labour turnover and migrant mobility power (see Chapter 3).

Table 2.1: The migrant labour regime: actors, terrains, and workplace effects

Actors	Migrant practices of mobility	State regulation of migration	Networks and intermediaries
Different forms	Transnational, multinational, onward, the multinational worker, chain migration, network migration.	Indentured labour, *Gastarbeiter*/guest worker programmes, temporary schemes, kafala, work permits, benched labour, point-based systems.	Gangmasters, *kangani*, brokers, agencies, families, kinships, communities, households, unions.
Common logic	Non-linear, household-based, not solely economic.	Tying migrant to employer, reducing mobility.	Facilitate recruitment, allows the outsourcing of labour management.
Workplace effects/social control	Worker-led temporariness, informal strikes.	Reduce migrant worker voice and collective action.	Ambivalent role: social control increased or decreased.
Turnover of migrant labour	Voluntary turnover, quitting as escape from precarity.	Rotation systems as an attempt to regulate turnover.	Ambivalent role: turnover of migrant workers increased/or networks help to control it.

Note: See 'Practices and forms of migration', 'States policies' and 'Networks and intermediaries' in the Glossary

As our cases showed, there is indeed a recurrent relationship between the emergence of temporary migration programmes and the need to control labour turnover as a voluntary expression of mobility and quitting by workers. We do not intend to suggest that migrants' rebellious practices always express themselves through higher levels of turnover (the latter may be true in certain sectors and under certain circumstances, such as the free movement of labour). What we argue, instead, is that there is a relationship between the introduction of new state-employer-managed temporary migration programmes (and other forms of regulation that limit migrants' mobility in the labour market), and high levels of worker-led turnover, which in turn can precede new migration flows, but also new labour conflicts inside and outside the workplaces. For instance, as shown in other studies in the case of the Bracero programme, it was the action of local Black farm workers, who refused to accept low wages and preferred to leave, that led agricultural lobbies to push the US government for the introduction of the scheme (Salinas, 2018).

In summary, the relationship between *migration management, autonomous mobility*, and *turnover* is not one of causation or aimed at the identification of a special agent of turnover (for example, the rebellious migrant who exercise quitting) but one that shows how migration is at the same time the source of labour instability and the driver of new forms of human mobility. In turn, new forms of relatively 'organized' migrations (described as multinational, onward, circulation) may be interpreted at the same time as the response of labour to poor working conditions, and as the organized response to changing migrant behaviours by capital and the state.

In a nutshell, the nature of multiple actors of today's mobility infrastructures (Xiang and Lindquist, 2014) maintain an historical continuity with colonial systems of labour control and rotation and with guest worker programmes. However they are constantly recombined in new configurations and assemblages of mobility where different actors organize their interests and attempt to regulate the market (Shire, 2020), while migrants continue to make, more or less explicitly, political claims (Cresswell, 2010). These claims are embedded in always evolving bordering techniques (Yuval-Davis, 2013).

Migrant regimes tend to adapt to both capital needs and the autonomy of migration, where the expansion of capitalist relations at the same time entraps and constrains, but also gives more leverage and power to workers, leading to ever evolving forms of circulation and regimentation, criss-crossed by racist discourses and racializing practices. In contrast to functionalistic and economistic readings of migration, we have seen how the autonomy of migration perspective and the mobility infrastructures approach unveil the impossibility of reading labour migration simply 'off' the politics of production (Bojadzijev et al, 2004), or reducing migrant subjectivity to what happens in the workplace or the labour market. Attempts by the state at reducing migration to a labour market strategy, while encompassing a significant amount of logistical and financial resources and relying on a multiplicity of formal and informal agents, tend to fail in the long term, showing how the ordinary practices of migrants and their 'mobility commons' (Papadopoulos and Tsianos, 2013) rather often defy or exceed state attempts to control migrant movements across borders.

Enclaves of Differentiated Labour

Labour mobility and immobility in China's EPZs

In 2010 at the Foxconn plant in Shenzhen, South China, just a short distance from Hong Kong, about 18 rural migrant workers between 17 and 25 years old attempted suicide, and 14 died as a result. Tian Yu, a 17-year-old woman from a village in Hubei province, was one of the survivors. She was the daughter of two migrant workers who emigrated in the 1990s to a Chinese coastal industrial district (Chan et al, 2020). Hired in February 2010, she worked at the Foxconn Longhua 'campus', which includes:

> multi-story factories, warehouses, dormitories, banks, two hospitals, a post office, a fire brigade with two fire engines, an exclusive television network, an educational institute, a library, a book store, soccer fields, basketball courts, tennis courts, track and field, swimming pools, cyber theatres, shops, supermarkets, cafeterias, restaurants, guest houses, and even a wedding dress shop. (Chan et al, 2020: 5)

Within the campus in 2010, about 400,000 workers employed by Foxconn were employed by Apple and many other electronics multinational companies. Yu worked for a month. When her wage was due she realized that she did not receive it, made an enquiry to her line manager and then moved to another Foxconn factory. After a day spent looking for the right office, being left without any money, she felt overwhelmed and desperate and jumped from her dormitory building (Chan et al, 2020).

The Longhua campus is located in one of the first Chinese special economic zones, established in 1980 (Pepper, 1988), that became a laboratory where foreign investors moved large parts of operations (Andors, 1988) thanks to incentives and administrative privileges offered by the local and national authorities. In these factories, migrant women suffer a double devaluation of their work and skills due to both their rural origins and their gender (Murphy, 2004). As in other parts of the world, the extension of global production networks in Export Processing Zones (EPZs) stands on the unstable base of long working hours, strict production schedules, supervised accommodation in company dormitories

(Pun and Smith, 2007), and low wages that barely allow individual workers to survive. The result is living conditions at the limits of endurance that lead to a chain of self-annihilation.

This system is based on the prevalence of a very young female migrant workforce and, critically, on its continuous rotation, in particular, in export-oriented factories. One of the crucial mechanisms underpinning the mobility of this labour is the hukou, the Chinese residence system. Since the early 1950s, the hukou system has separated the rural population from the urban one in economic and political terms by dividing them horizontally into two classes of citizenship, of which the lower one was largely, if not completely, trapped in the countryside (Pun, 2005). With the turning point of 1978, the exodus of young people from the countryside to the cities has assumed biblical proportions, and more than 250 million migrant workers till now have been able to move either within their own province, or outside their own region. In more recent years, this system has been somewhat softened: migrants arriving from areas adjacent to large industrial centres are sometimes given the option of converting their hukou from rural to urban as long as they renounce (or are forced to renounce) their land use rights. The land they previously owned in the countryside is often sold by the state to private companies for expanding the process of urbanization and industrialization in inner China (Chan, 2010: 661). Despite the reform of the hukou, the status of those who have left and are leaving the villages has mostly remained that of rural migrant worker. Migrant workers continue to be squeezed between two apparently separate worlds that make up two very different societies: that of the countryside, which in their eyes appears to be fading away, and that of the tough life of the factories. As a popular saying goes, they feel trapped: 'there is no future as a worker in the city, there is no point in returning to the village' (*dagong wu qiantu, huixiang wu yisi*) (Chan, 2010: 672). Most of the migrants are housed in dormitories in or close to the factory premises, so as to compress the workplace and living space and facilitate just-in-time, high-speed production. In the dormitories, the reproduction of human life is reduced to the bare minimum as the personal sphere is protected by a movable curtain, while the 'transmission of life' is either delayed or placed on the back of relatives who have remained in the countryside, or even completely thwarted in bitter renunciations. The personal relationships typical of the countryside end up loosening along the production chains where everyone finds themselves in the same anonymous position. Here, migrant workers live a time no longer marked by the rural system and agricultural production, but by the orders that flow in in real time from the four corners of the earth.

However, the dormitory system, as well as the canteens and other public places near the main industrial districts, has become a source of political debate for a generation of young and very young people. At the same time, though, the movements from factory to factory have become a learning opportunity for comparing working conditions, wages, hours, and quality of accommodation. Although the ability of migrant workers to organize themselves in the workplace and in the dormitories is weakened by the state and employers as they disperse workers at the end of each protest, this organizational impulse is found in an increasing number of plants (Smith and Pun, 2018). Migrant workers who are very mobile in the area are often able to support forms of "cellular activism' that allow the struggles to continue and spread. While researchers have argued that the progression of these workers' struggles could represent a turning point and the seed of a renewed class movement (Smith and Pun, 2018), in recent years political repression weakened the making of this 'new' working class. However, workers' spontaneous protests at Zhengzhou's Foxconn plant in 2022 to break the protective bubble raised by Foxconn to contain COVID-19 seems to testify to the difficulties of Chinese capital and government to manage labour conflicts even in this special economic zone of global production.

Global production networks and the place of labour

This chapter focuses on the role that migration and the mobility of labour play in relation to the labour process, exploring the dynamics at play in some specific localities exemplified by EPZs. We take the labour process and the wider labour regime (see Baglioni et al, 2022) involved in EPZs as paradigmatic locations of value extraction and of the international division of labour in contemporary global capitalism. Our approach to the labour process and migration recentres the question of mobility to the very functioning of capital accumulation in specific nodes of global production networks, and locates these areas in the international context of global production. In this regard we draw from different literature on the role of migrant workers and their exercise of mobility power in the workplace to challenge managerial control and escape degrading working conditions. Focusing on labour mobility power in special economic zones in the Global South and countries such as China and India, we reflect on some similar dynamics in very different production contexts and regulatory regimes in Europe and the Global North.

Since the 1980s, the global economy has seen a proliferation of potential areas for investments, generating a dispersion of workplaces that tend to be located in socially and politically adequate contexts for firms. These transformations have been analysed mainly through two theoretical approaches: global commodity (or value) chains (GVCs) (Gereffi et al, 1994) and global production networks (GPNs) (Henderson et al, 2002). Despite their considerable differences, which we don't have space to examine here, both the GPNs and GVCs approaches make it possible to rethink the forms of integration and stratification of capital on a global level. A broad review of these approaches from labour process scholars highlighted how the main weakness of GVCs' perspective is the poor consideration of 'the place of labour' in these chains, while the GPNs' approach may be criticized for claiming to build 'a theory of everything' (Thompson et al, 2015).

Until now, the expansion of global production worldwide has shaped three large 'factories of the world' at the international level: the European, the North American, and the South East Asian ones. Each of these areas contains internal and external forms of integration of labour process and segmented workforces in a differentiated way (UNCTAD, 2019). In Central and Latin America, thanks to the North American Free Trade Agreement (NAFTA) and other commercial agreements, North American, Asian, and Western European multinationals developed production networks in specific areas, for example the so-called *maquiladora* in Mexico. However, we shall not limit our gaze to the Global South to observe forms of differentiation and racialization in formally defined EPZs. Eastern European countries also became a sort of *maquiladora* (Ellingstad, 1997), producing manufacturing in particular in the electronics, automotive, and clothing sectors. Thanks to a 'state machine' that aims to attract foreign investment (Drahokoupil, 2008) as well as the presence of migrant workers, countries such as the Czech Republic, Hungary, Poland, Slovakia, and Romania have become more and more important in global production. In this process, not only Western producers, but also big Asian multinationals aim to move close to the markets where they can produce and sell their products more quickly and in larger quantities (Lee et al, 2013). Further, multinationals from Japan, the so-called 'Four Asian Tigers', and then the US started to move parts of production to various parts of Asia, contributing also to the economic development of China (Swain, 2011).[1] Since the mid-2000s, while China has tried to relocate part of production into its internal area as well as to other South East Asian countries, Mexico has expanded its *maquiladora* areas while continuing to stagnate in low wages, and Eastern Europe has specialized in some medium-low complexity production sectors in manufacturing, but with increasing intensity also in terms of service and technology levels.

The multiplication of new labour regimes and areas of production (Mezzadra and Neilson, 2013) means that the continuous reorganization of networks worldwide, namely the possibility to find new production sites, revitalizes and puts to work specific compositions of the workforce. The notion of global production indicates an uninterrupted process because firms continuously need new space and strive to reconstitute better conditions for profit (Harvey, 1989), responding to the politics of borders in both a commercial and political sense. Despite the construction of regional areas apparently converging from the legal point of view, that is, the common market of the EU, each zone represents a potential legal place of its own. The proliferation of legislations that regulate the functioning of these zones guarantees the creation of new areas where it is possible to set up or reset the conditions for an accumulation cycle, ensuring a wide choice to multinational companies. In fact, establishing facilities in some areas permits companies to avoid high tariff barriers to import/export, to obtain tax holidays, to transfer environmental costs, to benefit from a flexible labour market, and to rely on a specific migration regime. Undoubtedly, the state as an actor continues to be extremely significant in this context, influencing, for example, the power of trade unions (Chan, 2011). It is noticeable that even within the territory of a country of the Global North, like the post-Brexit UK in search of new routes for 'growth' outside of the EU, new investment zones have been proposed to attract investments through deregulated environments with tax advantages, planning liberalization, and lower environmental barriers for companies (Jolly, 2022).

However, multinationals may be faced with an 'obligated embeddedness' (Liu and Dicken, 2006) to invest in some areas rather than others due to international trade agreements.[2] Indeed, the role of both national and international institutions such as the World Trade Organization (WTO), and of the single states, is noticeable because the agreements on commercial trade between states or areas (NAFTA, EU) can explain the changeable geographical shape of the networks (Coe et al, 2012). The structure of supply chains responds to changes in economic opportunities in terms of agreements on commercial trade between states or areas, to the capacity of the states to attract foreign direct investment (FDI), and, critical for us, to the problem of managing and controlling labour inside and outside the production processes. These elements should be considered starting from concrete historical and geographical relations but without falling into a methodologically nationalist way of understanding the role of the state in shaping global supply chains, or indeed in moulding the local composition of the workforce. We rather emphasize the multi-scalarity of capitalist operations as well as labour agency across the local, national, and global levels (Baglioni et al, 2022) and the ways in which labour markets may be shaped from the bottom up (Peck and Theodore, 2010).

From this point of view, we also suggest that the specific role played by the state and local and international institutions, such as trade unions, NGOs, and temporary work agencies, as well as the place of migrant labour in a particular area, should also be considered in such multi-scalar analysis of global production.[3] From our perspective, the issue is that multinationals try to create and transform every space to develop fitting areas where it is possible to produce value (Hess and Yeung, 2006), which does not exclude the fact that they may encounter resistance by workers and local residents (Coe and Jordhus-Lier, 2011; Cumbers et al, 2008). Furthermore, companies not only rely on pre-existing production areas (Tsing, 2009), but also contribute to revitalizing new areas and mobilize particular workforce assemblages in certain locations (see also McDowell et al, 2009).

While GVCs and GPNs approaches provide critical insights into globally understanding the integration of production and services (Newsome et al, 2015), they have both overlooked the role of labour and its *heterogeneous composition*. Indeed, the lacuna of GVCs' and part of GPNs' approaches lies not only in underestimating the position of labour in those networks, but also in undervaluing the differentiated labour agency in responding to capital mobility, restructuring, and relocation. Labour agency should be considered as embedded in the power of global production (Henderson et al, 2002), that is, in the 'nexus of interconnected functions and operations of firms and non-firm institutions via which goods and services are produced and distributed' (Coe and Jordhus-Lier, 2011: 221). Similarly, the specific ways in which workers are incorporated into these networks of production and value chains, according to their embodied and socially constructed characteristics, is critical to understand the processes of differentiation of labour, coupling workers' exploitation with their 'differentiated agencies'. In this regard, we take inspiration from the recent re-elaboration of the notion of labour regime by labour geographers and development studies scholars (Baglioni et al, 2022: 82), who, drawing in turn from previous critical approaches (for example, Taylor and Rioux, 2018), define labour regimes as 'a set of social relations and institutions that make workers and shape and construct exploitation at multiple scales and through different spheres across the global economy'. A key starting point of the labour regime approach is that workers are not simply made in the workplace and according to particular politics of production, or shaped by national-level institutions (see Burawoy, 1985), but that transnational processes of social differentiation (along the lines of gender, race, core-periphery, and migration, to name some), occurring before and beyond the workplace, critically contribute to producing certain types of workers (Bhattacharyya, 2018; Taylor and Rioux, 2018). Going beyond a focus on the national level, the notion of the transnational labour process (Pun and Smith, 2007: 42) further illuminates the interlocking and multi-scalar nature of these processes, whereby employment relations need to be studied as embedded in transnational flows of labour, capital, and work organization practices that transcend the national and embrace the global.

Inspired by these approaches, and further centering the point of view of migration and mobility (see Chapter 1), we aim to analyse how labour processes worldwide and the mobility of workers within and across them should be connected to the specific configuration of the social, political, and historical context in which they are placed. Such place-based configuration is what makes a region 'plug in' and 'plug out' of todays' expanding and fragmenting global production, with critical consequences for work and workers. Therefore, we will analyse how the development of specific areas, namely EPZs, or what we will call enclaves of differentiated labour (EDL), allow for the assemblage and management of a specific workforce based on the intersectionality of nationality, gender, age, and race, which in turn shape different degrees of labour mobility power (Smith, 2006). We will then illustrate the differentiated abilities of workers to use such mobility power, not only in formally defined EPZs, but more broadly in workplaces characterized by high incidence of precarious employment arrangements and migrant labour in the Global North. If labour process theory (LPT) helps us recentre the 'relative autonomy' of the labour process (Edwards, 1990) and labour/capital relations in the workplace (see Chapter 1), we show how the specific composition of labour, including its relative (im)mobility in these production sites, as well as its gendered and racialized nature, have been underdeveloped in the field of labour studies, despite explicit calls to include them (for example, Newsome et al, 2015; Wolkowitz and Warhurst, 2010). On the contrary, we argue that the point of view of mobility unveils new angles to understand the potential conflicts between labour and capital at the level of the labour process in these areas of global production and beyond. The chapter concludes with analysing the ways in which migrant mobility practices as they emerge across different regulatory, industrial, and geographical contexts, may be positioned in a continuum of individual and collective agency and resistance to management control.

Localizing labour regimes: heterogeneity, time, and space

Smith and Meiksins (1995) note that globalization produces a homogenization of managerial techniques worldwide on the basis of 'best practice' in workplace relations (Selwyn, 2013: 82). This homogenization facilitates the repeatability and therefore replaceability of those practices. However, hiring practices, work organization, and labour relations are influenced by local conditions inside and outside the factory across countries (Xue, 2008: 87). On the one hand, global production stimulates the standardization of operations, but on the other hand it forces management to cope with diversity because every workplace mediates this incorporation of global labour rules on the basis of distinct territories (for example, Brown, 2019). The management of the workforce emerges as much from the top of the chain as from local governance standards (Tsing, 2009: 150). From this point of view, managers may need to develop anthropological lenses because the global space is increasingly differentiated from both the composition of the labour force and the ability to manage it. The social characteristics of the workforce available in each location are crucial in the construction of supply chains because companies have to confront different kinds of local communities, each one with their specific intersectionality. That is, every single workplace contains different combinations of workforces with a specific hierarchy of race, gender, nationality, and class that is disciplined on the basis of both global standards and local practices. Our argument is that *labour mobility contributes to this heterogenization*, both from above (when forced by employers) and below (from workers), as we will show in the following sections.

The notion that labour is highly localized finds its roots in the literature on local labour regimes. Jamie Peck, one of the key contributors to this literature in economic geography in the early 1990s and into the 2000s (Peck, 1989; see also Hanson and Pratt, 1992; Jonas, 1996; Peck and Theodore, 2010), illuminated the relevance of the subnational scale of labour markets' formation and functioning, and the importance of space and place in the articulation of the local labour market with the multiple levels of the global economy. As argued in his masterpiece *Work-Place* (Peck, 1996), locality or locales are at the origin of both the ways in which labour market dynamics are constituted by labour demand and supply (production and reproduction dynamics), as well as of the strategies of labour market institutions (comprising different actors, structures, but also norms and practices). Peck is indeed indebted to the earlier work of labour geographer Doreen Massey (1984), pioneer of the theorization of the spatial division of labour in capitalism. Authors like Jonas (1996) have elaborated the notion of a local labour control regime (more directly in dialogue with LPT perspectives), highlighting both the contingency and territorial embeddedness of time and space dynamics unfolding across the different spheres of work, consumption, and labour reproduction in these local markets (Jonas, 1996: 325, cited in Baglioni et al, 2022: 8). More recently, Peck (2022: 71) has highlighted the relationality and situatedness of local labour regimes against the temptation of considering them as bounded entities or else as 'free standing ideal types', arguing in favour of the power of labour regime analysis, as compared to LPT and labour market studies, for its ability to include 'the workplace setting–cum–scale, but at the same time attending to the dynamic spatiality of capitalist restructuring and *regulation*' (Peck, 2022: 63, our emphasis). Peck's approach may also be accused of daring to build a 'theory of everything', according to the same criticism made against labour geographers by labour process theorists (see Thompson et al, 2015). Operationalizing this approach to labour regime analysis may indeed present some challenges. And yet, the dimension of regulation as a critical component of the institutionalization of labour markets at different levels is central to our analysis, since without a regulatory focus it is impossible to understand the dynamics of labour migration, either as hard regulation operated by state and non–state actors, or as informal regulation acted by migrants from below (Bauder, 2006) and their networks (see Chapter 2). Moreover, involving both the spatiality of worker practices and the dynamics of regulation in capitalist accumulation allows us to explore how firms respond to the international mobility of labour in local contexts through ad hoc management strategies (see also MacKenzie and Martínez Lucio, 2019).

Multinational companies are in fact faced with the need to develop spatial and temporal strategies that can meet the needs of global production and those of clients. This means that globally multinationals operate a just-in-time production system and that various factories – where the global production is localized – function as enclaves in close cooperation and competition with each other (Dicken, 2003). Each step of the manufacturing process should be completed according to the times and needs of the market, neither before, nor later. This system allows multinationals to reduce waste of capital and to lower investment because firms need to speed up the turnover time of capital, that is to say, 'the time of production together with the time of circulation of exchange' (Harvey, 1989: 229) (see Chapter 1). The use of information technology is essential in this process to achieve a synchronization of machinery, parts to assembly, and the workforce. In fact, the application of information and digital technologies accelerates the construction of global networks and ever more pervasive expectations of flexibility that end up expanding and intensifying the working day (Towers et al, 2006). In this sense, managing global production produces a compression of space and time (Raworth and Kidder, 2009), that relies on both the social context and the composition of the workforce where this production is located.

In summary, space and time are central to these relations because capital and labour confront each other in a specific moment inside the workplace and in the reproduction sphere. The landscape where workers live and work is not a place without history; rather it is a product of history. Local and migrant workers can meet each other on the basis of the changes in the histories of migration and settlement in each location, and they usually take action drawing from the memory of past struggles, or indeed, its absence. On the other side, time is also important because migrant workers, for example, can remain in the workplace only for a while and be relatively little interested in gaining better working conditions in the long term (for example, Birke and Bluhm, 2020). Their temporariness may be considered by local workers or managers as an opportunistic behaviour (see Chapter 1), but migrants develop their agency within the externally enforced constraints of their temporary status and in the short time of a contract. Hence, alongside the relationality of labour regimes (Peck, 2022), *workers' agency* needs to be considered as a relational process not only displayed against capital, but also constructed and reconstructed with the entire workforce and inside a specific territory, and in the wider environment of a specific knot of global production: 'Workers are complex beings, with multiple identities that go far beyond the workplace, as citizens, consumers and family members' (Coe and Jordhus-Lier, 2011: 218). Indeed, scholars have often developed a limited reflection on the role of labour because they consider workers' action only in the visible, collective moments of stoppages and strikes through trade unions (Cumbers et al, 2008). Labour agency is rather a complex behavior related to both the spheres of production and reproduction, shaped not only by companies and employment regulation, but also by the state which tries to regulate who enters their territory, and their life and work, in and outside the factories. Also in this context, the state as an actor continues to be significant, struggling to shape '*who* is the worker, and *what it means* to be a worker for particular individuals and groups of people' (Coe and Jordhus-Lier, 2011: 223). In turn, labour agency develops from a combination of intersectional elements such as class, gender, race, and nationality (alongside many other social dimensions such as sexuality, age, disability, and ever emergent forms of intersectional differentiation) that become critical at particular historical conjunctures and in specific contexts (Brah, 2005; Yuval-Davis, 2006).

The racialization and genderization of migrant labour

While the intersection of multiple forms of social differentiation is central to understanding the use of labour mobility by migrants in the labour process, for the purpose of this chapter we highlight two dimensions of social difference which appear particularly relevant given our focus on migration: the racialization and genderization of migrant labour in the global economy. There are different forms of racialization and genderization operating at different levels: in the construction of global production and supply chains; connected with the specific institutions governing areas; and/ or built inside workplaces by managers and sometimes also by unions (see Chapter 5). Indeed, operationalizing intersectionality to produce a non-cumulative account of how social differences are embodied and co-constitute each other (McDowell, 2008, McCall, 2005) is a difficult and ambitious task.[4]

Since its emergence – in the late 19th century – the concept of racialization has been widely used by social scientists (Barot and Bird, 2001), shedding light on different aspects of how it works inside the labour process. To understand racialization, we need to move beyond the phenotypical Black and White dichotomy, which is theoretically imprecise and empirically less evident in countries hosting migration also from White areas (for example, Ignatiev, 1995). Differentiations based on race are fluid and mobile according to specific contexts and power dynamics, and groups or individuals can be racialized or de-racialized in specific situations because racialization is graded and always relational (Gans, 2017). Racialization is not only a causal factor determining migrants' segregation but also a product of a specific way to organize production, social reproduction, and to manage the labour force (Piro and Sacchetto, 2021).

Focusing on the materiality of racial exclusion and on processes and actions rather than on race and class as identities, Gargi Bhattacharyya's (2018) work on racial capitalism has taught us to focus on racialization as a historical process of differentiation which is necessary in capitalism for the purpose of value extraction. While we are not convinced by Bhattacharyya's emphasis on the exclusion of an 'edge-population', or surplus population, as the 'other or limit of the working class' (2018: 5), we found her attempt at reconciling separated debates on class and race as allegedly competitive forms of oppressions helpful to understand the place of racialized migrant labour in contemporary global capitalism. In other words, focusing on forms of racialization as division does not mean we have to abandon a class analysis of the labour process. As this author recognizes, the variety of capitalism perspectives in industrial relations and comparative global economy (Hall and Soskice, 2001) may risk to give the impression that capitalism can adapt to endlessly different circumstances, encountering a limited level of resistance. In contrast, other approaches in labour geography have rather emphasized the continuous remaking of spaces of exploitation and value extraction, whereby both subjects and political–economic institutions change according to local circumstances, including the social composition of labour (see for instance Brenner and Theodore, 2002; Coe and Jordhus-Lier, 2011). This does not mean that racial capitalism is a grand theory, but rather, it is a sensitivity that recognizes that processes of racialized exploitation (and expropriation) have been historically relevant in capitalist and class formations. For Bhattacharyya (2018: 9), critical illustrations of the relevance of the racial in contemporary capitalism are: the immigration controls and the multiplication of borders; the valorization of certain forms of difference in liberal multiethnic contexts, and workplaces celebrating specific forms of commodified difference; the differentiation between work and non-work in the distinction of productive and reproductive activity; and the rise of anti-racist movements for social justice.

As compared to Bhattacharyya, however, we move further away from any risks of fixing 'races' into specific bodies and processes of exclusion, dispossession, and expropriation, rather drawing from a more fluid understanding of the operations of borders as both excluding and including different groups of people: edge-population, migrants, women, minorities, and, more broadly, the 'mobile poor' (Anderson et al, 2009). We apply such a fluid approach to the management of migrant labour and its differentiations, specifically in relation to recruitment and production processes in the Global North and South, including in EPZs.

In dialogue with the important contributions of critical race and racialization theory (Matsuda, 1991; Crenshaw, 1989; Bhattacharyya, 2018; Bonacich et al, 2008, Roediger, 1991; Glenn, 1992), migration studies have indeed further illuminated how migration itself becomes racialized and gendered as state and capital change their interests and agenda vis-à-vis the different forms and speeds of peoples' movements across borders and labour markets. Critical migration scholarship has highlighted in particular how the racialization and 'illegalization' of migrants through state immigration controls and social/labour market dynamics contribute to social inferiorization (Olmos, 2019;

Erel et al, 2016). As a result, these racialized power dynamics segment and segregate certain groups of immigrants to low pay and poverty jobs. More broadly, a focus on the contemporary differentialist forms of racialization (Erel et al, 2016: 1342) brings to the fore the question of citizenship, the power of the state as well as capitalist organizations in differentially including migrant workers, while making visible how both 'migrants and settled communities emerge as uniquely racialized subjects through distinct, yet overlapping, hierarchies of legal status, gender, culture, class and social space' (Erel et al, 2016: 1347).

While treasuring the insights from migration scholarship, we focus on the debate studying the racialization of labour as a 'fundamental shaper of global capitalism' (Bonacich et al, 2008: 342; see also Roediger, 1991). According to these studies, which refuse a colour-blind notion of capitalism and exploitation, 'groups of workers are located within a hierarchical system of labour exploitation that affords certain groups more or less benefits than others depending on a group's racialized-gendered location' (Bonacich et al, 2008: 344). This hierarchical disposition takes place in the everyday co-constituted dimensions of work and workplaces. Such a view of racialization as a form of hierarchization attempts to go beyond functionalist accounts of segmentation (see also Chapter 1).

To explain racialization in the labour market, scholars have often relied on the dual labour market theory (Piore, 1979; Wilson and Portes, 1980). According to this theory, the primary market is accessed mainly by White local men, while youth, women, ethnic minorities and migrants remain largely concentrated into lower-paying and lower-status jobs. Thus, labour markets are often segregated rather than simply segmented or divided, according to gender and racial lines.[5] Other scholars, instead, recognize the pivotal role of the employers that rely on (or actively produce) racial meanings: in the process of recruitment of foreign workers, for instance, labour racialization is crucial to assign different tasks to different racialized groups (see Preibisch and Binford, 2007; Maldonado, 2009), sometimes also generating competition among them with the purpose of disciplining the workforce and reducing labour costs (Hellio, 2014). We will show more extensively in the following section how differently gendered group are also positioned in specific jobs and occupations according to their socially constructed characteristics and biases about their 'inherent abilities'. Some scholarships in migration and labour studies describe labour market segregation as the consequence of migrants' networks providing newcomers with labour opportunities in so-called ethnic niches (Sanders and Nee, 1996; McKay, 2007). Further, racial and gender stereotypes may be challenged or reinforced by racialized others through their everyday relations in the workplace (McDowell et al, 2007).

The recruitment and management of the labour force are indeed often depicted as technical and neutral practices, adopting a colour-blind understanding of organization and management. By doing so, the production of race and gender inside workplaces is formally neglected and the hierarchization among groups of workers is naturalized and de-problematized. Even in labour process literature there is very little research on the racialization practices adopted by managers, and how both managers and workers may contribute to these processes. Contrariwise, we maintain that the supply chain materially produces not only goods and services, but also unbalanced social relations and hierarchical patterns primarily based on race and gender differentiations.

Current transformations in the organization of production include: the implementation of new technologies; the resort to subcontracted labour; the hiring of migrants endowed with different migration status, also among core workers. All these elements increase labour force segmentation and segregation and, thus, (re)produce racialization and genderization at the site of production. For instance, research in the hospitality industry has shown how racialized migrants are hired through temporary and agency contracts into back of house occupations (McDowell et al, 2008), but also how complex gender, racial, and contractual divisions intersect to produce different combinations and power dynamics between workers according to the nature of the organization and its consumer market (Alberti and Iannuzzi, 2020). In the Italian meat industry, research highlighted how the processes of outsourcing and racialization intersect to support the segmentation of labour within the workplace. Further, findings emphasize that race can also be a factor of mobilization through the production of solidarities developed in the everyday struggles emerging within grass-roots organizations (Piro and Sacchetto, 2021).

Hampering working-class solidarity, racialization leads to an increase in competition and work rhythms and determines a general worsening of labour conditions, that affect not only migrants but also 'White' workers, that consider themselves as race-less. Unmasking racialization processes inside the plants may allow workers and trade unions to innovate their forms of mobilization, with positive effects also outside the factories and workplaces (Alberti and Però 2018).[6] This operation includes understanding and tackling the ways in which migrant workers reproduce social stereotypes and racializing/gendering practices among themselves, but also deconstruct them through mocking and solidarity (Cioce et al, 2022; Huang, 2021) (see Chapter 5 on organizing).

Bringing together this double sensitivity towards the intersectional racialization of labour and migration in global production as critical to foster processes of exploitation and expropriation, and labour regime analysis (McGrath-Champ et al, 2010; Peck, 2022; Baglioni et al, 2022), we now turn to observe the concrete places and localities where migrant labour is incorporated and assembled, reflecting different spatial techniques of aggregating and disciplining workers, but where labour also contests its valorization through individual and collective mobility practices.

Enclaves of differentiated labour (EDL)

Spaces with a special regulation take different names in the world because they can take many forms and have different purposes: EPZs, free zones, special economic zones, trade development zones, and industrial processing zones are just some of the many definitions (Singa Boyenge, 2007). International institutions such as the World Bank (1992), the International Labour Organization (ILO), the United Nations Centre on Transnational Corporations (UNCTC) (ILO/UNCTC, 1988) and the Organization for Economic Cooperation and Development (OECD) (Engman et al, 2007) use different definitions of these areas and modes in which workers and productions are organized, stressing the questions of government policy in establishing the specific jurisdiction that governs relations within them, the capacity to attract multinationals manufacturing goods for exports, free trade conditions, a liberal regulatory environment, and fiscal and financial incentives (see also Bach, 2011).

Dicken (2003: 179), one of the main scholars of economic globalization, had developed the concept of 'export enclaves' to highlight how EPZs emerged in the Global South countries at a particular time in the history of the international division of labour during the Cold War years, and how they have been used to justify a 'development policy': increasing exports by setting up manufacturing zones in the same countries that were producing (cheap) raw material to the global market (see also Neveling, 2015). We find this emphasis on the enclave form particularly relevant to the extent that it highlights how these special zones have been an historical instrument to international trade, but have also functioned as a political tool of economic liberalization when this took off in the 1970s.[7] Since the mid-1970s, these enclaves have proliferated: in 1975, there already existed 79 such EPZs in 25 countries, but by 1997, the number of countries with EPZs had risen to 93; throughout these 93 countries, 22.5 million workers were employed in 845 EPZs. The turn of the century heralded further expansion, and in 2006, EPZs accounted for more than US$200 billion in global exports, constituting about a quarter of the world's manufacturing and employing 66 million workers in 3,500 zones (Milberg and Amengual, 2008; Singa Boyenge, 2007; FIAS, 2008).[8] After a decade, in 2017, UNCTAD (2019: 138–9) highlighted that there were about 5,400 special economic zone and free-zone programmes in 147 different countries, employing about 90–100 million workers directly, and between 50 and 200 million workers indirectly; of these, 88 per cent were in so-called Global South economies (UNCTAD, 2019; Frick et al, 2019). Indeed, while they can be found in several countries across the world,

EPZs are concentrated in a handful of economies, including India, the Philippines, China, and the US. However, Europe is not exempt from the development of some unique forms of EDL, if more informally. Although only Poland hosts formal EPZs, Eastern European countries shifted their economic centre of gravity towards the European Union, building specific incentives for foreign investments. Scholars and analysts (for example, Farole and Akinci, 2011) have focused on the issue of freedom that the specific jurisdiction of these areas guarantee to enterprises: with import and export free of duties, exemption from paying corporate taxes, value added taxes (VAT), or other fiscal obligations; but also the fact that they are subjected to rare controls and labour enforcement, thus facilitating licencing and more freedom on regulatory processes (Milberg and Amengual, 2008).

While Lee (2005) notes that the increase of the number of EPZs is connected with the expansion of multinational enterprises worldwide, Organ (2006: 128) underline that 'free zones constitute the first stage of the integration of liberal trade and the national economy with the global economy'. This integration entails a *flexible rearrangement of sovereignty* where the capacity to differentiate national territory is a crucial point. Graduated sovereignty is a consequence of the changing role of the state, who become a 'manufacturer' of the different spaces of global production (Ong, 1999). Therefore, corporations and governments use the multi-regulation of space inside a territory as 'a spatial capital accumulation machine' where different rules are applied 'to corporations, and by extension workers, than in the rest of a given state' (Bach, 2011: 100). As Neilson (2014: 12) put it, 'their exceptionality is usually established within a normative frame and exists alongside a proliferation of norms that apply within their borders'. Regulation of land, worker rights, and tax regimes in these areas differ from country to country on the basis of the economic scope and the level of democracy within.

However, while regimenting and trapping labour in specific places, EPZs function as logistical hubs that are critical to manage the circulation of goods, capitals, and, critical for our argument, workers. Independently from the fact they physically host production, EPZs are a fundamental part of global production as commercial or technology centres because they fluidify the production and accumulation of value. To understand these zones (and the role of migrant labour in them) we suggest looking at the power relationships they constitute. In other words, these areas not only embody 'a heterogeneous constitution of sovereignty that mixes state, corporate, nongovernmental, and intergovernmental actors' (Neilson, 2014: 20), but shape and are shaped by a specific intersectionality of the workforce put to work. Therefore, the question of a differentiated labour regulation is of fundamental importance to delineate the nature of these unique areas. Following the reconceptualization of local labour control regime by Jonas (1996; 2020) we therefore propose for these areas to be defined as enclaves of differentiated labour (EDL) according to a definition that accentuates both their role in entrapping labour and constraining and differentiating its mobility power (Smith, 2006), as well as worker struggles over mobility and fixity in these same locations (see Brown, 2019, to be discussed later). Within the EDL, capital employs workers with similar characteristics to migrant labour, in the sense that they are subjected to a specific work regulation which is different from that of local workers.

From the point of view of the global economy, different EDLs should not be considered individually, but as a set of points connected with the surrounding area and also with the rest of the world. In other words, we need to look at EDL not only as an economic area to produce value, but also to establish a certain 'multi-scalar politics of production'. Michael Burawoy (1985) elaborated the concept of politics of production to indicate how not only the struggles between labour and capital in the workplace, but also the political norms and interventions by the state and other societal institutions (including social welfare and industrial relations mechanisms aimed at containing the most exploitative aspects of management control), contribute to shaping different factory regimes at the national level (see Baglioni et al, 2022: 4–5). Extending this notion of the politics of production in a multi-scalar fashion allows us to encompass the complexity and interconnectivity of production regimes along and across supply chains, foregrounding the paradigmatic character of *Enclaves of Differentiated Labour*. We therefore propose the concept of EDL as particular instantiations of how labour is organized in these exceptional, apparently peripheral, but indeed central, nodes of capital accumulation. These zones are paradigmatic of how labour is spatially regimented and its mobility entrapped under specific regulatory regimes, and of how the state itself allows for the disparaging of labour standards. By considering these EDL as unique forms but also illustrative of wider mechanisms of migrant labour management, we can apply our analysis not only to these institutionalized zones of regulatory exceptions, but also consider how each area is subject to specific governance mechanisms, incorporating specific compositions of labour, and managing its ongoing mobility. Understanding employers' practices in EDL towards specific groups of migrants, gendered and racialized workers, and how workers respond to them is part and parcel of this endeavor.

Gendered labour, turnover and worker agency in EPZs

EPZs are geared primarily to the production of finished or semi-finished goods for export based on intensive work processes and the repetitive tasks of low-skilled workers, usually under a labour regime involving restrictions on collective bargaining and trade union activity. These restrictions are accompanied by frequent daily discrimination and harassment of workers by managers, including blacklisting, threats, and physical violence (Milberg and Amengual, 2008, 33; Tejani, 2011: 264). As we will discuss later, the majority of workers employed in these enclaves or special zones are migrants arriving from abroad or internal migrants such as young women of rural origin. These workers tend to be perceived as docile and paid with poor wages (for example, Chant and McIlwaine, 1995; Safa, 1981; Nam, 1994).

Some scholars stress that women employed in these areas are marginalized to survival circuits, suffering harsh working conditions and trapped within the patriarchal system. Such an approach is attentive to the double subordination of women as workers, within the so-called new international division of labour, and as daughters and wives within families (Mies, 1986; Tiano, 1984). These views have however been criticized because they generalize the subordination and neglect the form of agencies of women. Indeed, the stereotypical representation of industrial women workers contributes to creating a monolithic vision of Global South (migrant) women as lacking the capacity to mobilize. The social and political construction of young workers without family responsibilities and dependent on male income, aims to legitimize low wages, long working hours, and the repetitiveness of the tasks to which they are designed (Fernández-Kelly, 1983). Gender stereotypes about women's nimble fingers, docility, and willingness as an explanation of the preponderance of women in export-oriented industries (Fuentes and Ehrenreich, 1983) is also contradicted by empirical evidence on the militancy and activism of (migrant) women in trade unions in Thailand (Porpora et al, 1989), in the export plants of South Korea (Sun, 1987), in the Mexican maquiladoras (Peña, 1997), and in the Chinese clothing industry (Pun et al, 2015) to name a few. Indeed, in the global assembly lines, female workers have been able to construct new forms of subjectivity that extend from the factory to daily reproduction (Mezzadri, 2017).

A more recent strand of literature has emphasized the gendered mechanisms of disciplining and controlling bodily movements that actively construct docile (female) bodies in work processes and in the private sphere (Salzinger, 2003).

The analysis of the formation of disciplined subjects, as a productive effect of power within the chains of global assembly, opens the way to the recognition of multiple forms of resistance. As Aihwa Ong (1997) pointed out, the daily practices put in place by male and female workers to defend themselves from control are also struggles over meanings, values, and cultural objectives. These cultural values are shaped, contested, and defended in different domains of power relations. Based on a long ethnographic research with women workers in a Nokia cell phone factory in Tamil Nadu in India, Madhumita Dutta (2020: 1370) underlined how 'there is much to work and workplaces beyond the logic of wages', as the workplace is a site that is vital for women 'in creating a sense of self-worth and identity'.[9] Women workers in the special economic zone of Tamil Nadu, for instance, were hired from rural villages and small towns through networks of recruiters. Despite their relatively small bargaining power in the workplace, they were able to develop a sense of autonomy and created 'some possibilities to negotiate everyday relations of caste and gender in their migrant labour spaces, such as sharing rooms and food with women from different castes', challenging and sometimes overcoming caste barriers (Dutta 2020: 1367). Workplaces can in fact become a space for political discussion and emancipation, where forms of activism and mobility grow. The experiences of work and mobility in these enclaves can foster emancipation processes, as it also appears from the case of *maquilas* in the Mexico northern border region, where in the 1980s the workforce consisted overwhelmingly of young Mexican women arriving mostly from urban and semi-urban centres rather than from the countryside (Fernàndez-Kelly, 1983: 210). A part of these migrants began to show greater autonomy, progressively gaining both a space for mobilization in the workplace and a degree of independence from the prevailing patriarchal authority in the domestic sphere (Iglesias, 2014) (see also Chapter 4).

Looking more closely at the relationship between *maquilas* and onward migration from Mexico to the US, Sassen (1996) highlighted the industrial apprenticeship that the mobile Mexican labour force need to undergo before setting foot in the US.[10] Similar processes were observed by Sassen (1990) in East Asia, where she studied the effects of FDIs flowing from the US into Global South countries as triggering processes of deruralization (and land expropriation) of the local population and reversing the directionality of labour mobility vis-à-vis that of capital (with proletarianized workers in East Asia becoming new migrants to the US).

The imperative of curbing the emancipatory and socially unpredictable effects of migration on women workers in particular through forms of resocialization, as in the Mexican maquila, shows capital's interest in controlling migrant labour in its various forms and across different production and social regimes, including by using sexist, gendered, and racialized stereotypes.[11] As Melissa W. Wright (2014) highlighted, processes of stigmatization are stronger for women who emigrated from other areas of Mexico, which, in the macho discourse, are represented as the cause of the phenomena of violence: while government officials advised setting up training courses for young mothers to raise awareness of the effects their 'emancipated lifestyle' would have on their children's health, some trade unions organized self-esteem courses for women in order to 'safeguard their moral values' (Salzinger, 2003: 39–40).

Regulating mobility in special zones and enclaves of global production does not function only through the allocation of occupations and tasks according to embodied characteristics, giving rise to labour segmentation as studied in migrant labour niches in the Global North (McDowell et al, 2007), or through the management of difference solely at the point of production (Roediger and Esch, 2012). As clearly shown by the case of EPZs, the management of labour mobility occurs also through the social and cultural disciplining of gendered/racialized migrant labour within and beyond the workplace. As an extreme case, consider how since the 1990s most of the northern area of Mexico has become the global capital of murders, and, in particular, of *feminicidios* (Segato, 2008), affecting young workers who emigrated from other areas of Mexico, were occupied in the maquila, and living in the suburbs. This systemic *feminicidios* (Monárrez, 2018) can be interpreted as an extreme attempt at curbing the emancipation processes of female (migrant) workers trying to support themselves thanks to access to income and, above all, to their different strategies of resistance to the rhetorical and material practices that define them as docile and subjectable. In other words, *feminicidios* can be interpreted as an extreme case of the restriction of their mobility power, understood as an act of emancipation from poverty and patriarchal oppression by these migrant women.

The critiques on stereotypical representations of female workers as passive subjects of highly exploitative regimes in EPZs point out the different forms of resistance put in place by women in those locales (for example, Pun, 2005), and how migrant women workers explicitly use the language of gender oppression to resist exploitative practices in the workplace. Also in Turkey, the strike in the Antalya Free Zone at Novamed, a subsidiary of the Germany-headquartered company Fresenius Medical Care (FMC), 'occurred in the context of the broader feminist struggle against [both] patriarchy' and the idea of women as a docile workforce (Ustubici, 2009; Fougner and Kurtoğlu, 2011). The strike, started on 26 September 2006 to improve working conditions at Novamed, was supported by external unions and national and international groups that contributed to visibilize women workers' conditions and their struggles (Fougner and Kurtoğlu, 2011). The transnational solidarity, in particular of feminist groups, was crucial for the success of the strike because it put pressure on management at the international level. Therefore, even highly exploited, gendered, and racialized subjects in these EDL, may experiment with different forms of resistance that challenge assumptions about their intrinsic docility and subjectification to the rhythms and spaces of entrapment that these enclaves impose on these workers' bodies and livelihoods.

Furthermore, the time management of labour mobility as turnover and migration is critical to understand the differentiation of worker agency in EPZs/EDL. During the 1980s, workers tended to be employed by a particular multinational corporation in a particular EPZ for about five years (ILO, 1998: 58–61), a temporal span that was unique to these zones and usually more marked than in the rest of the national industrial economy.[12] Connecting the question of the length of contract and employment with the question of labour mobility, it is not surprising that the Mexican *maquiladora* has been characterized for at least three decades by high turnover rates, with firms struggling to manage it, and sometimes being forced to close their businesses, with one firm closing shop after another in a kind of chain reaction (Sargent and Matthews 2009: 1071).

Like in Mexico, in the EPZs of the Philippines we witnessed an explicit connection between labour turnover and migration, sometimes induced by employers: 'High employee turnover, as a cost reducing practice, is often encouraged ... Thus, export-oriented industrialization can also lead to greater levels of rural-to-urban migration and a concomitant rise in urban unemployment' (Tyner, 2002: 70–71). The importance of rural–to–urban migration to allow for the sustenance and reproduction of EPZs is particularly evident in the case of China, where the state has developed a specific regime of migration controls that mould the rural population into a 'floating' labour supply of rural migrants into the industrialized centres, while maintaining their differentiated social vulnerabilities as compared to urban residents (see our introduction to this chapter).

The new division of labour brought about by China's so-called market reforms has entailed the entry of tens of millions of young women into serial factory-labour; typically aged between 16 and 29 and with a rural background, these women tend not to work in the factory for more than five to eight years. Their return to the countryside accords both with the principles of the patriarchal family and with those of an industrial efficiency in need of unspent neuromuscular systems. Uncertainty about production needs, long-hour shift systems, and the pressures for high productivity are the main elements that cause a sustained turnover among employees, requiring a continuous supply of new workers; when the company fails to attract sufficient workers it even looks for them among the students (Smith and Chan, 2015). The example of China however is also indicative of the turbulent nature of labour and migration and the need to constantly reform (and, recently, decentralize, Chan and Buckingham, 2008) the system of population management and mobility through its differentiation in terms of social and employment rights (Pun and Chan, 2013; Cheng and Selden, 1994). Recent data reports that:

> The number of rural migrant workers in China ranged at 295.6 million in 2022, comprising more than one third of the Chinese labor force. Due to the coronavirus pandemic, the number of migrant workers decreased slightly in 2020, but rebounded again in 2021 and 2022. Rural migrant laborers propelled the extraordinary boom of China's economy over the last decades but are still subject to discrimination and unfair treatment. (Statista, 2023)

Linking the role of worker spatial practices across production and reproduction activities with class struggle (see Chapter 1), Brown (2019) has recently studied the Savano-Seno special economic zone in Laos (which between 2006 and 2014 attracted FDIs from China, Thailand, and Vietnam to the value of about US$145.5 million). He shows how in Savannakhet, one of the zone localities where manufacturing firms have multiplied thanks to tax advantages and infrastructural benefits, many of the workers are indeed either Savannakhet residents (who, however, tend to become international migrants moving to Thailand thanks to the porous border between southern Laos and Thailand); or migrants from the more densely populated western areas close to the Thai border; or Thai migrants in search of higher wages. A large proportion of these migrants are female and they are favoured by employers given their alleged greater docility and attention to details. While arguing that Savannakhet residents and migrants' mobility constitutes another form of 'territorial coherence' across the Lao and Thai border, Brown (2019: 449) highlights how such ongoing cross-border migration also created problematic conditions such as a tight labour market and retention problems for employers. Workers, in fact, move both between the many firms springing up in the local labour market, and between their home village to conduct agricultural subsistence activities and employment in the factories. In response, employers are obliged to raise wages and bonuses, especially as a way to deal with labour turnover and to retain those workers who have already been trained.[13] Moreover, among the strategies of fixity implemented by the companies, some of the firms in the zone have coordinated regulation, establishing that workers who left their job were forbidden to join another firm in the same area within a period of six months (Brown, 2019: 451).[14]

Hence, returning to the wider questions of the poor working conditions in EPZs/EDL, the same conditions are often said to be the main cause of labour turnover that managers try opposing in different ways. The migrant composition of the workforce, alongside its gendered and racialized character, is therefore a crucial point of consideration for managers and may be 'reworked' from time to time to get the 'fair mix' to make labour processes smoother. This is possible thanks also to the state, who contributes to manage the relative (im)mobility of workers, through migration and employment policies (Chapter 2). Despite these constraints, migrant workers may still succeed at developing forms of resistance and solidarity in the special zones through their productive, reproductive, and 'spatial practices'.

As mentioned before, we do not need to limit our gaze to the so-called Global South to understand the significance and operation of EPZs as enclaves of labour differentiation, including the differentiation of labour mobility. The fact that enclaves have also emerged in the very core of Europe bears witness to the heterogeneity and internal stratification of systems of production well beyond a binary view of North vs South, West and East in the international division of labour, pointing to a more fragmented and heterogeneous picture globally (Mezzadra and Neilson, 2013). Eastern Europe, for instance, is particularly indicative of how flows of capital from the new centres of economic development, like China or Taiwan, condensate in specific locations where a particularly deregulated environment, and the availability of migrant workers from neighbouring regions and further afield, makes these regions attractive to processes of offshoring and the recruitment of migrant labour. In general, since the 1990s, within factories, the pace of production has intensified; this is especially the case in factories run by foreign capital. What we are seeing is a standardization of productive rhythms (Rinehart, 1999) that is constantly fine-tuned, imposes clearly defined deadlines, and tends towards 'closing the pores of the workday'. Local or foreign capitals encounter greater resistance to the imposition of the new work methods in older factories, whereas in the new, so-called greenfield factories (typically located in rural areas in which the workforce lacks previous industrial experience), the absence of viable employment alternatives promotes a kind of 'social truce' between workers and managers, at least for a few years. Employment in the new factories in Eastern Europe is again characterized by a high labour turnover rate which constrains firms to extend their recruitment area both socially and geographically. Up until the end of 2007, firms operating in the area around Bratislava – known as the Detroit of Eastern Europe – were forced by workforce shortages and high turnover rates to recruit workers from areas up to 100 km away (including areas outside the country), providing special bus transportation for workers (Perry and Power, 2007). In their efforts to address the shortage of labour power, business organizations did not look particularly at wage increases, but rather called for workforce imports to further reduce costs. In fact, foreign direct investment in Eastern Europe appears to increase the mobility of the labour force and may attract segments of neighbouring countries' working classes as well as from further afield (similar to what Sassen (1990) found in the 1980s between East Asia and the US). This is the case in the Czech Republic and Poland, Slovenia, and Hungary, but Slovakia, Romania, and Bulgaria are rapidly following the same steps.

Once they have emigrated, however, many workers in Eastern European EDL choose to set off again, this time to the countries of Western Europe, where wages are higher. Throughout the 1990s, the annual turnover rates for Polish, Bulgarian, and Romanian workers ranged from 30 to 40 per cent; average turnover rates were lower, during the same period, in countries where economic restructuring did not proceed as fast, such as Slovenia (Nesporova, 2002). These migration patterns in the informal EPZs of Eastern Europe remind us of the types of non-linear, multinational, multidirectional, and 'onward migration' identified in Chapter 2 (see Table 2.1). In this case, they show how they are connected to the phenomenon of labour turnover and what we understand as migrant mobility power.

Labour mobility power beyond EPZs

Moving beyond the specific context of EPZs and our notion of EDL, instances of migrant strategic behaviours around mobility (or, using Brown's (2018: 439) words, 'spatial practices') have also emerged in workplaces that do not fall under these terms, despite that they also present some of the EPZ/EDL key features, including a high presence of migrant labour, high turnover rates, and precarious employment conditions.

What we understand as migrant mobility power, mostly understood as an everyday practice to resist precarious and low-paid work and improve living and working conditions, has been originally illustrated in our own research in UK hospitality (Alberti, 2014) and in electronic manufacturing in Eastern Europe (Andrijasevic and Sacchetto, 2016). A range of subsequent studies both in the Global North and South have further evidenced instances of such practices of escape and reflected on their relatively unsettling effects vis-à-vis management. Beyond the manufacturing jobs that are usually associated with EPZs, migrant mobility practices expressed as high labour turnover have been found across a variety of low-wage and precarious jobs in both services and factory work: from transport, hotel and laundry (Baxter-Reid, 2016; 2021), tourism and hospitality work (Choi et al, 2017; Rydzik, and Anitha, 2020), to car washers (Clark and Colling, 2018), electronics (Pun, 2016), meat production (Birke and Bluhm, 2020; Theunissen et al, 2022), construction (Berntsen, 2016; Yea, and Chok, 2018), and agriculture (Piro, 2021).

In the EU context, high levels of turnover associated with migrant labour appear to emerge mostly in relation to systems of subcontracting and poorly regulated environments where workers on very temporary contracts tend to engage in 'job jumping' strategies rather than participating in collective action and unionization (for example, Berntsen, 2016; Wagner and Lillie, 2015), and where employers combine a series of flexibility and retention strategies by using temporary agencies to segment the workforce and manage turnover. For instance, in a study of management strategies and workers' use of labour mobility, Andrijasevic et al (2020) compare the practice of the same Taiwanese multinational (Foxconn) in the electronic industry in its Czech Republic subsidiaries with those of China to find a mixed use of temporary agencies employing 'free moving' EU nationals and the direct employment of non-EU migrants. The result is a high degree of contractual fragmentation, differential payment systems, and the partial immobilization of labour through dormitories. As the authors note, these management initiatives appear to be introduced to respond to the heterogeneity and mobility of the migrant workforce. These management strategies around contractual fragmentation and the use of different labour providers are aimed at limiting workers' high turnover behaviour rather than encouraging it: 'These management practices aim to curtail workers' exit and re-create dependency, so as to enable the subsidiary to cope with conditions of uncertainty and fluctuating demand in a highly competitive buyer-driven value chain' (Andrijasevic et al, 2020: 269).

It is precisely Foxconn's double effort to 'limit turnover and simultaneously guarantees flexibility' (Andrijasevic et al, 2020: 269) that shows in our view how contractual segmentation can be interpreted as a response to migrants' mobility practices (rather than preceding or 'producing' it – compare McCollum and Findlay, 2015), and that employers constantly struggle to reconcile their contradictory needs for both flexibility and retention (like under the just-in-time system model discussed earlier).

Similarly to what was observed by MacKenzie and Forde (2009) in a glass factory's recruitment strategy, sequentially targeting different nationalities of (newly arrived) migrant workers according to their changing availability to accept poor employment conditions, the very change in recruitment by Foxconn in the Czech Republic (from Slovak to EU migrants to non-EU) can be interpreted as an outward strategy to reduce labour costs, but also a reaction to collective worker actions, labour shortages, and high voluntary turnover. The significant finding in this context is that although initially the use of temporary employment agencies is meant to externalize the risks of managing a highly fluctuating workforce, in the end the problem of turnover is exacerbated. These patterns are visible not only in Eastern Europe but also in China, as employers struggle to respond to work strategies of moving from 'one factory-cum-dormitory' to another (Pun and Smith, 2007).

High levels of labour shortages have also been considered in very different sectors, such as the global hospitality industry, as a critical factor increasing 'turnover intentions' among migrants. Based on a survey of Chinese migrant workers in the restaurant industry in South Korea, Choi et al (2017: 55) argue that the increase in demand for migrant labour tends to reduce constraints to 'professional mobility', similarly to what happens for natives, increasing migrants' likelihood to engage in turnover and opportunities to move between companies. Writing from within management/organization studies, these authors' main concern is that, 'to alleviate turnover intentions, which is an *undesirable outcome* for migrant workers and for the organizations that employ them, it is necessary that both academics and practitioners devote attention to identifying what factors drive migrants' work adjustment, especially in industries like hospitality that have labor shortages' (Choi et al, 2017: 54).

It is not coincidence that, similarly to the just-in-time labour regime typical of EPZs discussed earlier, discussions on migrant temporariness in the workplace and high turnover of labour have emerged globally in contexts characterized by high fluctuation in demand, such as tourism and hospitality. While the specific nature of work and industry does not seem to determine the very occurrence of labour mobility and turnover, which rather appear as an almost universal phenomenon in the context of poor working conditions and low wages, the features of the local economy and its regulatory context of labour mobility contribute to explain variability across these studies. However, authors like Birke and Bluhm (2020) have shown how in the context of meat packaging in Germany, the specific occupations held by different groups of migrant workers (namely Eastern European EU migrants in slaughtering and packaging, and Syrian refugees in industrial cleaning), and their relative levels of skills and positions within the labour process, also critically influence the affordances of mobility power at the point of production. While both groups record high levels of turnover, creating critical retention problems, cleaners have much less leverage as compared to those with specialist skills such as meat cutting, who in contrast have a higher degree of bargaining power to force employers to raise their wages and secure their contracts. This is because companies in the industrial cleaning subsector find it easier to handle worker voluntary turnover, and because, 'in this situation a lack of experience becomes mainly a problem for the workers, not for the companies'(Birke and Bluhm 2020: 47) (rising risks of accidents and longer time needed to complete a task). In contrast, the ability to mobilize 'the threat to travel home or rather quit one job for another', usually moving to better-paid Nordic countries (Birke and Bluhm, 2020: 43), is higher for the slaughtering and packaging workers because they input directly and more visibly on produce quality and possible wastage (for example, by slowing down production), which is critical for employers confronting an increasingly demanding customer base. Hence insourcing rather than outsourcing or labour fragmentation under certain conditions may become a preferred response by management to reduce labour turnover and, critically, to increase control over the productivity of these migrant workers (Birke and Bluhm, 2020: 41).

The continuum of individual exit and collective voice

Beside the specific nature of work and occupations, the regulatory context engenders similarly important effects at the level of the mode of employment and production systems: sectors like construction in the context of the EU cross-border regime, where employers benefit from a highly competitive job market, have seen migrant 'posting' and subcontracting influencing differently employer ability to control worker movement as well as migrants' ability to quit (Wagner and Lillie, 2015; Theunissen et al, 2022).

In the case of the Dutch large construction sites studied by Berntsen (2016: 478), it was found that the work is highly mobile where 'the length of stay abroad spans between some weeks to several months but usually less than a year'. While lowering costs is one of the explicit ways in which employers exploit such competitive subcontracting and project-based labour regimes, they may also have to deal with situations where workers decide to form a group and move to a different employer and site by their own initiative. Critically, they may do so as a team, 'increasing their bargaining power with their future employers, as it will be more difficult to fire a group of workers than an individual'. Berntsen (2016: 484) argues that 'this is a way to both reclaim power and to resist, though in an undeclared manner, some power imbalances within the employment relationship'. Such mobility practices represent for us a form of 'turnover from below', with relatively disruptive effects for management, and perhaps some advantages for workers, rather than being fully at the advantage of the flexible and competitive pan-European system of labour management that dominates construction.

In the context of Scotland after the EU enlargement (when the UK immediately allowed the free entry of Accession 8 and Accession 2 country nationals from 2004 and 2007 respectively), Baxter-Reid (2016: 338) observed the behaviour of Eastern European workers who were managed under human resources management practices across transport, hotel, and laundry industries, and noted the extent to which migrants 'buy into the good worker rhetoric' about their assumed availability and willingness to work hard and flexibly. In this case, the management of their temporariness is presented as being far from smooth, rather 'the extraction of labour power was problematic, despite employing a group of workers who were perceived to be "good"'. This study contradicts the approach of the opportunistic behaviours of migrants: certainly there is an element of instrumentality and awareness of the feeble employment relations that attach them to their work, given the high insecurity and meagre pay prevalent in these sectors. Nevertheless, there is also an emphasis on the constraints that rather induce migrants to be as good as they need to be 'to cope with managerial strategies and the one-sided nature of the effort bargain' (Baxter-Reid 2016: 348).

More relevant for our discussion on the relatively unsettling and disrupting nature of labour mobility and turnover, Baxter-Reid (2016) critically questions the very sustainability of such management practices and highlights the precariousness of employers' strategies, and how management may be reactive rather than proactive in responding to the unpredictable labour market context, demands for services, as well as migrants' own decisions to withdraw their commitment and quit their jobs. Baxter-Reid (2016: 348) asks provocatively whether migrant work ethics has 'inbuilt obsolescence' (Mackenzie and Forde, 2009), or rather, is it the managerial strategies adopted in the context of high flexibility that quickly become obsolete?

In addition to these critical remarks, we highlight how the inability of such management strategies to fully control migrant mobility emerges not only from the uncertain conditions of these sectors and the economy at certain points in time, but from the very heterogeneity of labour, which is compounded by workers' unpredictable turnover and mobility power. We have seen previously how workers in Laos' special economic zone use their spatial practices and quit their jobs to respond to problems with management, and how management changed their practices explicitly in response to workers' 'propensity to move' by changing their 'labour control methods' (for example, raising wages and providing sick leave, Brown, 2019: 451). It is worth noticing that, in contrast to the EPZs, and considering the specifics of the local labour regimes described here, namely the relatively higher mobility power of EU nationals under the free movement of labour of the EU common market, the nature of the *regulatory framework*, beside the specific nature of the sector (compare Birke and Bluhm, 2020), appears to make a difference to the ability of these Eastern European workers as 'regional free movers' (Favell, 2008) to leave constraining employment relations as compared to posted workers and non-EU workers subject to immigration controls (Anderson, 2010).

However, in the meat industry in Belgium, characterized by a systematic reliance on 'posting' but also high levels of migrant labour turnover, Theunissen et al (2022) have recently demonstrated how posted workers also retain a level of mobility power, and try to overcome the structural vulnerability they are subject to because of their exceptional status (Lillie and Wagner, 2015), by leveraging the tensions between different sections of capital, namely the different interests of clients and subcontractors in controlling their labour effort and mobility. Their main argument is that by looking at the fragmentation of capital, not only that of labour, subcontractors themselves may come to encourage and orchestrate forms of collective turnover, as they coordinate worker reduction of effort (for example, to produce a high quantity of meat products rather than high quality as desired by the client firm) and rather encourage worker quitting and moving to other client firms (Theunissen et al, 2022: 14). While such a notion of collective mobility power is important because it overcomes individualistic understandings of migrant use of mobility, it points out more generally the importance of the fragmentation of capital as a source of new conflict between labour and capital. This point critically contributes to LPT:

Once capital is fragmented, the conflict between units of capital for the control over labour fundamentally complicates the struggle between capital and labour over labour power, expanding the practices capital deploys to control labour to include the coordination of workers' reduction of effort and increased mobility (for subcontractor capital) and advocacy ones (for client capital). (Theunissen et al, 2022: 15)

Indeed, the client capital company may end up playing a role that has traditionally rather been held by trade unions when they attempt to increase their control over workers' mobility, as well as control over the quality of production (usually degrading under subcontracting arrangements), by, for instance, advocating for better conditions, higher salary, and improved accommodations for posted workers (usually managed by the subcontractor).

Andrijasevic et al (2020: 273), reflecting on the effects of the internationalization of labour process practices across different locales, recognize explicitly the importance of relatively relaxed systems of free movement (whether in relation to intra–EU migration or internal migration in China) and the availability of a larger labour market for workers to be able to leverage their turnover power. However, they also remark how it is not simply the existence of a relatively regulated free movement regime in the EU, or the relaxation of the household registration system for internal migrants in China (Chan and Buckingham, 2008), that allow migrant workers to obtain a stronger bargaining position against manipulative employers. Migrants with relative freedom of movement weigh their opportunities, quit their jobs in a certain plant for another, or move to the service sector thanks to a range of collective practices involving the sharing of 'migrant capital' (Ryan et al, 2015), namely, a knowledge of the labour market, experiences of migration, and social networks (Andrijasevic et al, 2020: 273).

Similarly, migrant construction workers in the Netherlands (coming from a variety of southern and Eastern European countries) also use their social networks 'to make life abroad more liveable' (Berntsen, 2016: 482), but also as a source of practical assistance to deal with the cross-border dimension of labour management systems. Portuguese workers, for instance, try to obtain proof of work on behalf of other co-nationals from the agencies' subsidiaries in the country of destination to reclaim unpaid wages. Berntsen (2016) sees this as resilience rather than as resistant or reworking practices, with the main difference being that the latter are rather driven by a degree of critical consciousness about the exploitative nature of employment relations, while the earlier examples are 'simply' about surviving and reproducing the precarious and highly competitive system of labour management that constrains their lives. Under the different label of reworking (Katz, 2004), the disruptive effects of migrant workers jumping to better jobs is actually also evidenced in the construction sector: 'While employers try to retain labour until a project is finished, many workers are open to changing jobs *at short notice* when a better paying opportunity comes along' (our emphasis) (Berntsen, 2016: 483). Hence, rather than depicting this as merely an opportunistic or pragmatic response to cope with precarious employment, this author also recognizes that the sharing of collective knowledge and accumulated experience of 'savoir se mouvoir' – a 'know-how-to-move' (Tarrius, 1992, as cited in Morokvasic, 2004: 14) – are crucial for migrant workers to stay mobile and quit exploitative agencies. This in our view demonstrates the difficulty of separating individual and collective agency when exploring mobility power (Chapter 1).

Challenging the idea that in conditions of deregulated labour markets there is an easy match between employers' strategies and migrant workers' proclivity to accept poor and insecure jobs and simply serve the imperative of flexibility (Janta et al, 2011; McCollum and Findlay, 2015), we found that migrants employed in precarious jobs with loose employment relations, such as catering and hotel jobs, at times succeed in making a strategic use of their temporariness at work while developing independent plans to gain new skills, enrich their social lives, and reproduce their mobility transnationally (Alberti, 2014: 866). Again, the capacity of new and more settled migrants to rely on social networks of support and communal (material and immaterial) resources to sustain their precarious lives critically influenced their mobility power (see also Hagan et al, 2011; Datta et al, 2007).

Even in the case of the highly informalized work of car washers in England, Clark and Colling (2018: 332) found that migrant workers in the sector, while aware that these jobs were degrading for them as compared to their previous employment in their home country, accepted to engage in these jobs only temporarily and 'used informal networks to promote job mobility and help build skills to escape this work'. In the case of car washers, however, it was found that there were also lone movers who relied on temporary employment agencies and wider employment networks to engage in job hopping, although this led more often to poorer quality jobs (see also Caro et al, 2015). In fact, how Brown's study in the field of labour geography highlights, even in highly regimented production zones, workers are able to enact their spatial strategies and may leverage labour scarcity collectively in a highly competitive environment where zone and non-zone firms struggle to acquire labour in time.

Overall, the difference between LPT and labour and human geography approaches to migrant worker turnover as a form of agency may be that one of the primary interests of the former appears to be understanding the effect of labour mobility power on the process of production and within the boundaries of the workplace, while the second approach appears to have a sharper sensitivity towards the effects of state policies and control on regulating both labour market and community life for migrant and mobile workers. While building on Chris Smith's (2006: 392) interest in the disruptive and conflictual effects of labour mobility power (as an 'external' expression of mobility effort bargain) on employment relations, and vis-à-vis

Table 3.1: Forms of worker power and bargaining: the transnational migration lens

	Workplace	**Marketplace**	**Migration realm**
Individual	Individual work effort bargaining	Mobility effort bargaining or labour mobility power (Smith, 2006)	Turnover of migrant labour as migrant labour mobility power
Collective	Associational power (for example, strikes)	Coordinated/informal group mobility effort bargaining (Smith, 2006; Strauss and McGrath, 2017)	Migrant workers' mobility bargaining power
Individual and collective	Work effort bargaining	Mobility effort bargaining	Transnational labour mobility power

Note: See 'Forms of labour mobility power' in the Glossary

management practices, we explore the potentials and tensions of turnover and labour mobility power in relation to international migration and social reproduction in capitalism more broadly. We, thus, move beyond the tradition of LPT, which has historically focused on worker experiences at the point of production and treated migration as a separate topic. Our belief is that, to develop a fresh understanding of the social force of migrant labour, rather than focus on the mobility power of the abstract 'universal worker', it's crucial to overcome the binary framework of (collective) voice vs (individual) exit that has infused theorizations about worker resistance. Table 3.1 summarizes what our migration lens adds to the existing conceptualization of forms of worker power and bargaining (compare Table 1.1), as we will further elaborate in the concluding chapter.

Concluding remarks: management and labour between mobility and fixity

The aim of this chapter has been to show the ongoing efforts by capital to entrap and constrain workers' mobility power in the context of multi-regulated employment relations and managed mobility, across a range of labour processes and localized management regimes. Here, EPZs, or what we called enclaves of differentiated labour in global production, are particularly significant, relatively bounded locations, which exemplify the multiple forms of control and disciplining imposed over the mobility of workers and their working lives. In turn, our emphasis on heterogeneity of the workforce and on differentiation indicates the specific profile of the workforce in these zones, comprising mostly migrant, racialized, and gendered workers, and highlighting the centrality of controls on the embodied and embedded nature of their labour powers. And yet, as our critical analysis of empirical research shows, migrants' uncertain mobilities within and beyond EPZs/ EDL, far from being a mere solution to the historical problem of management of extracting surplus labour and managing turnover, is a source of further labour fragmentation and further complicates patterns of labour turnover. We conclude that migrant mobility practices, which should be seen as driven not only by economic motives but as embedded in larger social and transnational networks of support, constitute a critical aspect of the heterogeneity of the composition of labour in these crucial nodes of production, and need to be central to any analysis of changing labour processes and more or less interconnected local labour regimes (Baglioni et al, 2022) internationally.

More broadly, in this chapter we have demonstrated how labour turnover is not simply connected to the question of poor terms and conditions of employment, primarily low wages, antisocial working hours, repetitive nature of work, intense working patterns, and gender segmentation (as argued by early economic scholars of turnover, see Chapter 1). These are certainly some of the factors underpinning labour turnover, but they do not really consider the subjectivity of workers, the mobile composition of work, and the regulatory/sectoral/geographical/global production contexts. Through our discussion of case studies of the labour process and labour market dynamics, including relatively regimented local labour regimes (in and out of formally defined EPZs), we have shown how management and labour play a crucial match on the terrain of mobility and fixity, with far from linear and highly contradictory outcomes for both labour and capital.

On the one hand, management seems to put in place specific strategies of recruitment and management of a workforce that is relatively diverse and differentiated, to 'pacify' the most turbulent elements of mobility in favour of capital through either precarious working arrangements or relatively restrictive migration regimes. On the other hand, these very processes of labour mobility, initiated by workers in their origin country or in the country of immigration, also provide grounds for developing and consolidating forms of mobility power, and especially by migrant workers. Migrant mobility power is entrenched by the poor working conditions that are found in both manufacturing and increasingly precarizing service sectors (low salaries, long working hours, absence of trade unions), including in the Northern economies.

Yet, it is not just the poor quality of work that leads workers to leave their jobs and increase labour turnover, but the activation of social relationships in both the workplace and in the spaces of social reproduction, through the reliance on support networks and shared knowledge about the labour market, that allow workers to vote with their feet and quit exploitative jobs. The social networks that migrants build within and without the labour process appear to play a crucial role in sustaining mobility, but also in developing relatively informal forms of collective organization outside the traditional trade union model. Processes of genderization and racialization that are clearly at work in what we have called enclaves of differentiated labour may also be turned against the control of capital in the workplace, as we will further explore in Chapters 4 and 5.

The Field of Social Reproduction

Engineering social reproduction at Ford, 1910s

In 1913, at the Highland Park factory of the Ford Motor Company, the annual turnover rate reached 370 per cent. In January 1914, management shortened the workday from nine to eight hours and doubled the average daily wage from 2.50 to 5 dollars for those who had 'passed' Ford Sociological Department's meticulous inspections into the folds of personal and family life. The 'sociologists' analysed three different aspects of the lives of workers: social and biographical information; economic and financial situation of the worker and his family; habits, morality, and more generally the lifestyle of the worker and his family (Meyer III, 1981: 130). The Sociological Department was a specialist branch of Ford's management dedicated to establishing behavioral norms inside and outside the workplace, going from house to house to investigate the private lives of workers. The bundle of rules and norms set up by Ford to mould his workforce into prescribed social rules and turn them into good breadwinners and productive workers was imbued with patriarchal norms. Such control of the private sphere followed obsessive modes of surveillance, aiming to achieve forms of psychological domination that would modify workers' behavior not only among each other and vis-à-vis management, but that would also follow them into the sphere of social reproduction. The obsession with controlling the private sphere had been a hallmark of Henry Ford for a long period of time (Peña, 1997: 37).

The aim was also to establish rewarding and disciplinary mechanisms for those who would or would not comply with these norms. Such measures must be understood not merely as unilaterally introduced management strategies to better control the workforce, or increase productivity in the plants, but also to respond to and manage emerging workplace conflict, and for the stabilization/mobilization of the workforce. The family wage (May, 1982), for instance, was directly aimed at contrasting with the organizing efforts of the emerging grass-roots union the Industrial Workers of the World, and to increase productivity. Critically, it was also aimed at stabilizing the labour turnover of a workforce made up of three quarters male and, in large part, European migrant workers (Poles, Canadians, and also Germans, Russians, English, Austrians, Italians, and Hungarians) (Bates, 2012: 22).

As argued by Mohandesi and Teitelman (2017: 49), Fordism was a peculiar moment that saw the coincidence of an attempt at rationalizing production with that of attempting to rationalize people's lives, and therefore intervene in the sphere of the social reproductive work of women at home: 'wives were expected to budget the wage, keep the house tidy and raise the new generation. To assist with this work, the company provided loans to buy furniture, and kept a team of doctors and nurses to provide health advice'. There was also a nationalist element to such a project, whereby migrant workers where specifically monitored and disciplined to follow the North-American way of living. Non-compliance with the social norms and behaviors prescribed by Ford would have resulted in losing their jobs. The experiment effectively reduced labour turnover, but not in the long term.

Despite such attempts at rationalizing and nationalizing the workforce, the lifespan and destiny of the Sociological Department was due to be impacted by the changing profile and dynamics of the labour supplies available to work in the Fordist assembly lines. After having reduced labour turnover, Ford abolished the Sociological Department in 1921–22 as 'an adequate wage combined with a stern hand' were now deemed sufficient for the motivation of workers (Meyer III, 1981: 199). Simultaneously, a larger-scale recruitment of African American workers began thanks to the support of Christian ministers, policemen, and other notables of the Black community (Meier and Rudwick, 1979; Maloney and Whatley, 1995). African American workers were in large part made up of the first generation who had grown up outside slavery and who wanted to complete their emancipation by setting themselves at a long distance from the so-called Jim Crow code, that is, the set of laws that in the South supported racial segregation. However, in the labour market of Detroit of the time, African American workers were met with racist exclusion, and Ford hired these workers aware of the potential to maintain a strict 'color line' within the workplace (Bates, 2012). Labour relations at Ford remained marked by this control over workers' behavior beyond the workplace, involving 'how one voted, whether one was thrifty, what car one drove, how clean one's house was, and the nature of community institutions, most notably the churches' (Bates, 2012: 248).

During the 1930s, when a larger unionization process started at the Ford factories, the racial separation and the paternalistic industrial relations system started to crumble. Managers began to realize that the poor working conditions that increased labour turnover in the short run led to waves of strikes in the long run. As Ford's 'sociological' experiment highlights, however, labour turnover, and therefore workers' mobility, are strictly linked to social conflict, both when management seeks to eliminate or diminish them, and when workers actively participate in them. Crucially, the case of Ford shows how labour turnover and migration also affect management attempts at controlling the sphere of social reproduction to increase workers' efforts in the labour process, rather than being a mere technique to externalize or reduce the costs of labour renewal.

Reconnecting production and reproduction processes

Ford's organizational practices and his attention to his workers' lives outside the factory need to be looked at in relation, but not solely, to the debate on 'Fordism' as a method of discipline and labour control on the shop floor. The debate on Fordism has focused on the impact of assembly line production on workers, the regulation of labour relations, the deskilling process, the rigidity of management hierarchy, industrial conflict, and more generally the role of the state in supporting socio-productive systems (Aglietta, 2001; Bonefeld and Holloway, 1995). However, from the end of the 1940s and until the mid-1970s, in Western societies, the Fordist system paid extensive attention to the issue of social reproduction through specific welfare regimes, involving the provision of social benefits for those in full employment, with the aim of providing the constant renewal and social reproduction of the workforce, thanks to the unpaid work of women in the home.

The Ford experiment was indeed one of many in the industrial era: from truck systems[1] to company towns, employers attempted in various ways to tie workers to the enterprise by managing labour markets, social reproduction, and transport. If the social reproduction of workers nowadays is far more 'market-dependent', because of the privatization of welfare systems and the decomposition and fragmentation of production worldwide, still employers North and South strive to maintain a strict monitoring of the repercussions of social reproduction on the labour regime, and, when possible, intervene directly to manage it. While Marx focused his attention on forms of exploitation and the 'subsumption of labour' into the capitalist relation at the point of production, feminist scholarship has valuably highlighted how forms of exploitation are also shaped across realms of social reproduction, whereby forms of oppression co-constitute exploitation for waged and unwaged workers (Mezzadri, 2017: 72).

In this chapter we are not specifically interested in the debates on the value of reproductive vis-à-vis productive work, use and exchange value that characterize old and new theoretical controversies on social reproduction – especially within Marxist feminism (Dalla Costa and James, 1972; Mies, 1982; Mies, 1986; Laslett and Brenner, 1989; Federici, 2004; Arruzza, 2016; Mezzadri, 2017). We are certainly indebted to those debates for the ways in which they illuminate some of the fault lines in the complex relation between migrant labour, labour power, and social reproduction. However, we are particularly sensitive to attempts at making invisible the value of reproductive work as necessary not only for the reproduction of the commodity labour, but also for the creation and maintenance of communities (Bakker and Silvey, 2008), and therefore of 'capitalism overall' (Mezzadri, 2021). Further, we are sensitive to the fact that large parts of these activities fall on the shoulders of women and racialized migrants. Here we therefore look at how social reproduction activities are rather strictly interlinked and enmeshed with labour processes, and in particular with the mobility of labour across production and reproduction.

Recent analyses indicate that, while reproductive work has often been analysed as a distinct element of the labour process, the rearticulation of global production, thanks also to information technology, has led to the blurring of the boundary between these two spheres (Alberti et al, 2017). If the lifeblood of capital is based on labour power that has been shaped over many years of work inside families, schools, and supported by welfare provisions, the social reproduction of everyday life is also sustained by and through the mobility of labour (Yeates, 2004; Hochschild, 2003; Glick-Schiller, 2012; Lutz and Palenga-Möllenbeck, 2015). In the words of Teeple Hopkins (2017: 137), transnational social reproduction needs to be seen from the point of view of the persisting differentiation sustained by the politics of borders as well as by the stories of precariousness that cross those borders, and the processes of genderization and racialization that characterize them.[2]

However, the field of social reproduction is important not only to understand mobility patterns, but also to highlight the tensions in social relations and worker resistance. Reproductive practices come in fact to constitute a crucial element in the forms of organization and worker mobilization that develop at a political and economic level (Laslett and Brenner, 1989). It is at the crossroad of these two spheres, the productive and reproductive ones, that it is necessary to understand how 'capital organizes and hierarchizes human activities for the purpose of its reproduction' (Del Re, 2008: 112). Precisely because labour and reproduction processes intersect in different ways, it may be problematic to conceptualize the distinction between them (Kelly, 2009: 451; see also Strauss and Meehan, 2015). Still, such distinction may be emphasized and used politically (Federici, 2014; Teeple Hopkins, 2017).

According to Mezzadri (2019: 38), the activities in the reproduction of life are interlinked with the labour processes in at least three ways: 1) through the 'absorption of the systematic externalization of costs of social reproduction', for example cutting wages and social contributions and 'importing' migrants; 2) by expanding the control of the workforce beyond the formal working time and the labour process, as in the case of the dormitory labour regime; 3) through 'the expansion of formal subsumptions of labour, made possible by the fragmentation and decomposition of labour processes worldwide' (including for instance home work in sweatshops). How do these three modes of incorporation of social reproduction (understood as the reproduction of both labour and of capitalist social relations more broadly) map out onto the field of labour migration? And to what extent does the high turnover of labour through migrant mobility introduce elements of disturbance and disruptions in these processes of value generation, or rather merely contribute to subsidizing capital?

As we have seen in Chapter 1, labour process scholars have considered only tangentially the question of social reproduction, addressing primarily the reproduction of skills. The focus on skills, worker training, and education remained for a long time one of the only aspects of the regeneration of the workforce systematically studied in labour process research (for example, at least among the most prominent scholars of the labour process theory tradition in the Anglo-Saxon context). Only more recent discussions around 'embodied labour' in labour process scholarship have started to question Braverman's (1974) approach to skills, and rather emphasized the social construction of skills (Wolkowitz and Wahrhurst, 2010), for example in relation to the valorization of gendered and racialized bodies in the service economy. In our view, labour scholars strongly need to revisit the conception of skills by embracing a wider understanding of social reproduction, and indeed the role of migrant labour in shaping labour processes and control–resistance dynamics in and beyond the boundaries of work. Our refusal to oppose the sphere of reproduction with that of production allows us to understand how the former is not only at the service of the latter, but constitutes a space within which different forms of resistance and self-determination are forged, and where mobility power can grow. Considering the interdependency of these spheres, what is then the specific function of transnational migration in the field of social reproduction?

In what follows, we wear the lenses of transnational mobility (Chapter 1) to flesh out these dimensions elaborated by Mezzadri (2019). We identify four corresponding areas in the field of labour mobility where these modes of subsumption (and related conflicts/counter-practices) occur. These corresponding areas are: 1) international migration itself as a form of social reproduction which allows for the externalization of social reproduction costs for the country of destination, but also for the reproduction of life for the migrant and their family (Katz, 2001); 2) the role of transnational families and migrant social networks in providing a subsidy to capital and cheapening costs for employers; 3) the differential access to welfare between migrants and indigenous workers and the construction of discriminatory workfare states; 4) the role of migrant labour in dormitory regimes, where the main logic of subsumption of social reproduction is based on extending control over labouring bodies through spatial seclusion (Gambino, 2003), but where migrants can also find a support both for the reproduction and the organization of mobility and labour conflict. For each of these dimensions we also identify some 'counterpoints', or areas of tensions, that illustrate the relative autonomy of migration as a practice of social reproduction (to be discussed later). We further develop the implications of our theoretical extensions (Burawoy et al, 1991) in the concluding chapter, by proposing the concept of mobility skills as applied to the sphere of dormitory labour regime and further elaborating the notion of migrant labour mobility power across the spheres of production and reproduction.

The perspective that we propose here allows us not only to grasp the interdependence of the two spheres in the social formation of contemporary work and migration, but also to highlight the different forms of resistance and mobilization of workers inside and outside the workplace. The availability of an external community that supports and articulates work issues is undoubtedly an important aspect, often overlooked, in analysing the agency of workers and migrants (Coe and Jordhus-Lier, 2011), and key in defining fixity and mobility (see Chapter 1). In addition, attention to the realm of social reproduction in constituting alternative practices beyond the mere reproduction of capital, as highlighted by critical development and feminist scholars, critically contributes to our framework, as we illustrate later.

Feminist political economies and geographies of reproduction

The notion of social reproduction as discussed today was introduced by the feminist movement from the 1970s and refers to the whole of activities that allow for the maintenance and reproduction of a labour force (Picchio, 1992; Dalla Costa and James, 1972). More recently, however, there has been explicit emphasis on how social reproduction concerns the reproduction over time 'of capitalist life' more broadly: 'namely, human beings as well as the capitalist relations of production of which they are part' (Mezzadri, 2019: 36). Social reproduction comprises both the renewal and maintenance of life *and of the institutions and work necessary therein*, summarized in the following central components: biological reproduction of the human being; reproduction of the workforce; and the reproduction of the goods (environment, merchandises) and services necessary for the sustenance and care of the person (Bakker and Gill, 2019; Laslett and Brenner, 1989). In this sense, social reproduction involves various types of work – mental, manual, emotional (Laslett and Brenner, 1989: 383) – and it is usually supported by many institutions that contribute to it, on the basis of the specific social context: families, state, market, neighbourhood, and community (Massey, 1983). The notion of social reproduction has traditionally been used to analyse the unwaged work done by women in support of a male breadwinner employed in industrial work, and more generally to emphasize the oppression and reproduction of gender inequalities. In so doing, reproduction has been associated with reproductive labour, care, and housework.

We agree with feminist scholars who have argued that social reproduction is *not* just another way of saying domestic or care work. Social reproduction must be understood both as maintenance, rearing, and care of the workforce (Dalla Costa and James, 1972), and also as a condition and quality of life of subjects 'at work and outside work' (Mitchell et al, 2003: 433). Drawing from these perspectives, we endorse a notion of social reproduction as a general concept to describe the different daily activities individuals take care of and that compose the 'fleshy and messy and indeterminate stuff of everyday life' (Katz, 2001: 711). Cleaning, cooking, washing, accommodation, sexual relations, shopping, education, health, development and the maintenance of social relations, reproducing cultures and structures of belonging, participating in different social associations and organizations, helping children in their homework, learning and socialization, and the reproduction of labour, all constitute necessary components of making life.

It must be made clear however that recognizing how social reproduction encompasses much more than housework does not mean to obliterate the ongoing gendered and racialized social stratifications that dominate unpaid work and other activities in this realm, whereby women have historically been the main providers of the work needed to reproduce labour power. In the field of human geography, Doreen Massey (1984) was one of the first explaining how processes of uneven development in capitalism are the outcome of everyday social relations based on class and gender, but also of social welfare institutions and normative practices such as heterosexuality that contribute to reproduce economic inequalities over time and space. What the work of feminists has added to these perspectives, in particular the work of Federici (2004), is that mechanisms of social differentiation based on sex, gender, and race have operated well before the establishment of capitalism, and have critically contributed to the original process of capitalist accumulation and to the divisions within the working class. Labour scholars have in turn looked at the ways in which the working class has been shaped and transformed over time also in relation to other forms of social differentiation. From this point of view, social categories such as gender, citizenship, and skin color, for example, are immediately central to the reconstruction of the 'making of the working class' (Thompson, 1963), to refer to a title of a book that has been actually widely criticized by feminist historians (Scott, 1988).

Focusing on the relationship between capitalism, racism, and social reproduction, and drawing from the work of critical development scholar Sanyal, Bhattacharyya (2018: 37) has recently proposed a notion of racial capitalism as a pattern of 'differentiation of populations while also recuperating diverse economic activity into the logic of accumulation'. It is precisely the positioning of different types of subjects across the spheres of production and reproduction, work and non-work, and how they are constructed as participating more or less in capitalist formation, that deploys notions of racial differentiation. While we see the relevance of social reproduction and the valorization of differentiated bodies as critical to capital's primitive accumulation, we also believe in the value of taking reproduction processes into consideration together with the labour process as a way to analyse social and work relationships as co-constitutive (Mies, 1982). This approach, we argue, is especially needed to explore how worker mobility as an aspect of social reproduction (that is, the socially reproductive practices of migrants beyond the reproduction of wage labour) has immediate implications for the capitalist relations of production in the workplace, and for workers' opportunities of voice, empowerment, and resistance. What we mean is that power in labour relations can liberate forms of worker power also in the field of social reproduction, and vice versa: for example, when the enlargement of the sphere of welfare entitlements for migrants increases worker leverage to express union voice in the workplace.

Beyond institutional welfare, community-based forms of survival and networks of support may also provide resources to sustain the struggles of production in the workplace, as demonstrated by research about the coping tactics of precarious migrants in London (Datta et al, 2007). Their effects in terms of sustaining individuals and communities need to be recognized, despite the fact that migrant coping tactics often remain associated with relatively autonomous spaces of social reproduction, providing at best 'strained forms of survival' or 'precarious access to the essentials of life' (Bhattacharyya, 2018: 55). Still these spaces are the illustration that 'the requirement of production do not own all possibilities of remaking life' (Bhattacharyya, 2018: 55). While we recognize the importance of Bhattacharyya's remark that reproductive activities are not fully incorporated/subsumed into value for capital, in turn we acknowledge how formal access to social and financial resources to be able to reproduce oneself outside the constraints of waged work (at least for a period of time) is strongly influenced by state regulation of migrants and local citizens' individual entitlements to social assistance and social security.

Migration as a form of externalization of social reproduction

Human geographer Cindi Katz (2001) theorized the role of international migration in the rescaling of social reproduction globally, emphasizing how migration channels the transfer of variable capital across borders. Katz shed light on the fact that the reproduction process in the country of origin more or less directly supports the labour process in the country of destination: the rearing, education, and maintenance of the labourer prior to their emigration, and often during the emigration process, are often provided by the family or the state of origin. In this way, labour mobility is considered 'a direct transfer of wealth from generally poorer to richer countries' (Katz, 2001: 710). Similarly, research on informal labour in India (Mezzadri, 2017) has recently emphasized how rural–urban mobility, or more broadly circulatory labour movements, constitute a key mechanism in which reproductive activities participate in value generation in capitalism. Such circuits of labour, including the mobility of workers and rural migrants (outside of the formal labour commodity chain), are 'value–generative' in two ways: because they allow for the externalization of costs of social reproduction of the worker, and because they permit the cheapening of the costs of labour and commodities specifically. The externalization of costs is therefore made possible by the fact that, by maintaining their links with the community of origin, migrant strategies of social reproduction provide de facto a subsidy to capital.

In India, labour contractors facilitate the constant circulation of partially dispossessed peasants between their rural villages and the city to maintain the survival of these poor labourers. The partial dispossession of land or means of production implies that these workers can fall back to a form of 'social wage' when 'households, families, villages and communities of origin for workers—sustain value generation as they constantly reabsorb, regenerate and sustain labour when retrenched by capital' (Mezzadri 2021, 1197). So while this urban–rural circulation can be considered a form of survival it also externalizes the costs of social reproduction (see also Breman and van der Linden, 2014; Guérin, 2013; Guérin et al, 2013). If in India there are not proper worker dormitory regimes as in the case of China (Goodburn and Mishra, 2023), the 'partial dispossession' of Indian internal migrants, who still own their land but cannot rely on it for survival, being forced to sell their labour to the market, guarantees a 'social buffer zone' (Mezzadri, 2017: 72–3): migrants can fall back on the reproduction realm of their hometown to draw on a variety of resources (child and elderly care, health provisions, longer term housing) while reducing the costs of their socially necessary labour time. Hence the cheapening of labour's reproduction cost is made possible by the existence of informal networks of care and support, sustained in turn by long-established gender and racial regimes of oppression (Fernandez, 1997).

In the field of labour studies, the function of migrant labour in sustaining entire productive and reproductive systems was already highlighted by Michael Burawoy (1976) in his pioneering article comparing the system of migrant labour in South Africa and the Bracero programme of Mexican temporary rural workers in the US. While highlighting the role played by the country of origin in terms of the externalization of costs, differently from the contemporary readings of feminist geographers, Burawoy underlined the relative separation between the productive and reproductive fields. Critical for our analysis, the author also highlights the role of migration policies in controlling migrant labour and maintaining such separation over time. The reduction of costs occurs in turn through the spatial separation between the costs of maintenance and the reproduction of the same labour, that is, where the family of the migrant back in the country/area of origin (for example, Mexico) remained responsible for the overall reproductive and intergenerational costs, while the US employer was responsible only for the immediate maintenance of labour (Burawoy, 1976).

The control of reproduction can be realized not only through cross-border recruitment and the enforced return of migrants back to their countries, best exemplified by temporary immigration schemes now, as then, very popular with governments and employers (for example, Ruhs, 2006b; Ruhs and Martin, 2008). It emerges also through specific techniques for the control of migrants' social reproduction, for example in the way migration policies have historically hindered or banned family reunion (Burawoy, 1976). Family reunion would imply a partial transfer of social costs to the country of destination, and this may explain why it is resisted and restricted in many contemporary immigration policy regimes, or made conditional upon economic 'self-sufficiency' or the right to permanent residence (Schweitzer, 2015). Further, a worker who does not have to care for children and family members in their proximity is usually more available to work longer hours, hence more flexible and exploitable. Here also lies the 'functionality' of such sphere separation: (migrant) workers without family commitments may be interested or forced to become sheer living labour.

The control on migrants' reproduction in the Bracero programme shows a strong resemblance with what happened after the Second World War in some European countries, such as Germany and Switzerland, that adopted the guest workers programme (Castles and Kosack, 1973). Family reunification for *Gastarbeiter* was very limited during the 1960s and 1970s, and until 1964 in Switzerland, only migrants who had worked for at least ten years and got a residence permit for an indefinite period could apply for family reunion. While most migrants left their wives and children back in the country of origin, some arrived illegally in Switzerland and were kept secretly within the homes, or left under custody of other co-nationals or Swiss families living in the proximity (Barcella, 2012). The 'outsourcing of the reproduction' in this, as in many other cases, was aimed at maintaining a constant and young flow of migrants free from reproduction commitments. The cost of social reproduction, again, is 'dumped' on the shoulders of the families (often women) and households in the place of origin, thanks to migrants' remittances and to the unwaged work of women.

As shown by other research, migrant household relations and activities can become a source of protection and incentive for workers in the country of origin to refuse highly exploitative jobs, and push back against the intensification of work, as they draw from transnational remittance income sent by migrant members of the family (as in the case of data entry workers in Jamaica described by Mullings, 1999). Kelly (2009) shows how social mobility in Cavite, the Philippines, is supported by the income generated through the migration of family members rather than through the new jobs created in the export processing zones (EPZs), so that families are able to send their children to private schools drawing from remittance income.[3] However, remittances can also produce negative effects on migrants' agency because they can be 'forced' by the family to send money back, affecting their power relations in the workplace in the country of destination. Differently, in his incomparable analysis of migratory processes, Abdelmalek Sayad (2004) highlights how migrants can control reproduction in the country of origin through remittances by exactly knowing its costs.[4] However, the field of social reproduction remains fundamentally unstable, and its provisions uncertain, and is far from providing a constant and secure source of subsidy for capital. Still, the externalization of the reproduction costs of migrants may be pursued in a variety of forms by states and employers alike.

In the East Asian context, Diana Wong (2006), studying the social reproductive practices of migrants in Malaysia, has also highlighted the role of state migration policy as a form of control on both migrant labour and its reproduction. Wong researched the changing Malaysian migration regime since the economic crisis of the late 1990s', where migrants cannot marry either locals or fellow contract workers during the duration of their employment contract. Still today in Malaysia, which continues to be a major importer of migrant labour in the region, marriage with a Malaysian citizen is banned to migrant women on a Temporary Visit Pass visa, alongside the prohibition to bring their families with them and of getting pregnant (Miles et al, 2022). In other words, migrant temporary employment is made conditional upon the requirement to remain childless. As highlighted by Miles et al (2022), the justification of such draconian measures is that migrant workers are deemed to be employed on fixed term contracts and that creating a family would pose 'social problems and legal complications', making forced deportation the default.[5] Concerning marriage however, the Islamic law of Malaysia permits citizens to marry migrant workers, hence when this overrides the ban these spouses must forfeit their right to work under the permit. The interaction of religious laws and state policy shows the other side of reproductive and population controls when this is aimed at protecting citizens' rather than migrants' rights.

The question of the control on migrants' reproduction also has its socialist face. In the mid-1970s in Eastern European countries (and in particular in Hungary, Czechoslovakia, and East Germany) there were about 120,000 guest workers, while another 50,000 lived in Soviet Union (Pérez-López and Diaz-Briquets, 1990), having moved from other socialist countries.

Mobility was explained as a way to both resolve the demographic and labour problems of some countries, and as part of cooperative training programmes (Pérez-López and Diaz-Briquets, 1990: 279). Migrants from 'brother countries' moved to Eastern European countries, under the umbrella of different government agreements, signing a labour contract for some years, and in some cases were able to renew it. As in Western countries, in Eastern Europe labour migration during socialism was also linked to the widespread segmentation of the labour market, as migrants were hired for the dirty jobs and often made stay in dormitories provided by the firms (Pérez-López and Diaz-Briquets, 1990; Alamgir, 2014). Some scholars underlined how Vietnamese and Cubans, for example, could be targets of racism, partly because some governments put in place a colonial posture exploiting the asymmetries of power (Zatlin, 2007). In the treaty stipulated between Czechoslovakia and Vietnam in 1980, for example, the pregnancy and motherhoods of Vietnamese migrant women turned into a critical factor. Even if Vietnamese women could enjoy the same basic benefits as Czechoslovak workers, they first had to undergo a medical check before leaving Vietnam to prove they were not pregnant: 'When Vietnamese workers did arrive or become pregnant, the general policy was to return them home as soon as possible' (Alamgir, 2014: 146). Pregnancy, therefore, negated the reason for their stay, because a migrant's life had to remain restricted to the sphere of production.

While recent migration policies have made family reunion harder, it is important to recall how the pro-family policies of post-war immigration in Europe were preferred to replenish the workforce in former empires. For instance, the British government sponsored not only the arrival of migrants searching for work in sectors greedy for labour supplies (the Windrush ship carrying hundreds of Caribbean migrants in 1948 is an emblematic moment of such facilitated mass immigration at times of labour shortages), but also actively promoted family members' migration, such as in the case of the Bangladeshi communities that moved from specific regions of Bangladesh to heavy industry districts in the Midlands to find work as labourers (Gardner, 2009). The spouses of Caribbean migrants and migrants from other former British colonies in Africa meanwhile found work in the then growing public sector, as civil servants and health and social workers, despite ongoing xenophobic backlash, including within the labour movement against othered minorities (Joshi and Carter, 1984).

After the Second World War, the bilateral treaties between Italy and Belgium also guaranteed Italian migrants the right to settle permanently in Belgium. Since Italian migrants were recruited in the mines, Belgium authorities and the capital city hoped that a family reunification could favour migrants' settlements, while also helping to increase Belgium's birth rate (Gabaccia and Iacovetta, 2002). There is no space here to include the issue of how migration may be used as a demographic/re-population strategy by governments in countries affected by ageing populations and labour shortages, but the example of post-war migration to Belgium certainly illuminates the different drivers of controls and the governance of migration at the intersection of migration and social reproduction, within and beyond the control of the productive sphere.[6] In the well-known case of the strawberry pickers in Spain, migrant mothers with dependent children back home are explicitly favoured by employers compared to other categories as they are perceived as more 'acquiescent' guest workers and keen to return home once the seasonal work is completed (Corrado, 2017; Glass et al, 2014), demonstrating the ongoing relevance of temporal regimes of migration management (Chapter 2). These examples also demonstrate the continuing interest by the state in controlling the social reproduction activities of non-citizens while dumping onto the shoulders of the working poor (and their social kin, networks, and family ties) the costs for socially reproducing labour (Arruzza, 2016).

Transnational networks and social reproduction

While it is important to understand reproduction from the point of view of capital and the state, we also need to understand the tensions that migrants' socially reproductive practices and strategies bring into the sphere of subjectivity and cultural practices, as these also have a bearing on the labour process. Indeed, while migrants 'subsidize' the local economy of the country of immigration by relying on their transnational and local community resources, when they move across borders they are not just responding to economic needs, but move for a mix of reasons, including the desire to break away from systems of oppression back in their home countries and to look for spaces of appropriation and liberation. According to this reading, migration's diverse motives variously influence both transnational and local practices of social reproduction and mobility. Highlighting the implications of the social reproductive practices of migrants for the sphere of production does not mean to reduce migration to economic processes because migrants move for reasons beyond individually calculated cost-benefit analyses. Indeed, it would be misleading to reduce migration to a function of capitalist reproduction.

The role of transnational migrant networks (whether of kin or coethnic) in supporting the social reproduction of migration has been widely illustrated by the migration literature (Glick Shiller et al, 1995; Conradson and Latham, 2005a; Faist, 2006), stressing how they can facilitate the initial migration from the country of origin and provide continuous support in the country of destination. Among the activities that are inherent to the sphere of social reproduction we may include practices as diverse as: providing information to potential migrants who can facilitate early accommodation and operate as intermediaries for job opportunities, as well as support emotional and financial needs (Vertovec, 2002; Ryan et al, 2015).

In the European context, Ciupijus et al (2020) illustrated the role of kinships and ethnic networks in facilitating migrants' transnational exit and mobility power across the labour markets of different member states. Similarly to our endeavour, Ciupijus and colleagues point out that the drivers of such movements transcend readings of labour market mobility that have tended to associate migrants with the *homo economicus*. They argue that what we call migrants' mobility power, or transnational exit, is being 'moulded within kinship and ethnicity networks across transnational social spaces' (Ciupijus et al, 2020: 2), borrowing a term originally developed by Faist (2006: 3).[7] A critical theoretical aspect of this perspective is to switch the focus from the country of destination to what happens between leaving their country and entering the new labour market in the country of immigration. This passage encapsulates a transnational experience of relocation, which critically depends on the action and support of kinships, families, and communities, rather than the sole individual (Sporton, 2013).

Preserving family ties for both affective and economic reasons, and the wellbeing of family networks (for example, children finishing school), is also an element that explains the link between kinship and mobility. Such affective kinships make migration movements and their temporality less opportunistic in terms of the monetary gains. One critical finding from our point of view is about what Ciupijus et al (2020) call 'the actualization of labour power' through mobility, which does not simply follow the law of supply and demand. In this sense, labour intermediaries and migrant brokers are part and parcel of what they describe as the complex social process that occurs between the country of origin and the labour market of destination (see also Chapter 2). Even though their research does not use theories of social reproduction, the interviews with Eastern European migrants moving to the UK demonstrates the role played by friends and family members in providing support at arrival, and a series of supportive practices (for example, providing accommodation and critical information about the local labour market, and in initiating the very mobility choice by 'verifying' migratory routes). Ethnic networks also appear to facilitate secondary movement within the country of immigration, thus allowing for job switching and reskilling (accreditation, improving one's English language skills), and 'to act successfully in professional jobs designed to offer services to other post-2004 CEE [Eastern European] migrants' (Ciupijus et al, 2020: 10). Here is where the community dimension allows mobility to occur and for labour mobility to be sustained once migrants and their families are settled. Unpaid or informal home-based work, such as a 'telephone nanny' and Polish language tuition for the children of migrants, are other examples of where we see the emergence of socially reproductive work (as understood by feminist scholars), sustaining mobility as pertaining to the field of social reproduction. In the London hospitality sector, Alberti (2011) had found similar dynamics where, for instance, young and educated Brazilian migrants, temporarily engaged in the catering industry as agency workers, would organize their social time for sharing food and houseware; putting together their limited income to recover from the intensive rhythm of work; supporting each other's precarious lives; gathering financial resources to afford a more plentiful if constrained leisure time; and, not least, building connections for possible onward geographical mobility. While those coethnic and hybrid networks served as a coping strategy against precarious work and to provide new jobs or self-development opportunities in the UK or abroad, their gains exceeded the sphere of labour reproduction for the market, or indeed merely economic or financially oriented aims. The fact that migration itself can trigger demands for non-market services, and new forms of unpaid or low-paid work that are necessary to reproduce the transnational family, may be understood as an instance when the social reproductive labour of migrants is not completely or immediately recuperated by the needs of the market but rather supports the reproduction of mobility and the (migrant) worker family as such.

Drawing from Marx's original theorization of social reproduction, encapsulating the historical ways in which 'the class of free workers' has been formed and maintained, Cravey (2005) highlights the interdependencies as well as tensions between the spheres of production and reproduction: on the one hand the costs of producing labour power are externalized through migration, but on the other the everyday reproduction of the worker becomes more and more *reliant* on the networks of support and circuits of resources made possible by migrant transnational ways of living. In the workings of migrant networks lies a double movement whereby, on the one hand, these communities 'lower the necessary labour time' (Cravey, 2004: 196) of future migrants, and, on the other, serve to reproduce and inspire new migrations. The circulation of labour across the fields of production and reproduction therefore creates a continuous tension in highly mobile life situations, enlightening the contradictory nature of migrant transnational lives.

The role of transnational families in sustaining entire production systems, communities back home, and global (gender and class) inequalities has been the subject of research by feminist geographers as well as migration scholars (for example, Baldassar and Merla, 2014; Riccio, 2008; Zontini, 2010). The work of Cravey (2005) is particularly inspiring for us in that, drawing from the transnationalism of migrants in North Carolina, it theorizes the implications of globalization for production and social reproduction, respectively described as 'scaling up' and 'scaling down' processes of valorization. Here, not only macro-economic restructuring of production, but also changes in the subjective and cultural processes of migrants interacting with a variety of structures of oppression (including gender and race) in the country of origin and destination are considered:

> Gender relations, as well as sexual expression and desire, are all altered by the need to find spaces of social reproduction to substitute for family and household forms not available in North Carolina. That is, when they migrate to the US South, Latinos and Latinas creatively *adapt to, and substitute for,* the loss of two important sites of social reproduction in their daily lives: household/family systems of support and state-funded channels of social provision. (Cravey, 2005: 358; author's emphasis)

Compared to the 'subsidizing role' of migrant households/family illustrated in the work of Mezzadri (2019, 2021) for the Indian sweatshop regime, here subsidies to capital are 'recreated' by the practices of survival and the building of new cultural communities by Latin American immigrants adapting their new lives in North Carolina. In addition, Cravey's account of the 'scaling down' of social reproduction is fundamental to understand the role of migrant labour in systems of labour exploitation by showing how capital does not simply 'reduce the cost of social reproduction of labour power' by 'importing migrant workers'. Scaling down rather involves a *continuum* of exploitation that migrants experience for the sake of their reproductive capacities through the maintenance of strong links back home. In other words, by hiring migrants the state relies on the fact that they base their livelihoods on the existence of support networks in the country of origin, while a highly networked community and household relationships in the country of destination provide a wealth of material and psychological resources that allow their longer term self-sustenance.[8] From the use of their local store that becomes a community centre, the night club, and the flea market, Cravey's ethnography shows how migrants develop these practices into 'resistant' spaces of social reproduction, whose transformative and conflicting elements emerge in particular through the cultural field (Cravey, 2004: 193). Through hybridizing national and gender identities in their leisure time, Latino and Latina migrants conserve and at the same time remake their Latino culture, 'reappropriating' these community spaces as Mexican, thus compensating for those sets of relationships and networks of support that migration disrupts and displaces (compare Harvey, 2018). Cravey is indeed well aware that those reappropriation practices occur in a context of labour exploitation whereby (in that particular region of the US) migrants mostly provide temporary racialized supplies of labour to a hyper-exploited agricultural sector. At the same time as they are subject to immigration rules that strip them of full protections and dispatch them as labourers with lesser rights, they remake and transform oppressive gender relations and desires through their migrations. These outcomes must be considered beyond merely economic relationships.[9]

Similarly, Teeple Hopkins (2017: 144), studying domestic workers from the Philippines in the Canadian context, argues that the community space of the church for Filipino and Filipina live-in caregivers provides an important source of psychological support and informal care. These forms of support in the realm of social reproduction have various ramifications and implications: as the emotional sphere, where workers need recharging from difficult and exhausting work; in terms of physical necessity if they decide to quit their employer and quickly find new accommodation; and materially, in the sense of facilitating access to new employers or financial support. The role of faith groups and social centres is, for Teeple Hopkins, an example of 'the stretching of space' alongside that of time, which proves the need to keep distinguishing between the space of paid reproductive work and that of unpaid social reproduction. In this sense, the author extends both the argument of Silvia Federici (2014), and that of Barbara Ellen Smith and Jamie Winders (2015), who make a spatial and temporal argument to counter the idea of the total blurring of the sphere of production and reproduction for migrant domestic workers: live-in domestic workers shows that when work and home coincides, it is hard to distinguish between the two spheres. Still, it remains politically important to recognize the two as separate as they unfold in the real lives of these workers. Such distinction means to acknowledge that these workers are still doing unpaid reproductive work in addition to paid domestic and care work. Overall, in Teeple Hopkins's (2017: 143) interviews with Filipina workers, it emerges that even though the employers exploit the continuum of productive and reproductive work when they extrapolate unpaid overtime from their domestic helpers, the workers keep the distinction between the two areas in their mind when they rather describe the extension of the working day as simply 'abuse of her time'.[10] Silvia Federici (1975) had indeed already argued about the importance of visibilizing the realm of reproduction as separate from production, as doing this is a political strategy that illuminates the extraction of value from women's work as well as its erasure from capitalist processes of accumulation. Similarly, Smith and Winders (2015) show how hostile immigration laws in some of the US states, by criminalizing the use of transportation, lodging, and schooling by undocumented migrants, widened the separation between migrants' social spaces and working spaces, and eventually restricted the spaces of social reproduction for migrants and their children afraid of exposing themselves to the authorities.

Overall, we can conclude with Cravey (2005) that it is this 'downscaling' of the cost of social reproduction from the public to the private spheres that requires both the separation (Burawoy, 1976) as well as the ongoing connection of migrant members with their diaspora communities, and with family members across borders. So, we agree that it is politically and methodologically important to understand the specificity and separateness of production and reproduction processes in terms of migrant lives, but we also stress how their mutual dependency is theoretically key. Maintaining this double view, it appears that the point of view of transnational migration illuminates the wider role of social reproduction in the globalized economy because it shows how the reproductive work of transnational families, alongside the exclusion of migrants from social welfare protections, and migrants' incorporation in the precarious economy, are critical in supporting productive systems in the country of immigration, while still allowing for the reproduction of migrant communities across borders.

Differential access to welfare and social reproductive strategies

Some authors suggest that migrants can move for welfare reasons, as Western European countries often have wealthier systems than other countries. Analysing the European Union enlargement, Kvist (2004), for example, considers that mobility processes from East to West could be seen as a means to access the national welfare system, sometimes exporting the benefits into the home country. However, in most countries of the Global North, non-citizens are excluded from entitlements to welfare benefits (see Cohen et al, 2002). Border controls extend into the sphere of social life by excluding immigrants and asylum seekers from social assistance and means-based benefits. In this sense, the costs of the social reproduction of migrant labour are outsourced twice: by employers in destination countries receiving 'ready-made' labour, and by leaving the burden of unpaid activities occurring in the house to the family and the community, which are systematically used as subsidies for the maintenance of the same labour (especially in contexts where neither the state nor employers bear any welfare costs such as pension contributions or social security benefits).

Similar to the distinction between waged and unwaged, value producing and non-value producing work (Mezzadri, 2019), determining who is entitled or not to social protections (including social contributions, health services, and out of work social assistance) has always been a largely political issue managed by the administration and production of legal categories of entitlement (Picchio, 1992). Migrants as non-citizens are the archetype figure of the construction of the welfare state. Critical migration scholarship has masterfully illustrated the complex ways in which the functioning of migration controls is not only aimed at controlling the employment relation (Anderson, 2010), but also pointed at the maintenance of societal precariousness through different categories of entitlement and 'deservingness' (Cohen et al, 2002).[11] As critically argued by Tom Vickers in his research on the intersection of welfare, migration and class formation in the context of Brexit-Britain: 'immigration control and state welfare describe two dimensions of state intervention that actively structure the operation and reproduction of waged labour that is vital to capitalism' (Vickers, 2020: 5).

According to most immigration systems across the Global North and South, migrants are allowed to bring their families in when they can demonstrate economic 'self-sufficiency' and do not become a burden on the welfare state of the country of immigration, and are usually excluded from any 'recourse to public funds' (Ruhs, 2013; Anderson and Hughes, 2015; Riedner, 2015). Even in the common market of the European Union, the welfare restrictions imposed on those who cannot prove to be 'active' in the labour market or do only 'marginal' work, including those who are in principle covered by 'equal treatment' in the areas of social welfare and taxation, such as EU 'free movers' (Schiek et al, 2015), prove the persistence of differential access to state-supported social reproduction (to be discussed later). Fostering regimes of precarious employment also for higher skilled immigration – allegedly enjoying freedom of movement but forced to accept low-paid and insecure jobs for the purpose of claiming social benefits (see also Simola, 2018) – welfare and migration controls extend into the disciplining of migrant labouring and non-labouring bodies.

While there is only very limited research on the struggles, strategies, and demands of migrant workers in the field of welfare benefits, there is indeed literature on the intersection of migration and welfare controls (Cohen et al, 2002), and on the effects of welfare restrictions and exclusion perpetuating migrants' precariousness (O'Brien, 2015; Sanguinetti, 2016; Dwyer et al, 2019; Simola, 2018). This research clearly needs to be expanded in relation to migrant work. Migrant strategies in the field of welfare claims are indeed critical to understand labour mobility power, because welfare provisions may also directly support the maintenance of migrants' mobility across and within labour markets, including temporary migrants. Research on precarious workers has demonstrated, for instance, how seasonally employed migrants in the hotel industry in Italy make a strategic use of the existing unemployment benefits to survive non-seasonal periods of worklessness and maintain their transnational families between Italy and different African countries (Iannuzzi, 2021). Carlotta Benvegnù (2018), in a comparative research on the logistics sector, highlighted how while in France migrants (recruited as temporary agency workers and relying on relatively wealthy unemployment benefits) develop a strong mobility across different warehouses looking for better working conditions, in Italy (where unemployment benefits are poorer and workers are hired as permanent workers by cooperative of convenience), migrants have less room for manoeuvre to set up forms of autonomous mobility. In research on Bangladeshi migrant workers in the Fincantieri shipyards in Italy, Al Amin Rabby (2022) highlights how workers subject to renewal of their permit to stay, or waiting for a permit, are sought after by employers, while those with long-term residence permits can move easily in the labour market and prefer short-term contracts to go to visit family for a longer time while still being able to rely on (poor) unemployment benefits.

Temporary work and dependency on welfare in the country of immigration are in fact both necessary to survive the high costs of living and working for low wages (especially in costly global cities). In turn, such conditionalities allow capital and the state to reproduce this type of migrant labour as precarious.[12] The ongoing reproduction of mobility for the same individual or household (and the resources needed for it) have been more seldomly observed in this literature, and this is the new research agenda tackled by emergent research on multiple, multinational, or onward migrations (Mas Giralt, 2017; Paul and Yeoh, 2020) (see Chapter 2). The uncertainty of the outcome of any mobility decision that suggests that onward migration is characterized by 'the continuous re-evaluation of migration opportunities' (Morad and Sacchetto, 2020: 165), rather than rationally preplanned routes, demonstrates in our view the very instability of the terrain of social reproduction and the ways in which this interacts with social dynamics in the sphere of production and labour. When stricter state migration policies introduce new obstacles to the (already long and complex) regularization process and attainment of social security, these may become a reason for migrants to look for a different destination. Morad and colleagues' (2021) study of the strategies of Italian–Bangladeshis in the UK at the time of Brexit highlighted their selective approach to the welfare state and labour market: given the relatively meagre wages they gain in the UK gig economy – which are not sufficient to support their families – it is more convenient for them to keep applying for rent support and work part-time. These 'onward-migrants', once in the new location, also experiment with their own strategic use of welfare benefits to afford both housing and a decent family time. Onward and multinational migration are therefore not merely driven by economic calculation by the individual, but by more complex factors in the sphere of social reproduction, often playing out at the household level. These experiences of welfare and labour coping strategies by migrant workers may be understood as 'battles of indeterminacy': caught between labour, capital, and state welfare controls, migrants are captured by the impossibility of planning time for leisure. In turn, migrant welfare strategies generate intermittencies of labour supply and a preference for part-time work which may be problematic for employers in the longer term.

Beyond the welfare regime, it's important to recognize how community-based forms of social reproductive strategies may also provide resources to influence, directly or indirectly, labour relations inside workplaces across the whole economy. Brown (2019), for instance, in his study on the Savan-Seno special economic zone in Laos, highlights how an agrarian subsistence economy could be advantageous for firms, as it appears as a subsidy for social reproduction, permitting them to maintain lower wages. However, managers need to cope with workers' activities outside factories. These activities, as in the case of small crops in Laos, can guarantee workers more bargaining power than full proletarian workers. Similarly, in Guatemala's Free Zone, young female indigenous Maya combine different economic strategies, including working for subsistence, producing small goods to sell informally, and also producing for export (Goldín, 2012). While in the first years these young women hoped that employment in manufacturing could support a modern way of life, and improve their ability to negotiate household relations thanks to the access to cash (Fernàndez-Kelly, 1983; Salzinger, 2003), they soon understood that their working conditions inside these plants were hard, with extensive exploitation and lack of respect. Analysing the experiences of this EPZ's garment workers, as well as people not working in the maquila industry, Goldín underlines that workers manage labour turnover to regulate high levels of exploitation at work *and* the needs of reproduction. Therefore, labour turnover should not be analysed as helpless and desperate reactions to the power of capital, but as an option for workers to take hold of their lives. Indeed, Goldín (2011: 139) suggests 'a framework whereby labor conditions and sources of support at home are linked to turnover of young workers in the maquila'.

Bhattacharyya (2018: 53), in a similar spirit, draws from the work of Cindi Katz, exploring the ways in which the field of social reproduction may offer spaces with 'the possibility of resisting the forces of global capitalism'. Are all activities which attain the field of reproduction immediately absorbed in the sphere of capitalist wage relations? While both Katz and Bhattacharyya seem sceptical about understanding social reproduction as a source of revolutionary and anti-capitalist practices (see Chapter 1), they remain open to the idea that, partially at least, some of these activities maintain a level of autonomy from the mere reproduction of capitalist social relations: on the one hand, social reproduction cannot be revolutionary because it remakes 'the very social relations and material forms that are so problematic' (Katz, 2001: 718). On the other hand, Bhattacharyya, while maintaining a relatively bleak view of what may happen to those unwaged populations who are left outside social protection and minimum security, considers the possibility that alternative, non-capitalist forms of survival and struggles may emerge directly in the sphere of social reproduction.

The question for us is therefore to better understand what other transformative practices and disruptions are possible in those 'exceeding spaces', and to what extent they are transformative of other forms of oppression based on race and gender, including but not limited to the workplace. Whether or not directly at the point of production, or solely in the field of reproductive practices, they still carry implications for capitalist social relations that rely on racism and patriarchy to control workers in the workplace (Brah, 1993; see also Chapter 3). Turning to the fields of labour process studies and the sociology of work may help in providing illustrations of the disruptive or creative nature of socially reproductive practices when they intersect with labour (im)mobility: how have these other perspectives tackled the relationship between migration and social reproduction? In particular, if mobility can be considered as one of the reproductive capacities that workers want to preserve and strive for, as shown earlier, how do we understand the existing regimes of 'labour mobility capture', such as dormitory regimes across Global North and South countries, their functioning, and fault lines? In what ways do they constitute contested terrains for the reproduction of migrant labour and rather generate new sources of worker power?

The multiple functions of worker dormitories

In the past decade critical labour process scholars conducted international research that spanned the fields of production and reproduction in innovative ways, looking in particular at capital's strategies to control and reduce the costs of social reproduction of the workforce through new regimes of (im)mobilization and circulation of labour. Building on Burawoy's (1985) notion of labour regime, Smith (2003) and Pun and Smith (2007) have introduced and elaborated the concept of dormitory labour regime as a form of production that has political effects on the labour process and on social reproduction. Pun Ngai and Chris Smith (2007) highlighted the emergence of the dormitory labour regime in managing internal migration in mainland China as a crucial mechanism integrating the workplace and the space of everyday life for the purpose of controlling and disciplining labour (and extending labour time). Worker dormitories allow not only to capture the workforce, locating workers in controllable places in proximity of the site of production, and monitoring more closely the time and space of their production and reproduction activities, but also to dispose of them when capital no longer requires that labour (see Chapter 1). Concentration and circulation of the workforce are the two opposite poles of the management of labour power in dormitory labour regimes. Together, they make possible for the employers: 'the holding down of wages and the lengthening of the working day' for a 'hybrid, transient workforce … circulating between factory and countryside' (Pun and Smith, 2007: 31). Workers' circulation, in fact, is mostly analysed in terms of providing the employers with an ever-regenerating workforce of permanently young workers. Moreover, workers' circulation is discussed as favouring the employers as it 'removes the discontented and more vociferous workers from the workplace' (Pun and Smith, 2007: 43). This reminds us of the critical view of turnover as detrimental to collectivism considered in Chapter 1.

This notion of dormitory labour regime has been adopted by most other authors in the analysis of an ongoing phenomena that became widespread worldwide in the last twenty years. It is important to note how early studies of dormitories can be found in feminist political economy and geography, where again the research by Cravey (1998) demonstrated how dormitories divided by gender in Mexican maquiladoras are particularly functional to managerial control that extends into the sphere of workers' everyday reproduction. While the dormitory labour regime follows the rationale of control and extraction of value, at the same time the life in the dormitory generates elements of tensions and resistance (Pun and Smith, 2007). For instance, with spatial proximity augmented in the dormitory, social and ethnic networks can also strengthen migrants' control over their own mobility, hence the dormitory becomes a site of resistance and class formation: a way to organize, individually or collectively, forms of power (Bal, 2016). Based on the recent analysis (Ceccagno and Sacchetto, 2020), we identify the following multiple characteristics of dormitories vis-à-vis the reproduction of labour power, namely as:

1) A strategy to capture and expand a pool of a just-in-time's workforce for the needs of production. Here mobility is considered mostly as orchestrated by management and sometimes with state support. For example, the kafala system in the Gulf countries, the *Gastarbeiter* programme in Europe, and the Bracero programme in the US (as shown in Chapter 2).
2) A site of coercion and control over the workers, blurring the space of work and non-work to the point of creating a total institution, whose main aims are to reduce and 'downscale' (see earlier discussion) labour reproduction costs and to restrain the freedom of workers by limiting their voice and controlling their associational power (Smith, 2003).
3) A space where ethnic and family networks both reinforce and moderate controls over labour mobility, but which also permits building forms of mobility.
4) A site of class recomposition and collective action, to gather knowledge about labour markets and strengthen what we call mobility skills.

Just-in-time management regimes

The most evident case of workers' mobility orchestrated by states and their agencies on the basis of the employers' needs is described by Xiang and Lindquist (2014). Analysing the mobility pattern of Asian migrants in South East Asia, the authors show how, thanks to the actions of labour intermediaries and migration brokers, migrant recruitment and accommodation in dormitories are aimed at expanding the labour market to satisfy just-in-time needs and managing labour turnover. In this way, employers are no longer constrained to recruit in the local labour market where workers have the support of a community and a specific culture of work, but can entrust to migrants whose only concern is to maximize wages (Smith, 2003).

If the COVID-19 pandemic was perhaps the most obvious episode of how the state and capital control the (im)mobility of migrant workers through dormitories, there are other important historical examples that show how both have been striving to manage labour time and spatial mobility through housing workers near the place of work, and the gendered and racialized dynamics of such control mechanisms. For instance, Brinton (1993) studied how Japanese silk factories depended on a constant supply of migrant women workers, but that this also presented with high levels of female labour turnover. Tsurumi (1992), in contrast, studied Japanese dormitories to house women workers in thread mills, showing how these were disciplinary management methods but also used to reduce the turnover of labour.

The case of China today is in our view particularly exemplary of how both management and the state have a common interest in immobilizing labour as a way to respond to the needs of just-in-time production. Additionally, dormitory labour regimes in China need to be understood in the context of wider social transformations in terms of rural to urban and urban to urban migration, with the rise and population growth of new middle-range cities as new migrant destinations within China, and the partial relaxation of the *hukou* system (Wang et al, 2015; Pun, 2007). The use of the dormitory regimes is not a mere retention strategy to hold on to scarce skills in the firm, but one aiming to 'capture single migrant workers for short period of tenure in order to maximise the utilisation of labour services during the working day' (Smith, 2003: 334). Studying the dormitory labour regime of China's Southern Pearl River Delta, and comparing the latter with paternalistic managerial regimes in China and internationally (for example, in Japan), Smith (2003: 345) was initially interested in exploring the benefits for management from having labour available 'on tap': 'as they can rely on increasing overtime when demand dictates without fear that workers will refuse. … This is far harder where there is a clear market, spatial and familial separation between "home" and "work".'

The integration of production and reproduction is in fact possible because the dormitories are near the factory, workers have no family needs, and they are relieved from housework duties beside taking care of the minimum needed for their individual daily reproduction. Research comparing working hours in footwear and sporting apparel supply chain factories in China and Thailand (Smyth et al, 2013: 395) underlines that living in a labour accommodation regime 'has a positive and significant effect on working in excess of 60 hours per week'. In China, dormitories facilitate longer working hours even if they are located in urban areas because migrants feel entrapped in strong disciplinary systems (Fan, 2004).

Employer-driven mobility on the basis of an immobile capital, and worker isolation in accommodation, are main concepts also in the analysis of posted workers in Europe. Posted workers, dispatched from one member state to another of the EU as services rather than labour, and for defined periods of time (Hayes and Novitz, 2013), are by definition denied the possibility of building up political, economic, and social resources as compared to more permanent migrants (Caro et al, 2015: 1602). Posted workers' mobility to different European countries is indeed temporary, and often their working lives are made more precarious as posting is in turn based on sub-contractual arrangements between firms (Danaj and Simola, 2015; Fellini et al, 2007). Construction, as well as shipbuilding and meat sectors, account for about two million posted workers across Europe, for jobs that can last from a few months to years (Wagner, 2018; Engbersen et al, 2013; European Commission, 2016).[13] Accommodation arranged for posted workers is often in substandard housing (that is, inexpensive hotels, barracks) where they share the rooms with colleagues in remote areas with sporadic contacts among locals and suffering from a segregation that is strengthened by language barriers (Caro et al, 2015).

In both the Asian and the European cases, therefore, we witness a trend towards moving an international workforce across national boundaries on the basis of predetermined and precise production needs. From this point of view, dormitories work as an efficient mechanism to regulate labour performance by increasing control over the reproduction of migrant labour: 'just-in-time production has its counterpart in the just-in-time reproduction of the dormitory system' (Schling, 2014: 48).

It clearly appears that securing labour involves the reproduction of such labour power over time and space together with the attached skills. In this sense, controlling mobility means controlling the reproduction of labour power and skills in the longer term, not only its immediate expendability. Far from being an Asia-only phenomenon, the reconfiguration of space and time in the factories of Chinese entrepreneurs in Italy in garment production, through the housing of workers at their place of work, allows the outsourcing of social reproduction by placing socially reproductive tasks out to other workers (Ceccagno, 2017). In this context, the outsourcing of the costs of job flexibility guarantees an 'expansion' of the sphere of production to the detriment of that of social reproduction, which shrinks and becomes impoverished in order to manage production's needs (Smith and Winders, 2008). With Ferruccio Gambino (2016) we may say that in the dormitory labour regime, the reproduction of human life, as well as any other activity, is in fact expelled (outsourced to the worker or their family) because the primary objective remains the production of value for capital.

Total institutions

Considering the multiple functions of dormitories, they have been analysed as total institutions (Lucas et al, 2013), which means recognizing their function in extending the time of work and control across the spaces of production and reproduction. Scholars underline that the dormitory labour regime is an oppressive system of control where curfews are widespread. The literature shows that as much as at the production site, control in the dormitories is overt, publicly displayed, and punishment-oriented (Ceccagno and Sacchetto, 2020; Ceccagno, 2017). The regimental approach is also evident in the spatiality and characterization of the dormitories that are often described as incorporated into the factory grounds, or close to them, often fenced on four sides by walls, with entrance gates guarded around the clock by security guards (Pun, 2005). This regimental order dictates who can stay in the dorm, for how long, who can be a roommate, what can be done, and what is forbidden in the dormitory premises. Such intrusive controls remind us of the practices of Ford's Sociological Department, but go beyond them as the boundary of work and life are further blurred.

Analysing migrant farm workers that move from Mexico and Central America to the US, Kraemer Diaz et al (2016) illustrate how they are accommodated by employers in isolated and overcrowded labour camps. The harsh conditions of these total institutions contribute to increase their aggressiveness, 'because of the forced relationship among a small group of people for extended period of times at work and play' (Kraemer Diaz et al, 2016: 548). The practice of spatially segregating migrant workers is analysed as a powerful labour management tool that makes it possible to take advantage of the unrestricted availability of a migrant workforce, and, critically for our discussion, to shelter employers from the high labour turnover rate, and to depress wages demand (Pun and Smith, 2007).

Studying the everyday experiences of agricultural migrant workers in the south of Italy, Sanò and Piro (2017) and Piro (2021) have similarly highlighted these patterns of seclusion (Gambino, 2003) to describe how, despite their formal freedoms, migrants are de facto constrained in a situation of immobility, being accommodated in proximity of the greenhouses and strictly controlled by employers. However, they have also highlighted how the overlapping spaces of work and dwelling open up spaces for new family strategies of social reproduction when workers are hired as couples. Other disciplinary tools used to control and contain the workers' mobility include the company holding the workers' passports for 'safe-keeping' reasons, and the threat of deportation (Azmeh, 2014). The institutionalization of low-wage migrant flows by government is a factor that influences the spatial separation and exclusion of workers from society in the country of destination. In research on Chinese-owned construction sites in Cambodia, where Chinese and Cambodian workers are employed, Ivan Franceschini (2020) highlights how employers use language barriers and segregation in accommodation to prevent the rise of a cohesive front among workers. Local institutions and trade unions being extremely weak, employers can manage the workforce without any mediation, undermining worker solidarity.

As we saw in Chapter 2, migrants moving from Asian countries have to undergo country of destination migration policy, restricting migrant workers' self-determination because they cannot choose or change employer and are exposed to stringent segregation, living in isolated places. Nepalese workers in South Korea are in fact temporary sojourners under the government Employment Permit System, and are accommodated by employers in containers or crumbling houses (Seo and Skelton, 2017). The sponsorship system, and similar models with a strong link between employer and migrant workers, is the rule in the Persian Gulf countries where 'sociospatial segregation is the norm' (Gardner, 2012: 43). Started in the 1930s, the construction of labour camps for migrants supported the development of the oil industry and was widespread as an apparatus to manage and control migrants, leading to severe consequences for their health (Kamrava and Babar, 2012). In the United Arab Emirates, for example, they suffer from the so-called Dubai Syndrome, which includes depression and thoughts of self-harm (Al-Maskari et al, 2011) because they live in isolated areas under crowded and miserable conditions (Bruslé, 2012).

The ambivalent role of ethnic and family networks

The management's struggle at retaining the workforce is more effective when it counts on, or even strives to secure, the help of the workers' family members employed in the same factory, or else people sharing the same place of origin. The reliance on ethnic networks has been described by scholars as substantially unchanged over the last decades. For instance, in the 1990s, Lee (1995) highlighted the role of family members in limiting workers hopping from one job to another. Even when they were willing to move to higher paying factory jobs, young women could be vetoed by older relatives, especially when these relatives lived with the women in the same dormitory rooms, as a form of control of the young women's behavior. One decade later, in the 2000s, Pun (2005) pointed out that family bonds among coworkers reinforce control over the workforce. She referred to the 'cartography of dormitory labour' making up mutual obligations as well as mutual control and group discipline in the workplace. Beyond dormitories, research in Western Europe has more broadly illustrated the ambivalent role of ethnic enclave and migrant coethnic networks in both supporting job seeking, but also restricting the job opportunities of undocumented migrants (Bloch, 2013). Workers' networks, more often than not, are indeed discussed as a double-edged sword in that they contribute to hamper and not only facilitate workers' mobility. Xiang (2012), for example, points to the pressures from family members and local communities back home, thanks to which migrant workers do not try to overstay or change employer, but return back home, as planned by the states and the agency. Nevertheless, social networks can work differently. In fact, isolating workers away from their community network may be an outward strategy in some contexts to respond to and limit their resourcefulness. Bonded or coercive forms of labour may be supported, for instance, by national and local authorities' willingness to adopt working arrangements that include the seclusion of workers. Azmeh (2014) emphasizes that the discriminating factor shaping locational choices by international manufacturing firms lies in favouring the dormitory labour regime that is considered crucial for cutting the social ties of the workforce: recruiting migrants globally without any social networks and putting them to work in qualifying industrial zones and inside dormitories has been crucial for employers to build a 'working machine' satisfying the needs of US buyers in Jordan. In sum, the dormitory arrangements, by tackling the very fabric of relations among workers and communities, represent 'the cornerstone of the social control of workers in the workplace' (Azmeh, 2014: 508), with critical implications in the sphere of worker organizing practices. However, even where there are coercive practices carried out by employers to limit migrant mobility, migrants may use escape, despite the risk of losing their personal documentation; according to trade union records in Jordan, around 10,000 workers have escaped the EPZs in a few years, leaving their passports in the hands of the companies (Azmeh, 2014: 507).

One of the most recent and explicit employer anti-social network strategies has been developed in the global mining industry, through the replacement of company towns by a 'fly-in/fly-out (FI-FO)' labour regime. Mining companies put in place a strong transformation from company town to a long-distance commuting model (Manky, 2016), with a separation of production and reproduction process, weakening social bonds both at work and in the local communities (Ellem, 2016). Long-distance commuting has been implemented thanks both to technological improvements in the mines, that allow employers to recruit technicians that don't want to live in a company town, and to improved transport connections. Miners are moved from the city on a weekly basis to the mine and companies build accommodation close to the workplace to lodge workers. With the families residing in the city, workers are pushed to work for longer hours, exposing them to substance abuse (Aroca, 2001). Overall, the spatial reorganization of reproduction processes impacts on the bargaining power of the workers because they are scattered across the country and are more interested in their personal lives than in union activities (Manky, 2016). Indeed the construction of appropriate spaces for social reproduction can produce an individualization of the labour force with an erosion of social relations. Therefore, the organization of dormitories by employers affects workers' collective bargaining, weakening the associational power of workers (Smyth et al, 2013: 401).

Transnational family dynamics and the availability of resources for social reproduction (or lack of them), including during the migratory process, beside the specific conditions of the dormitory and its coercive functions, influence the 'affordability' of turnover as mobility power for these workers.

Class recomposition and collective action

The reconfiguration of reproductive work through dormitories is strictly connected not only to the labour process, but also to the forms of solidarity and workers' organization (Pun and Smith, 2007). The importance of hybrid, composed class formations and opportunities for conscientization in dormitories, despite the efforts of employers at limiting workers' associational power through spatial seclusion and the extension of working time, has been emphasized by a part of the literature (Ceccagno and Sacchetto, 2020).

In this process, not only purely class-based identities, but also gender and ethnic ones provide the social glue to resist the complete commodification of labour. Contrary to the view that workers' sense of collectivism stems solely from class-based factors, China's mostly female migrant workers have been found developing a sense of class identity drawing on the powerful influence of kinship, ethnicity, and gender (Pun, 2005). In research on Foxconn's plants in Europe, Andrijasevic and Sacchetto (2016) underlined how the dormitory is a space in which EU migrant workers rebuild new forms of sociality which are often superficial and occur between compatriots, but which can constitute an important foothold to cling to the isolation in which they find themselves, as well as the opportunity for an exchange of information on the different labour markets in Europe and sometimes even outside Europe. For workers, dormitories can become the spaces to establish new relationships and to understand what is going on in the factory, but also in other parts of the European labour market. Therefore, for EU workers, the dormitory regime also opens up some spaces of agency: circulating information to broaden labour market prospects, and reinforcing the workers' ability to handle the hardships of the factory life. Developing this argument, Ceccagno and Sacchetto (2020) suggest not to look at the single dormitory but at the multiplicity of accommodations at work available for migrants. From this point of view, the web of dormitories in Europe – as well as in other countries – can be considered as a chessboard where migrants 'can jump from one square to another in search of better conditions', and also a place where workers develop associational power (Ceccagno and Sacchetto, 2020: 310).

Living together in cheap accommodation may elicit forms of solidarity among migrants that spill over into the workplace, thus also creating a high turnover of labour that 'can be identified as a protest against this labour management regime' (Smith, 2003: 335). In his book, Charanpal Singh Bal (2016: 216) argues that migrant workers were able to organize strikes in the Dubai construction sector thanks to the concentration of workers in labour camps, where word of mouth travelled fast without highly structured forms of organization. A camp, therefore, on the one hand appears as a controlling institution atomizing workers, and on the other, it enhances the propensity of workers for collective action.

Recognizing the benefits of mobility and movement for class consciousness is quite rare, considering decades of theories and assumption about the negative effects of migration on collectivism. With Pun Ngai (2007: 255), we believe, however, that while used for the purpose of capital interest in the high circulation of labour, and inhibiting the possibility of long-term collective resistance, dormitories may actually create the conditions for class formation, nurturing class consciousness and collectivism in the longer run: 'No doubt the dormitory labor system, in concentrating and yet circulating labor, provides the basis for and facilitating class actions in the future' (Pun, 2007: 255). Indeed, the specific shape and form of the spatial restriction under which labour is trapped configures different degrees of 'affordability' of labour mobility power, as the case of EPZs demonstrate. Table 4.1 summarizes the different roles or functions played by worker dormitories in the management of mobility, with a focus on social reproduction and labour control, and the relative effects on worker associational power.

Concluding remarks: differential mobility powers in social reproduction

In this chapter we have considered migrant mobility practices as forms of reproductive work that sustains migration, as both facilitator and disruptor of processes of capitalist accumulation by allowing for the reduction and downscaling (Cravey, 2005) of the social costs of reproducing and

Table 4.1: The ambivalent functions of dormitories in social reproduction and labour control

Functions	Associational power decreased	Associational power increased
Just-in-time regimes	Just-in-time reproduction of workforce	Increased turnover leads to strikes
Total institutions	Spatial seclusion + extension of working time	Creation of tight social ties
Ethnic networks	Increase exploitation and dependency	Facilitate bonding, collectivism
Class formation	Weakened class identity	Dormitories as anchors for migrant workers and sources of socialization

Note: See 'Forms of worker power' in the Glossary

maintaining labour power. The scope of this chapter has been to show how tensions observed about the ambivalent nature of labour mobility, and its problematic effects for management when turnover is initiated by workers (Chapters 1 and 3), can be better grasped in relation to social reproduction and transnational migration.

The forms of agency and resistance available to the workers appeared strongly influenced not only by the conditions of their social reproduction in loco (for example, the presence of dormitories and the receiving country's migration and welfare policy), but also by the forms of reproduction that occur across their extended or stretched transnational households. Having families in their home countries waiting for the money, or having incurred debts to migrate, can create dependencies, and therefore lower what we understand as migrant labour turnover power. Azmeh's (2014) study in Middle Eastern EPZs confirms in turn insights emerging from other research that illustrated how transnational labour migration profoundly reshapes the ways in which social reproduction is organized across borders (Kofman, 2012). This is true even without the need to look at migration, as in the case of non-migrant EPZ workers in Laos and Guatemala, who manage their own turnover based on the overall organization of the family and on their life experiences (see Goldín, 2011; 2012; Chapter 1).

Turnover can therefore be considered a long-term strategy that allows workers to cope with harsh conditions at work, with scarce opportunity to improve their working conditions, and in the space of reproduction, where it is possible not only to gain time to spend with children, parents, or friends, but also to find other ways to satisfy their needs. Labour turnover in this instance clearly offers some chance to workers to control their lives, because they can enjoy some kind of flexibility and decide to work or not to work, to leave or not to leave, to take time to explore alternative workplaces or alternatives to becoming employees. Labour turnover can be, therefore, a space of agency for workers as well as a strategy for capital to deal with global competition (Goldín, 2012; Pun, 2005; Tiano, 1984; Salzinger, 2003; Wright, 2006). This is why turnover maintains an intrinsic ambivalence in terms of the conflict between capital and labour (see Chapter 1).

The intersection between the spheres of production and reproduction, considered at the start of the chapter, remains complex in terms of the role of families in facilitating or hindering mobility: while family networks may create greater dependency on work (for example, the need to send remittances back home and thus discourage the migrants from choosing quitting), the absence of local family networks and the disembeddedness of migrants in the territory may be beneficial to the employers, increasing their reliability on this labour. In the case of the EPZs studied by Azmeh, it was the temporary and just-in-time nature of product demand in global production that explained their preference for migrant labour; because of their lack of social ties with the local communities, employers assumed migrants would be more easily subjugated and controlled (Azmeh, 2014: 509).

This notion of disembeddedness is critical to understand how capital reduces the cost of social reproduction not solely in monetary terms, but by hiring workers with limited social resources as well as caring responsibilities. We have shown how migration regimes can be very prescriptive of what kind of workers are wanted in terms of their reproductive 'profile', like the 'childless' strawberry pickers (Corrado, 2017; Glass et al, 2014), or the migrants banned from marrying and having children in Malaysia (Miles et al, 2022). In addition, the kinds of relationships that migrants develop with the local workforce on the basis of their cultural backgrounds have a bearing on their relative embeddedness and mobility power. In Malaysia, when a relatively relaxed system of (legal and illegal) flows, mainly from Indonesia, turned into a more controlled system of guest workers (and drop in illegal flows) in 1997, Wong (2006: 214) noted that this shift from a regional migration system based on cultural affinity and settlement, to an orderly system of rotation of migrant labour, was explicitly aimed at maintaining social and cultural distance between workers.

Overall, migrants may be more or less successful in utilizing their labour turnover power according to a series of circumstances: whether it is the degree of workplace coercion and immigration controls imposed by the country's government or workplace regimes (most evident in the case of worker dormitories); or the nature of work and product market and the relative bargaining power of workers; or, crucially for our discussion, the normative expectations, dependencies, and practices of migrant transnational families, and migrants' levels of dis/embeddedness with the local community. All these aspects weigh a great deal in terms of shaping the relative 'affordability' of turnover for workers. We can therefore conclude that the differential forms and degrees of mobility – emerging already in the field of social reproduction rather than solely in the labour process – are critically influenced by gender and racialization dynamics and social norms, as well as by the social and cultural practices of the families and communities that sustain or hinder migrant mobility at work. The spheres of production and social reproduction explain together the irreducible social power of, as well as the relative barriers to, the exercise of labour mobility as a relatively troublesome practice for capital and the state.

5

Migrant Organizing

Migrant women strike in 1970s German plants

On 13 August 1973, at the Pierburg Autoparts factory, which supplied carburetors to many West German automobile industries in Neuss (North Rhine-Westphalia), a group of Greek, Turkish, and Yugoslav women workers began a wildcat strike to demand compliance with what had been achieved in previous strikes since 1970: the abolition of the so-called Light Wage Category I. This category was created in 1955 to overcome the illegal 'women's wage category', declared unconstitutional by the German Federal Labour Court. Of the 3,600 workers employed at the Pierburg factory, 2,100 were migrants, with an overwhelming number of migrant women (almost half of all employees) hired under the Light Wage Category I (Bojadzijev, 2008: 163). The union and workers' council offered no support to the strikers, considering their action 'illegal'. After four days during which police brutally attacked female (and male) foreign workers, finally, the strikers received the solidarity of West German higher skilled coworkers. The support from the 'privileged' White and native working class was key to win the struggle. For migrants, 'the gratitude for the privilege to be accepted into the paradise of the industrial wage ... inevitably turns into an antagonistic awareness' (Groppo, 1974: 170).

The early 1970s West Germany was criss-crossed by a long wave of official and unofficial strikes revealing the 'multinational' nature of workers' behaviour, that had grown despite the guest workers' programme (see Chapter 2). About 2.3 million migrant workers (of which at least 700,000 were women), were legally employed in West Germany's economy, while another 300,000–500,000 were without documents (Kosack, 1976: 371; Groppo, 1974: 169). About three quarters of all migrant workers were employed in construction and in large exporting manufacturing firms (Roth, 1974). Most of them arrived through the *Gastarbeiter* programme with a two-year contract, living in 'company-supplied housing, with rent deducted from their paychecks', where managers enforced strict rules on worker behaviour (Miller, 2013: 230). The relationship between West Germans, employed more often than not in skilled occupations, and migrant workers, recruited as low-skilled, expressed varying degrees of conflict but also of solidarity across the 1960s and 1970s (Castles and Kosack, 1973). However, in the early 1970s, about 20 per cent of migrant workers were unionized (Miller, 2013).

Even if the political activities of migrant workers in West Germany has been concealed for a long time, it is now well documented that they organized demonstrations and strikes in particular during the 1960s and 1970s, protesting 'against the stratification of skills and wages along ethnic lines'.[1] Migrants organized strikes in the mines, automotive, and construction sectors with and without the help of unions, and sometimes also wildcat strikes.

The political construction of skilled and unskilled labour ended up exacerbating divisions, also because the qualifications of German workers meant a command over the work of others. This stratification in the labour market and inside labour processes based on nationality and gender was not new in West Germany. Analysing the immigration labour regime from 1870 to 1978, Rhoades (1978) notes a continuity of management of migrant workers. After 1870, a large local population moved from the rural to the urban and industrial areas, where migrants from Poland, Italy, the Netherlands, Belgium, France, and Switzerland fulfilled the needs of industrial, construction, mines, and agricultural jobs. This first wave of immigration also worried Max Weber (1924: 456–7) about the 'Polonization' that was occurring in the east of the country because Polish workers with their differently constructed stomachs would pull the German workers down 'to a more Eastern cultural level'. The racial construction of labour market segmentation identified by Max Weber at the end of the 19th century not only provided the basis for future scholars to build critical categories to understand the present society and economy, but also revealed rooted racializing assumptions and biases about the nature of labour segmentation that run until today.

The forced labour rotation of the different nationality groups managed by employers, as well as labour turnover put in place by workers, allowed employers to weaken the local labour movement and limit strikes. Different nationality groups were played one against the other, but German labour unions also concurred to undermine workers' power, arguably in order to 'protect' local workers, asking the government not to use migrants as strike breakers and to establish annual quotas (Rhoades, 1978: 559). The legacy of the Nazi period (where the deployment of foreign workers was influenced by the Nazi hierarchy of 'races', see Chapter 2) was evident until the post-Second World War period, when millions of migrants arrived in Germany as guest workers, that is, only on a temporary basis (Hachtmann, 2010). The migrant workers' rotation 'had the same effect on the position of immigrant in Germany, France and Switzerland as does colour prejudice in Britain' (Castles and Kosack, 1973: 463). Having the worst jobs and social conditions, migrants developed a high labour turnover (Castles and Kosack, 1973: 118). Such long-lasting migrant labour regimes influenced the mentality of workers in West Germany, producing a social and political segmentation of the labour market which became entrenched: skilled jobs remained the arena for German workers, while migrant workers (and women) tended to be employed in unskilled and repetitive jobs.

The history and the legacy of the racial and gender segregation of migrants in the case of Germany is emblematic of both how unions have contributed to the racialized differential inclusion of migrant workers, and how migrants have successfully organized collectively despite the relative welcome received from organized labour. But Pierburg Autoparts factory was not an isolated case in Europe, and local workers often attempted to defend their 'national' privilege to maintain tolerable forms of exploitation. Ten years before, in May 1965 in Britain, the first significant strike of migrant workers took place at Courtaulds Red Scar Mill in Preston. When management tried to force Asian workers to take care of more machines for a slight wage increase, migrants refused and went on strike, but White (local) workers and managers collaborated with management to resolve the dispute and the strike failed (Sivanandan, 1981: 121). Similar forms of complicity of local workers and management against migrant worker labour conflicts have also been registered in other European workplaces, and unions have often been associated with protectionist policies (Jefferys, 2007). However, we can also register many cases where local workers and unions try to break down the form of segregation in the name of a united international working class, sometimes under the pressure of racialized migrants and minorities workers from within the labour movement.[2]

Three types of workers' power

Considering the history of the racialized segregation of migrant workers within labour markets and in the labour movement itself, and the debate on forms of worker power reviewed in Chapter 1, we build here on recent literature to identify and further develop three types of worker power: structural (Wright, 2000), associational (Silver, 2003), and mobility bargaining power (Strauss and McGrath, 2017). Distinguishing these categories and their interrelations within and beyond the power resource approach (Wright, 2000) is a critical step, in our view, to illuminate the tensions of migrant labour turnover vis-à-vis not only employers, but also trade unions, and the relatively disruptive nature of the mobility of labour both at the point of production and when migrants face nationalistic and protectionist forms of worker organizations.

Originally Erik Olin Wright distinguished between two main types of workplace-based worker powers: associational and structural. Associational power is described by Wright (2000: 962) as the 'result from the formation of collective organizations of workers', including unions, parties, works councils, and also community organizations. In contrast, structural power consists of the 'power that results simply from the location of workers within the economic system'. Wright included under the latter: 'The power of workers as individuals that results directly from tight labor markets or from the strategic location of a particular group of workers within a key industrial sector' (Wright, 2000: 962).

Since Wright's early categorization there has been a rich debate on the 'power resource approach', reflecting on the relative strengths and limitation of such a framework to understand contemporary challenges of union organization and the antagonistic nature of class struggle. Whether the resource framework is helpful to highlight the importance of a relational approach, where the exercise of worker power is a direct and relatively constant reflection of historical antagonism between capital and labour (Gallas, 2018), or whether it is used to identify specific forms and realms in which power resources are used by workers and allies (Schmalz et al, 2018: 119), what we notice is that very few have applied this framework to the field of migrant labour and its collective organization.[3]

Exploring in more depth the origins of Wright's framework may help unpack some of its usefulness as well as its limitations to better understand migrant labour power or 'labour mobility power' more broadly (Smith, 2006). Indeed, Wright (2000) first elaborated the distinction between structural and associational power with the aim of defining 'positive class compromise'. By reinterpreting Marxian social theory this author was interested in the ways in which capitalist and workers' material interests would find mutual benefits across the exchange, production, and political spheres, rather seeking opportunities for coordination and predictable outcomes through positive class compromise (see also Streeck, 1992).

Precisely those factors that Wright highlights as important to maintain the class compromise demonstrate a contrario their capacity as sources of instability and as constituting uncompromising antagonism. First of all, in the sphere of exchange, Wright points out how 'having a labor force with a particular mix of skills in a labor market that provides predictable and adequate supplies of labor' is one of the key interests of capitalists, while under conditions of tight labour supply, worker associational power may contribute to wage restraint at the level of market exchange:

> Wage restraint is an especially complex collective action problem: individual capitalists need to be prevented from defecting from the wage-restraint agreement … (given the unavailability of workers in the labor market), and individual workers (and unions) need to be prevented from defecting from the agreement by trying to maximize wages under tight labor market conditions. (Wright, 2000: 980)

This is exactly what migrants may refuse to do. Restraining labour is what migrants ignore when, moved by their interests as migrants (for example, driven by the 'double frame of reference', Piore, 1979), they break away from this associational agreement and try to maximize wages for themselves. A second area where we notice the disruptive power of turnover emerging in specular ways from Wright's framework is in the sphere of production, and lies in the temporal dimension of 'class compromise', or what we have understood elsewhere as the power of temporariness. Wright (2000: 981) argues that the permanent or open-ended employment contract that some workers manage to obtain from their employers (also thanks to their strength and class struggles) provides a sense of job security and financial predictability that increases their loyalty and cooperation with their employer. However, it is precisely this loyalty and security over time that migrants are led to reject based on their experience of labour relations as racialized minorities. In this sense they escape the dimensions of capitalists' and workers' material interests in 'positive class compromise'.

Overall, considering the strengths and limitations of Wright's original conceptualization, we integrate it with Beverly Silver's (2003: 13) distinction between two subtypes of structural bargaining power: workplace and marketplace bargaining power. While the first one results from the strategic location of workers within an integrated labour process, the latter is based on the ability of workers to move to other sources for their reproduction (relative to whether they have scarce skills, if there are low levels of unemployment, or the availability of alternative sources of survival and nonwage forms of income). Marketplace bargaining power is reversed when firms try to undermine it through the mobilization of a large pool of labour, firm relocation, and technology fixes involving the mobility of capital (Silver, 2003). As part of the first strategy, migrants have often been represented as a mass of workers pushing on the factory's gates to obtain a job with worse working conditions than locals. In this way, migrants have been accused of being the culprit of unions' decline and working class fragmentation. Scott (2013: 1094) argued that 'migration regulates labour in a negative sense by dividing the working class along national, ethnic, racial, religious, linguistic and cultural lines'.

However, the working class was born as mixte and has been forcefully nationalized only during the 20th century (van der Linden, 2008; Moulier-Boutang, 1998). For instance, Satnam Virdee (2014) develops a unique reconstruction of the history of the English working class from the Victorian era until the 1990s, highlighting its characteristic nature as a multiethnic formation. Besides providing a clear example of working class mixte in a country with a long history of colonialism, Virdee's approach overcomes a victimizing or accusatory approach to migrants as either passive recipients of integration policies, or as the culprits of working-class segmentation and racial divisions. On the contrary, he shows how migrants and racialized minorities have often taken on themselves the burden of unveiling and fighting racism from within the labour movement. As has been noted, in some cases union strategies can also directly or indirectly support racism in the workers' movement itself (Silver, 2003; Burawoy, 1976).

On the one hand, the presence of migrants may well work as a disciplinary force for local workers who are put under competitive pressure by others who are considered easily disposable and replaceable. On the other hand, more often than not, the employment of migrants allows local workers to maintain better jobs and working conditions. Afonso and Devitt (2016) argue in this regard that, as long as there is a level of dual segmentation in the labour market, and migrants do not substitute for indigenous workers, migration can be beneficial in that indigenous workers can retain their advantageous conditions (see Chapter 1). In fact, migrants tend to be employed in workplaces that are already segmented in terms of tasks, contractual status, citizenship, and subcontracting, and where collectivism has taken the colour of White privilege. The making of this stratification is managed by local workers, unions, employers, and other labour market and social institutions (Iannuzzi and Sacchetto, 2020).

Since what has been called, without irony, 'the 30 glorious years' or the 'golden age of capitalism' (1947–73), the racial division of labour in all Western Europe produced 'ethnic jobs', and migrant workers responded to their disadvantaged conditions both through quitting and by developing collective action in the workplace (Sivanandan, 1981: 113). What we find is that the more local workers are integrated into institutional systems, the more the agency of migrant workers can find opposition because local workers defend their immediate interests (Piro and Sacchetto, 2021). In turn, migrants are often described as scarcely interested in unions because they perceive unions as useless in the short time of their stay, or have little trust in their ability to promote better working conditions. Migrants hired on temporary contracts indeed have lower incentives to organize through unions, preferring an individual bargaining with employers (for example, Thompson et al, 2013).[4] Differently from local workers, migrants often aim to maximize the effort and to obtain more money in the short run. This behaviour has been seen as 'predatory' because migrants contact unions only ex post when they have some problems with pay and working conditions (Refslund, 2016). Some scholars underline how migrants' behaviour is linked to the time they spend in the country (Bauder, 2006), but we should also consider that familiarization to the workplace and daily life in the country of destination is influenced by migrants' wider settlement, educational or mobility plans, their social networks and family life, and their perceptions of the countries' social, economic, and cultural environment – as well as that of origin.

Arguably, working in an unskilled and non-standard job puts all workers in a condition of lacking interest in long-term employment, or in a slow career inside the same workplace. This weak attachment can generate absenteeism, whether or not sickness related. As Hopkins (2014: 229) noted in sectors requiring low-skilled jobs, 'absence must also be considered as a form of industrial conflict'. In the context of the tightening of managerial control, absence is part of workplace bargaining (Edwards and Scullion, 1982). As Granovetter (1973) highlights, through the development of different (strong and weak) ties, workers are able to move across different labour markets; because they have a high knowledge of different workplaces and labour market mechanisms, they are able to speedily find other employment, and also compare wages, hourly standards, and quotas of production (see Chapter 3). If this mobility has historically had to deal with immigration controls and with national and international institutions (Chapter 2), the information that migrant workers share in relatively more fluid labour markets allows them to develop exit practices that constitute another form of worker power, similar to what other authors have recently theorized as mobility bargaining power.

As we have seen before, Strauss and McGrath (2017) develop the notion of 'mobility bargaining' by drawing from the previous literature and combining marketplace mobility and associational power. Reflecting on the constraints that migration controls exert on free labour relations, and migrant workers' precariousness in the context of Canada, Strauss and McGrath (2017) showed how migrants' mobility strategies are important precisely because employers look for a supply of labour which is largely prevented from exercising mobility bargaining power, such as through the effects of immigration controls that hinder migrant voice and autonomy in the workplace (see also Fudge, 2012; Bogg and Novitz, 2012; Novitz and Andrijasevic, 2020).[5]

Beverly Silver's (2003) research on the relationship between capital accumulation and collective struggles across the Global North and South had indeed already shown how under certain conditions, workers develop forms of community/social power and sources of leverage outside the workplace, despite a relatively weaker structural power at the point of production: critically, they do so in association with other non-traditional union actors, social movement campaigns for living wages, and civil society groups. Such associational forces, we argue (building from the insights of Strauss and McGrath's research on migrants' 'unfree labour relations'), may in turn influence migrants' ability to use their marketplace mobility power, drawing from alternative resources for reproducing life across their local and transnational communities (see Chapter 4).

Overall, we believe that these categories of worker power need to be seen as *a continuum* across different scholars and traditions/disciplines. The relationship between forms of worker behaviour, organized labour, and migrant exit power must be understood as part of this wider framework, conceptualizing different forms of worker power as contested and mutually related. In our view, one of the major limitations of trade union practices has been precisely to overlook the power of mobility bargaining by migrants and racialized others, and in understanding the importance that freedom of movement in the labour market and across borders has for precarious migrants. While migrants are often unfairly accused of opportunistic behaviours, a form of opportunism may be detected in some unions' approach towards migrants and community groups as they try to 'tap in' to non-unionized groups to replenish their declining membership (see Chapter 1 and to be discussed later).

Establishing these conceptual connections is necessary before looking at the historically specific forms of politics and tensions that shape industrial relations research on migrant labour, and the opportunities for migrants' collective action. As we do so, we need to unpack the deep-rooted preconceptions underpinning turnover and racialized labour since the origins of Fordism, through an examination of the rationale for racial management practices, as well as of how racism within the labour movement has reflected a form of suspicion towards migration, turnover and mobility more broadly.

In terms of the emphasis on the combination of marketplace with associational power, Strauss and McGrath (2017) have illuminated the importance of labour mobility power for migrants in relatively unfree labour relations (see also Reid-Musson, 2014). They critically highlighted the fact that migration controls curtail both labour mobility and workplace-based associational power (see Table 1.1) through the 'institutionalization of forms of unfree labour relations endogenous to precarious migrant status' (Strauss and McGrath (2017: 205). Drawing from their work, we argue that associational/community forces inside or outside the workplace may influence migrants' ability to use their marketplace mobility power through migration and to collectively improve their conditions. We will further develop this contribution in our concluding chapter (Table 6.1).

Race management: temporariness against sedentarism

The turnover of migrant labour expressed in the form of migrant transiency and temporary status in the workplace is one of the reasons for trade unions' historical reluctance to believe and invest in the inclusion and organization of migrant workers (Castles and Kosack, 1973; Piore, 1979; Fitzgerald and Hardy, 2010). The argument that migrants are unorganizable or 'not worth the effort' precisely because of their transient passage in the workplace is easy to encounter both in the early scholarship and still in contemporary accounts on unions and migrant workers. Looking at labour mobility in the first decades of the 20th century, the labour historian Jacoby (1983) provides an essential perspective on how organized labour has often expressed a degree of suspicion, if not outward antipathy, towards workers who were highly mobile. In relatively moralized terms, the literature of that time has variously judged the habit of turnover by certain groups of workers. As we will see, this viewpoint has been largely contested by the Industrial Workers of the World (IWW), which tried to organize the highly mobile workers, mostly European migrants and African Americans, in the first decades of the 20th century.

What we see as an association of high turnover with less skilled, disaffected workers by trade unions, was indeed the result of shifts in working practices, employment dynamics, and unions strategies across time. In the first period of industrial capitalism we see a supportive role of trade unions toward workers on the move through institutions such as the *Tour de France* and the *Wanderpflicht*.[6] Also in the US, initially, it was the skilled workers who were considered more mobile, and their capacity to hop from one employer to another was part of 'learning a trade' and was therefore considered positively, not only by the workers and the employers, but also by the trade unions. The craft unions in particular facilitated the skilled worker's propensity to move. Unions were not interested in mobility as such, but in the control of the labour market and to spread relevant information (Hobsbawm, 1951). However, by the end of the 19th century, the system was on the decline in Europe, and at the beginning of the 20th century in the US (Ulman, 1965). Since the early postwar period suspicion towards mobility started to infiltrate workers' organization and their representatives. From this account we start noticing the complexity of trade unions' stance towards turnover in general and migrant workers' temporariness and mobility in particular: while on the one hand the act of quitting in the face of lack of work improvements was considered a valid practice, migrants were also assumed to be less likely to participate in strikes because of the time commitment and presence required by industrial action. Such concern was expressed despite 'spectacular strikes' and quitting levels that might have corresponded, indicating the complementary rather than the contrary nature of turnover and collective action (see Chapter 1 and conclusions).

In order to understand how trade unions contributed to the stigmatization of migrant labour in the workplace, and its racialization, we need to go back (Chapters 1 and 4) to the first decades of the 20th century in the US, where the fluid labour market appeared more integrated as compared to the period that saw immigration restrictions introduced after the First World War. Indeed, despite or precisely because of this situation of general fluidity and high worker turnover, significant forms of segmentation and divisions in the workforce emerged, which highlight the bottom-up acts both of workers and trade unions in influencing forms of racialization of temporary and segregated groups. While the rate of turnover rose significantly between 1910 and 1920, these were also the years when employers attempted specific substitution as well as union repression strategies in order to lower wages in key sectors of the industrializing economy:

During the 1910s and 1920s a number of large employers became dissatisfied with productivity problems associated with high turnover and simultaneously sought to stave off union organization of their workplaces. In consequence, they began to improve conditions for workers in their firms, developed welfare capitalism and rewarded workers with firm-specific and general human capital through the formation of internal labour markets. (Fishback, 1997: 10)

While this author confirms some of the arguments made in Chapter 1 that welfare capitalism and the birth of human relations can be interpreted as a response by employers to high levels of labour turnover, we also need to see that a new racial politics by employers and racialized dynamics by and within trade unions emerged to 'curb' the problem of high turnover. In particular, Fishback's (1997) study of the relationship between turnover, exit, and voice dynamics in a coal mine of the time in West Virginia highlighted how processes of racial segregation through separate housing for certain migrant groups, and the phenomenon of monopsony (the advantage derived by being the only 'buyer of labour'), were explicitly used by employers to limit workers' exit. However, and critical for our discussion here, it appears that these management strategies to hamper the high mobility of coal miners were also influenced by the behaviour of White local workers towards racialized immigrants and Afro-Americans. On the one hand, employers took 'race as proxy for skills' and only after experimentation allowed Black workers to progress in certain sectors. On the other, lower income and opportunities for Black workers were also the outcome of the action of coworkers and their unions, who pressurized employers to hire Black workers for the lower skilled positions but applied exclusionary or separatist practices towards Black workers:

> Most white workers at the time refused to take directions from blacks, which meant that there were almost no black managers except in all-black work forces ... Meanwhile, many white workers pressed employers to hire blacks. The pressure was most visibly manifested in the actions of labour unions. The vast majority of union excluded blacks. Some like the railroad porters established separate organizations. (Fishback, 1997: 27–8)

Also in the German Ruhr mining industry at the beginning of the 20th century, unions discredited Poles and blamed them for causing accidents as they didn't speak German and had high turnover rates (Kulczycki, 1989). While evidence shows that migrants did not quit as often as other local miners did, the lack of solidarity pushed migrants to self-organize and create a separate Polish trade union in 1902. As John J. Kulczycki (1989: 55) bitterly notes: 'Differences of culture and origin among the Ruhr's coal miners did not divide them as much as their response to these differences'.

Indeed, such racist dynamics within the labour movement must be understood in relation to management strategies of division and segmentation of the workforce. Roediger and Esch (2012) make a critical contribution in this regard, looking at management's use of race to manage different groups of workers in the first decades of the 20th century US as well as worker counter-practices. In the nascent Taylorist factory, different ethnicities of workers were positioned in different jobs and industries according to their allegedly intrinsic or natural traits, but also in this way divided and disciplined. And yet, it was the shift to stricter immigration policy with the introduction of the Johnson–Reed Act in 1924 that exposed the limitation of race management in terms of failing to tame the rebellions of White immigrants who were critically involved in the great wave of strikes of 1917–22.[7] Among them there were not only White militants from craft unions but also new migrant workers and Black workers (Montgomery, 1987). Roediger and Esch (2012) therefore show the role of immigration policy in restricting immigration precisely once immigrant workers started joining the ranks of activists, but also the limitation of the racial strategies of workers' divisions operated by employers at the workplace level. Their analysis of the changes post-First World War are also important because they show how the growing incorporation of African Americans into the industrial workforce was in turn a response to those immigration restrictions. It was also the increasing suspicion towards White immigrants, whereby Eastern and Southern European migrants were considered particularly dangerous and responsible for 'Bolshevik sabotage', which fear by the management increased after the war, with a strong repression of the IWW (Cartosio, 2007). The forms of concentration of race management and segregation of African Americans in the dirtiest and most labour intensive jobs, such as in the foundry, was allegedly also driven by their assumed higher 'loyalty' as compared to the European immigrants, who were perceived as rebellious and recalcitrant.[8] As Roediger and Esch (2012) highlight, the question of turnover appears therefore strictly linked with the emergence of migration controls, the incapacity of industrialists to take a clear stance on immigration and quota policies, and the processes of racial segregation within the workforce accentuated by perceptions of lack of loyalty and quitting practices by workers.

Within the US context the debate on the attempts to unionize workers in the southern bituminous coal field at the end of the 20th century is a crucial episode in the history of trade unions organizing across racial lines and has produced strong controversy. Gutman (1968)'s study of the life and career of the black miner Richard L. Davis, highlights the industrial conflict, unions' organization struggles, as well as strikebreaking, racial and class violence happening in the mines at the time. Davis' biography offers examples of racism but also of first steps towards inter-racial cooperation and unionization among African Americans and White mine workers. Criticizing Gutman, Hill (1996) accuses him to create a myth of the United Mine Workers as and advanced model of interracial solidarity. Differently, Hill stresses how the racist attitudes of the White leaders and members of the union reproduced the primacy of race, and how unions, as racialized formations, tend to reinforce inequalities in the working class.[9]

Drawing from archives on litigation cases over workers' allegedly racist behaviours, Hill (1996) highlighted the forms of opportunism by apparently inclusive unions such as the CIO recruiting Black workers into their ranks in sectors where Afro Americans were highly present: while since the late 1930s the CIO was known to be more inclusive of Black workers than the craft unions under the AFL, Hill argues that in reality the CIO tolerated ongoing exclusionary practices on the shopfloor. More critically for us, Hill (1996: 201) still acknowledges the genuine inter-racial solidarity and self-organization of Blacks in sectors where they were highly concentrated, such as in the case of the United Packinghouse Workers of America.

The stark contrast between craft and industrial unionism in the history of the North American labour movement, and its relationship with interracialism, is evident in the history of the IWW, the combative and revolutionary union that emerged in the US. Since its formation in 1905, the IWW distanced itself ideologically from the business-style unionism of the AFL, refusing contracts with employers and favouring direct action by the rank and files and a focus on job control.[10] While the latter two elements, understood as practical syndicalism, were indeed shared by the more business oriented AFL, Kimeldorf (1999: 2) emphasizes that the skills and racial composition of the workforce represented by the IWW and their inclusive approach towards 'the unskilled, recent immigrants, women, and workers of color', as opposed to the mostly 'native-born, skilled, white craftsmen' affiliated with the AFL, were underlying factors of their different logics of collective action.

The inclusive methods of rotation of Black and White leaders among its ranks,[11] the involvement of activists from Black movements, as well as the ability to control hiring and defend wages and conditions (without adopting the restrictive practices of the AFL's closed shop model), allowed the Local 8 of the IWW Marine Transport Workers Industrial Union in Philadelphia to build a successful series of strikes and to win the same wages for all workers on the docks:

By bringing the entire dockside labour force under the same organizational umbrella, Local 8 was able to establish a viable portwide presence for contesting the shipowners' ability to whipsaw Blacks against whites, Poles against Italians, even one gang against another. Interracial industrial unionism thus emerged as a sound, if unstable, strategy for levelling the field of combat. (Kimeldorf, 1999: 46)

Critically for our discussion, one of the tactics used by Local 8 workers on the docks was to respond to employers' anti-union attacks with situational power sources, that is, quitting work in response to any firing of union members, as in during the strike of 1913, when after five workers were sacked for holding on to their union badges, 300 workers walked out and managed to bring to a halt the whole operation of the International Mercantile Marine Company, leading the largest employers to cave in soon after (Kimeldorf, 1999: 38). Further, racial conflicts and employers' attacks on the efforts of the IWW during its 'golden decade' of battles in the ports of Philadelphia after 1913 fatally contributed to the demise of the IWW as a mass industrial union in the US, and partly explain why the great majority of workers eventually left the IWW for the more compromising AFL.[12] If also within the IWW, interethnic problems arise from time to time (Dreyfus, 1997), the IWW were quite successful in organizing African Americans. Rather, as Dana Frank (1998) underlined, the real Achilles heel of the IWW should be identified as the question of gender and what Francis Shor (1992) calls 'virile syndicalism'.

Labour historians have made important observations as to how craft and occupational identity as gendered and racialized constructions, alongside the wider 'social construction of skills' (Phillips and Taylor, 1980), are crucial to the formation of working class communities, and how a 'moral topography' attached to the occupational map arises, with exclusionary consequences not only for women, but also for migrant workers (Withers, 1991).

Alongside the tendency to blame migrants (especially the low-skilled ones) as being 'guilty' of higher turnover rates, or for choosing quitting rather than striking, unions' suspicion towards mobility can be seen a contrario through the moralization of the working-class attachment to their communities. Here the notion of sedentarism is presented as a positive trait of traditional working-class behaviour. The industrial relations literature, for instance, illustrates (and sometimes perhaps romanticizes) the strong historical connections between the emergence of territorially settled worker communities and the origin of early unionism, based on common occupational identities: in the British context, for instance, Wills and Simms (2004) highlight how trade unionism in its original historic form manifested both strong roots in the local community and a distinct industrial identity. They argue that in the wake of industrialization, working class communities developed their sense of collectivity through working and living together in proximity, and on the basis of a relatively homogenous occupational identity (for example, in the cases of 'mining villages, ports, textile towns, engineering centres and urban neighbourhoods' where workers in the late 1800s started to fund mutual societies, working men's clubs, and trade unions; see also Beynon and Austrin, 1994).

Masculine and sedentarist values are apparent, for instance, in how 'pride in the tradition of hardship' (a typical code of masculinity) is combined with a male sense of place and camaraderie in particular labour politics (McDowell, 1999: 102). Similarly, social historians showed how male associations, including craft guilds, chambers of commerce, and professional bodies, existed to promote the pursuit of business but also to foster a certain version of male conviviality (Tosh, 2005). The gendered nature of labour politics is not exclusive to the history of the UK, and different examples of masculinist politics can be found in countries across the Anglo-Saxon world (McDowell and Massey, 1984; Milkman, 1985; Shor, 1992) and beyond. Defined as a 'vulnerable group' (Kawar, 2004), migrant women, especially from the Global South, have been labelled as workers with reduced defence capabilities, representing them as weak victims in need of protection. And yet, as our vignette highlights, in the experiences of migrant women working in relatively low-skilled jobs, conditions of vulnerability coexist with radical forms of resistance (Christopoulou and Lazaridis, 2012). Moreover, the stigmatization of temporariness tends to be stronger for women migrant workers as they are supposed to stay in the labour market for as long as their families need financial support.

The historical literature on gender relations in the trade union movement has developed if only properly from the 1980s, providing rich evidence and accounts of how women have been marginalized within trade unions and more broadly illustrating the gendered nature of the organized labour movement since its original constitution (Boston, 1987; see also Pearson et al, 2010). In contrast, the place of migrant (and racialized) labour within the labour movement and in relation to the trade union approach to migration and mobility historically (including their ambivalent role in fighting or reproducing sexual and racial stereotypes within the workforce) has received only partial attention (Ignatiev, 1995; Roediger, 1991; Sivanandan, 1990).

In essence, what the historical cases show is that turnover is racialized not only in terms of the ways in which it is associated with low-skilled workers perceived as disloyal, but also as the subject of both management and organized labour responses. These actors exercise more or less explicit forms of racism, racialization, and divisions. We may detect an almost cyclical pattern in the process of management first responding to high turnover levels through labour racial segregation, then monopsony, and finally attacks on unionization: initially immigration and 'unfettered markets' are promoted (for example, through relaxed migration policies) to facilitate the arrival of new immigrants at lower wages, but this is then followed by a restrictive drive. Specifically, when migrant labour turnover becomes too high and affects productivity, stricter forms of segregation are imposed, and often with the complacency of the unions and workers' practices on the shop floor. As we saw earlier, these processes resemble recent dynamics of borders opening and closing for different categories of 'low' and 'high skilled' migrants according to patterns of recruitment and retention (see Alberti and Cutter, 2022), or resemble various 'transitional measures' applied to migrant workers from poorer member states, such as in the case of Eastern European migrants joining the labour market and acquiring free movement rights at different speeds. The further insights of Fishback (1997) are about the active role of trade unions and local workers in shaping these dynamics, rather than a sole focus on the interests of employers and the state in reproducing or curbing labour turnover. The process of racial segregation therefore appears central to explaining the management of turnover (Chapter 1) and the repression of solidarity.

Unions' immobility and migrant mobility: an ongoing dilemma

In the 1990s, one of the first publications on trade unions and migrant labour in seven north-western European countries had proposed a stylized account of the three dilemmas that trade unions in industrial economies confront when migrant labour appears: reject their very recruitment or cooperate with employers hiring migrants; accept and actively integrate them into the local unions or exclude them; organize them on the basis of their specific needs or on an equal basis with the local workers – if they opted for inclusion (Penninx and Roosblad, 2000). Each of these dilemmas contained anticipated challenges, most of them regarding the risks of broadening or restricting the bargaining power of local workers vis-à-vis the expansion of the union constituency though accepting migration. These dilemmas matter to the extent that they all reflect historical tensions intrinsic to nationally based labour organizations (Meardi, 2012a; Giles, 2000) who have privileged the interests of 'members' (often strictly defined and equated with nationals/citizen workers), or attempted to influence state policy to regulate immigration and ensure equal terms and conditions for migrants (Penninx and Roosblad, 2000). Acknowledging the nationally specific approaches to migrant workers highlighted in comparative industrial relations research (Marino et al, 2017a), a general trend emerges when unions seem to continue to struggle to identify their sources of leverage to win grievances: theoretically at least, they seem to know that if more workers are unionized independently of their background or passport, less competition on wages and conditions would follow. But in practice, they seem to still be concerned about representing their 'core members' interests, assumed to be different from those of foreign or otherwise marginalized workers who are, in the main, likely to remain outside mainstream union organizing efforts (for a critical review, see Doellgast et al, 2018), and rather adopt a relatively open or closed approach to migration according to circumstances (to be discussed later).

The study by Penninx and Roosblad (2000) was certainly important as it provided contextualized knowledge of union dilemmas in comparative perspective, by looking at the different factors that produced different results across the countries observed: from the position and power that unions enjoyed in each national context; to the socio-economic environment where they operated; to the public discourse on immigration (and civil society related attitude) in a particular period and country; to the very characteristics of the migrant population to be 'integrated'. Taking into account all these different factors, the main result of the Penninx and Roosblad (2000: 183) study was that between 1960 and 1993 the positions across European countries differed greatly according to the national system of industrial relations, highlighting an ambivalent attitude towards migrants in a continuous tension between exclusion and inclusion, equal and special treatment (Krings, 2009; Pugliese, 2000; Alberti et al, 2013; Marino et al, 2017a). However, it remains unclear how exactly unions were able to 'equally include' migrant workers into their ranks and protect workers from a 'race to the bottom'. In fact, while in some European countries trade unions have actively promoted the integration of migrants both in the workplace and in society as a way of tackling inequalities (for example, Adler et al, 2014), in others they have played a clear role in the segmentation of the labour market (Castles and Kosack, 1973; Erne and Imboden, 2015).

The fact that unions have been uninterested in migrants, or even actively drawing boundaries between the domestic and foreign workforces, is clearly discernible in both Western and Eastern European countries today. Reviewing the position and activities of trade unions towards migrant workers in the Czech Republic, for instance, Marek Čaněk (2017) has pointed out how, since the 1990s Czech unions have refrained from developing inclusive policies towards non-EU migrants. These include the more culturally and 'racially compatible' Ukrainians because of their understanding of labour migration as cheap labour exerting downward pressure on the standards of indigenous workers. Considering the specific labour market locations of migrants in low unionized and most segmented sections, often characterized by agency employment, Čaněk (2017: 323) points out how: 'The migrant workers' precarious legal status has mostly been seen as a necessary protective boundary maintaining the privilege of the domestic workers rather than a barrier to equal wage and labour standards between the domestic and migrant workers in the labour market'. Using Silver's (2003) framework on the distinctive actions of capital, state, and workers' own boundary-drawing respectively via labour market segmentation, citizenship, and exclusionary class identities, Čaněk (2017) illustrates how Czech unions have drawn from existing divisions between domestic and migrant workers to increase their bargaining power and preserve their own advantage as a section of the working class. In this context, the behaviours of migrants may be seen as a necessary response to the indifference or exclusion received by trade unions. As a consequence: 'Migrant workers have mostly pursued individualistic strategies including exit strategies. An important role has been played, first, by the intermediaries that have provided support and/or exploited the workers, and second, by non-governmental organizations that have been providing legal and social services' (Čaněk, 2017: 322–3).

The question of equal or differential treatment, or what we called elsewhere the universalistic or particularistic approaches (Alberti et al, 2013) to migrant incorporation into trade unions actually strikes at the core of what we see as a binary view of inclusion and exclusion of migrants in established labour organizations. It can be that at times precisely inclusion on the grounds of equality may result in discriminating against migrants by overlooking their specific needs as racialized workers affected by immigration controls, for example, for those facing particular forms of precarity related to their work permit and migration status (for example, Alberti and Danaj, 2017; Iannuzzi and Sacchetto, 2020).

Despite some emerging critiques of ethnocentrism persisting in their structures and cultures (McGovern, 2007; Lee and Tapia, 2021), unions in the EU have been largely concentrated on national workers' interests (Krings, 2009). It is worth noticing in this regard the contradictory outcome that the introduction of temporary recruitment programmes was seen as proof of the stronger unions' ability to negotiate with the state over the first dilemma, that is: migrants were welcome, yes, where they were needed, but only temporarily. The complacency or even complicity of unions in supporting and co-producing guest worker schemes is indeed an element that complexifies our understanding of the logistics of migrant labour (see chapter 2) as directly co-constituted by the action of different actors, including social partners like trade unions, and should be considered through the lens of differential (and temporally conditioned) inclusion rather than a true opening of trade unions to migrants.[13]

In turn, the position of trade unions is strongly influenced by the wider regulatory and institutional environment at the national level, but their relationship is not always a straightforward one. Comparing Danish and British unions, Wrench (2004) highlighted how the more inclusive stance of unions towards migrants can be understood as a consequence of the decline of their influence in the national framework: without including marginalized groups it was difficult for unions to relaunch themselves and revitalize. Marino (2012) has understood these trends in original ways, in terms of an 'institutional embeddedness paradox', whereby, in contrast to the original interpretation of the three dilemmas, an inverse relationship between union institutional embeddedness and their willingness and capacity to organize migrants emerges. Comparatively studying Dutch and Italian unions, Marino (2012) found that the Italian unions were weaker in terms of their role in jointly regulating industrial relations with the state and employers as compared to the Dutch corporatist tradition, and yet still they were rather more effective at reaching out to migrant workers and developing a 'special approach' through servicing and support in relation to migrants' specific grievances (for example, work permits and regularization). Roosblad (2013) confirms this tendency as she observes the inverse trajectory of Dutch unions, who, precisely as they witness their institutional decline, also become keener to incorporate new groups, including undocumented migrants. The cases of Italy and Spain are particularly interesting, whereby an already relatively unstable system of industrial relations has allowed unions to maintain a regulatory role in terms of providing support services and regularization advice to migrants (Marino, 2012).

While these critical approaches are relevant in that they introduce a renewed dynamism in rigid, path-dependency approaches in comparative industrial relations research on migration (chapter 1), they also provide an opportunity to reflect on unions' 'opportunistic' approaches to migrant recruitment as a strategy to reinvigorate their own organizations (Turner, 2011). As highlighted by Tapia's (2013) critical study of labour community coalitions in the field of migrant rights in the UK, processes of organizational change and culture changes may well occur 'as a strategy to revitalize trade unions over bargaining and negotiating', thus linking migrant organizing with questions of union institutional survival. More broadly, as Alberti and Però (2018: 698) underline, large parts of research on migrant organizing and union renewal maintain an institutional focus, privileging the analysis of trade union strategy; or move to the questions of the 'organizational cultures' and labour community organizations and their institutional rationale for coalitions. Shifting the gaze to migrants' perspectives in relation to these observations, the alleged 'opportunism of migrant workers' (see previous discussion) may be therefore considered as specular to the opportunism of unions amidst their crisis of 'institutional embeddedness', whereas migrants' integration may become just another strategy of union survival.

The question of migration has posed challenges to trade unions not only from the point of view of their institutional structures and their relative openness to migrants and migration, but also because unions seem to have developed inadequate responses to the very questions of labour mobility and free movement of labour. In light of what some have called the Europeanization of employment relations, and the 'unprecedented degree of inequality' triggered by the European enlargement and the extension of the framework of free movement to workers in member states with significantly lower wages, comparatist industrial relations scholars were pushed to revise their union dilemmas framework (Meardi, 2012b: 104). Evaluating the inclusion vs exclusion dilemma in the new context, Marino et al (2017a) are positive that, despite growing racism and xenophobia, unions have generally strengthened their internationalist and inclusive stance towards migrants (see Marino, 2012; Adler et al, 2014, for instance), but they also acknowledge how growing populism and hostility to immigration since the 2000s across the West has worked against this.[14]

The question of free movement, and especially in the context of the EU enlargement which included the incorporation of countries with much lower wages, has indeed represented key challenges for European trade unions (Hyman, 2005). A strand of industrial relations literature has in fact voiced the concerns of unions around free movement of labour, especially where it was argued to be the cause of social dumping on locals' wages and labour standards (Krings, 2009; Cremers, 2016). In other words, in the new EU's free movement framework context, the point was no longer to oppose migration, but to what extent and how to influence its regulation.[15] Marino et al (2017b: 370) conclude noticing that it has been in particular in those countries with higher levels of regulation that the discussion on social dumping has been more prominent, whereby by 'social dumping' is meant the employer attempts 'of undermining or evading existing social regulations with the aim of gaining a short-term competitive advantage over their competitors' (Bernaciak, 2015: 11).

These discussions find their roots in the early examination of trade unions' relationship with migrant labour in the 1970s (for example, Castles and Kosack, 1973, see also Chapter 1), where the idea of unfair competition is very much associated with migrants as a reserve army of labour diminishing union bargaining leverage. What is often overlooked in these debates about the impact of free movement of labour is that there are indeed important differences between different types of mobility within the EU common market, starting from the difference between free movement of workers and services (Meardi, 2012a). It is too often ignored in the literature on intra-EU migration and industrial relations that posted workers may actually exert a greater pressure on wages precisely on the basis of not being treated as free moving workers under EU law, but as services deprived of the equal treatment and protections guaranteed under the EU citizenship regulations (Novitz and Andrijasevic, 2020). Overlooking such differences means banalizing the question of mobility of labour and the ways in which it is differently protected under the law, and its tension with economic freedoms as a central ambivalence of the EU project.

According to Marino et al (2017a), the development of the union debate on social dumping caused by intra-EU migration must be understood in the framework of EU institutions prioritizing economic freedoms over social protections. One of the reasons why these debates might have been less prominent in Mediterranean countries as compared to northern and western ones is attributed to the fact that in these countries migrants were already more starkly segregated into low paid and informal sectors of the economy, where, according to dual labour market theories, there is less competition between different segments of the workforce. Therefore, unions appear more tolerant of migration precisely where the interests of the indigenous membership may not be as directly impacted because the high levels of segmentation 'shield' them from downward pressure on wages (see Erne and Imboden, 2015; Afonso and Devitt, 2016). We have already developed our critique to labour market segmentation theories and institutionalist readings of international migration in Chapter 1, but certainly an important lesson from the 'institutionalists' is that all the variables or elements that shape union stances on migration are influenced by the relative strength of industrial relations/social regulation existing in different contexts, and the extent to which unions rely on a relatively established compromise of power sharing with state and employers. This makes the exclusion of migrant labour more or less strategic to maintain or change the status quo in terms of the existing structures of social dialogue. The merit of the analysis by Marino et al (2017b: 359) is that it acknowledged how, while social dumping discourses are not intrinsically anti-immigrant, they did have the effect of increasing the growing ambivalence of labour organizations towards migrant workers in the form of EU free movement (Neergaard and Woolfson, 2017, on Sweden), with negative consequences in terms of spreading anti-immigrant feelings within the union rank and files.[16] And yet, as powerfully argued by Milkman (2020) in the context of the US, one of the key limitations of the industrial relations literature, and of the unions' position, has been not to see the difference between migrant labour being the outcome rather than the cause of degrading labour conditions in the national labour market.

All of these accounts in industrial relations, while critically identifying the institutional conflicts and dynamics in the field of migrant labour today, reproduce in our view a functionalistic idea of migration as responding to national dynamics, rather than a full actor shaping and contributing to their development. While constituting a pathbreaking work in the sociology of work and migration – introducing for the first time a theorization of the stance that trade unions take vis-à-vis migrant labour – Penninx and Roosblad's research and their revised version (Marino et al, 2017a) remained limited to comparisons across Western economies and to a focus on the point of view of trade unions themselves, their policy, and structures. This limitation continues to characterize the literature on migrant workers in industrial relations more broadly, whereby empirical research had tended to focus on a national level or comparative industrial relations (for example, Connolly et al, 2014; Martínez Lucio and Perrett 2009; Fitzgerald and Hardy, 2010), even when highlighting aspects of transnational organizing (Lillie and

Sippola, 2011; Greer et al, 2013), and only marginally taking into account the experience of migrant workers themselves as they organize through unions (Adler et al, 2014; Holgate, 2005). Only recently there seems to be more recognition from within industrial relations research that the points of view of migrant workers need to be foregrounded, and issues of migrant agency and their collective mobilization potential brought to the centre of the analysis (Berntsen, 2016; Refslund, 2016). However, what is still lacking from these accounts is yet again the subjective experience, voice, and leverage of migrant workers themselves, whether through forms of self-organization and grass-roots mobilization (Alberti and Però, 2018), networking outside unions (Roca and Martín Díaz, 2017), or through forms of an invisible politics of escape and mobility (Papadopoulos et al, 2008; Sacchetto and Vianello, 2015). There is at least a growing recognition in industrial relations debates that if unions continue to act as 'agents of labour market regulations' rather than act as social and political actors (Marino et al, 2017b: 338), they will overlook the increasingly important questions of social citizenship (see Chapter 1) and the wider precariousness of migrants that influences their ability to improve their material conditions. Recentering turnover as a form of worker (and migrant) agency aims to change precisely this perspective. Unpacking the tensions between individual and collective forms of action is also important to uncover the meaning of migrants' transnational practices of exit and contestation vis-à-vis the continuing nationalism of trade unions or their ambivalence towards migrants – as well as the racialized effects of state regulation (see Grappi, 2021).

Union–NGO alliances and separate organizing

In the conclusions of the symposium organized by the International Labour Organization (ILO) on Asia Pacific trade unions in 1999, participants recognized that in this area, 'migrant workers have traditionally been ignored or opposed by unions' (Raghwan and Sebastian, 2000: 6). In fact, trade unions in Asian countries have a history of hostility against migrants which is long lasting: until recently they have been explicitly against immigration and at times have officially demanded the deportation of migrants. The Japanese union federation, Rengō, still campaigns against the entry of migrant workers. Similarly, the Taiwan Labour Front demanded the 'human deportation' of migrant workers in 1998, while the Chinese Federation of Labour in the 2010s was still opposed to labour migration in general. In Kuwait, many of the members of the Kuwait Trade Union Federation (KTUF) 'are employers of domestic workers themselves, resulting in conflicts of interest that may partially explain their lack of work on this issue' (Varia, 2011: 285). On their part, Thai and Malayan unions have been historically in favour of the expulsion of migrants (Ford, 2019). Nevertheless, in the last 20 years in Asia a growing sensitivity towards migration has also developed, permitting some unions and NGOs to promote, at least in some countries, the protection of migrant workers' rights. In this context, the comparative research of seven Asian countries and unions' engagement with migrants conducted by Michele Forde has critically shown how a recent shift in tactics by local unions in their pro-migrants campaign has been facilitated by financial and political support by the international labour movement: namely a series of programmes by the Global Union Federation (GUF) in the Asian region on temporary migration. In contrast to northern European experiences, where unions might have failed to organize migrant workers taking into consideration the overlapping or intersectional forms of oppression, 'in Asia the opposite is true: there, foreign workers have been seen first and foremost *as migrants* – whose presence disrupt the local labour market and harms the local labour force – rather than as part of a global collectivity of workers' (Ford, 2019: 2). Ford's corollary argument is that this factor (alongside the overall limited power of unions in the Asian context) has led to a situation where it is rather non-governmental organizations (NGOs) (and faith groups) that have been more successful in advocating and supporting the cause of migrant workers (Piper and Yamanaka, 2008). Stronger collaboration between unions and NGOs as well as regional advocacy networks have emerged in the past couple of decades in some Asian countries (for example, Ford and Piper, 2007; Piper and Uhlin, 2002), which provide a way forward to find more representation of migrants at the international level of labour standards and protections.

Overall, Ford's (2019) comparative study shows how local trade unions combine different strategies but are also more likely to move to a less exclusionary approach in those countries where GUFs have been most active. This happened despite draconian approaches by East Asian countries which tend to implement illiberal regimes in the field of migration policy.[17] Despite ongoing limitations in the forms and outcomes of migrant organizing in the Asia-Pacific region, Ford (2019: 150) remains positive that the evidence demonstrates the 'potential advantages for mainstream unions of engaging with temporary labour migrants in situations where they are poorly integrated into the industrial relations system or where militancy is low'. In particular, the Hong Kong case with the domestic workers organizing efforts and their successes in making the legislative frameworks more migrant-friendly 'demonstrates that the temporary labour migrants employed in informal sector occupations can be unionised and that doing so through separate but affiliated structures can strengthen the political voice of the labour movement, even if mainstream unions remain weak.' (Ford, 2019: 150).

This evidence shows the importance of transnational collaboration (including with the country of origin) to move away from the nationalistic/

universalistic approach that has characterized union response to (temporary) migration in the Global North and South. It also shows, in comparison to the longer entrenched history of union policies for the integration of migrants in Western countries, how a more recent history of union engagement with immigration may sometimes imply a more prominent role for non-union organizations, such as civil society and migrant advocacy groups, and opens up new avenues for migrant organizing.

While interest in temporary labour migration by the international labour movement can be found in Europe in relation to intra-EU migration and posting (Arnholtz and Lillie, 2020), the Asia–Pacific region remains a unique case due to the intense interregional mobility in a wider range of industries and sectors.[18] Ford's study is indeed relevant to our discussion on migrant organizing and labour turnover, because it focuses on the specific challenges of temporary migration for trade unions, going to the core of the tension between those who believe that 'temporary migration can never be good and therefore should be restricted' and those who recognize it as a strategy that migrants use anyway to improve their lives and that of their children (Ford, 2019: 2). This tension has been explored specifically in the debate on US trade unions and migration (especially over guest workers), where representatives of the second stance have emphasized the importance of guaranteeing the labour and human rights of temporary migrants, rather than focusing on restricting temporary migration per se (Ness, 2011). While recognizing the important role of NGOs at mobilizing migrants *as workers* in forms of collective action (usually associated to classic industrial action such as strikes), their full incorporation in the trade union movement and ability to 'access the destination country's industrial relations institutions' are believed to be necessary steps if the aim is to equip migrants with full labour citizenship and 'if they are to benefit of the protections afforded to them by virtue of their status as workers' (Ford, 2019: 3). This argument however maintains a level of methodological nationalism and differs from the one developed by Gordon (2006) in the context of the US, where temporary migrants would also rather immediately access full labour citizenship under a transnational framework and cross-border agreements between the country of origin and destination (see Conclusion).

When, however, Asian unions have managed to recruit temporary workers, this has happened under a strategy of separate organizing 'by which migrant workers focused associations are formed, and where possible, registered as migrant-only unions – with or without the support of a mainstream union' (Ford, 2019: 9), partly confirming trade unions' overall scepticism at successfully organizing immigrant workers. In countries like Japan and Taiwan, for instance, unions have had limited results in their efforts at involving migrants, including when they have attempted the creation of special structures for migrants. Migrant temporary status is what has made 'organizing' less easy or common: 'the degree of complexity associated with organizing increases considerably when the target is temporary labour migrants because of their outsider status, their position in the labour market and their temporal limits imposed by their contracts' (Ford, 2019: 114).

Similarly, in the EU context, there have been several cases where migrants have been included but under specific branches, either based on their migrant status and ethnicity, such as in the case of Polish workers in the UK (Ciupijus et al, 2020; James and Karmowska, 2012); or through ad hoc committees with more advocacy and lobbying rather than industrial organizing roles (the case of Unite studied by Alberti et al, 2013); or through the creation of separate social movements or community groups more or less affiliated with existing union branches (for example, Jiang and Korczynski, 2016); or explicitly under the wider category of migrant worker unions in transnational contexts (for example, Greer et al, 2013). In the context of Italy, special treatment has been perceived with suspicion as 'separatist' in that it can produce or foster divisions in the membership (Marino, 2012). In this regard, the question of race in industrial relations research, and the racializing practices of unions giving rise to forms of segregation that are often separated from that of nationality, contribute to neglect the fact that specific issues suffered by migrants such as turnover are always already racialized, as we showed earlier.

In these instances of creating separate or special structures, indeed, results have been mixed, with relatively beneficial outcomes for workers finding new communities of support and opening the unions to the realities of different languages and cultures (for example, Ciupijus et al, 2020; Marino et al, 2017a), but also confirming the unions' only temporary investment in those structures and the partial legitimizing of internal self-segregation of migrants around special grievances, in turn reproducing the dichotomy between work and migration issues (Alberti and Però, 2018). Others have shown how in multiethnic settings migrant workers may spontaneously develop hybrid forms of 'lingua franca' through which they attempt to recompose divisions and attempt to overcome barriers to collective action and participatory organizing, away from union assimilationist approaches (Cioce et al, 2022).

In sum, in the words of Jefferys (2007: 387) on the limits of 'separatist' approaches to minority and migrant organizing within established unions:

> Specialisation does have some advantages. It shows that the 'majority' union has a place for 'minority' workers. But where that 'place' relies on 'majority' goodwill, and where the 'majority' are still not prepared to take up discrimination issues as union issues affecting all workers, then there remains unease. In particular, the 'segregation' or delegation of responsibility for anti-racism to a minority of interested activists

(whether black or white), can reinforce a sense of exclusion: the idea that minority workers' rights are about special pleading rather than about all workers' rights. (Jefferys, 2007: 387)

The protagonism of migrants in the creation of new union structures from within, however, has been only partially considered. Recent research on migrant self-organizing within union structures, such as that of Rogalewski (2018), explored how migrant workers from Poland managed to persuade the established unions to start a new wave of industrial action. Their educational background mattered in terms of their organizing potential, but also the fact that they were met by an open approach by trade unions who focused on their recruitment and mobilization as a chance for regenerating the whole sector. Here the question of the importance of labour composition as well as the 'union opportunism', viewing migrants as a 'fill-in' or renewal strategy to resuscitate a moribund labour movement, returns critically to the debate. Moreover, as Rogalewski (2018: 424) argues, a central question is that 'all approaches adopted by Western European trade unions towards Eastern European migrants have taken place within the framework of the "special versus equal treatment dilemma, with many trade unions opting for the special treatment approach"'. This has been the case at least for Dutch unions, the German agricultural and construction union IG BAU, and the Irish Congress of Trade Unions, but with limited results. Similarly, British unions' relative success at organizing and integrating Eastern European migrants remain piecemeal, with workers mostly concentrated in fragmented and non-union sections of the economy (Hardy, 2021; Fitzgerald and Hardy, 2010).

The research by Rogalewski brings us back to the distinction between universalistic and particularistic approaches that unions may adopt when dealing with migrant workers, respectively leveraging their common worker/occupational and class identity, or the specific issues they face as migrants (non-citizens) and racialized minorities (Ford, 2019; Alberti et al, 2013). They also highlight the need to overcome such a binary approach to equal and special treatment as an either/or strategy. As shown by Rogalewski (2018), when unions set up specific structures for migrant workers, these may not be necessarily or always effective; while these particularistic bodies may be beneficial in terms of creating safe spaces for minorities to organize around specific issues, their effectiveness in terms of long-term sustainability varies from country to country and union to union. Further, the majority of industrial relations scholars still tend to focus on the contractual (and temporal) limitations of migrants' ability to join trade unions, but with concerning omissions of questions related to race and intersectionality (for example, Hyman and Gumbrell-McCormick, 2020; Thomas, 2020).[19]

Overall, industrial relations research on migrant workers demonstrates more awareness than before about the failures of sustained integration of migrants in trade unions and how this has to do with short-lived funding;[20] the lack of democratic self-organizing structures (Marino, 2015); and the fact that ad hoc initiatives are often based on the action of individual officers rather than being embedded in a wider union strategy (Rogalewski, 2018). In our view, such limited funding and short-term investments in organizing migrants partly reflects the ongoing refusal of unions to deal with temporariness as a structural element of contemporary labour. As argued by Alberti and Però (2018), instead of seeing migrant workers as an exceptional and temporary figure of labour, migrant workers may be rather understood as emblematic embodiments of the contemporary traits of an increasingly diverse, transient, and precarious workforce which requires sustained organizational efforts.

In terms of the capacity of migrant workers to organize in separate groups, and the unions to focus on specific identities to mobilize them, issues of race and nationality have been considered, and 'like with like recruitment' (Holgate, 2005) – for example when the union hires an organizer that speaks the language of the migrants – and the creation of informal/community-based collective initiatives are fundamental steps to foster migrants' sense of empowerment and collective action (Tapia, 2013; see also Ciupijus et al, 2020). The problem with industrial relations approaches to migrant workers, however, remains in our view that of reproducing in a functionalistic manner these crystallized notions of 'special vs equal' treatment, particularistic and universalistic approaches, and the insistence about the primacy of either (Ford, 2019), as if migrants were not always at the same time migrants with their own issues and workers with specific issues linked to being migrants. It is rather paramount to consider the fluidity of these social locations and their different strategic value in terms of aggregating and dividing workers in historically situated struggles, a perspective that a more nuanced view on migrant labour critical of union schematic approaches may help to support. In this regard, the emergence of fully separated independent unions of migrant and precarious workers has been discussed as a move away from separate or segregated organizing within established unions (Però, 2020; Weghmann, 2022), which we will explore later.

Migrant self-organization and collective action within and without unions

Instead of focusing on union 'internal logics of action' (Connolly et al, 2014) for creating new strategies of inclusion towards migrant workers (whether on the basis of ethnicity, social rights, or migration status), we shift the focus to the perspective of migrant workers' self-activity in the labour movement. In fact, even in a context of unions that accept migration (second dilemma), what if migrants refuse to become part of these unions because they do not feel adequately represented in their specific issues and interests? More broadly, how do we interpret the rise of indie unions in countries of the West (Però, 2020; Benvegnù et al, 2018) and beyond when these have involved, in particular, precarious workers, migrants, and minorities in the context of post-crises austerity politics and the ongoing decline of traditional unions?

Constable (2009) showed, for instance, how, in the case of Hong Kong, foreign domestic workers have been successful at self-organizing for their rights. Thanks to the fact that they were already covered by labour laws and the national industrial relations system, but also to the additional activism of NGOs in the field of migration, migrants have been able to organize more successfully and improve their terms and conditions also through collaboration with both 'migrant labour NGOs and mainstream unions' (Ford, 2019: 150). In contrast to other countries in the region, the unique context of Hong Kong as a postcolonial 'global city' explains the specific forms that migrant workers' organizing (and female migrant domestic workers in particular) have taken in this location, including their ability to bring their protests into the public realm (Constable, 2009). Arguing that the subjectivities of these migrants as feminized domestic labour subject to specific practices of exploitation are critically shaped by the dynamics of 'inter-ethnic affiliations'[21] (where Filipina and Indonesian workers meet in domestic shelters as growingly politicized spaces with the help of unions, NGOs, and grass-roots organizations),[22] the opportunities for their action will not be understood without considering the socio-historical context of post-1997 Hong Kong as a neoliberal space of exception. As shown by Aihwa Ong (2006), the exercise of civil rights, including by those excluded from the benefits of citizenship such as temporary migrant workers, is allowed in the special administrative region of Hong Kong and rather accommodated by the government as long as they continue to provide the needed labour that benefits the upper and middle classes of Hong Kong residents (Constable, 2009: 155). A critical point of note by Constable (2009: 162) is that these women workers are not demanding permanent residence or the right to citizenship, but the mobile and temporary dimension is rather assumed into a discourse of 'flexible noncitizenship (that) provides assurance that they cannot remain there permanently', and rather advocate for their rights as workers and as humans. Both mobility and voice seem therefore to coexist as product and symptoms of the transnational framing of their demands, as articulated by the NGO and activist organizations with which they are affiliated (rather than focusing on local rights only).

More recently, and drawing from the case of Singapore's migrant worker rights movement, Lenore Lyons (2009) has argued that while migrant advocacy groups, NGOs, and unions have showed interest in transborder organizing, they remain focused on local claims to improve the conditions of migrant women workers (questioning that transnational activism is a necessary outcome of migrant worker organizing), and focused on the national level of advocacy and lobbying (for example, with government and agencies). In contrast to Hong Kong there are also lower levels of transethnic solidarity, and the author explains how this may have to do with 'the limited presence of grass-root migrant worker organizations' (Lyons, 2009: 109). It is remarkable that organizing efforts have happened despite migrant structural temporariness and where union movements are likely to be weak, and non-union organizations, such as labour NGOs, have been most active.[23]

Recent literature in industrial relations has indeed tried to overcome the prejudices about the impossibility of organizing migrant workers, questioning the extent to which trade union resources have supported migrant integration adequately, the degree of sustainability and time limitations of migrant-oriented initiatives (Rogalewski, 2018), and the occasions on which migrants have actually decided to self-organize/break away from established unions to set up their own independent unions (Però, 2020; Weghmann, 2022; Cillo and Pradella, 2018; Benvegnù et al, 2022). A helpful development has started with those looking at how migrants develop forms of collective action. This represents an important shift away from seeing migrants as essentially vulnerable workers (TUC, 2008).

Based on recent research across EU member states, Refslund and Sippola (2022) have critically demonstrated how it is possible to create instrumental collectivist solutions including both migrants and indigenous workers, developing a conceptual framework with four preconditions: workers' closeness; feeling of unity; common problem perception; and reference groups. These preconditions, they argue, are crucial for migrant workers to develop collective labour market strategies that can overcome individualistic strategies and encourage more pro-union activities. And yet, even in these critical readings that look at worker collective action and class formation, aiming to understand the reasons for conflict and why 'gaps between migrant workers and host-country workers may form', a degree of suspicion towards migrant transnational mobility remains (Refslund and Sippola, 2022: 1004). There is also increasing awareness of one limitation of comparative studies of trade union strategies to integrate migrant workers: that the relative success of union strategy lies in measuring solely migrant formal inclusion in industrial relations processes (Arnholtz and Refslund, 2019; Berntsen and Lillie, 2016). More attention should rather be paid to informal dynamics between migrants in the process of collective mobilization (Rogalewski, 2022), whereby it is argued that workers become mobilized and cognitively liberated (McAdam, 1999) thanks to the creation of informal spaces for workers and the use of particularistic policies by the union. Similarly, forms of interstitial trade unions also emerged among Spanish migrants in the EU relying on solidarity networks as a response to the tensions between mainstream unions and migrant labour (Roca and Martín-Díaz, 2017). Hence the enabling of migrant collective action seems here related to the use of particularistic approaches that highlight migrants' specific needs (for example, the creation of informal language groups in Rogalewski's (2018) case). However, in our view, even this approach, critically differentiating between processes of formal and informal inclusion, fails to encompass the subjectivity of migrant labour, since the departure point of these studies remains trade union revitalization strategy.

Moving the focus outside established union structure, Weghmann (2022) has shown how community ties have been central to the development of migrant independent unions in the UK, such as the Independent Workers' Union of Great Britain (IWGB) and United Voice of the World, organizing migrants and ethnic minority in both the platform and non-platform gig economy of the UK. Here an outward refusal of institutional racism within the union has played a key role in the process of autonomization of existing groups of workers and the creation of new structures from below. This does not mean that these small grass-roots unions, usually keen to use more horizontal participatory methods of decision making, are also not themselves subject to the risk of hierarchization and bureaucratization, but at least they have recentered migrant workers' leadership as a taken for granted factor within the decision making progress of these unions. Weghmann (2022) rather emphasizes the rank and file approach to unionism recently championed by the work of Ness (2014) on the revival of syndicalist grass-roots unions in the US. This approach differs from traditional ones on union organizing in that it refuses top-down or integrationist strategies towards minorities and precarious workers, but rather points to the bottom-up emergence of worker organizations modelled on more traditional forms of class struggle and industrial rank and file unions.[24] The main argument by Ness is that traditional unions, based on partnership models and class compromise, are unfit to represent workers in the new era (Ness, 2014: 11), and that instead a focus on worker self-activity, participatory forms, and rank and file tactics both across the Global North and South is the only way to break the impasse of the labour movement. Key elements of such an approach, also adopted in the formation of migrant indie unions in the UK (Kirkpatrick, 2014; Weghmann, 2022), France (Benvegnù et al, 2022), and Italy (Cobbe and Grappi, 2011; Grappi, 2021), among others, are the preference for immediate and direct action by workers, the partial refusal to engage with formalized practices of union recognition and collective bargaining procedures (Moyer-Lee and Lopez, 2017), as well as the rejection of top-down models of professional organizers appointed to organize (migrant) workers in greenfield sectors (Ness, 2014). Similarly, Cillo and Pradella (2018) see the emerging strikes by migrants in the logistics sector of Italy since the economic crisis of 2008 as an opportunity for class international recomposition and union renewal in other sectors. They argue that the development of just-in-time production in logistics strengthens worker bargaining power at the point of production, including that of migrants, despite the racialization of employment relations.

Looking beyond union politics per se, Grappi (2021) has critically argued that one key aspect of migrant autonomous struggles in Italy, at least since the 1990s (including in the expanding logistics sector and by the so-called undocumented), has targeted not only particularly disadvantageous labour conditions, but also the wider 'injustice of migration laws and the different forms of institutional racism they entail'.[25] Indeed, another important aspect that, in the context of migrant-led indie unions, Weghmann (2022) attributes to the relative success of these small unions lies in the fact that they are based on the networks of support of racialized communities. Formed on the initiative of minority and migrant workers, their self-organization has developed into campaigns and disputes primarily based on pay and conditions, and they have successfully brought disadvantaged migrant contract workers in-house, or improved their wages, but also reclaimed dignity and respect given the racialized profile of its constituents. In this regard, Weghmann draws widely from the work of Sivanandan (1981) and his emphasis on the possibilities of overcoming union institutionalized racism through 'inter-racial' class action, and acknowledges how 'the power of solidarity in enabling and maintaining strike action, which is especially important for less powerful groups of workers' (Weghmann, 2022: 135) is ultimately necessary to develop worker power and successful class struggles.[26]

Sivanandan's (1981) own analysis of the Grunwick strike led him to the conclusion that Black 'communities of resistance' were more suitable to support these migrant workers in their workplace struggles considering the limited support from mainstream unions. In the contemporary case of United Voices of the World, the notion that the union was in itself a community (see also Però, 2020) meant that it provided emotional support and a variety of material and immaterial resources to break the isolation of initially non-unionized migrant workers, and supported them in building workplace power (Weghmann, 2022: 141).[27] The racialized dimension of migrants' sense of injustice, however, is not really tackled in Weghmann's account, as she concentrates on migrant workers' preference for forms of direct action and horizonal power structures, in polemic with that of established unions. Indeed, we have seen across a multitude of cases how ethnic communities and wider social movements based on intersectional solidarities encompassing class, race, ethnicity, and migration status have been rather key — more than established trade unions — in supporting precarious migrant workers in their campaigns (Jiang and Korczynski, 2016; Cioce et al, 2022; Tapia and Alberti, 2019; Holgate et al, 2012).

Concluding remarks: recentering migrant agency

Through this overview of the historical and contemporary literature on trade unions and migrant workers, what is clear to us is that migrants have historically demonstrated a level of antagonism and protagonism which unions, more or less purposefully, have often remained blind to. The emergence of autonomous formations among migrant workers is therefore not a coincidence, but rather the outcome of the ongoing difficulty of established unions in understanding migrant temporariness, and, using the worker power framework, their 'mobility bargaining power'. Similarly, despite genuine attempts, unions seem to have struggled to come to terms with migrant agency and self-organization dynamics against institutionalized racism. The latter appears to operate within the precarious economy and within trade union structures themselves.

Overall, we embrace an actor-centred, anti-institutionalist view of migrant organizing (Alberti and Però, 2018), pointing out the forms of self-organization by migrant workers, especially where migrants have felt 'let down' by recognized unions in the workplace, when unions failed to understand the implications of free movement of labour (for example, see Meardi, 2012a; 2012b), and where political differences and not just the existence of special issues have pushed for the creation of separate unions (for example, Weghmann, 2022). Some grass-roots unions in the migrant gig economy (for example, Cillo and Pradella, 2018) have indeed been formed as a response to the gap of representation of migrant-specific needs in relation to rampant processes of restructuring, while in other cases migrant members' committees have been formed as part of internal union structures (Tapia and Turner, 2013; Marino, 2015; Connolly et al, 2014).

However, we agree with Weghmann (2022: 145) that we should not assume that (fully) separate organizing is the only model or 'that low paid, Black and Minority Ethnic or migrant workers cannot organize within established unions'. The reality on the ground is much more fluid, and it indicates that while forms of institutional racism and persistent nationalism remain in the fabric of trade unions North and South, East and West, with relatively different levels of hostility towards temporary migrants, a variety of different formula have indeed emerged in terms of relatively autonomous constellations of alliances and collective formations within, outside, and across trade unions in the terrain of migrant labour. The very question of union recognition, for instance, or the willingness to negotiate formally with employers, may be important also for migrant workers organized under autonomous unions (Kirk, 2018). Union recognition might however be rejected as a strategy by the same indie unions as they raise their profile and start winning grievances without formal recognition (Weghmann, 2022). Ongoing attention to the democratic nature of decision-making structures of unions and the access to resources for mobilizing and for active participation by migrant workers are indeed central to the durability and radicality of any form of worker organization, whether in established or 'indie' unions – maintaining that the latter are not intrinsically excluded from processes of bureaucratization and hierarchization.

It appears that renewed concerns over migrant mobility have brought front stage the historical union dilemmas: is it worth for trade unions to put effort into the inclusion of the new version of Piore's (1979) 'birds of passage'? Industrial relations research not focusing specifically on migration points out that ultimately organizing is about building sustainable and democratic bottom-up structures of participation, where the specific issues of workers are acknowledged across the boundaries of the workplace and the community (McAlevey, 2016; Holgate et al, 2018; Marino, 2015). This focus on organizational capacity constitutes a new element of the industrial relations debate on migrant labour organizing, which helps in moving towards a more open approach where migrants are not simply passive recipients of union integration strategies, but become themselves active change-makers and transform their own labour institutions from below. This literature may not move away completely from an institutionalist approach to trade unions and migrant workers, but brings back to the fore the questions of 'whose voice' is represented in those structures, suggesting that if migrants themselves may be given more prominence inside unions, then wider organizational and social change may follow even within traditional trade unions (Rogalewski, 2018). The links between union renewal and migrant organizing (see also Turner, 2011) brings the discussion to a different level beyond entrenched integrationist approaches about the survival of unions as self-enclosed, members-serving organizations (see Chapter 1), protecting the interests of 'shielded' workers in an increasingly segmented labour market.

To conclude, recentering migrant agency is key to the future development of industrial relations research on migrant organizing, diversity, and intersectionality, and, not least, internal union democracy, and the ability to think 'outside the box', both when they collaborate with other actors (as we have witnessed in the Asian context) or attempt to renew their own structures. We have seen how one response to ongoing forms of exclusion of migrants or segregation within trade unions has been the creation of separate migrant or ethnic-based unions both in East Asia and in the European context, and that mixed outcomes in terms of sustainable self-organizing structures have emerged. In our view however, what Ford (2019) calls 'separate organizing' may be interpreted as the outcome of established unions' inability to actively engage precarious migrant workers, who may decide to leave mainstream unions and form their own grass-roots or independent unions, sometimes through the help of their communities and their sense of racial injustice. Rather than calling it separate organizing, we prefer seeing these recent efforts by migrants as forms of self-organization and indicative of processes of autonomization/empowerment away from traditional union structures that often appear unable to include or create sustainable rooms for different constituencies. In contrast, existing unions may rather consider building new structures that are in themselves flexible and reflect intersectional forms of solidarity.

Conclusion: Rethinking Worker Power Through Mobility

Points of tension and resistance in labour mobility regimes: migrants' logistics

As we considered the political regulation of migration in Chapter 1 and 2, we found that the tempo, patterns, and dynamics of labour mobility today are the outcome of formal and informal processes shaped by a variety of actors or agents: from state agencies and governments directly controlling the flows of migrants across borders; to private brokers and organizations profiteering from restricted entry; to migrants' own informal networks following, adapting, and circumventing existing barriers through their own infrastructures of mobility and support.

In terms of the logic or logistics of such cross-border movements, while migrant labour has been historically seen in the Global North as a 'supplement' to the domestic workforce, todays' reorganization of the labour market takes rather the shape of a more layered, 'porous', or 'differential' border regime (Bojadžijev et al, 2004), reflecting the need for an increasingly flexible and just-in-time supply of labour, structural to the current modes of production (Chapter 3). Against this background, we argue that a central tension in contemporary migration regimes is that the greater complexity of regulation requires more rather than less intermediation, which in turn gives rise to new forms of informalization and deregulation, that ultimately tend to increase the exploitability of labour on the move.

Within the field of economic sociology, Shire (2020) has recently injected a more dynamic view into mainstream institutional perspectives of labour markets and migration infrastructures, by arguing that migration contributes to the making of transnational markets, which however remain relatively unstable and far from consolidated institutions. Similarly to Bauder (2006), Shire (2020: 442) highlights the regulatory functions of migration in the management of labour circulation, but differently from previous accounts she sees more positively the action of multiple entities (from states, to migrant organizations, and trade unions) in 're-embedding regulatory paths to transnational labour exchanges'. While for Xiang and

181

Lindquist (2014), infrastructures are mainly forces of deregulation and neoliberalism, Shire believes that these intermediaries can also intervene positively by negotiating the rules and practices of selling and buying labour across borders.[1]

These notions of coordination and cooperation among the different 'agents' of migration (often with conflicting interests) are indeed central to Shire's analysis, which is based on the idea that mobility cannot occur without establishing a form of social order (Sayad, 2004): the emphasis here is on identifying opportunities of regulation of both competitive dynamics in the international market for labour, and for establishing labour standards through 'increasingly formalized migration channels' (Shire, 2020: 435). Demystifying the idea, common to industrial relations debates, that labour migration is an issue for specialists: 'Migrant labour markets are fundamentally the same as other labour markets in how they must find solutions to the risks market actors face in the commodification, reproduction and *transformation* of labour power' (Shire, 2020: 442, authors' emphasis).

We agree that migrant labour is paradigmatic of wider processes in capitalist labour markets, such as the ongoing indeterminacy of labour capture (Edwards, 1990) and the 'transformation problem' (Deutschmann, 2002). And yet, migrants also represent a 'normal exception' (Mometti and Ricciardi, 2011) in the sense that the control and rebelliousness of migrant workers present unique characteristics that make transnational labour markets function differently from national ones, with the role of migration policy being critical in shaping forms of unfree labour (Strauss and McGrath, 2017). Shire's emphasis on coordination as an attempt by private and public actors to find solutions to the essential turbulence and uncertainty characterizing the reproduction of labour power and its commodification remains important to highlight how various actors may be forced to come together.[2]

From within employment relations research, MacKenzie and Martínez Lucio (2019) have recently applied the notion of regulatory spaces to the field of international migration, arguing that the intrinsic imbalance of power between labour and capital (and of employment relations as inherently contested and unstable) makes any attempt to regulate cross-border migration, and the relationships between multiple actors, not only unstable, but as also conflicting and 'power-laden, competitive rather than cooperative' (Alberti and Cutter, 2022: 440). Following this latter approach, we emphasize that the reproduction of labour power and labour mobility are intrinsically contested terrains, and this is why transnational markets need to constantly find new compromises on the ways labour is exchanged. Critically, this is also to allow for the continuation of labour mobility, or indeed the immobilization of labour in specific circumstances (Harvey, 2006). Therefore, we question the predictability and systematic nature of regulatory forms, but also the importance of government intervention in eliciting the continued circulation of labour under capitalism. According to Xiang's (2020: 522) more recent notion of the gyroscope economy, even under exceptional circumstances, such as enforced lockdowns in the context of the recent global health crisis, we witnessed the continuation of labour mobility and goods circulation, including in the most regimented contexts of China and other East Asian countries who adopted a zero-tolerance policy during COVID-19. For Xiang (2020: 521), mobility did not stop but actually intensify 'like a gyroscope, which cannot balance unless spun fast'. The economies of many countries have appeared to have become almost dependent on such constant movement of people, capital flows, information, and technologies, whereby, even during unprecedented forms of state border closure, such as during the peak of the COVID-19 pandemic, specific cohorts of migrants have been (more or less forcibly) moved to serve the ongoing labour needs of immobilized economies.[3] (see also OECD 2020b).

It is our view that, in such hypermobile but still regimented economies, migration policies may need to remain relatively fluid and adaptable, while performing a double function: on the one hand reassure citizens that the borders are sovereign and their social, physical, and economic security is protected by a vigilant, protective state; and on the other, that the needs of the economy or the market are fulfilled – even if this means hiring ad hoc labour from abroad. In this sense, hypermobility and draconian policies in the area of labour mobility controls run hand in hand rather than being opposite aspects of capitalist markets. As already envisaged by Papadopoulos et al (2008), post-liberal migration regimes have become a characteristic of todays' migration policies, in correspondence with increasing levels of precariousness for the majority of the population. The spontaneous movement of people therefore occurs alongside the ongoing attempt by states and employers at filtering, restricting, and taming the subjective forms of migrants' everyday practices. But these practices are carried on in ever increasingly tense markets that appear further away from coordinated models, and are rather marked by increasingly polarized mobility politics and 'migrant (own) logistics'.

Labour and social mobility power

In Chapter 3, we focused on the ongoing efforts by capital to entrap and constrain workers' mobility power in the context of relatively deregulated employment relations and managed mobility, in global production and localized management regimes. In dialogue with recent elaboration of local labour regimes theory in development and labour geographies (Baglioni et al, 2022), as well as from labour process approaches to global production networks (Newsome et al, 2015), we have centered the point of view of migration and mobility to provide a more finely-grained understanding of international labour processes and the mobility of workers within and across them. We have therefore elaborated a place-based perspective of migrant labour under an intersectional lens, and considered the specific configurations of the social, political, and historical contexts in which workers are placed. We have considered the development of enclaves of differentiated labour (EDL) as paradigmatic sites to understands the power dynamics of control and escape in the assemblage and management of a specific (gendered and racialized) workforce. Analysing EDL, we applied an intersectional sensitivity that understands not only nationality, gender, age, and race, but also mobility itself (and migrant spatial practices) as shaping the different degrees of power by migrant workers in particular.

EDL in the Global South are telling examples of how contemporary forms of control and disciplining concern mostly migrant, racialized, and feminized workers in these exceptional sites of labour value's extraction and reproduction. EDL are indeed particularly illustrative of how labour can be stripped from fundamental rights and freedom vis-à-vis the assumption of 'free-wage labour' (Strauss and McGrath, 2017). However, beyond EDL/EPZs as the formal regimes of labour entrapment and assemblage, where state and private actors coordinate their activities to ensure lowest cost and greater availability of labour supplies, the precarizing sectors of the service and manufacturing economies of the Global North appear to show similar patterns of segregation and fragmentation as well as migrants' mobile practices of refusal of underpaid and unfree labour.

We concluded that if labour process theory helps us recentre the 'relative autonomy' of the labour process (Edwards, 1990) and labour/capital relations in the workplace (see Chapter 1), the specific composition of labour in each site of global production, including its relative (im)mobility, further illuminates how labour turnover as mobility power of migrants represents a unique challenge for management in its desire to keep labour in place and dispense of it when no longer needed. In other words, migrants' uncertain mobilities, far from providing a straightforward solution to the historical problem of management at extracting surplus labour and 'the transformation problem', represent both source of further labour fragmentation and make the predictability of labour turnover harder rather than easier. Such unpredictability, we have shown, is not simply reducible to the material conditions that migrant workers experience in the sectors in which they are employed (that tend to be characterized by poor quality of work, low wages, contractual insecurity, and high turnover), but also critically depends on the development of social relationships with other migrants or indigenous workers across both the spaces of production and social reproduction. In particular, through the development of shared knowledge on new routes and labour markets, as well as of new 'skills' that equip them with new resources to engage in onward journeys after relatively brief periods of stasis. These 'commoning practices' include the use of support networks for their survival in periods of unemployment or in between jobs, whereby workers are able to exercise their quitting power and move out from exploitative jobs (Andrijasevic et al, 2020; Alberti, 2014). We also showed that the social networks that migrants build within and without the labour process appear to play a crucial role in sustaining mobility, but also in developing relatively informal social practices of collective organization and bargaining outside the traditional trade union model (Ryan et al, 2015; Berntsen, 2016; Theunissen et al, 2022).

In essence, moving away from an individualistic understanding of migrant labour mobility power as opportunistic, calculative, and a mere tactic of survival, and against some interpretations of mobility strategies as individual responses by solo migrants acting as a monad in the labour market, we rather emphasize both the social dimensions of labour mobility power as always already embedded in (relatively informal) collective practices, collective (class) formations, and networks of mutual support, and the outward challenge to management.

It is in this context that the affective (rather than merely rational or calculative) dimension of migration needs to be brought to the fore, to rethink labour mobility power as part of the double indeterminacy of labour (Smith, 2006), thus reasserting labour as a collective and relational subject. Indeed, in addition to the need to bring back the dimensions of conflict, protest, and negotiation of workers on the move, the subjective dimension of multinational, transnational, and onward migration under new regimes of controls also needs to be emphasized. Paul and Yeoh (2020) in this regard have critically discussed the dimensions of the new unsettled regimes of labour mobility, characterized by a feeling of uncertainty at the subjective level with important implications for the very sustainability of such migration regimes, where the affective relations sustaining migration play an important if underexplored role. Multinational migration under these circumstances may be driven just as much by disenchantment and anxiety, as much as by excitement and aspiration (Paul and Yeoh 2020: 357). However, other researches highlighted that multinational migration can also be the product of the affective/subjective impacts of migration restrictions on migrants, and not just pull and push factors as direct outcomes of policies or labour market regimes, moving labour across countries or continents according to the temporal logics of employers' demand and state policy (compare Xiang, 2007).

In other words, the mobility power of migrants is not just about a cost-benefit calculation by rational labour market actors (compare McCollum and Findlay, 2015), but an irreducible force shaped by subjective and material motives that make it fundamentally unpredictable in its processes and outcomes. These elements of uncertainty, related to the intrinsically subjective nature of migration, may also be related to the uncertainties of labour's own capacity of reproduction across borders. Indeed, the ways in which migrants and their families survive and reproduce themselves despite or through the logistics of migrant labour have been largely overlooked in the literature, beside some exceptions in feminist geography and feminist-Marxist scholarship (for example, Katz, 2001; Strauss and Meehan, 2015). Similarly to the mobility practices within and across workplaces observed in Chapter 3, migrants' reproductive practices beyond the workplace also create problems for the management of turnover, revealing an additional dimension to the 'social mobility power' of migrants beyond the labour process. Therefore, we now move from the logistics of migrant labour and the labour process to the field of social reproduction, to map out the tensions that migration may generate within and across these fields, and how these tensions may be related to the overall crisis of social reproduction that capitalism faces routinely, and most dramatically today.

Social reproduction as terrain of struggle: mobility skills

In Chapter 4 on migration and social reproduction we have drawn mostly from the insights of feminist scholarship to understand how migration can itself be considered a strategy of social reproduction for workers in the Global South, arguing that (alongside the workplace) the household, the community, and migrant social ties with the country of origin and destination are crucial sites of regeneration of their ability to move (contributing to the sustenance of entire families and states through remittances). At the same time, we highlight how the reproductive labour of migrants is a site of tension, where capital control of mobility for the scope of managing the sphere of social reproduction, encompassing the reproduction of the workforce and of life itself, is challenged by migrants' own mobility and settlement choices. Foregrounding the intersection of reproduction and production spheres in the field of migration makes it possible to understand how the former is not only at the service of the latter, but constitutes a space within which workers develop various forms of resistance and self-determination.

Going beyond the focus on reproduction as limited to the production of individuals as labourers in a capitalist system, by separating the 'waged labourers' from means of sustenance, Mitchell et al (2004: 13) highlighted the hybrid nature of the capitalist economy where there are pockets of economic activities that exist outside or in relation to capitalism, but that are not purely capitalist and rather involve non-market, reciprocal relations (see also Gibson-Graham, 1996). Firstly, this means that class relations are not solely created through coercion to paid work, but also encompass all the activities carried out in social reproduction. In fact, forms of coercion to work (whether paid or unpaid) can occur not only through the formal economic separation from the means of production, but also through coercion of other types, such as that coming from 'an ethnic group, a husband, a coyote (people smuggler), or a parent' (Strauss and Meehan, 2015: 8). Secondly, material spaces of social reproduction must be pragmatically studied as coexistent systems of racism and patriarchy intertwined with capitalism (Strauss and Meehan, 2015: 10). Most importantly for our discussion, migration shows precisely how the alienation of labour from its 'owner' may occur in other spaces than the site of its reproduction, namely in a different nation state (see also Buroway, 1976). We believe that the point of view of feminist geography offers an important key to understanding mobility as itself a key practice of social reproduction.

Our analysis of the use of worker dormitories, in particular, revealed how they may be considered infrastructures and nodes in the logistics of living labour and its reproduction. We argue that these institutions, by concentrating labour spatially and restricting worker movement in time, have been and continue to be critical components of the management of labour mobility internationally, especially as voluntary mobility became more complex and larger in scale. They also show the 'Janus face' of the temporary (im)mobilization or emplacement of labour for the purpose of both production (capital control) and reproduction (migrant labour self-reproduction). Worker dormitories fulfil the double function of tying labour in place but also constituting helpful 'station stops' or 'anchors' (see Chapter 4) for migrant workers on the move searching for better opportunities in their multinational/multilocational journeys. Considered as a single workplace, such as in the case of Foxconn in China, the dormitory labour regime (Pun and Smith, 2007) seems to play the role attributed to it by the employers of coercing a labour force into a situation where workers' behaviours and productivity are controlled more closely. However, considering the multiple forms of living at work in the context of the EU-regulated freedom of movement, scholars shed light on the growing empowerment of migrant workers in dormitory-like systems in terms of developing their exit strategies (Ceccagno and Sacchetto, 2020). If we understand these spaces as a network of accommodations, instead of a single workplace, it becomes clearer that the dormitory regime plays a crucial role in facilitating and even promoting transnational exit strategies, within and without the EDL. Facilitating the mobility of the workforce, the labour accommodation regime allows workers to enjoy new forms of mobility power and develop better knowledge about the running of different labour markets. 'Accommodation labour regimes' can in fact encourage workers' bonds and networks, facilitating mobility and resistance, as they are also able to shift a balance of power inside the workplace.[4] In this sense, the dormitory becomes the archetype of mobility control as well as the site where mobility skills are shared, transmitted, and multiplied.

It is in this context that we develop our contribution to the debate on migration and social reproduction, as we note that significant social and class relationships are forged since migrants are able to develop specific skills across these fields. These specific abilities are not so much linked to a particular labour process, but concern their capacity to move in different labour markets, constituting themselves as a multinational labour force. Overall, we suggest that the mobility of migrants between workplaces and geographical areas allows them to develop knowledge of different labour markets and build a specific form of shared expertise: *transnational mobility skills*. Mobility skills constitute the engine of the infrastructures of migrant continuous movement across labour markets, and at the same time elude the migrant labour regime, as they do not always follow the mere logic of wage differentials and migrant dual frame of reference (Piore, 1979; Waldinger and Lichter, 2003), but are rather concerned about the reproduction of life and household/community relations, that may transcend economic reasoning or calculations (Chapter 4). Mobility skills are central to understanding the drivers and tensions of the mechanics of living labour today, including when borders become apparently less porous, as they help to recentre the mobility power of migrants as a central force of institutional and social change, across different infrastructures.

Overcoming the duality of power in skills/work effort vs power in mobility, our argument highlights the unpredictable effects of labour mobility on the labour process and the community, foregrounding the relationship between migration and skills beyond the workplace (see Table 6.1). That is, rather than focusing on the skills that are valorized by capital in the labour process for the scope of producing commodities for the market and creating profits (Braverman, 1974), we understand mobility

Table 6.1: Forms of worker power across production and reproduction

	Workplace	Migration	Community/ Societal
Individual	Effort power	Migrant labour turnover as migrant labour mobility power	Mobility skills
Collective	Associational power	Transnational mobility bargaining	
Individual *and* collective	Migrant labour turnover power	Migrants' social mobility power	Social mobility power

Note: See 'Migrant labour mobility practices and power forms' in the Glossary skills as knowledge and affective capabilities of migrants in reproducing their own movement and their capacity to move beyond borders and across (trans) national labour markets. Mobility skills include, for instance, the ability to access useful knowledge about better jobs, strategize over one's labour market mobility accordingly, and manage productive and reproductive resources as mobile subjects. This approach overcomes an employer or state-driven view of skills as fixed endowment and 'human resources', and rather points to the social construction of skills and their situational and process-based nature (Alberti and Cutter, 2022).[5]

Returning to the question of labour (mobility) controls at the core of labour process theory, and what our notion of labour mobility skills adds to that debate, we acknowledge that new forms of Taylorism and close monitoring and control of the workforce have become pervasive, as predicted by Braverman, and have led to the erosion of worker autonomy and their 'de-skilling': that is, from the Taylorization of services in call centres (Taylor and Bain, 1999) to the new forms of algorithmic management emerging in the spreading forms of platform, gig, and crowdwork (Wood and Lehdonvirta, 2021), where migrants are often employed (Van Doorn et al, 2022). And yet, what we have definitely not seen in the transformations of work in the 21st century is the degradation of the mobility skills of migrants.[6] The debate about the Great Resignation in the US and other Western countries in the context of the COVID-19 may further illustrate that the ability to quit as a generalized attribute of wage labour (rather than of migrant labour specifically) is further amplified in a context where a global health crisis has exposed the contradictions of poor quality work in so-called essential sectors and the difficulty of capital to retain workers: although only some might have afforded to quit, still the post-lockdown reopening has witnessed the withdrawal from low-paid sector jobs by thousands of individuals, including migrant workers.[7] In this context, migrants' skillfulness about how to manage and maintain their own occupational and geographical mobility (Ciupijus et al, 2020) becomes even more important in a transnational labour market where both the certification of skills and complex regulatory immigration in 'transnational skills regimes' (Collins, 2021) tend to overlap and filter different categories of wanted and unwanted migrants.

It must be said that such mobility skills are not merely 'absorbed' by the international market for labour, nor are they a mere individualist strategy of survival or competition. Papadopoulos and Tsianos (2013) have illustrated the 'imperceptible' practices of undocumented migrants crossing European borders by sharing locations, maps, and survival tips to facilitate their onward migration in a context of illegalization and punitive restrictions (an ensemble of tactics and resources that the authors have called 'mobility commons'); similarly, migrant workers in their workplaces and constrained accommodations may also develop a reservoir of common knowledge to sustain their capacity to be mobile and escape exploitative conditions. In this sense, mobility skills are therefore not just about labour market bargaining power (see Chapter 4), the capacity of the individual to leave a job and find a new employer according to their skills and credentials. They are also about leveraging a possibility to make working and living conditions more bearable (at least for some time), or otherwise reproduce their social lives in excess of what is required for the reproduction of capital, that is, refusing precarious work through transnational exit power and everyday mobility practices.

We therefore shift our gaze to those activities that are required by migrants to sustain their movement across borders as well as their working lives, including access to new labour markets and legal forms of employment, which at times also require forms of conflict and negotiation that may take an explicit collective form.

Beyond structural vs associational worker power: transnational mobility bargaining

Moving to the final thematic chapter, we started our discussion on the trade unions' (historical and ongoing) 'dilemmas' vis-à-vis migrant labour, focusing on the heated question of the relationship between trade union organization and migrant temporariness/labour mobility. The latter has been historically reflected in the uneasy stance of trade unions towards the question of how to tackle labour turnover, where initially worker mobility was considered a legitimate practice and then stigmatized as an individualistic response by workers undermining collective action. The historical review of the literature in particular has shown the racialization (and genderization) by trade unions of labour turnover (as embodied by migrant and ethnic minority workers), constituting the other face of 'racial management' in the workplace as a way to maintain divisions in the workforce (Roediger and Esch, 2012).

Reading these historical trends in light of the ongoing discomfort or even unwillingness of trade unions to develop a clear stance towards the question of labour mobility (Meardi, 2012a), we may conclude that the contested nature of free movement (as in the EU common market), and cross-border movement (for example, in the context of the Mexican border with the US, or in the regimented forms of temporary migration in East Asia), ultimately indicate the ongoing intractable nature of migration in contemporary capitalism. De Genova (2017) has argued that such intractability or incorrigibility are signs of migrants' struggles against border regimes and has maintained that autonomy and freedom of movement are human facts to which borders reactively respond with restriction and deportability. While this notion of intractability has been applied to the field of migrant border struggles and undocumented migration in particular, we transplant this concept to the field of migrant labour vis-à-vis organized labour (unions). To illustrate this point, we noted how the relatively entrenched nature of the Western industrial relations debates on unions and migrant workers, fossilized into the false binary between special versus equal treatment models (Penninx and Roosblad, 2000), continue to be reflected in contemporary debates on separate union structures for temporary migrants, reflecting the long-standing union dilemmas of inclusion/exclusion (Ford, 2019). Our concern is that such an approach inadvertently reproposes a passive view of migrant workers as either too vulnerable to organize, or simply disinterested in such attempts (because of their temporary status), and rather obscures migrant protagonism and activism inside and outside unions structures.

The review of both the historical and contemporary literature on migrant workplace organizing shows that migrant workers themselves have rather been pushing the boundaries of union membership from within and without, while exposing the racialized nature of union organizations (Lee and Tapia, 2021). The emerging forms of migrant self-organization and prolific collaborations between (grass-roots) unions, NGOs, community groups, and social movements have recently brought about an innovative wave of migrant organizing in different countries (Ford and Piper, 2007; Constable, 2009; Adler et al, 2014). Moving away from unproductive discussions about the best organizing strategy or models, we need to recognize the fluidity and multiplicity of forms of organizations within, across, and beyond traditional union structures (whether based on industrial, workplace, geographical or sectoral units).

As we mentioned, a critical knot to understand barriers within the labour movement is that of the historical and ongoing institutional racism within unions and how this is related to migrant temporariness. Using Wright's (2000) terminology, we argue that both the associational and structural power of workers (independently from their migration status) need to be understood as *a continuum* rather than polar opposites, and in context, and putting the onus on existing trade union strategies and their relative adequacy rather than the relative unwillingness of migrants to get involved in industrial action/ labour associations. What we notice is that if unions start taking seriously the transnational dimension of migrants' lives, and the opportunities that arise precisely from cross-border organizing, migrant labour may rather be seen as a source of conflict in the country of destination, and as a source of bargaining with origin countries. In this way, mobility becomes 'normalized' as an intrinsic aspect of all labour rather than seeing it as an existential threat or a weakness to organized labour.

After a critical consideration of the tensions between the internationalism of trade unions and the ways in which the national level regulation and social dialogue influence union positions on migration (Chapters 1 and 5), it seems to us that governments and unions alike appear to share a general cry of 'lost control'. Industrial relations scholars interested in the inclusion of migrant workers still complain that what unions have 'relinquished' is precisely the ability to control national markets (for example, Penninx, 2017). In turn, what the sparse examples of international union collaboration in the context of free movement in the EU tend to illustrate is rather often the absence of union transnational contacts with migrants on the ground.[8] This is where our critique to methodological nationalism becomes more relevant as we explain further later.

In the context of the EU having no choice but to accept the process of Europeanization, unions have rather attempted some modest interventions to reregulate the market by building forms of coordination across borders (beside attempting migrant incorporation at the local level). But there has been a dimension of free movement of labour that has been mostly overlooked by scholars and unions, which concerns the effects of migrants' act of leaving their country of origin, as Meardi critically reminds us:

> Even if the 'voice' of employees in the new member states has remained feeble, their massive 'exit' has forced employers, and to a lesser extent governments, to important concessions, leading to higher than expected wage growth and some improvements in employment conditions. Moreover, the labour market effects of exit have in turn resulted in more attention to voice, with multiple instances of trade union revitalization and newly found assertiveness. (Meardi, 2012b: 105)[9]

This reversal of the gaze, looking at the effects of migrant exit in the country of origin's wages, conditions, and industrial action, is critical to our discussion as it contributes to deconstruct the methodological nationalism in which most of the industrial relations literature, including the one on migration, is trapped (Chapter 1). It also helps to evaluate the potential for transnational organizing in the context of free movement of labour. Indeed, despite growing tensions, examples of transnational cooperation between unions in country of origin and destination have emerged around the four freedoms.[10] For Meardi (2012a), the reasons for union immobility in this context are to be attributed to unions clinging to a nationalistic frame of industrial relations (Giles, 2000), and being attached to homogenizing categories of workers' 'organic solidarity', which make them unable to grasp the multiple affiliations and diversity of solidarities expressed by migrants from different political cultures and histories of struggles.[11]

Another necessary reversal of the gaze from the side of industrial relations' traditional view of migrant labour requires us to start seeing migrant mobility not as an element of weakness but as a form of empowerment for workers, especially if solid connections are built between countries of origin and destination.[12] In the context of the US, Jennifer Gordon (2006) has tackled more directly the dilemmas of free movement and national labour unions, examining the effects of the unionization of migrant guest workers from Mexico preparing to work in the tobacco plants of North Carolina, originally advancing the notion of 'transnational labour citizenship' and highlighting the role that unions themselves could play in empowering mobile workers.[13]

The shift to a pro-migrants stance and openness to organizing undocumented workers has been a critical development in the US labour movement since the early 2000s (not coincidentally in the context of protests against immigration reform and guest worker schemes waged by migrants themselves), but Gordon develops the additional argument that to really succeed in improving working conditions for all workers, unions must accept the inevitability of continuous movement, and so its temporariness. As suggested by Gordon (2006: 505), worker organizations should rather acquire a central role in ensuring migrants' terms and conditions as they continue to move across borders: this includes revising their membership rules, 'normative expectations of solidarity', and, critically for our discussion in Chapter 5 on migrant autonomous organizing, develop democratic processes within their organizations. Drawing from these insights we develop Strauss and McGrath's notion of labour mobility bargaining (see Chapter 3) into its transnational dimension through the notion of *transnational mobility bargaining power*, exercised by migrant workers in particular, but also by any worker involved in transnational work and labour organizing. Through this notion, we renew our quest to overcome methodological nationalism in the field of industrial relations and union organizing practices, hoping that recognizing the power of transnational bargaining and mobility itself on both destination and origin countries, and emphasizing the responsibility of unions in taking transnational mobility seriously, may help to overcome the entrenched suspicion and biases against mobility, and rather reappropriate the power of mobility as an inevitable dimension of labour organizing in today's 'precarious worlds' (Strauss and Meehan, 2015).

Concluding remarks: the politics of migrant labour

As we complete the final draft of the book (June 2023), the second largest shipwreck of asylum seekers crossing the Mediterranean leaves more than 500 missing bodies in the sea, with 78 confirmed deaths and 108 survivors. It is still to be established what the responsibility of the Greek coastguards has been in failing to provide rescue to those escaping in search of better lives. As we witness with disconcertment yet another boat disaster at the border of Europe, we reflect on one limit of this book, which has been not to engage with the vast and critical literature on refugees and asylum seekers, including the work experiences of those who manage to make it to their destination. The criminalization of asylum seeking by European governments, and the denial of legal access to work for those in the limbo of temporary 'humanitarian permits' are indeed part and parcel of the racialized and gendered border and migrant regimes that attempt to control and precarize migrant people, or at times indeed, let them die. As the environmental crisis worsens, adding to global expanding socio-economic inequalities, we can only expect more rather than less crossings and, as governments tighten legal routes, for irregular migration to grow.

Taking into account the multiplicity of autonomous collective and independent actions by migrants inside and outside established worker organizations, and through our overview of migrants' transnational practices of social reproduction, we have attempted to build an understanding of migration itself as a creative and life-sustaining strategy of both social reproduction and labour conflict. This approach moves away from a static and victimizing view of the 'function' of migrant labour as a mere recuperation strategy by capital vis-à-vis labour indeterminacy, or as an easy cost reduction strategy by employers. Rather, understanding the *excessive* reproductive mobility practices of migrants as always already constructed collectively across families, kinship networks, paid, and unpaid activities, we demonstrated the *relationship between social reproduction, labour mobility, and worker turnover* as a differentiated field of contestation for workers. As Goldín (2011: 152) critically remarked: 'Turnover is the shape that labour takes in global capitalism'.

Overcoming the false dichotomies between production and reproduction, individual and collective practices, migrant vs indigenous workers, we hope to help reverse the mainstream image of migrants as the ultimate form of vulnerable labour still dominating the industrial relations and labour studies literature and some of the migration scholarship. As part of the same effort, we also argue for the need to overcome binary views related more broadly to the discussion of worker power and in particular the historical counterposing of exit and voice (Hirschman, 1970), the former as intrinsically individualist, and collective the latter. Instead, we have shown how migrant turnover may both originate and lead to collective practices that at times take the form of the decision to flee unacceptable conditions or lead to overt protest and collective action. The continuum between exit and voice, and their non-linear developments and interconnections, needs instead to be brought to the front to understand the realities of mobility power. We need to acknowledge how the everyday mobility practices of migrants as subjects who experience particular constraints to their freedom of movement are continuously differentiated by state and management policies in the Global North and South. Mobility is indeed specifically restrained for migrant workers, but in truth for all the hundreds of millions of people who are currently facing the overlapping spiralling crises of social and environmental reproduction, and the degradation and precarization of work and living standards unfolding in our capitalist societies.

The contemporary situation shows how the global race for sourcing forces of labour continues to unfold and to be contested, whereby labour migration flows may follow a logic of their own and exceed governmental and capital expectations, whereas migrant workers strive to set themselves free from the new ties that sponsorship and temporary programmes, hostile environments, and regional systems of body shopping impose on them under new forms of unfree or semi-free waged labour. Even when the power of labour appears almost depleted (with declining union organization, a severe cost of living crisis, and precarious livelihoods across the Global North and South), workers and migrant workers in particular continue organizing on the ground, either by relying on their networks of everyday reproduction and survival, or by developing new organizational forms to confront capital and regain terrain vis-à-vis employers and the state in more coordinated and collective forms (Atzeni and Sacchetto, 2023). We have argued, however, that both individual and collective forms of protest, moving from structural mobility bargaining power at the point of production to *social mobility power* across the field of production and social reproduction, constitute power sources within a continuum of resistance, that characterizes the historically indeterminate relationship between capital and labour.

Our perspective has centered labour mobility and the relevance of social reproduction in order to understand the politics of labour control and worker power in todays' increasingly differentiated and heterogeneous markets, from the enclaves of differentiated labour of East Asia and Latin America to the precarizing migrant sectors of the Global North. We hope to renew attention to the subjective as well as structural and regulatory aspects of transnational migration and their importance for work and employment relations, by foregrounding the point of view of migrant labour.

With our historical sensitivity in reassessing the development of labour turnover and migration patterns across world regions and periods, and with a critical discussion of the underlying biases that still discourage labour organizations to engage fully with the questions of migration, labour mobility, and temporariness, we also hope to have illuminated some concrete pathways to promote the improvement of the many lives of those on the move, as well as the common interests of their more settled counterparts, accepting that global mobilities will continue to be a legitimate and normal response to the compelling challenges of our uneven and fragile capitalist world.

Glossary

Forms of worker power

Associational power: form of worker power based on the collective organization of workers (unions, political parties, community groups) (Wright, 2000; Silver, 2003).

Coordinated mobility effort bargaining: labour mobility power or mobility effort bargaining, may also be exercised informally by groups of workers: 'the individual or work group can also use the threat of exit to re-negotiate the internal work bargain within the firm – improving wages, changing jobs, gaining additional training resources, changing line management' (Smith 2006: 391).

Marketplace or mobility bargaining power: 'form of power exerted by workers in relation to their ability to exit employment relations in a tight labour market' (Strauss and McGrath, 2017: 204, drawing from Silver, 2003).

Structural effort power: strategic position based on worker labour power at the point of production (Wright, 2000).

Practices and forms of migration

Multinational migration: umbrella term encompassing the transient, irregular, multi-directional, and 'stone-stepping nature' of migration (Paul and Yeoh, 2020: 7). Also emphasizes the different nature or directionality of these movements, not always upwards in terms of the preferred destination but also 'lateral'.

Multinational worker: this concept recentres mobility, focusing on how migrants share knowledge about job searches and strategize around their opportunities to find employment, comparing wages, terms and conditions, and quality of life across different workplaces and countries (Andrijasevic and Sacchetto, 2016: 222).

Onward migration: migratory movements from the country of arrival to a third country (Mas Giralt, 2017; Paul and Yeoh, 2020), characterized by 'the continuous re-evaluation of migration opportunities' (Morad and Sacchetto, 2020: 165) rather than rationally pre-planned routes.

Transnational migration: indicates non-linear, household-based migration choices and patterns. While understanding migratory flows beyond methodological nationalism, transnational migration studies still maintained a focus on how already settled migrants create transnational ties mostly between countries of origin and settlement (Glick Schiller et al, 1995; Faist, 2006).

State policies

Benched labour: one of the key functions of the logistics of migrant body shopping. This notion was elaborated by Xiang (2007) in the context of the 'Indian triangle', whereby intermediaries manage labour across borders and provide 'ready-made' skilled workers to the market on demand. Hiring but then leaving workers 'on the bench' is a practice considered profitable by the body shops because it provides a pool of labour on site and also a labour reservoir.

Circular migration programmes: new version of guest worker schemes (Castles, 2006; Ruhs and Martin, 2008). These schemes reflect initiatives by supranational institutions adopting developmental narratives about 'win-win-win' solutions for country of origin and destination *and* for individual migrant workers (Vertovec, 2009; Castles and Ozkul, 2014).

Gastarbeiter: The 'guest worker' migrant labour system introduced in the Federal Republic of Germany (FRG) after the Second World War to facilitate the recruitment of migrant workers to respond to increasing demand. It was based on bilateral agreements between European states. Migrant workers were not allowed to settle or bring their families to the FRG, but were expected to go back to their country of origin when their work permit expired (for example, Castles and Kosack, 1973).

Indentured labour system: a form of labour in which a person is contractually bound to an employer for a specific time period, usually to repay a loan (for travel and/or living expenses), and in which breaches of the contract are punishable. Different forms of indentured labour existed in different world regions (from precolonial Asia to eighteen century British and French America (Hoefte, 2018: 363)).

Kafala: regime of migration in some Arab and Persian Gulf countries, based on sponsorship and developed after the 1970s. Under this system, the state gives sponsorship permits to local individuals or companies (*kafeel)* to employ migrant workers under temporary contracts. The *kafeel* should cover travel expenses and provide housing to the migrant worker, who is bound to the sponsor for his/her contract period and residence permit. These migrants have no right to family reunion or settlement.

Point-based systems: in place in many countries around the world today, it attributes a set of points to visa applicants according to migrants' individual 'assets' (education, income) and skills profile. On paper it favours highly-skilled migration, but in practice promotes informal migration in low-skilled sectors. It maintains the principle that the migrant's work/ residence permit depends on a sponsoring employer and therefore increases precarious employment of migrants (Anderson, 2010).

Networks and intermediaries

Intermediaries: actors that facilitate and mediate access to the labour market for workers while providing labour supplies to employers. Intermediaries can take different forms and can be legal and illegal. Intermediaries may focus on facilitating migration only, or both mobility and job searches. Intermediary actors include: local authorities, recruitment agencies, brokers, gangmasters, coyotes, *calos, taikongs, dalal,* religious organizations, employers, migrants' communities, and networks (Xiang and Lindquist, 2014). Institutional intermediaries are actors that can facilitate, manage, and obstruct mobility, including for instance NGOs, international organizations, trade unions, and global labour federations (for example, see Ford, 2019).

Migration system, chain migration, and network migration: these concepts aim to stress the self-perpetuating nature of migration beyond factors triggering the labour flow, such as state policy (for example, Faist, 2006; Miller and Castles, 2009).

'Mobility infrastructures' perspective: a critical framework to understand the operation of organized migration 'from below', including migrants' own networks, migrant private brokers, and state agencies, employers, and international bodies. It encapsulates a form of 'delegation of state authority to private actors as part of a process of deregulation and neoliberal globalization' (Shire, 2020: 442; see also Lindquist et al, 2012; Xiang, 2007).

Forms of labour mobility power

Labour mobility power: individual capacity to exit a job and employment relation; equivalent to labour turnover (Smith, 2006; Baldamus, 1961).

Migrant workers' mobility bargaining power: brings together structural and associational power, comprising the forms of power exerted by migrant workers as marketplace labour mobility power (Alberti, 2016; Silver, 2003; Strauss and McGrath, 2017) with direct or indirect effects on the workplace.

Mobility effort bargaining: 'the application of workers' power over where to sell their labour services to the concept of work effort ... For workers, mobility power is manifest in the time involved with network building, the resources used at work for the planning of job moves, and the use of mobility threats to create strategic rewards' (Smith, 2006: 391).

Transnational labour mobility power: it emerges when labour mobility power is exercised across borders, for example including collective effects of individual exit and migration on workers' wages and conditions in origin country (see Meardi, 2007).

Migrant labour mobility practices and power forms

Migrant labour turnover or migrant labour mobility power: we develop this notion to indicate the power to quit of migrant workers exerted in the absence of social bargaining rights (for example, Reid–Musson, 2014).

Mobility skills: types of soft skills used by workers to facilitate their occupational mobility; they may be exercised by workers independently from their migrant status, while the other two concepts (migrant labour turnover and transnational mobility power) are specific to migrants as they face the constraints of migration controls and migrant labour regimes.

Social mobility power: This is based on the reproductive work of families, kinship, and social networks but remains ambivalent in that it increases both support and forms of social control, subsidizes capital, but also allows for the reproduction of migrants beyond capital (see Chapter 4 and the ambivalent role of dormitories, Table 4.1).

Transnational mobility power or transnational mobility bargaining: for example, collective effects of individual exit and migration on worker wages and conditions in origin country (see Meardi, 2007).

Transnational mobility skills: skills that migrant workers develop as they move across workplaces and borders regarding opportunities to access useful knowledge about job opportunities, strategize their labour market mobility, and manage their productive and reproductive resources (for example, Andrijasevic and Sacchetto, 2016).

Notes

Introduction

[1] According to the newly created 'International Labour Migration Statistics' (ILMS) database, under the Arab States the following 12 countries are included: Bahrain, Iraq, Jordan, Kuwait, Lebanon, Occupied Palestinian Territory, Oman, Qatar, Saudi Arabia, Syrian Arab Republic, United Arab Emirates, Yemen (ILO, 2018; IOM, 2021).

[2] Among the OECD destination countries, Poland was the one receiving the highest number of temporary labour migrants in 2018, namely 1.1 million migrant workers on temporary work permits entering the country from outside the EU, predominantly Ukrainians, and 27,000 from inside the EU single market (OECD, 2019: 16).

[3] In the words of the OECD: 'These statistics enable the assessment of the degree of fluidity in the labour market as well as identifying the areas of economic activity where the turnover of labour is rapid. Data are broken down by professional status – employees, self-employed, total employment – sex, five-year and broad age groups' (OECD, 2020a).

[4] See European Commission (2010), available from: https://ec.europa.eu/employment_social/eie/chap3-2_en.html

[5] For research adopting a Global South's perspective on labour turnover, see Qin et al (2019).

[6] For an historical approach in the field of management studies, see Bruce (2005).

[7] For pioneering work and the first efforts at theorization, see Diemer (1917); Slichter (1919); March and Simon (1958); Price (1977); Mobley (1982).

[8] We should add also the Pacific and Indian middle passage that involved about 4 million people (Christopher et al, 2007).

[9] Natives in the Americas also suffered from forms of slavery: it is estimated that from 1492 to the end of the 19th century, 2.5 to 5 million natives were enslaved. This slavery, especially female slavery, was widespread from Mexico to Argentina, but without excluding North America (Reséndez, 2016: 324). While between approximately 1550 and 1650 different European states tolerated the departure of their citizens willing to embark for the New World, later these movements were regulated through the institution of the indentured contract lasting from five to seven years. To this form of indentured labour one could add the prisoner labourers who were deported to the New World by the European colonial powers (Hoerder, 2002).

[10] Free and unfree African Americans, as well as Whites, built the so-called 'Underground Railroad' that helped perhaps as many as 100,000 slaves to move from the southern to the northern US states, but also to Canada and Mexico (Lucassen and van Voss, 2019).

[11] While the notion of spatial fix was introduced by Harvey to explain capital's ability to use mobility to its advantage, Herod (2001: 256) provides a helpful application in the field of labour geography highlighting the debate around worker agency: 'space can be used by both capital and labor – and by different segments within these two categories – to further political and economic agendas'. Structuralist approaches to the geography of labour (as opposed to labour geography) fail to see workers as 'active geographical agents'.

In order to see workers and their organizations as active geographical agents, there is a need 'to understand how various groups of workers went about constructing spatial fixes in pursuit of their varied political and economic objectives' (Herod 2001: XIII).

[12] As argued by Morrison et al (2013: 7), despite important advances even in migration scholarship 'methodological nationalism remains an issue and research focus still relies on concepts and preoccupations emerging from national politics of host countries'.

[13] For instance, Alesina et al (2004), among the most prominent writers on the links between migration and welfare, argue that, in order to perceive the redistribution of benefits as fair, citizens of destination countries want to see immigration controls as a safeguard against 'undeserving' strangers. Benefits conditionality for migrant claimants is considered necessary if generous welfare systems have to survive for citizens (see also Chauvin et al, 2013).

[14] According to Bruce (2005: 493), exploring the first comprehensive empirical study of the costs of turnover by the General Electric manager Mr Alexander, 'in electrical and other types of machine-building firms, quit rates increased by 329 per cent between 1913–14 and 1917–18 as war orders flooded in from Europe'.

[15] The study by Smith et al (2004: 374) in Japanese transnational corporation (TNC) manufacturing firms showed how in the context of a declining bureaucracy, non-unionism, and eroding national bargaining, alternative non-wage forms of retention may be favoured, through increases in soft or cultural forms of human resources management and in reward strategies including 'loyalty bonuses, Christmas parties, social activities, games and rewards for suggestions, quality and other performance inducements'.

[16] This text sent to the newspaper *L'Humanitè* in 1973 was then published in Balibar (1974).

[17] Moving to the example of the East German Democratic Republic, from the 1960s to 1980s, migrant workers coming from other communist countries received a five-year contract, so that they did not have the right to family housing and could contract a marriage only with a German partner and after receiving permission from the state (Schrover, 2018: 462).

Chapter 1

[1] While the US Bureau of Labour Statistics originally used turnover to refer to the number of replacements needed, in order to fulfil the concern of employers to maintain the workforce, the authors suggest to keep into account all three elements of analysis: '1) the number of employee hired (accessions); 2) number leaving (separations); and 3) the number of replacements required to keep up the workforce' (Brissenden and Frankel, 1922: 8).

[2] As Dubofsky (1995: 126) notes, 'The First World War years witnessed an unparalleled explosion of labor unrest. Strikes increase dramatically in 1916; they reached their highest level ever in 1917; and peaked in terms of numbers of workers involved in 1919 when over four million workers (almost 25% of all private-sector employees) struck'. During the Second World War labour conflict in the firms also remained high (Glaberman, 1980).

[3] This was true also in the USSR, where labour turnover remained high in particular after 1956 when the strict labour legislation against mobility approved in 1940 during the Second World War was abrogated. On the basis of a large research conducted by some Soviet economists, Fakiolas (1962: 23) underlines that the five most important causes of labour turnover in 1960 were linked to 'return to parents' home town', 'grievances against the wage level', 'inadequacy or complete lack of living accommodation', 'job maladjustment', and 'bad working conditions'.

[4] An emphasis on individuals' choices and their economic utility to explain turnover behaviour among workers has also dominated more recent accounts of turnover in organization studies, even though there have been some attempts to bring a more

dynamic approach to the framework that includes social conflicts (for example, March and Simon, 1958) and less individualistic (community/family) and 'off work' drivers of turnover intentions, such as through embeddedness theories (Mitchell et al, 2001) that explain both turnover behaviours and organizations' responses.

[5] As Blackett (1928: 12–13) noted: 'It is a mistake to suppose that the reduction of labor turnover is under all circumstances a net advantage. There are industries which thrive best in a mobile labor market because the business is by nature seasonal or subject to unexpected changes in volume. These industries tend to locate in large cities or to build up around them communities where labor moves easily from one employment to another'.

[6] Recently, in the context of labour shortages following the COVID-19 pandemic, we have witnessed the introduction of specific contractual clauses that penalize workers who decide to leave their employers earlier than a prescribed time, including in low-paid manual occupations (Boeri et al, 2022).

[7] An important issue observed by studying differences between national contexts is how the structure of a labour market can influence the sort of vocational training available to workers (Thelen, 2004; Teague and Donaghey, 2018). When state and employers don't invest in training there is a tendency to look for alternative sources of skills and 'outsource' the reproduction of skills to other countries. This is a typical example of the 'substitution function' of migration, that is, when immigration is used by employers/governments if national training and vocational education institutions have failed to reproduce the needed skills in a certain labour market. However, we will see how replacing skills through migration is far from a straightforward process that state or capital can simply take for granted.

[8] For a critique of the enthusiastic apologists of the so-called golden age during the thirty glorious years (1945–75), see Gambino (1996).

[9] Interestingly, in that article, Hirschman (1978) was exploring the political scientists' critique and the contribution that the notion of exit can provide to understandings of political behaviour vis-à-vis the state (rather than private capitalist organizations), a topic that could be relevant in understanding the relationship between the state and migration.

[10] It is worth noting that Smith's conceptual distinction between 'mobility-effort bargaining' and 'work-effort bargaining' (Smith, 2006: 392) is not one drawing differences between individual and collective forms of labour power, but rather focuses on the mobilization of external (labour market) and internal (workplace) *bargaining resources* by workers. And yet, while work effort tends to be associated also by Smith to a collective and formalized organizational form (trade union/work group), mobility effort bargaining is understood as pertaining to both 'individual' or 'possible group' (Table 1, Smith, 2006: 392).

[11] If we compare Smith's (2006) original theorization with our table on worker power (resource based approach) it is relevant to look at the 'resource requirement' feature of his table whereby work effort is associated to formal organization and mobility effort to more informal one: networks of contracts, external market power, strong labour market demands. So in this sense labour mobility power leverages resources in the labour market rather than in the labour process and therefore differs from the structural labour market at the point of production. Here is where Silver (2003) distinction between marketplace and workplace based structural power is helpful.

[12] Also, Marcel van der Linden (2008: 175–8) highlights many cases of 'collective exit' in particular among slaves, indentured laborers, journeymen, and sailors.

[13] See also Linebaugh and Rediker (2000).

[14] In most Western countries, for example, workers can access unemployment benefits only if they are fired or their contract expired.

[15] Balibar (2004) has illustrated this point with reference to the workings of freedom of movement within Europe, which (while arguably bringing many material advantages to EU citizens) exists because the movement from the outside is filtered and selected.

Chapter 2

[1] In 2020, after pressures from FIFA, governments, and NGOs, the emir of Qatar abolished the kafala sponsorship system, even if full implementation of this new rule is not clear. At the same time, the emir increased the minimum monthly wage to 1,000 Qatari riyal (about €230); see Human Rights Watch (2019) Qatar: Migrant Workers Strike Over Work Conditions. Online Publication. Available from https://www.hrw.org/news/2019/08/08/qatar-migrant-workers-strike-over-work-conditions. Accessed 22 March 2021. Saudi Arabia also abolished the kafala sponsorship system in 2020.

[2] The six GCC countries are: Bahrain, Kuwait, Oman, Qatar, Saudi Arabia, and the United Arab Emirates.

[3] https://www.theguardian.com/global-development/2021/feb/23/revealed-migrant-worker-deaths-qatar-fifa-world-cup-2022 [last accessed 11 November 2022]. On the working conditions and the responsibility chain during the construction of infrastructure for the FIFA World Cup, see also Millward (2017).

[4] Next to migrant workers we also find some thousands of Western expats working mainly as managers and technicians (Naufal and Genc, 2012).

[5] As Gibson and Graham (1986: 141) noted analysing this system in Gulf countries: 'Embedded in the labour contract are the roots of worker disenfranchisement. The economic "freedom" to sell labour power has been separated and isolated from the political freedoms of speech, assembly and organisation.'

[6] In his research on Zimbabwean workers in South African border farms, Maxim Bolt (2015) shed light on the fact that the concepts of displacement and labour migration are not alternatives but stay in a dynamic relationship, as displaced Zimbabweans that cross the border into South Africa become labour migrants only *at their places of work* after being recruited by farmers (Bolt, 2015: 8).

[7] For example, migrants in the Gulf tend to be housed en masse in labour camps which help the formation of mass-worker-households where 'common grievances are shared and fomented' (Bal, 2016: 219), in contrast to the migrants in Singapore who are much more dispersed. While both countries tend to apply draconian measures, banning workers from exercising collective bargaining, threatening migrants with wage withdrawal, and prohibiting them from returning to the country if they engage in protests, more recently ad hoc and informal collective bargaining have emerged, especially in Dubai, where workers managed to obtain concessions on minimum wage standards. And yet, in terms of institutional actors' responses, 'while authorities in Singapore have responded to unrest with a mix of coercive and cooptive measures, their counterparts in Dubai have recently moved to legalize strikes within labour camps, in addition to existing coercive practices of arrest and deportation' (Bal, 2016: 212).

[8] In using the term 'living labour' we refer to the tradition of Italian operaism that in turn has rehabilitated the Marxian term to indicate the 'diversity of encounters' between capital and labour and the multiplicity of labour forms which are not to be merely assimilated to capital's myriad forms of subsumption (Mezzadra, 2011b: 160).

[9] See also the literature on 'transnational social spaces' by Faist et al (2013).

[10] Migration policy to attract high-skilled workers has its problems, as the failure of Germany's programme to recruit 20,000 high-tech Indian migrants highlights (Poros, 2001).

[11] Between 1919 and 1934, about twenty-four treaties were signed in Europe, while from 1937 to 1943 Germany alone signed a total of sixteen labour treaties. After 1945, the number of labour treaties rose to forty, often based on 'ILO's model' and with some convergence of structure and content (Rass, 2012: 201).

[12] Bosma et al (2012) consider: family and community based; public and private agencies; and national and international agencies (as the nation state).

[13] Hoerder (2002: 390) notes that 'in 1921 the population of Singapore and Malaya of 3.3 million included 1.6 million Malays, 1.2 million Chinese, 0.5 million Indians, and some 60,000 others'.

[14] The characteristics of the kangani system were: recruitment based on kinship and family networks, and no contract or fixed period of service, meaning workers were legally free to leave. However, forms of constraints were as strong as in the indentured system, through, for example, indebtedness. Violence was also the main system to manage Indian migrant workers, because it allowed for the preservation of social distance between 'coolies' and their bosses (Ramasamy, 1992: 99).

[15] In 1910, the Malayan government prohibited indentured contract labour. However, for Indians, the last indenture contract ended in 1913, and for Chinese in 1914 (Kaur, 2012).

[16] In 1937, about 30,000 Chinese labourers, mainly employed in rubber estates, went on strike asking for better wages and living conditions. Labour militancy was supported by the Malayan Communist Party, but expanded also thanks to the weakening of Chinese (and then Indian) contractors' power, and thanks to the widespread 'moral economy' based on the idea of a just treatment for workers (Nonini, 1993: 236).

[17] However, after their first experiences, some of the migrant workers moved autonomously to other factories and farms thanks to the wide opportunities in the labour market, with high job turnover rates in the mines in the Ruhr area in particular (Kulczycki 1993: 135).

[18] Recruitment of migrant workers by the Nazi regime was justified as temporary and was arranged with friendly allies (as in, Italy and Romania) with bilateral agreements, but also by moving workers from occupied territories. Some of these migrants, about 750,000, mainly from Eastern Europe, remained in Germany after the war refusing to be repatriated (Rhoades, 1978: 563).

[19] Forced labour also increased in the USSR during the Second World War, and in 1941 'there were 2.9–3.5 million forced laborers' (Hoerder, 2002: 466).

[20] In particular, migrants' rates were high in Switzerland (16.0 per cent of total population), Belgium (7.1 per cent), France (6.4 per cent), Great Britain (5.0 per cent), and Germany (4.8 per cent).

[21] The process of the UK's withdrawal from the Commonwealth free movement area started in 1962 and culminated in 1968 with the Commonwealth Immigrants Act. This act abolished free mobility of Commonwealth subjects, establishing that a 'Citizen of the United Kingdom and Colonies' could only 'live and work in the UK if they, or at least one of their parents or grandparents, had been born, adopted, registered, or naturalized in the UK' (Yeo et al, 2022: 6) creating a de facto 'two tier system of citizenship rights based on parentage' (see Taylor, 2017).

[22] Stephen Castles (2006) later addressed the question of guest worker government schemes as a paradigmatic example of migration policies and asked provocatively if we are now in the presence of a 'resurrection' of the 1950–70 programmes to import labour migrants in Western countries, although in different forms. Castles highlights how, in the context of the EU, the European Commission put in place schemes to recruit high-skilled labour, although failed to set up plans for lower-skilled migrants.

[23] As Sayad (2004: 56) underlined: 'Any study which neglects the conditions of origin of emigrants is condemned to give only a partial and ethnocentric view of the phenomenon. On the one hand, such studies give consideration only to the immigrant, not to the emigrant, as if his existence began at the moment he arrived in France. On the other hand, the implicit and explicit problematic of such studies is always the immigrant's adaptation to the 'welcoming' society'.

[24] The Philippines entered the international labour market during the Vietnam War when the US needed civilian labour to work in the warring country (Woodward, 1988: 125). Despite the creation by the government of relevant offices in 1974 (that is, the Philippines

Overseas Employment Development Board and the National Seaman's Board), it was not until 1982 that remittances started to become substantial as the Philippine government decided to play a more active role in the management of out-migration. The 1982 creation of the Philippines Overseas Employment Administration (POEA), into which the two previous offices merged, is the cornerstone of a new organization, selection, and control of the sale of the Filipino labour force abroad. In those years, other countries were also preparing the tools to export migrants in large quantities: after Bangladesh in 1976, Sri Lanka also created the State Office for the Export of Labour in 1980 (Tyner, 1998).

[25] On the level of remittances see, for example, IOM (2021).

[26] The Chinese contractor system was an indirect form of labour control organized by recruiters or brokers who had some previous experience in Malaya and included a 'kinship-based' migration network in China (Kaur, 2012: 239). Nonini (1993) reconstructs how labourers, labelled 'little pigs', were organized in gangs under the control of the contractor that paid wages, retrieving his expenses for recruitment. Migrant workers were under a 'truck system', forced to acquire food and other commodities from the contractor at a higher price than on the free market. Debt bondage for the cost of their passage and for commodities, direct threats, and native-place ties were the main form of control of this workforce. In some cases, labourers were locked in their houses and barracks from 6 pm to 6 am (Ramasamy, 1992: 93).

[27] As Ramasamy (1992: 99) notes: '*Kangani* was not a mediator of conflicts between labour and capital; he was very much an agent of capital and his primary role was to subject labour to the rigorous discipline required by the plantation production system'. Wage payments to migrants were routed through *kanganies*, while they were paid a fixed monthly wage and a commission for every one of the workers he (*sic*) recruited who came out to work.

[28] Generally, Indian migrants often suffered a severer control on plantations than Chinese migrants. Further, Chinese migrants could enjoy more freedom than Indians in Malaya because they were bound only by their financial obligations and after that they were free to move (Kaur, 2012: 241–2).

[29] Obviously, we should also consider the millions of workers who made the many middle passages, and in particular the slave trade of Africans that passed through different forms of 'mediation' (Christopher et al, 2007). Further, as Bosma et al (2012: 6) note 'labour recruiters were also a widespread phenomenon before the rise of industrial capitalism'.

[30] The recruitment industry in this case is characterized by different kinds of actors: small and medium-sized agencies regularly registered and licenced and with ethical recruitment practices; small and medium-sized agencies without proper registration and licence; subagents or brokers with and without registration and licence; social networks based on family members, relatives, friends, and other village members; sponsors (such as the *kafalas* regime in GCC countries) and agents in destination countries (Martin, 2017; Wickramasekara and Baruah, 2017).

[31] 'After the First World War, the ILO tried to create standards for the recruitment of foreign workers. In the 1920s and 1930s, attempts were made to take stock of how many people moved in order to find work' (Schrover, 2018: 453).

[32] As Wadauer et al (2012: 189) note, 'job placement should be examined as a field of relations between state policies (enacted by local, provincial, and federal levels of state authority), trade unions, employers, philanthropists, scholars, commercially run agencies, and – if nothing else – job seekers'.

[33] Although the ILO Private Employment Agencies Convention 181/1997 prohibited charging workers with fees, this system is largely the rule. To migrate to some GCC countries, Bangladeshi and Pakistani migrants pay the highest fees, accounting

approximately for six to nine months' wages, Egyptians about five months' wages, Indians two to three months' wages, and Filipinos one month's wage (Martin, 2017).

[34] In the case of skilled workers, intermediaries can be paid only by the employer or the governments, without any charge for workers, as in the case of skilled workers placed in the EU and US, where fees for employers and governments can be up US$10,000 for each worker (Gammeltoft-Hansen and Sorensen, 2013).

Chapter 3

[1] US investment abroad started in the 1950s. Tracing the history of mobile capital across advanced and emerging economies since the 1960s in the form of foreign direct investments (FDIs), and their directionality in relation to ongoing and successive immigration flows, Saskia Sassen (1990) focussed on East Asian migrations to the US between the 1970s and 1980s, successfully showing how the movement of migrants can be seen as a direct response to the arrival of FDIs in these countries.

[2] To avoid Brazil's high tariff barriers, Foxconn opened new plants in this high ICT consumer population; producing in Brazil also gives Foxconn preferential access to Mercosur markets such as Argentina, Paraguay, and Uruguay.

[3] See, for instance, the work of Michele Ford (2019) on the role of global unions and temporary migration in East Asia.

[4] We are aware of the limitation of focusing on two main dimensions of social difference to understand intersection with others (migration status, age, disability, North-South divisions) as a partial rendering of social phenomena, but we chose to focus on processes of racialization and genderization here as they have more effective explanatory power in this context, that is, for the specific purpose of understanding the differentiation of mobility across and through the labour process in EPZs and (migrant) precarious employment settings more broadly.

[5] According to Silver (2003), labour market segmentation (actuated by capital), is coupled with limitations to citizenship (imposed by the states), and with the formation of exclusive identities based on differences other than class, such as race and gender (see also Bonacich et al, 2008).

[6] Obviously, workplaces need to be considered in continuity with local and national contexts hosting them; so, the 'manufacturing of race' at the point of production has to be understood in connection with phenomena of race formation in the public space and with broader political orientation in managing migration and labour markets (see also Piro and Sacchetto, 2021).

[7] In any case, the first modern free zone is often considered the Shannon Free Zone in Ireland, established in 1959.

[8] FIAS (2008) estimates that the share in exports of manufactured goods in free zones constituted 40.8 per cent of all world exports.

[9] As Bonfiglioli (2020) stresses on the basis of oral history interviews with former women workers at the Arena knitwear factory in Pula (Croatia), while in socialist Yugoslavia, female industrial workers participated in the discourses and practices of workers' self-management, despite their hard work and their low wages, the post-socialist transition poses a challenge to the values, ways of life, and worldviews of these women.

[10] However, it should be noted that the migrations of Mexicans to the northern border pre-date the maquila programme, and that some of those employed in the *maquilas* had already experienced migration to the US, hence we cannot trace linear patterns of transnational migration as a movement from A to B even when we use concepts such as onward or multinational migrations (see Chapters 1 and 4).

[11] Sexist discourses and practices have crystallized on a cultural level in a term widely used in the northern border area of Mexico's Free Zone to define these female

workers as *maquilocas*, a derogatory adjective made up of the words *maquiladora* (manufacturing) and *loca* (mad), full of stigmatizing sexual and moral connotations because *loca* is used also as a synonym for prostitute or unfaithful woman (Sánchez and Ravelo, 2010: 20).

[12] The case of Mexico is exemplar: in the 1980s, while in the Mexican manufacturing sector as a whole the average duration of employment was 15 years, in Mexico's EPZs the duration was on average five years (Williams and Passe-Smith, 1989: 7; Peña, 1997).

[13] As a factory manager reported: 'Before we deducted their salary, their wages, but now we don't deduct. It's many things we have changed to do more incentives for them (...) to make them motivated and happy to stay working with us' (Brown, 2019: 451).

[14] On this topic see also Boeri et al (2022).

Chapter 4

[1] The truck system is a way of paying workers' wages by means other than money, usually vouchers or chits spendable only at a company store, where commodities are often overvalued. In other cases, the so-called truck-system consists of making it 'obligatory for the employee to buy with his (her) wage-income those consumer goods which the employer offers for sale' (van der Linden, 2008: 29). The Truck Act of 1831 in Great Britain was designed to eliminate the truck system. However, this practice remains widespread in different countries and includes several practices. For Brazil see, for example, Issa, 2017.

[2] In the 1920s and 1930s, farmers in the southern US preferred Mexican workers because they didn't settle, as Chinese and Japanese did, and they could be hosted in employer-owned housing where they could be better controlled (Guerin-Gonzales, 1994).

[3] Maintaining a piece of land in the country of origin for an internal migrant in India provides a form of subsidy for capital in the urban temporary residence, who can rely on the migrant ability to reproduce itself by falling back on the rural household, but it is also a survival strategy by migrant workers who cannot rely on permanency at work (see Mezzadri, 2021).

[4] As an Algerian emigrant to France says: 'I send a postal order and I ask them to send me accounts, to tell me how they have spent the money ... I know what they need ... 100,000 [old] francs every three months, that's their 'due', that's enough, unless there are exceptional expenses' (Sayad, 2004: 70).

[5] Critically 'Women migrant workers testing positive for STIs are also deported, on the basis that they are no longer fit to work' (Miles et al, 2022: 1681).

[6] Migration policy as a population management is after all a requisite that continues to characterize many immigration systems around the world and is particularly common in the case of temporary workers' schemes.

[7] According to Faist (2006: 3) 'Terms such as transnational social spaces, transnational social fields or transnational social formations usually refer to sustained ties of geographically mobile persons, networks and organizations across the borders across multiple nation-states.'

[8] Even just the possibility of finding fresh Mexican vegetables at the local market and the ability to maintain and nourish their religious practices with the rest of their community are critical sources of cultural and material survival in a foreign environment for Latinos and Latinas in North Carolina (Cravey, 2004: 191).

[9] In their research on the female children of immigrants in Italy, Frisina and Hawthorne (2018) highlights how they use aesthetics and the female body in struggles for social and legal recognition.

[10] This experience is reported also among Romanian workers in the agriculture sector of southern Italy (Piro, 2021).

[11] Gwyneth Lonergan (2015) stresses how migrant women considered 'undesirable' in the UK are often dissuaded from having children, while having to demonstrate to be self-sufficient

and well-integrated if they want to receive any state support. These dynamics appear to follow the same logic of applying the notion of deservingness as a way to justify migrants' exclusion from any type of social assistance (Chauvin et al, 2013).

[12] This follows a similar logic to the one identified in the working of the 'workfare system' more broadly, see Peck (2003); Greer (2016).

[13] http://europa.eu/rapid/press-release_MEMO-16-467_en.htm

Chapter 5

[1] Simon Goeke (2014: 168, 176) underlines that West Germany unions were worried that migrants could be infiltrated by communists and they would be politically active in Germany. However, unions appreciated migrants' activities against the regime back in their homeland, as in the case of Greek, Spanish, and Portuguese migrants.

[2] According to Virdee (2014), only by looking at the ways in which racialized outsiders publicly shared and articulated the experience of oppression, exploitation, and struggles abroad and at home is it possible to explain the forms of working-class radicalization in Britain. In essence, activists, in particular freed slaves of African descent who migrated from the colonies to the imperial motherland, critically contributed to building links between working-class radicalism and the campaign to abolish slavery in the British Empire.

[3] Schmalz et al (2018: 119) finds it useful to further classify worker power forms into 'institutional power', using legally fixed rights to claim entitlements, and societal power, when workers gain strength through cooperating with other actors. Gallas (2018) in contrast highlights the risks of turning 'class power' into compartmentalized worker/organizational capacities that disrupt the notion of intrinsically asymmetric relations of power between labour and capital, and the antagonist essence of class struggle.

[4] However, the literature has also demonstrated some positive examples of posted and temporary workers organized through unions or developing collective action even under their temporary and posted condition (see Chapter 3 and Arnholtz and Lillie, 2020).

[5] Assessing the importance of mobility bargaining and its link to exit, Strauss and McGrath (2017: 204) highlight the fact that its relevance emerges precisely as it appears constrained by the institutionalization of forms of unfree labour relations endogenous to precarious migrant status: via tying international migrants to an employer (or to employment more generally), and through time restrictions to their permits, migrants are limited in their 'ability to exit the employment relations in a tight labour market' or use the labour market to negotiate better conditions (Strauss and McGrath, 2017: 204).

[6] As Eric Hobsbawm (1951: 299) highlighted: 'The story of nineteenth-century labour is one of movement and migration'. The constitutions of the early national unions required local secretaries to furnish reports on the conditions of the trade in their area and assist travelling members in finding jobs. Some unions even had 'travelling loan systems', which gave members money to finance a search for work if none was to be found near home.

[7] 'During and after the war came massive, militant strikes, concentrated in one of the largest waves in US history between 1917 and 1922. In the year after the end of the war alone a staggering four million workers struck' (Roediger and Esch, 2012: 175-6).

[8] While the Great Migration of African Americans moving from rural areas and towns of the South, and arriving in the larger cities of the North-east and Midwest, were looking for the so-called Second Emancipation (Sernett, 1997), the US government started to state immigration restrictions.

[9] However, the controversy was not only about race versus class, but also about methodological approaches to the of study of racism and inter-racialism inside unions, whereby the New Labour History of which Gutman was one prominent voice, also considered micro histories and biographies.

[10] As stated in the well-known Article II of the Constitution of the IWW (1905): 'It is the aim of the IWW to build world-wide working-class solidarity. The IWW therefore actively opposes bigotry and discrimination on and off the job. No wage or salaried worker shall be excluded from the IWW or barred from holding union office because of race, ethnicity, sex, nationality, creed, disability, sexual orientation, or conviction and charges history.'

[11] As also reported by one of the radical Black magazines of the time, *The Messenger*, Local 8 was the only integrated union in the country with a biracial system of rotation, where every month an African American president was assisted by a White vice, to then reverse the pattern the following month (Kimeldorf, 1999: 39).

[12] Solidarity on the docks was indeed fragile: with an unusual economic downturn and the outward attack of hostile employers – who mass-sacked striking workers on the Philadelphia Waterfront in 1915, using Black workers from the South as strikebreakers to divide the organizing dock workers – the IWW had to learn the hard lesson of interracial conflicts on the docks as violent riots erupted among the workers towards the end of the decade, eventually leading to the disunity of Black and White workers on the Waterfront and the defeat of the IWW more broadly (although parts of its syndicalist practice and focus on job control remains in the much more conservative AFL) (Kimeldorf, 1999).

[13] For a wider discussion on unions' ambivalent stance towards temporary programmes in the US, see Ness (2011).

[14] For an example of union ambivalence towards migration during the Brexit Referendum, see also Fitzgerald et al (2022).

[15] It was recognized that unions usually tended to be aligned with the choices of their government about when and how to open their borders to new accession countries' migrants with lower wages. Indeed unions tended to either be in favour of gradual transitions or immediate opening of their labour market to workers from the new member states, as mobility was beneficial to the extent that it did not undermine local workers conditions (Hyland, in Marino et al, 2017a; see also Crawford, 2020). The fact that the European Court of Justice has delivered some critical decisions in favour of economic freedoms at the expenses of the 'social dimension' of the EU single market has increased industrial relations scholars' scepticism towards the ability of the Europeanization process to avoid deepening inequalities (for example, Woolfson et al (2010) on the Laval case limiting collective bargaining rights and industrial action in the name of freedom of services in Sweden).

[16] In countries like the UK and Ireland, where the unions initially failed to oppose the lack of transitional measures at the time of the enlargement, it was the later austerity crisis and the attack on working conditions, but also the parallel health and housing crises, that led to increasing hostility towards migrant labour from the EU specifically (culminating with the Brexit vote of 2016). While the Trades Union Congress (TUC), the umbrella organization bringing together most unions in the UK, adopted a (weak) Remain position in the referendum, they also 'flirted' with the notion that free movement has been among the causes for employers' ability to push down wages and conditions.

[17] The 'opportunity structures' for migrant organizing and the relative effectiveness of the intervention of the GUFs, encouraging local unions to develop work on migration, vary greatly according to the diversity and political landscape of each country: from semi-authoritarian governments such as Malaysia, Singapore, and Thailand to more liberal and more democratic ones like Japan (Ford, 2019). This means that while the GUFs may develop a comprehensive strategy across the region to encourage local unions to integrate and organize migrant (temporary) workers, ultimately *the national context* and the identity of the individual unions will determine the actual level of engagement.

[18] In contrast, industrial relations research on union efforts to integrate temporary migrant workers from outside the EU is extremely scarce and often rather workplace or country based.

[19] In the recent special issue by Gumbrell-McCormick and Hyman (2020), the action of unions in challenging migrant inferior conditions and divisions in the workforce has been tackled, considering important questions of workforce segmentation and opportunities for cross-border organizing, but without considering any issues related to race, gender, and migration status intersections as barriers to mobilization.

[20] See for instance James and Karmowska (2012) on the experience of attempts at creating a Polish migrants branch in the UK.

[21] In this context, migrant women develop a specific form of political subjectivity highly 'entwined in a critique of the global', where they 'come to see themselves ... as global labourers whose voices belong and deserve to be heard in public spaces that reach beyond their household workplaces' (Constable, 2009: 161).

[22] On the multiethnic nature of grass-roots migrant organization in Hong Kong, see also Hsia (2009).

[23] Despite its similarities with Thailand in terms of the large numbers of irregular migrant workers, limited industrial relations, and one of the most restrictive immigration regimes in the region, the IndustriAll organizing drive in the electronics industry in 2010 (although not limited to migrants per se but rather aimed to reinvigorate the union as a whole) led to important outcomes, such as successful collective bargaining agreements that included migrant workers and organized more than 900 workers at electronics multinational companies (Ford, 2019: 145).

[24] See also Atzeni and Ness (2018) for a wider perspective on the return of independent rank and file unions not only in the US but also in South America and internationally.

[25] There is an important reversal of the gaze here from movements of solidarity towards migrants to political movements led by migrants' own subjectivity, which in turn finds its roots in the migrant-led struggles and protests started since the 1990s, such as the sans-papier in France, where racialized migrants and the children of migrants have highlighted the role of migration laws in shaping the particular forms of segregation and racialization experienced by migrants as second-class citizens or permanent aliens. On anti-racist practices in Italy, see Frisina and Hawthorne (2018).

[26] It is worth noting that the 1974 wildcat strike by Asian workers at Imperial Typewriters, and the Grunwick strike of 1976–78 ended with the abandonment of the grievances concerning Asian and Caribbean workers by the official unions. In this context, Sivanandan wonders bitterly whether better outcomes would have been achieved if migrant workers 'would have done better to rely on the Black community and Black organizations for their support than to look to the trade unions – who finally betrayed them' (Sivanandan, 1990: 85).

[27] This notion of community is to be differentiated from that of community unionism, where it is other actors away from the workplace, such as faith-based groups and civil society organizations, that organize workers instead of unions (for example, Wills and Simms, 2004; Stewart et al, 2009).

Conclusion

[1] In this regard, it is important to notice another theoretical difference between Xiang and Lindquist's understanding of migration infrastructures and Shire's one: while the former draw from an actor–network framework where migrants' infrastructures and networks become in a way self-sustaining and self-serving (Xiang and Lindquist, 2014: 124), Shire's (2020: 438) approach to economic sociology emphasize the politics of labour controls. It is indeed both the 'voluntary and competitive nature of markets'

that produce instability in the system of cross-border mobility of labour, and that makes this process inherently political and based on unresolved 'heterogeneous interests and power imbalances'.

2 As discussed in the debate about segmented labour markets in Chapter 1, national actors/social partners may agree to a certain level of labour mobility where the role of migrant labour's inferior status in a context of relatively regulated free movement may still reproduce forms of privileges and 'shielding' of labour protection for the other half (Erne and Imboden, 2015).

3 For example, see the debate about the dual position of temporary migrants in the context of labour shortages, between 'the need for essential labour' and the 'threat of mobile people' (Deneva, 2021); for a wider picture on the politics of mobility during pandemic times in similar sectors but various regions, see also Tagliacozzo et al (2021) and Paul (2020).

4 Dormitories become a source of information where rights and power arise from the information network shaped by workers themselves: as 'disseminators of information, the dormitories may be acting as de facto unions' (Smyth et al, 2013: 403).

5 This emphasis on the socially constructed nature of skills is also important because it is critical of the use of skills categories in migration policy and academic research (Liu-Farrer et al, 2021). Diverse actors are indeed involved in the making, identification, and evaluation of migrant skills, which remain contested and contextualized. Skills are constantly constructed and reconstructed in the labour market alongside their value, and as McGovern (2020) suggests, the actual skills put to work in the workplace are often learned on the job in a tacit way.

6 Regarding the question of deskilling, we are not arguing that this phenomenon may not be still prevalent, especially in the migrant section of the workforce. Deskilling occurred for instance in the case of the Bangladeshi-Italians that moved to the UK following the economic crisis and increasing racism in Italy in the late 2000s; and yet at the same time their ability to engage in forms of onward or multinational migration has actually increased thanks to the existence of first and second generation postcolonial Bangladeshi migrant communities in the UK and extended transnational networks (Morad et al, 2021).

7 It is not coincidence that in a country like the UK, impacted by both Brexit and COVID-19 crises in the same period of time, the results are still visible in the persistent shortages of skills and labour in migrant-reliant sectors as well as the growing rates of 'inactive' population who are not even looking for work often due to worsening health conditions (for example, Long Covid), but de facto refusing to stay or return to low-paying and intensive jobs (ONS 2022).

8 For example, in the infamous Lindsey Refinery dispute, the slogan 'British jobs for British workers' was highlighted in the media as fostering a sense of divisions between indigenous and migrant workers, while in fact it had been initially used by right-wing parties, then reused by Prime Minister Brown, and then reused by some of the rank and files in protest against overly exploited Italian and Portuguese contractors (see Ince et al, 2015).

9 The same author, interested in the impact of the East European enlargement of the EU on industrial relations and migration, noticed in fact that in 2007, strike levels in a country like Poland and other new member states increased, in contrast to declining industrial action in the old members (Carley, 2008, cited in Meardi, 2012b: 105).

10 Greer et al (2013) have looked at the individual case of the 'European migrant workers branch' set up by the German construction union IG BAU, describing the difficulties that the European migrant branch has encountered, such as the unilateral nature of the initiative causing criticism from Polish construction unions. While this experiment was only partially successful – critically also because of the lack of buy-in from Polish

unions – solidarity and cross-border support and even common action did develop between Polish and German unions.

[11] See for instance Milkman (2000) on the advantage of the Latino and Latina's experience of collectivism that informed the wave of organizing in California.

[12] For international examples of cross-border labour organizing in response of the globalization of capital, see Silver (2003) and McCallum (2013).

[13] Tying the juridical status of migrant workers to membership of trade union organizations operating transnationally (substituting for the tie with the employer sponsor) is the central mechanism proposed by Gordon (2006) already in the 2000s, alongside the principle that it is through worker organizing, rather than solely government enforcement of minimum labour standards, that migrants' conditions can be protected and downward pressure on local workers avoided.

References

Ackroyd, S. and Thompson, P. (1999) *Organizational Misbehaviour*, London: Sage.

Adler, L.H., Tapia, M., and Turner, L. (eds) (2014) *Mobilizing Against Inequality: Unions, Immigrant Workers, and the Crisis of Capitalism*, Ithaca: Cornell University Press.

Afonso, A. (2017) 'Freer labour markets, more rules? How transnational labour mobility can strengthen collective bargaining', in J.E. Dølvik and L. Eldring (eds) *Labour Mobility in the Enlarged Single European Market*, Bingley UK Emerald Group Publishing Limited, pp 159–82.

Afonso, A. and Devitt, C. (2016) 'Comparative political economy and international migration', *Socio-Economic Review*, 14(3): 591–613.

Aglietta, M. (2001) *A Theory of Capitalist Regulation: The US Experience* [1979], London: Verso.

Alamgir, A.K. (2014) 'Recalcitrant women: internationalism and the redefinition of welfare limits in the Czechoslovak-Vietnamese labor exchange program', *Slavic Review*, 73(1): 133–55.

Alberti, G. (2011) Transient Working Lives: Migrant Women's Everyday Politics in London's Hospitality Industry, unpublished PhD thesis, Cardiff University.

Alberti, G. (2014) 'Mobility strategies, "mobility differentials" and "transnational exit": the experiences of precarious migrants in London's hospitality jobs', *Work, Employment and Society*, 28(6): 865–81.

Alberti, G. (2016) 'A new status for migrant workers: restrictions of the free movement of labour in the EU', *Mondi Migranti*, 3: 33–49.

Alberti, G. (2017) 'The government of migration through workfare in the UK: towards a shrinking space of mobility and social rights?', *Movements. Journal for Critical Migration and Border Regime Studies*, 3(1): 1–19.

Alberti, G. (2019) 'The expansion of the labour market and the politics of migration', in G. Gall (ed) *The Politics of Labour Work and Employment*, Cheltenham/Northampton: Edward Elgar.

Alberti, G. and Danaj, S. (2017) 'Posting and agency work in British construction and hospitality: the role of regulation in differentiating the experiences of migrants', *The International Journal of Human Resource Management*, 28(21): 1–24.

Alberti, G. and Però, D. (2018) 'Migrating industrial relations: migrant workers' initiative within and outside trade unions', *British Journal of Industrial Relations*, 56(4): 693–715.

Alberti, G. and Iannuzzi, F.E. (2020) 'Embodied intersectionality and the intersectional management of hotel labour: the everyday experiences of social differentiation in customer-oriented work', *Gender, Work & Organization*, 27(6): 1165–80.

Alberti, G. and Cutter, J. (2022) 'Labour migration policy post-Brexit: The contested meaning of regulation by old and new actors', *Industrial Relations Journal*, 53(5): 430–45.

Alberti, G., Holgate, J. and Tapia, M. (2013) 'Organising migrants as workers or as migrant workers? Intersectionality, trade unions and precarious work', *The International Journal of Human Resource Management*, 24(22): 4132–48.

Alberti, G., Sacchetto, D., and Vianello, F.A. (2017) 'Spazio e tempo nei processi produttivi e riproduttivi', *Sociologia del lavoro*, 146: 7–23.

Alberti, G., Bessa, I., Hardy, K., Trappmann, V., and Umney, C. (2018) 'In, against and beyond precarity: work in insecure times', *Work, Employment & Society*, 32(3): 447–57.

Alesina, A., Glaeser, E., and Glaeser, E.L. (2004) *Fighting Poverty in the US and Europe: A World of Difference*, Oxford: Oxford University Press.

Alexander, M. (1917) 'The cost of labor turnover', *Bulletin of the U.S. Bureau of Labor Statistics*, 227: 13–27.

Alho, R. and Sippola, M. (2019) 'Estonian migrants' aspiration for social citizenship in Finland: embracing the Finnish welfare state and distancing from the "non-deserving"', *Journal of International Migration and Integration*, 20(2): 341–59.

Al-Maskari, F., Shah, S.M., Al-Sharhan, R., Al-Haj, E., Al-Kaabi, K., Khonji, D., Schneider, J.D., Nagelkerke, N.J., and Bernsen, R.M. (2011) 'Prevalence of depression and suicidal behaviors among male migrant workers in United Arab Emirates', *Journal of Immigrant and Minority Health*, 13: 1027–32.

Ambrosini, M. (2018) *Irregular Immigration in Southern Europe. Actors, Dynamics and Governance*, Cham: Palgrave Macmillan.

Amelina, A. and Faist T. (2012) 'De-naturalizing nation states in research methodologies: key concepts of transnational studies in migration', *Ethnic and Racial Studies*, 35(10): 1707–24.

Anderson, B. (2010) 'Migration, immigration controls and the fashioning of precarious workers', *Work, Employment and Society*, 24(2): 300–17.

Anderson, B. (2013) *Us and Them? The Dangerous Politics of Immigration Control*, Oxford: Oxford University Press.

Anderson, B. (2017) 'Towards a new politics of migration?', *Ethnic and Racial Studies*, 40(9): 1527–37.

Anderson, B. and Davidson, J.O.C. (2004) *Trafficking – a Demand Led Problem?*, Stockholm: Save the Children Sweden.

Anderson, B. and Hughes, V. (eds) (2015) *Citizenship and its Others*, Basingstoke: Palgrave Macmillan.

Anderson, B., Sharma, N., and Wright, C. (2009) 'Why no borders?', *Refuge*, 26(2): 5–18.

Andors, P. (1988) 'Women and work in Shenzhen', *Bulletin of Concerned Asian Scholars*, 20(3): 22–41.

Andrijasevic, R. and Sacchetto, D. (2016) 'From labour migration to labour mobility? The return of the multinational worker in Europe', *Transfer: European Review of Labour and Research*, 22(2): 219–31.

Andrijasevic, R. and Sacchetto, D. (2017) 'Disappearing workers': Foxconn in Europe and the changing role of temporary work agencies', *Work, Employment and Society*, 31(1): 54–70.

Andrijasevic, R. and Novitz, T. (2020) 'Supply chains and unfree labor: regulatory failure in the case of Samsung Electronics in Slovakia, *Journal of Human Trafficking*, 6(2): 195–208.

Andrijasevic, R., Pun, N., and Sacchetto, D. (2020) 'One firm, two countries, one workplace model? The case of Foxconn's internationalization', *The Economic and Labour Relations Review*, 31(2): 262–78.

Andrikopoulos, A. and Duyvendak, J.W. (2020) 'Migration, mobility and the dynamics of kinship: new barriers, new assemblages', *Ethnography*, 21(3): 299–318.

Arnholtz, J. and Refslund, B. (2019) 'Active enactment and virtuous circles of employment relations: how Danish unions organised the transnationalised Copenhagen Metro construction project', *Work, Employment and Society*, 33(4): 682–99.

Arnholtz, J. and Lillie, N. (eds) (2020) *Posted Work in the European Union*, London: Routledge.

Aroca, P. (2001) 'Impacts and development in local economies based on mining: the case of the Chilean II region', *Resources Policy*, 27(2): 119–34.

Arruzza, C. (2016) 'Functionalist, determinist, reductionist: social reproduction feminism and its critics', *Science & Society*, 80(1): 9–30.

Atzeni, M. (2016) 'Beyond trade unions' strategy? The social construction of precarious workers organizing in the city of Buenos Aires', *Labor History*, 57(2): 193–214.

Atzeni, M. and Ness, I. (eds) (2018) *Global Perspectives on Workers' and Labour Organizations*, Berlin: Springer.

Atzeni, M., and Sacchetto, D. (2023) 'Locating labour conflict and its organising forms in contemporary times: between class and the reproduction of capitalism', *Global Labour Journal*, 14(3): 207-19.

Axelsson, L., Hedberg, C., Pettersson, N., and Zhang, Q. (2022) 'Re-visiting the 'black box' of migration: state-intermediary co-production of regulatory spaces of labour migration', *Journal of Ethnic and Migration Studies*, 48(3): 594–612.

Azmeh, S. (2014) 'Labour in global production networks: workers in the qualifying industrial zones (QIZs) of Egypt and Jordan', *Global Networks*, 14(4): 495–513.

Babar, Z. (2017) *Arab Migrant Communities in the GCC: Media and Politics in the Wake of the Arab Uprisings*, Oxford: Oxford University Press.

Babar, Z. (2021) 'Purveyors of dreams: labour recruiters in the Pakistan to Saudi Arabia migration corridor', *Migration and Development*, 10(1): 68–85.

Bach, N. (2011) 'Modernity and the urban imagination in economic zones', *Theory, Culture, and Society*, 28(5): 98–122.

Bada, X. and Gleeson, S. (2020) 'Transnational networks for portable migrant labor rights in North America', in D. Dijkzeul and M. Fauser (eds) *Diaspora Organizations in International Affairs*, London: Routlegde, pp 43–63.

Baglioni, E., Campling, L., Coe, N.M., and Smith, A. (2022) 'Introduction: Labour Regime and Global Production', in E. Baglioni, L. Campling, N.M. Coe, and A. Smith (eds) *Labour Regime and Global Production*, Newcastle: Agenda Publishing, pp 1–28.

Bakker, I. and Silvey, R. (2008) 'Introduction: Social reproduction and global transformations from the everyday to the global' in I. Bakker and R. Silvey (eds) *Beyond States and Markets: The Challenges of Social Reproduction*, London: Routledge, pp 1–16.

Bakker, I. and Gill, S. (2019) 'Rethinking power, production, and social reproduction: towards variegated social reproduction', *Capital and Class*, 43(4): 503–23.

Bakker, L., Dagevos, J., and Engbersen, G. (2017) 'Explaining the refugee gap: a longitudinal study on labour market participation of refugees in the Netherlands', *Journal of Ethnic and Migration Studies*, 43(11): 1775–91.

Bal, C.S. (2016) *Production Politics and Migrant Labour Regimes*, New York: Palgrave Macmillan.

Baldamus, W.G. (1961) *Efficiency and Effort*, London: Tavistock.

Baldassar, L. and Merla, L. (2014) 'Introduction: Transnational family caregiving through the lens of circulation', in L. Baldassar and L. Merla (eds) *Transnational Families, Migration and the Circulation of Care: Understanding Mobility and Absence in Family Life*, London: Routledge, pp 3–24.

Balibar, E. (1974) *Cinq Études du Matérialisme historique*, Paris: Maspéro.

Balibar, E. (2004) *We, the People of Europe? Reflections on Transnational Citizenship*, Princeton: Princeton University Press.

Barcella, P. (2012) '*Venuti qui per cercare lavoro'. Gli emigrati italiani nella Svizzera del secondo dopoguerra*, Bellinzona: Fondazione Pellegrini Canevascini.

Barot, R. and Bird, J. (2001) 'Racialization: the genealogy and critique of a concept', *Ethnic and Racial Studies*, 24(4): 601–18.

Bartel, A. and Borjas, G. (1981) 'Wage growth and job turnover: An empirical analysis', in S. Rosen (ed) *Studies in Labor Markets*, Chicago: University of Chicago Press, pp 65–90.

Bates, B. (2012) *The Making of Black Detroit in the Age of Henry Ford*, Chapel Hill, NC: University of North Carolina Press.

Bauder, H. (2006) *Labor Movement. How Migration Regulates Labor Markets*, New York: Oxford University Press.

Baxter-Reid, H. (2016) 'Buying into the 'good worker' rhetoric or being as good as they need to be? The effort bargaining process of new migrant workers', *Human Resource Management Journal*, 26(3): 337–50.

Baxter-Reid, H. (2021) 'Developing mobility power tactics and strategies: the experiences of Central Eastern European workers in Scotland', *Employee Relations*, 44(1): 244–58.

Benvegnù, C. (2018) Nelle officine della circolazione: un'etnografia del lavoro logistico tra il Grand Paris e la metropoli diffusa veneta, PhD thesis, University of Padova.

Benvegnù, C., Haidinger, B. and Sacchetto, D. (2018) 'Restructuring labour relations and employment in the European logistics sector. Unions' responses to a segmented workforce', in V. Doellgast, N. Lillie, and V. Pugliano (eds) *Reconstructing Solidarity. Labour Unions, Precarious Work, and the Politics of Institutional Change in Europe*, Oxford: Oxford University Press, pp 83–104.

Benvegnù, C., Gaborieau, D., and Tranchant, L. (2022) 'Fragmented but widespread microconflicts: current limits and future possibilities for organizing precarious workers in the French logistics sector', *New Global Studies*, 16(1): 69–90.

Bernaciak, M. (2015) 'Introduction: social dumping and the EU integration process', in M. Bernaciak (ed) *Market Expansion and Social Dumping in Europe*, London: Routledge, pp 1–22.

Berntsen, L. (2016) 'Reworking labour practices: on the agency of unorganized mobile migrant construction workers', *Work, Employment and Society*, 30(3): 472–88.

Berntsen, L. and Lillie, N. (2016) 'Hyper-mobile migrant workers and Dutch trade union representation strategies at the Eemshaven construction sites', *Economic and Industrial Democracy*, 37(1): 171–87.

Beynon, H. (1973) *Working for Ford*, London: Penguin Books.

Beynon, H. and Austrin, T. (1994) *Masters and Men*. London: Rivers Oram.

Bhattacharyya, G. (2018) *Rethinking Racial Capitalism: Questions of Reproduction and Survival*, London: Rowman and Littlefield.

Bickerton, C.J. (2019) 'The limits of differentiation: capitalist diversity and labour mobility as drivers of Brexit', *Comparative European Politics*, 17(2): 231–45.

Blustein, D.L. (2006). *The Psychology of Working: A New Perspective for Career Development, Counseling, and Public Policy*. Lawrence Erlbaum: Mahwah, NJ.

Bigo, D. and Guild, E. (2005) *Controlling Frontiers: Free Movement into and Within Europe*, Aldershot: Ashgate.

Birke, P. and Bluhm, F. (2020) 'Migrant labour and workers' struggles: the German meatpacking industry as contested terrain', *Global Labour Journal*, 10(1): 34–51.

Blackett, O.W. (1928) *Factory Labor Turnover in Michigan*, Ann Arbor: University of Michigan.

Bloch, A. (2013) 'The labour market experiences and strategies of young undocumented migrants', *Work, Employment and Society*, 27(2): 272–87.

Boeri, T., Garnero, A., and Luisetto, L.G. (2022) 'The use of non-compete agreements in the Italian labour market. Report prepared for the XXIV European Conference of the Fondazione Ing. Rodolfo Debenedetti, 12 September, Chioggia', *Fondazione Rodolfo Debenedetti*, [online], Available from: https://www.frdb.org/wp-content/uploads/2022/05/Summary_Garnero_et_al_ENG.pdf. Accessed April 2022,

Bogg, A. and Novitz, T. (2012) 'Investigating voice at work', *Comparative Labor Law & Policy Journal*, 33(3): 323–54.

Bojadžjev, M. (2008) *Die windige Internationale. Rassismus und Kämpfe der Migration*, Münster: Westfälisches Dampfboot.

Bojadžjev, M. and Karakayali, S. (2007) 'Autonomie der Migration: 10 Thesen zu einer Methode', in Transit Migration Forschungsgruppe (ed) *Turbulente Ränder. Neue Perspektiven auf Migration an den Grenzen Europas*, Bielefeld: Transcript, pp 203–9.

Bojadžijev, M., Karakayali, S., and Tsianos, V. (2004) 'Das Gespenst der Migration. Krise des Nationalstaats und Autonomie der Migration', *Fantômas*, 5: 24–7.

Bojadžjev, M., Karakayali, S., and Tsianos, V. (2004) 'L'enigma dell'arrivo', in S. Mezzadra (ed) *I confini della libertà. Per un'analisi politica delle migrazioni contemporanee*, Roma: DeriveApprodi, pp 125–41.

Bolt, M. (2015) *Zimbabwe's Migrants and South Africa's Border Farms. The Roots of Impermanence*, Cambridge: Cambridge University Press.

Bolt, E.E.T., Winterton, J., and Cafferkey, K. (2022) 'A century of labour turnover research: A systematic literature review', *International Journal of Management Reviews*, 24(4): 555–76.

Bonacich, E.M., Alimahomed, S., and Wilson, J.B. (2008) 'The racialization of global labor', *American Behavioral Scientist*, 52(3): 342–55.

Bonefeld, W. and Holloway, J. (eds) (1995) *Global Capital, National State and the Politics of Money*, New York: St. Martin's Press.

Bonfiglioli, C. (2020) 'Post-socialist deindustrialisation and its gendered structure of feeling: the devaluation of women's work in the Croatian garment industry', *Labor History*, 61(1): 36–47.

Bosma, U., van Nederveen Meerkerk, E., and Sarkar, A. (2012) 'Mediating labour: an introduction', *International Review of Social History*, 57(S20): 1–15.

Boston, S. (1987) *Women Workers and the Trade Unions*, London: Lawrence & Wishart.

Bourdieu, P. (2004) 'Preface', in A. Sayad *The Suffering of the Immigrant*, Cambridge: Polity Press, pp xi–xiv.

Brah, A. (1993) '"Race" and "culture" in the gendering of labour markets: South Asian young Muslim women and the labour market', *New Community* (19)3: 441–458.

Brah, A. (2005) *Cartographies of Diaspora: Contesting Identities*, London: Routledge.

Braverman, H. (1974) *Labor and Monopoly Capital: The Degradation of Work in the Twentieth Century*, London: Monthly Review Press.

Breen, T.H. (1973) 'A changing labor force and race relations in Virginia 1660–1710', *Journal of Social History*, 7(1): 3–25.

Breman, J. (1990) *Labour Migration and Rural Transformation in Colonial Asia*, Amsterdam: Comparative Asian Studies, Free University Press.

Breman, J. and Van der Linden, M. (2014) 'Informalizing the economy: the return of the social question at a global level', *Development and Change*, 45(5): 920–40.

Brenner, N. (1998) 'Between fixity and motion: accumulation, territorial organization and the historical geography of spatial scales', *Environment and Planning D: Society and Space*, 16(4): 459–81.

Brenner, N. and Theodore, N. (2002) 'Cities and geographies of "actually existed neoliberalism"', *Antipode*, 34(3): 349–79.

Brinton, M.C. (1993) *Women and the Economic Miracle: Gender and Work in Post War Japan*, Berkeley and Los Angeles: University of California Press.

Brissenden, P.F. and Frankel, E. (1922) *Labor Turnover in Industry: A Statistical Analysis*, New York: Macmillan Company.

Brown, J.A. (2019) 'Territorial (in) coherence: labour and special economic zones in Laos's border manufacturing', *Antipode*, 51(2): 438–57.

Brown, D. and McIntosh, S. (2000) 'Job satisfaction and labour turnover in the retail and hotel sectors', in W. Salverda, C. Lucifora, and B. Nolan (eds) *Policy Measures for Low-Wage Employment in Europe*, Cheltenham: Edward Elgar, pp 218–37.

Bruce, K. (2005) 'Magnus Alexander, the economists and the issue of labour turnover', *Business History*, 47(4): 493–510.

Bruslé, T. (2012) 'What kind of place is this? Daily life, privacy and the inmate metaphor in a Nepalese workers' labour camp (Qatar)', *South Asia Multidisciplinary Academic Journal*, 6: 1–29.

Buckley, C. (1995) 'The myth of managed migration: migration control and market in the Soviet period', *Slavic Review*, 54(4): 896–916.

Burawoy, M. (1976), 'The functions and reproduction of migrant labor: comparative material from Southern Africa and the United States', *American Journal of Sociology*, 81(5): 1050–87.

Burawoy, M. (1979) *Manufacturing Consent: Changes in the Labour Process under Monopoly Capitalism*, Chicago: University of Chicago Press.

Burawoy, M. (1985) *The Politics of Production*, London: Verso.

Burawoy, M., Burton, A., Ferguson, A.A., and Fox, K.J. (1991) *Ethnography Unbound: Power and Resistance in the Modern Metropolis*, Berkeley: University of California Press.

Çağlar, A. (2016) 'Still "migrants" after all those years: foundational mobilities, temporal frames and emplacement of migrants', *Journal of Ethnic and Migration Studies*, 42(6): 952–69.

Çağlar, A. and Glick Schiller, N. (2018) *Migrants and City-Making: Dispossession, Displacement, and Urban Regeneration*, Durham, NC and London: Duke University Press.

Calmfors, L., and Driffill, J. (1988) 'Bargaining structure, corporatism and macroeconomic performance', *Economic Policy*, 3(6): 13–61.

Campbell, C. (1993) 'Do firms pay efficiency wages? Evidence with data at the firm level', *Journal of Labor Economics*, 11(3): 442–70.

Čaněk, M. (2017) 'Trade unions and migration in the Czech Republic, 2004–15', in S. Marino, J. Roosblad and R. Penninx (eds) *Trade Unions and Migrant Workers*, Cheltenham: Edward Elgar Publishing, pp 307–27.

Caraway, T.L. (2007) *Assembling Women. The Feminization of Global Manufacturing*, New York: Cornell University Press.

Carley, M. (2008) *Industrial Relations Developments in Europe 2007*. Dublin: European Foundation for the Improvement of Working and Living Conditions.

Caro, E., Berntsen, L., Lillie, N., and Wagner, I. (2015) 'Posted migration and segregation in the European construction sector', *Journal of Ethnic and Migration Studies*, 41(10): 1600–20.

Carter, S.B. and Savoca, E. (1990) 'Labor mobility and lengthy jobs in nineteenth-century America', *Journal of Economic History*, 50(1): 1–16.

Cartosio, B. (ed) (2007) *Wobbly! L'Industrial Workers of the World e il suo tempo*, Milano: Shake.

Caruso, F. (2016) 'Dal caporalato alle agenzie di lavoro temporaneo: i braccianti rumeni nell'agricoltura mediterranea', *Mondi Migranti*, 1(3): 51–64.

Castles, S. (2004) 'Why migration policies fail', *Ethnic and Racial Studies*, 27(2): 205–27.

Castles, S. (2006) 'Guestworkers in Europe: a resurrection?', *International Migration Review*, 40(4): 741–66.

Castles, S. (2010) 'Understanding global migration: a social transformation perspective', *Journal of Ethnic and Migration Studies*, 36(10): 1565–86.

Castles, S. (2011) 'Migration, crisis, and the global labour market', *Globalizations*, 8(3): 311–24.

Castles, S. and Kosack, G. (1973) *Immigrant Workers and Class Structure in Western Europe*, London: Oxford University Press.

Castles, S. and Ozkul, D. (2014) 'Circular migration, triple win or a new label for temporary migration?' in G. Battistella (ed) *Global and Asian Perspectives on International Migration*, Switzerland: Springer International Publishing, pp 27–36.

Castles, S., Miller, M.J., and Ammendola, G. (2003) *The Age of Migration: International Population Movements in the Modern World*, New York: The Guilford Press.

Ceccagno, A. (2017) *City Making & Global Labor Regimes. Chinese Immigrants and Italy's Fast Fashion Industry*, Cham: Palgrave Macmillan.

Ceccagno, A. and Sacchetto, D. (2020) 'The mobility of workers living at work in Europe', *Current Sociology*, 68(3): 299–315.

Ceccagno, A. and Gao, R. (2022) 'The making of a skilled worker: the transnational mixed embeddedness of migrant workers', *Mobilities*, 18(2): 250–266.

Chan, A. (2011) 'Strikes in China export industries in comparative perspective', *The China Journal*, 65: 27–51.

Chan, J. and Selden, M. (2017) 'The labour politics of China's rural migrant workers', *Globalizations*, 14(2): 259–71.

Chan, J., Selden, M., and Pun, N. (2020) *Dying for an iPhone: Apple, Foxconn, and the Lives of China's Workers*, London: Pluto.

Chan, K.W. (2010) 'The global financial crisis and migrant workers in China: "there is no future as a labourer; returning to the village has no meaning"', *International Journal of Urban and Regional Research*, 34(3): 659–77.

Chan, K.W. and Buckingham, W. (2008) 'Is China abolishing the hukou system?', *The China Quarterly*, 195: 582–606. doi:10.1017/S0305741008000787.

Chant, S. and McIlwaine, C. (1995) *Women of a Lesser Cost: Female Labour, Foreign Exchange and Philippine Development*, London: Pluto Press.

Chapman B.J. and Prior, H. (1986) 'Sex differences in labour turnover in the Australian Public Service', *Economic Record*, 62(4): 497–505.

Chauvin, S., Garcés-Mascareñas, B., and Kraler, A. (2013) 'Employment and migrant deservingness', *International Migration*, 51(6): 80–5.

Cheng, T. and Selden, M. (1994) 'The origins and social consequences of China's hukou system', *The China Quarterly*, 139: 644–68.

Choi, H.-M., Kim, W.G., and McGinley, S. (2017) 'The extension of the theory of person-organization fit toward hospitality migrant worker', *International Journal of Hospitality Management*, 62: 53–66.

Choldin, H.M. (1973) 'Kinship networks in the migration process', *International Migration Review*, 7(2): 163–76.

Christopher, E., Pybus, C., and Rediker, M. (eds) (2007) *Many Middle Passages. Forced Migration and the Making of the Modern World*, Berkeley: University of California Press.

Christopoulou, N. and Lazaridis, G. (2012) 'Vulnerability, silence and pathways to resistance: The case of migrant women in Greece', in S. Fitzgerald (ed) *Regulating the International Movement of Women: From Protection to Control*, New York: Routledge, pp 92–110.

Cillo, R. and Pradella, L. (2018) 'New immigrant struggles in Italy's logistics industry', *Comparative European Politics*, 16(1): 67–84.

Cioce, G., Korczynski, M., and Però, D. (2022) 'The improvised language of solidarity: Linguistic practices in the participatory labour-organizing processes of multi-ethnic migrant workers', *Human Relations*, Available from: https://doi.org/10.1177/00187267221119775. Accessed 21 November 2022.

Ciupijus, Z., Forde, C., and MacKenzie, R. (2020) 'Micro-and meso-regulatory spaces of labour mobility power: The role of ethnic and kinship networks in shaping work-related movements of post-2004 Central Eastern European migrants to the United Kingdom', *Population, Space and Place*, 26(5): e2300: 1–12.

Clark, I. and Colling, T. (2018) 'Work in Britain's informal economy: learning from road-side hand car washes', *British Journal of Industrial Relations*, 56(2): 320–41.

Cleaver, H. (1992) 'The inversion of class perspective in Marxian theory: From valorisation to self-valorisation', in W. Bonefeld, R. Gunn and K. Psychopedis (eds) *Open Marxism, Volume II: Theory and Practice*. London: Pluto, pp 106–44.

Cobble, D.S. (1991) 'Organizing the postindustrial work force: lessons from the history of waitress unionism', *ILR Review*, 44(3): 419–36.

Cobbe, L. and Grappi, G. (2011) 'Primo marzo, percorsi di uno sciopero inatteso', in M. Ricciardi and F. Mometti (eds) *La normale eccezione. Lotte migranti in Italia,* Rome: Edizioni Alegre, pp 55–90.

Coe, N.M. and Jordhus-Lier, D.C. (2011) 'Constrained agency? Re-evaluating the geographies of labour', *Progress in Human Geography*, 35(2): 211–33.

Coe, N.M., Johns, J.L., and Ward, K. (2012) 'Limits to expansion: transnational corporations and territorial embeddedness in the Japanese temporary staffing market', *Global Networks*, 12(1): 22–47.

Cohen, R. (1987) *The New Helots: Migrants in the International Division of Labour*, Aldershot: Avebury.

Cohen, S., Humphries, B., and Mynott, E. (eds) (2002) *From Immigration Controls to Welfare Controls*, New York: Routledge.

Collins, F.L. (2021) '"Give me my pathway!": multinational migration, transnational skills regimes and migrant subjectification', *Global Networks*, 21(1): 18–39.

Connolly, H. and Sellers, B. (2017) 'Trade unions and migrant workers in the UK: Organizing in a cold climate', in Stefania Marino, Judith Roosblad, and Rinus Penninx (eds) *Trade Unions and Migrant Workers: New Contexts and Challenges in Europe*, Cheltenham: Edward Elgar Publishing, pp 224–43.

Connolly, H., Marino, S., and Lucio, M.M. (2014) 'Trade union renewal and the challenges of representation: Strategies towards migrant and ethnic minority workers in the Netherlands, Spain and the United Kingdom', *European Journal of Industrial Relations*, 20(1): 5–20.

Conradson, D. and Latham, A. (2005a) *Ordinary and Middling Transnationalism*, London: Routledge.

Conradson, D. and Latham, A. (2005b) 'Transnational urbanism: attending to everyday practices and mobilities', *Journal of Ethnic and Migration Studies*, 31(2): 227–33.

Constable, N. (2009) 'Migrant workers and the many states of protest in Hong Kong', *Critical Asian Studies,* 41(1): 143–64.

Corrado, A. (2017) *Migrant Crop Pickers in Italy and Spain. International Politics*, Berlin: Heinrich Boll Stiftung.

Cowie, J. (1999) *Capital Moves: RCA's Seventy-year Quest for Cheap Labor*, New York: The New Press.

Cranston, S., Schapendonk, J., and Spaan, E. (2018) 'New directions in exploring the migration industries: Introduction to special issue', *Journal of Ethnic and Migration Studies*, 44(4): 543–57.

Cravey, A.J. (1998) *Women and Work in Mexico's Maquiladoras*, Washington DC: Rowman & Littlefield.

Cravey, A.J. (2004) 'Toque una ranchera, por favor', in K. Mitchell, S.A. Marston, and C. Katz (eds, 2012) *Life's Work: Geographies of Social Reproduction*, Malden: Wiley-Blackwell, pp 185–202.

Cravey, A.J. (2005) 'Desire, work and transnational identity', *Ethnography*, 6(3): 357–83.

Crawford, R. (2020) 'Why the new points-based immigration system threatens everyone's rights at work', *Trade Union Congress (TUC)*, [online] 19 February, Available from: https://www.tuc.org.uk/blogs/why-new-poi nts-based-immigration-system-threatens-everyones-rights-work. Accessed 15 June 2020.

Cremers, J. (2016) 'Economic freedoms and labour standards in the European Union', *Transfer: European Review of Labour and Research*, 22(2): 149–62.

Cremers, J., Dølvik, J.E., and Bosch, G. (2007) 'Posting of workers in the single market: attempts to prevent social dumping and regime competition in the EU', *Industrial Relations Journal*, 38(6): 524–41.

Crenshaw, K. (1989) 'Demarginalizing the intersection of race and sex: a black feminist critique of antidiscrimination doctrine, feminist theory and antiracist politics', *University of Chicago Legal Forum*, 1989(1) article 8: 139–67.

Cresswell, T. (2010) 'Towards a politics of mobility', *Environment and Planning D*, 28(1): 17–31.

Crețan, R. and Light, D. (2020) 'Covid-19 in Romania: transnational labour, geopolitics, and the Roma "outsiders"', *Eurasian Geography and Economics*, 61(4–5): 559–72.

Cumbers, A., Nativel, C., and Routledge, P. (2008) 'Labour agency and union positionalities in global production networks', *Journal of Economic Geography*, 8(3): 369–87.

Currie, S. (2007) 'De-skilled and devalued: the labour market experience of Polish migrants in the UK following EU enlargement', *International Journal of Comparative Labour Law and Industrial Relations*, 23(1): 83–116.

Dajani, D. (2021) 'Refuge under austerity: the UK's refugee settlement schemes and the multiplying practices of bordering', *Ethnic and Racial Studies*, 44(1): 58–76.

Dalla Costa, M. and James, S. (1972) *The Power of Women and the Subversion of the Community*, Bristol: Falling Water Press.

Damir-Geilsdorf, S. and Pelican, M. (2018) 'Between regular and irregular employment: subverting the kafala system in the GCC countries', *Migration and Development*, 8(2): 155–75.

Danaj, S. and Sippola, M. (2015) 'Organizing posted workers in the construction sector', in J. Drahokoupil (ed) *The Outsourcing Challenge*, Brussels: ETUI, pp 217–36.

Datta, K., McIlwaine, C., Evans, Y., Herbert, J., May, J., and Wills, J. (2007) 'From coping strategies to tactics: London's low-pay economy and migrant labour', *British Journal of Industrial Relations*, 45(2): 404–32.

De Genova, N. (2002) 'Migrant "Illegality" and Deportability in Everyday Life', *Annual Review of Anthropology*, 31(1): 419–47.

De Genova, N. (2005) *Working the Boundary. Race, Space, and Illegality in Mexican Chicago*, Durham, NC and London: Duke University Press.

De Genova, N. (2013) '"We are of the connections": migration, methodological nationalism, and "militant research"', *Postcolonial Studies*, 16(3): 250–8.

De Genova, N. (ed) (2017) *The Borders of 'Europe': Autonomy of Migration, Tactics of Bordering*, Durham, NC: Duke University Press.

Del Re, A. (2008) 'Produzione-riproduzione', in V.A. *Lessico Marxiano concetti per ripensare il presente*, Roma: Manifestolibri, pp 109–21.

Della Puppa, F., Montagna, N., and Kofman, E. (2021) 'Onward migration and intra-European mobilities: a critical and theoretical overview', *International Migration*, 59: 16–28.

Dench, S., Hurstfield, J., Hill, D., and Akroyd, K. (2006) 'Employers' use of migrant labour. main report', *Home Office*, [online], Available from https://www.employment-studies.co.uk/resource/employers-use-migrant-labour. Accessed 30 March 2008.

Deneva, N. (2021) 'Essential workers with dangerous bodies: the Covid-19 crisis and East European migrants', *Sociological Problems*, 53(2): 538–60.

Deutschmann, C. (2002) *Postindustrielle Industriesoziologie: Theoretische Grundlagen, Arbeitsverhaeltnisse und soziale Identitaeten*, Weinheim: Juventa.

Devitt, C. (2011) 'Varieties of capitalism, variation in labor immigration', *Journal of Ethnic and Migration Studies*, 37(4): 579–96.

Dicken, P. (2003) *Global Shift: Reshaping the Global Economic Map in the 21st Century*, London: Sage.

Diemer, H. (1917) 'Causes of "turnover" among college faculties', *The Annals of the American Academy of Political and Social Science*, 71(1): 216–24.

Dimitriadis, I. (2023) *Migrant Construction Workers in Times of Crisis*, Cham: Palgrave Macmillan.

Doellgast, V., Lillie, N., and Pulignano, V. (2018) 'From dualization to solidarity: halting the cycle of precarity', in V. Doellgast, N. Lillie and V. Pulignano (eds) *Reconstructing Solidarity*, Oxford: Oxford University Press, pp 1–41.

Douglas, J.H. (1959), 'Labor Turnover', in E.R.A. Seligman and A. Johnson (eds) *Encyclopedia of the Social Sciences*, New York: The MacMillan Company, pp 709–13.

Douglas, P. (1918) 'The problem of labor turnover', *American Economic Review*, 8(June): 306–16.

Drahokoupil, J. (2008) 'The investment-promotion machines: the politics of foreign direct investment promotion in central and Eastern Europe', *Europe-Asia Studies*, 60(2): 197–225.

Dreyfus, P. (1997) 'The IWW and the limits of interethnic organizing', *Labor History*, 38(1): 450–70.

Dubofsky, M. (1995) 'Labour unrest in the United States, 1906–90', *Review (Fernand Braudel Center)*, 18(1): 125–35.

Dumitrescu, R. (2022) 'Non-EU foreign workers in Romania to require written agreement of first employer to change jobs', Romania-Insider. com, [online], 3 November, Available from: https://www.romania-insi der.com/asian-foreign-workers-romania-written-agreement-first-emplo yer-change-jobs-nov-2022. Accessed 5 June 2021.

Dutta, M. (2020) 'Workplace, emotional bonds and agency: everyday gendered experiences of work in an export processing zone in Tamil Nadu, India', *Environment and Planning A: Economy and Space*, 52(7): 1357–74.

Dwyer, P. (2005) 'Governance, forced migration and welfare', *Social Policy & Administration*, 39(6): 622–39.

Dwyer, P. (2016) 'Citizenship, conduct and conditionality: sanction and support in the 21st century UK welfare state', *Social Policy Review*, 28: 41–62.

Dwyer, P.J., Scullion, L., Jones, K., and Stewart, A. (2019) 'The impact of conditionality on the welfare rights of EU migrants in the UK', *Policy & Politics*, 47(1): 133–50.

Dyer-Witheford, N. (1994) 'Autonomist Marxism and the information society', *Capital and Class*, 18(1): 85–125.

Edwards, P.K. (1990) 'Understanding conflict in the labour process: the logic and autonomy of struggle', in D. Knights and H. Willmott (eds) *Labour Process Theory. Studies in the Labour Process*, London: Palgrave Macmillan, pp 125–52.

Edwards, P.K. and Scullion, H. (1982) *The Social Organization of Industrial Conflict*, Oxford: Blackwell.

Ehrenreich, B. and Hochschild, A.R. (eds) (2003) *Global Woman: Nannies, Maids, and Sex Workers in the New Economy*, New York: Metropolitan Books.

Elger, T. and Smith, C. (2005) *Assembling Work: Remaking Factory Regimes in Japanese Multinationals in Britain*, Oxford: Oxford University Press.

Ellem, B. (2016) 'Geographies of the labour process: automation and the spatiality of mining', *Work, Employment and Society*, 30(6): 932–48.

Ellingstad, M. (1997) 'The maquiladora syndrome: central European prospects', *Europe-Asia Studies*, 49(1): 7–21.

Elson, D. and Pearson, R. (1981) '"Nimble fingers make cheap workers": an analysis of women's employment in third world export manufacturing', *Feminist Review*, 7(1): 87–107.

Engbersen, G., Leerkes, A., Scholten, P., and Snel, E. (2017) 'The intra-EU mobility regime: differentiation, stratification and contradictions', *Migration Studies*, 5(3): 337–55.

Engbersen, G., Leerkes, A., Grabowska-Lusinska, I., Snel, E., and Burgers, J. (2013) 'On the differential attachments of migrants from Central and Eastern Europe: a typology of labour migration', *Journal of Ethnic and Migration Studies*, 39(6): 959–81.

Engman, M., Onodera, O., and Pinali, E. (2007) *Export Processing Zones: Past and Future Role in Trade and Development*, Working Party of the Trade Committee, OECD Trade Policy Working Paper No. 53, Paris: OECD.

Erel, U., Murji, K., and Nahaboo, Z. (2016) 'Understanding the contemporary race–migration nexus', *Ethnic and Racial Studies*, 29(8): 1339–60.

Erne, R. and Imboden, N. (2015) 'Equal pay by gender and by nationality: a comparative analysis of Switzerland's unequal equal pay policy regimes across time', *Cambridge Journal of Economics*, 39(2): 655–74.

European Commission (2010) Employment in Europe 2010, [online], Available from:https://ec.europa.eu/employment_social/eie. Accessed 30 November 2021.

European Commission (2016), *Revision of the Posting of Workers Directive*, https://ec.europa.eu/commission/presscorner/detail/en/MEMO_16_467

Everton, W.J., Jolton, J.A., and Mastrangelo, P.M. (2007) 'Be nice and fair or else: understanding reasons for employees' deviant behavior', *Journal of Management Development*, 26(2): 117–31.

Faist, T. (2006) 'The transnational social spaces of migration', COMCAD Working Papers, 10: 1-8 *SSOAR Open Access*, [online] Available from: https://nbn-resolving.org/ urn:nbn:de:0168-ssoar-350692. Accessed 11 February 2021.

Faist, T. (2014) 'On the transnational social question: how social inequalities are reproduced in Europe', *Journal of European Social Policy*, 24(3): 207–22.

Faist, T., Fauser, M., and Reisenauer, E. (2013) *Transnational Migration*, Cambridge: Polity Press.

Fakiolas, R. (1962) 'Problem of labour mobility in the USSR', *Soviet Studies*, 14(1): 16–40.

Fan, C.C. (2004) 'The state, the migrant labor regime, and maiden workers in China', *Political Geography*, 23(3): 283–305.

Farole, T. and Akinci, G. (eds) (2011) *Special Economic Zones: Progress, Emerging Challenges, and Future Directions*, Washington: World Bank Publications.

Favell, A. (2008) *Eurostars and Eurocities: Free Movement and Mobility in an Integrating Europe*, Oxford: Blackwell.

Favell, A. and Recchi, E. (2020) 'Mobilities, neo-nationalism and the lockdown of Europe: will the European Union survive?', COMPAS, [online] 14 April, Available from: https://www.compas.ox.ac.uk/2020/mobilities-and-the-lockdown-of-europe-will-the-european-union-surv ive/. Accessed 13 June 2020.

Federici, S. (1975) *Wages Against Housework*, Bristol: Falling Wall Press.

Federici, S. (2004) *Caliban and the Witch: Women, The Body, and Primitive Accumulation*, New York: Autonomedia.

Federici, S. (2014) 'Revolution at point zero: housework, reproduction, and feminist struggle', *Revija za sociologiju*, 44(2): 179–89.

Fellini, I., Ferro, A., and Fullin, G. (2007) 'Recruitment processes and labour mobility: the construction industry in Europe', *Work, Employment and Society*, 21(2): 277–98.

Fernandez, B. (2021) 'Racialised institutional humiliation through the Kafala', *Journal of Ethnic and Migration Studies*, 47(19): 4344–61.

Fernandez, L. (1997) *Producing Workers: The Politics of Gender, Class, and Culture in the Calcutta Jute Mills*, Philadelphia: University of Pennsylvania Press.

Fernández-Kelly, M.P. (1983) *For We Are Sold, I and My People: Women and Industry in Mexico's Frontier*, Albany, NY: State University of New York Press.

FIAS (2008) *Special Economic Zones: Performance, Lessons Learned and Implications for Zone Development. Final Report to U.S. Agency for International Development*, Washington DC: The World Bank Group.

Fiedler, M., Georgi, F., Hielscher, L., Ratfisch, P., Riedner, L., Schwab, V., and Sontowski, S. (2017) 'Contested movements to and through Europe. Introduction', *Movements. Journal for Critical Migration and Border Regime Studies*, 3(1): 1–10.

Fielding, A. (1993) 'Migrations, institutions and politics: the evolution of European migration policies', in R. King (ed) *Mass Migration in Europe*, London: Belhaven, pp 40–62.

Fine, J. (2006) *Worker Centers: Organizing Communities at the Edge of the Dream*, Ithaca, NY: ILR Press.

Fine, J. (2007) 'A marriage made in heaven? Mismatches and misunderstandings between worker centres and unions', *British Journal of Industrial Relations*, 45(2): 335–60.

Fishback, P.V. (1997) *Operations of 'Unfettered' Labor Markets at the Turn of the Century*, Cambridge: NBER.

Fisher, B. (1917) 'Determining cost of turnover of labor', *The Annals of the American Academy of Political and Social Science*, 71(1): 44–50.

Fitzgerald, I. and Hardy, J. (2010) ' "Thinking outside the box"? Trade union organizing strategies and Polish migrant workers in the United Kingdom', *British Journal of Industrial Relations*, 48(1): 131–50.

Fitzgerald, I., Beadle, R., and Rowan, K. (2022) 'Trade unions and the 2016 UK European Union referendum', *Economic and Industrial Democracy*, 43(1): 388–409.

Ford, M. (2019) *From Migrant to Worker: Global Unions and Temporary Labor Migration in Asia*, Ithaca–London: Cornell University Press.

Ford, M. and Piper, N. (2007) 'Southern sites of female agency: informal regimes and female migrant labour resistance in East and Southeast Asia', in J. Hobson and L. Seabrooke (eds) *Everyday Politics of the World Economy*, Cambridge: Cambridge University Press, pp 63–80.

Forde, C. and MacKenzie, R. (2009) 'Employers' use of low-skilled migrant workers: Assessing the implications for human resource management', *International Journal of Manpower*, 30(5): 437–52.

Forde, C.J., Mackenzie, R., Ciupijus, Z., and Alberti, G. (2015), 'Understanding the connections between temporary employment agencies and migration', *International Journal of Comparative Labour Law and Industrial Relations*, 31(4): 357–70.

Foucault, M. (1975) *Discipline and Punish: The Birth of the Prison*, New York: Vintage.

Fougner, T. and Kurtoğlu, A. (2011) 'Transnational labour solidarity and social movement unionism: insights from and beyond a women workers' strike in Turkey', *British Journal of Industrial Relations*, 49(2): 353–75.

Franceschini, I. (2020) 'As far apart as earth and sky: a survey of Chinese and Cambodian construction workers in Sihanoukville', *Critical Asian Studies*, 52(4): 512–29.

Frank, D. (1998) 'White working-class women and the race question, *International Labor and Working-Class History*, 54: 80–102.

Frick, S., Rodríguez-Pose, A., and Wong, M. (2019) 'Toward economically dynamic special economic zones in emerging countries', *Economic Geography*, 95(1): 30–64.

Friedman, M. (1964) *Capitalism and Freedom* (4th edn), Chicago: University of Chicago Press.

Frisina, A. and Hawthorne, C. (2018) 'Italians with veils and Afros: gender, beauty, and the everyday anti-racism of the daughters of immigrants in Italy', *Journal of Ethnic and Migration Studies*, 44(5): 718–35.

Fröbel, F., Jurgen, H., and Otto, K. (1977) *Die neue international Arbeitsteilung. Strukturelle Arbeitslosigkeit in den Industrielandern und die Industrialisierung der Entwicklungslander*, Reinbek: Rowohlt.

Fudge, J. (2012) 'Precarious migrant status and precarious employment: the paradox of international rights for migrant workers', *Comparative Labour Law and Policy Journal*, 34: 95–132.

Fudge, J. and Strauss, K. (2014) *Temporary Work, Agencies and Unfree Labour: Insecurity in the New World of Work*, London: Routledge.

Fuentes, A. and Ehrenreich B. (1983) *Women in the Global Factory*, Boston, MA: South End Press.

Gabaccia, D. and Iacovetta, F. (eds) (2002) *Women, Gender, and Transnational Lives: Italian Workers of the World*, Toronto: University of Toronto Press.

Gallas, A (2018) Class power and union capacities: a research note on the power resources approach. *Global Labour Journal* 9(3): 348–352.

Gambino, F. (2003) *Migranti nella tempesta*, Verona: Ombre Corte.

Gambino, F. (2016) 'The early outsourcing of the electronics industry and its feeders', in J. Drahokoupil, R. Andrijasevic and D. Sacchetto (eds) *Flexible Workforces and Low Profit Margins: Electronics Assembly between Europe and China*, Brussels: Etui, pp 223–36.

Gambino, F. and Sacchetto, D. (2014) 'The shifting maelstrom: from plantations to assembly lines', in M. van der Linden and K.H. Roth (eds) *Beyond Marx: Theorising the Global Labour Relations of the Twenty First Century*, Leiden: Brill, pp 89–120.

Gambino, R. (1996) 'A critique of the Fordism and the regulation school', *The Commoner*, 12: 39–62.

Gammeltoft-Hansen, T. and Nyberg Sorensen, N. (2013) *The Migration Industry and the Commercialization of International Migration*, New York: Routledge.

Gans, H.J. (2017) 'Racialization and racialization research', *Ethnic and Racial Studies*, 40(3): 341–52.

Gao, Ru (2020) *Women's empowerment in translocal mobility and the globalised assembly line of low-end labour force (re)production: Chinese female migration in Italy*, PhD thesis, University of Padova.

Gardner, A. (2012) 'Why do they keep coming? Labor migrants in the Persian Gulf states', in M. Kamrava and Z. Babar (eds) *Labor Migrants in the Persian Gulf States*, London: Hurst & Company, pp 41–58.

Gardner, K. (2009) 'Lives in motion: the life-course, movement and migration in Bangladesh', *Journal of South Asian Development*, 4(2): 229–51.

Gereffi, G., Korzeniewicz, M., and Korzeniewicz, R. (1994) 'Introduction: global commodity chains', in G. Gereffi and M. Korzeniewicz (eds) *Commodity Chains and Global Capitalism*, Westport, CT: Praeger, pp 1–14.

Gibson-Graham, J.K. (1996) *The End of Capitalism (As We Knew It)*, Oxford: Blackwell.

Gibson, K. and Graham, J. (1986) 'Situating migrants in theory: the case of Filipino migrant contract construction workers', *Capital and Class*, 10(2): 130–49.

Giles, A. (2000) 'Globalisation and industrial relations theory', *Journal of Industrial Relations*, 42(2): 173–94.

Glaberman, M. (1980) *Wartime Strikes: The Struggle Against the No Strike Pledge in the UAW During World War II*, Detroit: Bewick Editions.

Glass, C.M., Mannon, S., and Petrzelka, P. (2014) 'Good mothers as guest workers', *International Journal of Sociology*, 44(3): 8–22.

Gleeson, S. (2013) 'Shifting agendas, evolving coalitions: advocating for immigrant worker rights in Houston', *WorkingUSA*, 16(2): 207–26.

Glenn, E.N. (1992) 'From servitude to service work: historical continuities in the racial division of paid reproductive labor', *Signs: Journal of Women in Culture and Society*, 18(1): 1–43.

Glick Schiller, N.G. (2012) 'Unravelling the migration and development web: research and policy implications, *International Migration*, 50(3): 92–7.

Glick Schiller, N. and Çağlar, A. (2011) 'Locality and globality: building a comparative analytical framework in migration and urban studies' in N. Glick Schiller and A. Çağlar (eds) *Locating Migration: Rescaling Cities and Migrants*, Ithaca, NY: Cornell University Press, pp 60–81.

Glick Schiller, N., Basch, L., and Szanton-Blanc, C. (1995) 'From immigrant to transmigrant: theorizing transnational migration', *Anthropological Quarterly*, 68(1): 48–63.

Glick Schiller, N.G., Çağlar, A., and Guldbrandsen, T.C. (2006) 'Beyond the ethnic lens: locality, globality, and born-again incorporation', *American Ethnologist*, 33(4): 612–33.

Goeke, S. (2014) 'The multinational working class? Political activism and labour migration in West Germany during the 1960s and 1970s', *Journal of Contemporary History*, 49(1): 160–82.

Gold, S.J. (2005) 'Migrant networks: a summary and critique of relational approaches to international migration', in M. Romero and E. Margolis (eds) *The Blackwell Companion to Social Inequalities*, Malden, MA: Blackwell, pp 257–85.

Goldín, L.R. (2011) 'Labor turnover among maquila workers of Highland Guatemala: resistance and semiproletarianization in global capitalism', *Latin American Research Review*, 46(3): 133–56.

Goldín, L.R. (2012) 'From despair to resistance: Maya workers in the maquilas of Guatemala', *Anthropology of Work Review*, 33(1): 25–33.

Goodburn, C. and Mishra, S. (2023) 'Beyond the dormitory labour regime: comparing Chinese and Indian workplace–residence systems as strategies of migrant labour control', *Work, Employment and Society*, Online First, pp 1–22.

Gordon, J.L. (2005) *Suburban Sweatshops: The fight for immigrant rights*, Cambridge, MA: Harvard University Press.

Gordon, J. (2006) 'Transnational labor citizenship', *Southern California Law Review*, 80(3): 503–88.

Goss, J. and Lindquist, B. (1995) 'Conceptualizing international labor migration: a structuration perspective', *International Migration Review*, 29(2): 317–51.

Granovetter, M. (1973) 'The strength of weak ties', *American Journal of Sociology*, 78(6): 1360–80.

Grappi, G. (2021) 'Migration and the contested politics of justice: an introduction', in G. Grappi (ed) *Migration and the Contested Politics of Justice*, New York: Routledge, pp 1–20.

Gray, N. and Clare, N. (2022) 'From autonomous to autonomist geography', *Progress in Human Geography*, 46(5): 1185–206.

Greer, I. (2016) 'Welfare reform, precarity and the re-commodification of labour', *Work, Employment and Society*, 30(1): 162–73.

Greer, I., Ciupijus, Z., and Lillie, N. (2013) 'The European Migrant Workers Union and the barriers to transnational industrial citizenship', *European Journal of Industrial Relations*, 19(1): 5–20.

Groppo, B. (1974) 'Sviluppo economico e ciclo dell'emigrazione in Germania Occidentale', in A. Serafini (ed) *L'operaio multinazionale in Europa*, Milano: Feltrinelli, pp 149–80.

Groutsis, D., van den Broek, D., and Harvey, W.S. (2015) 'Transformations in network governance: the case of migration intermediaries', *Journal of Ethnic and Migration Studies*, 41(10): 1558–76.

Guérin, I. (2013) 'Bonded labour, agrarian changes and capitalism: emerging patterns in South India', *Journal of Agrarian Change*, 13(3): 405–23.

Guerin I, D'Espallier B and Venkatasubramanian G (2013) Debt in rural South India: Fragmentation, social regulation, and discrimination. *Journal of Development Studies*, 49(9): 1155–1171.

Guerin-Gonzales, C. (1994) *Mexican Workers and American Dreams: Immigration, Repatriation, and California Farm Labor, 1900–1939*, New Brunswick, NJ: Rutgers University Press.

Gutman, H.G. (1973) 'Work, culture, and society in industrializing America: 1815–1919', *American Historical Review*, 78(3): 531–88.

Gutman, H.G. (1968) 'The Negro and the United Mine Workers of America. The Career and Letters of Richard L. Davis and Some things of Their Meaning: 1890–1900', in Julius Jacobson (ed) *The Negro and the American Labor Movement*. Garden City: New York, pp 49–127.

Hachtmann, R. (2010) 'Fordism and unfree labour: aspects of the work deployment of concentration camp prisoners in German industry between 1941 and 1944', *International Review of Social History*, 55(3): 485–513.

Hagan, J., Lowe, N., and Quingla, C. (2011) 'Skills on the move: rethinking the relationship between human capital and immigrant economic mobility', *Work and Occupations*, 38(2): 149–78.

Hála, J. (2007) 'Unions criticise unequal treatment of temporary agency workers', *Eurofound*, [online] 28 January, Available from: http://www.eurofound.europa.eu/eiro/2006/11/articles/cz0611049i.htm. Accessed 11 November 2022.

Hall, D.T. (2004) 'The protean career: a quarter-century journey', *Journal of Vocational Behavior*, 65(1): 1–13.

Hall, P.A. and Soskice, D. (2001) 'An introduction to varieties of capitalism', in P.A. Hall and D. Soskice (eds) *Varieties of Capitalism. The Institutional Foundations of Comparative Advantage*, Oxford: Oxford University Press, pp 1–68.

Halpern, R. and Horowitz, R. (1996) *Meatpackers: An Oral History of Black Packinghouse Workers and the Struggle for Racial and Economic Equality*, New York: Twayne.

Hammer, A. and Adham, A. (2022) 'Mobility power, state and the "Sponsored Labour Regime" in Saudi capitalism', *Work, Employment and Society*, 1–20. Available from: https://doi.org/10.1177/09500170221080373.

Hansen, B.R. and Zechner, M. (2017) 'Intersecting mobilities. Declassing and migration from the viewpoint of organising within and against precarity', *Movements. Journal for Critical Migration and Border Regime Studies*, 3(1): 109–28.

Hanson, S. and Pratt, G. (1992) 'Dynamic dependencies: a geographic investigation of local labor markets', *Economic Geography*, 68(4): 373–405.

Hardt, M. and Negri, A. (2000) *Empire*, Cambridge, MA: Harvard University Press.

Hardy, J. (2021) *Nothing to Lose but our Chains: Work and Resistance in the Twenty-First Century*, London: Pluto Press.

Harvey, D. (1989) *The Condition of Postmodernity*, Oxford: Blackwell.

Harvey, D. (2006) *Spaces of Global Capitalism: Towards a Theory of Uneven Geographical Development*, London: Verso.

Harvey, D. (2018) *The Limits to Capital* [1982], London: Verso books.

Hastings, T. (2016) 'Moral matters: de-romanticising worker agency and charting future directions for labour geography', *Geography Compass*, 10(7): 307–18.

Hayes L. and Novitz, T. (2013) 'Workers without footprint. The legal fiction of migrant workers as posted workers', in B. Ryan (ed) *Labour Migration in Hard Times*, London: Institute of Employment Rights, pp 99–118.

Hellio, E. (2014) '"We don't have women in boxes": channelling seasonal mobility of female farmworkers between Morocco and Andalusia', in Jörg Gertel and Sarah Ruth Sippel (eds) *Seasonal Workers in Mediterranean Agriculture*, New York: Routledge, pp 159–82.

Henderson, J., Dicken, P., Hess, M., Coe, N., and Yeung, H.W.-C. (2002) 'Global production networks and the analysis of economic development', *Review of International Political Economy*, 9(39): 436–64.

Hernández-León, R. (2013) 'Conceptualizing the migration industry', in T. Gammeltoft-Hansen and N.N. Sørensen (eds) *The Migration Industry and the Commercialization of International Migration*, Abingdon: Routledge, pp 24–44.

Herod, A. (2001) *Labor Geographies: Workers and the Landscapes of Capitalism*, New York and London: The Guilford Press.

Hess, M. and Yeung, H.W.-C. (2006) 'Whither global production networks in economic geography? Past, present, and future', *Environment and Planning A*, 38(7): 1193–204.

Heyes, J. (2009) 'EU labour migration: government and social partner policies in the UK', in B. Galgóczi, J. Leschke, and A. Watt (eds) *EU Labour Migration since Enlargement*, Aldershot: Ashgate, pp 51–68.

Hill, H. (1996) 'The problem of race in American labor history', *Reviews in American History*, 24(2): 189–208.

Hirschman, A.O. (1970) *Exit, Voice, and Loyalty: Responses to decline in firms, organizations, and states*, Harvard: Harvard University Press.

Hirschman, A.O. (1978) 'Exit, voice, and the state', *World Politics*, 31(1): 90–107.

Hirschman, A. (1982) *Shifting Involvements. Private Interest and Public Action*, Princeton, NJ: Princeton University Press.

Hoang, L.A. (2016) 'Vietnamese migrant networks in Taiwan: the curse and boon of social capital', *Ethnic and Racial Studies*, 39(4): 690–707.

Hoang, L. and Yeoh, B. (eds) (2015) *Transnational Labour Migration, Remittances and the Changing Family in Asia*, Basingstoke: Palgrave Macmillan.

Hobsbawm, E.J. (1951) 'The tramping artizan', *Economic History Review* 3(3): 299–320.

Hochschild, A. (2003) *The Commercialization of Intimate Life*, Berkeley: University of California Press.

Hodkinson, S.N., Lewis, H., Waite, L., and Dwyer, P. (2021) 'Fighting or fuelling forced labour? The Modern Slavery Act 2015, irregular migrants and the vulnerabilising role of the UK's hostile environment', *Critical Social Policy*, 41(1): 68–90.

Hoefte, R. (2018) 'Indentured labour', in K. Hofmeester and M. van der Linden (eds) *Handbook Global History of Work*, Walter de Gruyter, pp 363–76.

Hoerder, D. (2002) *Cultures in Contact: World Migration in the Second Millennium*, Durham, NC: Duke University Press.

Hofmeester, K. and van der Linden, M. (eds) (2018) *Handbook Global History of Work*, Berlin: Oldenbourg De Gruyter.

Holgate, J. (2005) 'Organizing migrant workers: a case study of working conditions and unionization in a London sandwich factory', *Work, Employment and Society*, 19(3): 463–80.

Holgate, J., Simms, M., and Tapia, M. (2018) 'The limitations of the theory and practice of mobilization in trade union organizing', *Economic and Industrial Democracy*, 39(4): 599–616.

Holgate, J., Keles, J., Pollert, A., and Kumarappen, L. (2012) 'Workplace problems among Kurdish workers in London: experiences of an "invisible" community and the role of community organisations as support networks', *Journal of Ethnic and Migration Studies*, 38(4): 595–612.

Hom, P.W. and Griffith, R.W. (1995) *Employee Turnover*, Cincinnati, OH: South-Western.

Hom, P.W., Lee, T.W., Shaw, J.D., and Hausknecht, J.P. (2017) 'One hundred years of employee turnover theory and research', *Journal of Applied Psychology*, 102(3): 530–45.

Hondagneu-Sotelo, P. (1994) *Gendered Transitions: Mexican Experiences of Immigration*, Berkeley, CA: University of California Press.

Honig, B. (2001) *Democracy and the Foreigner*, Princeton: Princeton University Press.

Hopkins, B. (2014) 'Explaining variations in absence rates: temporary and agency workers in the food manufacturing sector', *Human Resource Management Journal*, 24(2): 227–40.

Hopkins, T.K. and Wallerstein, I. (1977) 'Patterns of development of the modern world-system', *Review (Fernand Braudel Center)*, 1(2): 111–45.

Horáková, M. (2011) 'International labour migration in the Czech Republic', Prague RILSA *Bulletin*, 27.

Hsia, H.C. (2009) 'The making of a transnational grassroots migrant movement: a case study of Hong Kong's Asian Migrants' Coordinating Body', *Critical Asian Studies*, 41(1): 113–41.

Huang, T.J. (2021) 'Negotiating the workplace: Second-generation Asian American professionals' early experiences', *Journal of Ethnic and Migration Studies*, 47(11): 2477–96.

Human Rights Watch (2019) Qatar: Migrant Workers Strike Over Work Conditions. Online Publication. Available from: https://www.hrw.org/news/2019/08/08/qatar-migrant-workers-strike-over-work-conditions. Accessed 22 March 2021.

Huff, G. and Caggiano, G. (2008) 'Globalization and labor market integration in late nineteenth and early twentieth-century Asia', *Research in Economic History*, 25: 285–347.

Hutchinson, S.T., Villalobos, J.R., and Beruvides, M.G. (1997) 'Effects of high labour turnover in a serial assembly environment', *International Journal of Production Research*, 35(11): 3201–24.

Hyman, R. (2005) 'Trade Unions and the politics of European integration', *Economic and Industrial Democracy*, 26(1): 9–40.

Hyman, R. and Gumbrell-McCormick, R. (2020) '(How) can international trade union organisations be democratic?', *Transfer*, 26(3): 253–72.

Iannuzzi, F.E. (2021) *Assemblare le differenze. Il lavoro nell'industria alberghiera veneziana*, Milano: Guerini.

Iannuzzi, F.E. and Sacchetto, D. (2020) 'Outsourcing and workers' resistance practices in Venice's hotel industry: the role of migrants employed by cooperatives', *Economic and Industrial Democracy*, 43(2): 877–97.

Iglesias, P.N. (2014) *La flor más bella de la maquiladora: historias de vida de la mujer obrera en Tijuana*, Tijuana: El Colegio de la Frontera Norte.

Ignatiev, N. (1995) *How the Irish Became White*, New York: Routledge.

ILO/UNCTC (1988) *Economic and Social Effects of Multinational Enterprises in Export Processing Zones*, Geneva: International Labour Office, [online] 13 September, Available from: https://www.ilo.org/global/publications/ilo-bookstore/order-online/books/WCMS_PUBL_9221061949_EN/lang--en/index.htm. Accessed 12 March 2020.

ILO (1997) 'As migrant ranks swell, temporary guest workers increasingly replacing immigrants private employment agencies send millions overseas to work', International Labour Organization [Press Release: ILO/97/9] 18 April, Available from https://www.ilo.org/global/about-the-ilo/newsroom/news/WCMS_008048/lang--en/index.htm#n1. Accessed 21 February 2020.

ILO (1998) *Export Processing Zones Growing Steadily*, Geneva: ILO.

ILO (2003), *Employment and Social Policy in Respect of Export Processing Zones (EPZs)*, Geneva: ILO.

ILO (2004) *Towards a Fair Deal for Migrant Workers in the Global Economy*, Geneva: ILO, Available from: https://www.ilo.org/public/english/standards/relm/ilc/ilc92/pdf/rep-vi.pdf. Accessed 15 May 2021.

ILO (2018) *Global Estimates on International Migrant Workers*, Geneva: ILO, Available from: https://www.ilo.org/global/publications/books/WCMS_652001. Accessed December 2022.

Ince, A., Featherstone, D., Cumbers, A., MacKinnon, D., and Strauss, K. (2015) 'British jobs for British workers? Negotiating work, nation, and globalisation through the Lindsey Oil Refinery disputes', *Antipode*, 47(1): 139–57.

IOM (2021) *World Migration Report 2022*, IOM: Geneva, Available from https://publications.iom.int/books/world-migration-report-2022. Accessed 3 January 2022.

Issa, D. (2017) 'Reification and the human commodity: theorizing modern slavery in Brazil', *Latin American Perspectives*, 44(6): 90–106.

Jacoby, S.M. (1983) 'Industrial labor mobility in historical perspective', *Industrial Relations*, 22(2): 261–80.

Jacoby, S.M. (1985) *Employing Bureaucracy: Managers, Unions, and the Transformation of Work in American Industry, 1900–1945*, New York: Columbia University Press.

Jacoby, S. (1991) *Masters to Managers: Historical and Comparative Perspectives on American Employers*, New York: Columbia University Press.

Jacoby, S.M. and Sharma, S. (1992) 'Employment duration and industrial labor mobility in the United States, 1880–1980', *Journal of Economic History*, 52(1): 161–80.

James, P. and Karmowska, J. (2012) 'Accommodating difference? British trade unions and Polish migrant workers', *Journal of Workplace Rights*, 15(2): 169–89.

Janta, H., Ladkin, A., Brown, L., and Lugosi, P. (2011) 'Employment experiences of Polish migrant workers in the UK hospitality sector', *Tourism Management*, 32(5): 1006–19.

Jefferys, S. (2007) 'Why do unions find fighting workplace racism difficult?', *Transfer*, 13(3): 377–95.

Jiang, Z. and Korczynski, M. (2016) 'When the "unorganizable" organize: The collective mobilization of migrant domestic workers in London, *Human Relations*, 69(3): 813–38.

Jolly, J. (2022) 'Kwasi Kwarteng announces 'investment zones' with huge tax cuts for businesses', *The Guardian*, [online] 23 September, Available from: https://www.theguardian.com/uk-news/2022/sep/23/kwasi-kwart eng-mini-budget-announces-investment-zones-with-huge-tax-cuts-for-businesses. Accessed 24 September 2022.

Jonas, A. (1996) 'Local labour control regimes: uneven development and the social regulation of pro-duction', *Regional Studies*, 30(4): 323–38.

Jonas, A. (2020) 'Labor control regime', in A. Kobayashi (ed) *The International Encyclopedia of Human Geography* (2nd edn), viii, Oxford: Elsevier, pp 53–7.

Jordhus-Lier, D. (2014) 'Fragmentation revisited: flexibility, differentiation and solidarity in hotels', in D. Jordhus-Lier and A. Underthun (eds) *A Hospitable World? Organising Work and Workers in Hotels and Tourist Resorts*, London and New York: Routledge, pp 39–51.

Joshi, S. and Carter, B. (1984) 'The role of labour in the creation of a racist Britain', *Race & Class*, 25(3): 53–70.

Kamrava, M. and Babar, Z. (2012) *Migrant Labor in the Persian Gulf*, New York: Columbia University Press.

Karakayali, S. and Bojadžijev, M. (2007) 'Autonomie der Migration. 10 Thesen zu einer Methode', in Transit Migration Forschungsgruppe (eds) *Turbulente Ränder. Neue Perspektiven auf Migration an den Grenzen Europas*, Bielefeld: Transcript Verlag, pp 203–10.

Katz, C. (2001) 'Vagabond capitalism and the necessity of social reproduction', *Antipode*, 33(4): 709–28.

Katz, C. (2004) *Growing Up Global: Economic Restructuring and Children's Everyday Lives*, Minneapolis, MN: University of Minnesota Press.

Kaur, A. (2010) 'Labour migration trends and policy challenges in Southeast Asia', *Policy and Society*, 29(4): 385–97.

Kaur, A. (2012) 'Labour brokers in migration: understanding historical and contemporary transnational migration regimes in Malaya/Malaysia', *International Review of Social History*, 57(S20): 225–52.

Kawar, M. (2004) 'Gender and migration: why are women more vulnerable', in F. Reysoo and C. Verschuur (eds) *Femmes et mouvement: genre, migrations et nouvelle division international du travail*, Geneva: Colloquium Graduate Institute of Development Studies, pp 71–87.

Kelly, J. (1998) *Rethinking Industrial Relations: Mobilization, Collectivism and Long Waves*, London: Routledge.

Kelly, P. (2009) 'From global production networks to global reproduction networks: households, migration, and regional development in Cavite, the Philippines', *Regional Studies*, 43(3): 449–61.

Kimeldorf, H. (1999) *Battling for American Labor: Wobblies, Wraft workers, and the Making of the Union Movement*, Berkeley and Los Angeles: University of California Press.

King, R. and Pratsinakis, M. (2020) 'Special issue introduction: exploring the lived experiences of intra-EU mobility in an era of complex economic and political change', *International Migration*, 58(1): 5–14.

King, R., Money, J., and Murawska, M. (2011) 'Twenty years of JEMS: a geographical content analysis', *Journal of Ethnic and Migration Studies*, 37(9): 1539–50.

King, R., Black, R., Collyer, M., Fielding, A., and Skeldon, R. (2010) *People on the Move: An Atlas of Migration*, Berkeley: University of California Press.

Kirk, E. (2018) 'The (re) organisation of conflict at work: mobilisation, counter-mobilisation and the displacement of grievance expressions', *Economic and Industrial Democracy*, 39(4): 639–60.

Kirkpatrick, J. (2014) 'The IWW cleaners branch union in the United Kingdom', in I. Ness (ed) *New Forms of Worker Organization: The Syndicalist and Autonomist Restoration of Class Struggle Unionism*, Oakland, CA: PM Press, pp 233–57.

Kofman, E. (2012) 'Rethinking care through social reproduction: articulating circuits of migration', *Social Politics*, 19(1): 142–62.

Kosack, G. (1976) 'Migrant women: the move to Western Europe – a step towards emancipation?', *Race & Class*, 17(4): 369–80.

Kraemer Diaz, A.E., Weir, M.M., Isom, S., Quandt, S.A., Chen, H., and Arcury, T.A. (2016) 'Aggression among male migrant farmworkers living in camps in eastern North Carolina', *Journal of Immigrant and Minority Health*, 18(3): 542–51.

Krings, T. (2009) 'A race to the bottom? Trade unions, EU enlargement and the free movement of labour', *European Journal of Industrial Relations*, 15(1): 49–69.

Kulczycki, J.J. (1989) '"Scapegoating" the foreign worker: Job turnover, accidents, and diseases among Polish coal miners in the German Ruhr', *Polish American Studies*, 46(1): 42–60.

Kulczycki, J.J. (1993) 'Scapegoating the foreign worker: job turnover, accidents, and disease among Polish coal miners in the German Ruhr, 1871–1914', in C. Guerin-Gonzales and C. Strikwerda (eds) *The Politics of Immigrant Workers. Labor Activism and Migration in the World Economy since 1830*, New York: Holmes & Meier, pp 133–52.

Kvist, J. (2004) 'Does EU enlargement start a race to the bottom? Strategic interaction among EU member states in social policy', *Journal of European Social Policy*, 14(3): 301–18.

Lai, P.C., Soltani, E., and Baum, T. (2008) 'Distancing flexibility in the hotel industry: the role of employment agencies as labour suppliers', *The International Journal of Human Resource Management*, 19(1): 132–52.

Lam, L. and Triandafyllidou, A. (2021) 'An unlikely stepping stone? Exploring how platform work shapes newcomer migrant integration', *Transitions: Journal of Transient Migration*, 5(1): 11–29.

Lan, P.C. (2006) *Global Cinderellas: Migrant Domestics and Newly Rich Employers in Taiwan*, Durham, NC: Duke University Press.

Laslett, B. and Brenner, J. (1989) 'Gender and social reproduction: historical perspectives', *Annual Review of Sociology*, 15(1): 381–404.

Lee, C.K. (1995) 'Engendering the worlds of labor: women workers, labor markets, and production politics in the South China economic miracle', *American Sociological Review*, 60(3): 378–97.

Lee, C.K. (1998) *Gender and the South China Miracle*, Berkeley: University of California Press.

Lee, C. (2005) 'Development of free economic zones and labor standards: a case study of free economic zones in Korea', Cornell University: International Programs Visiting Fellow Working Papers [online], Available from: https://ecommons.cornell.edu/handle/1813/89761. Accessed 1 September 2023.

Lee, J., Gereffi, G., and Nathan, D. (2013) 'Mobile phones: Who benefits in shifting global value chains?', *Capturing the Gains: Revised Summit Briefing, No. 6.1*. Available from: https://papers.ssrn.com/sol3/papers.cfm?abstract_id=2265845

Lee, S.K. (2017) 'The three worlds of emigration policy: towards a theory of sending state regimes', *Journal of Ethnic and Migration Studies*, 43(9): 1453–71.

Lee, T.L. and Tapia, M. (2021) 'Confronting race and other social identity erasures: the case for critical industrial relations theory', *ILR Review*, 74(3): 637–62.

Lefebvre, H. (1991) *The Production of Space* [1974], Oxford: Blackwell.

Lewis, H., Dwyer, P., Hodkinson, S., and Waite, L. (2015) 'Hyper-precarious lives: migrants, work and forced labour in the Global North', *Progress in Human Geography*, 39(5): 580–600.

Lillie, N. (2012) 'Subcontracting, posted migrants and labour market segmentation in Finland', *British Journal of Industrial Relations*, 50(1): 148–67.

Lillie, N. and Greer, I. (2007) 'Industrial relations, migration, and neoliberal politics: the case of the European construction sector', *Politics & Society*, 35(4): 551–81.

Lillie, N. and Sippola, M. (2011) 'National unions and transnational workers: the case of Olkiluoto 3, Finland', *Work, Employment and Society*, 25(2): 292–308.

Lillie, N. and Wagner, I. (2015) 'Subcontracting, insecurity and posted work: evidence from construction, meat processing and ship building', in Jan Drahokoupil (ed) *The Outsourcing Challenge: Organizing Workers Across Fragmented Production Networks*, Brussels: ETUI, pp 157–74.

Lillie, N., Berntsen, L., Wagner, I., and Danaj, S. (2019) 'A comparative analysis of union responses to posted work in four European countries', in J. Arnholtz and N. Lillie (eds) *Posted Work in the European Union – The Political Economy of Free Movement*, London: Routledge, pp 89–108.

Lin, W., Lindquist, J., Xiang, B., and Yeoh, B.S. (2017) 'Migration infrastructures and the production of migrant mobilities', *Mobilities*, 12(2): 167–74.

Lincoln, D. (2009) 'Labour migration in the global division of labour: migrant workers in Mauritius', *International Migration*, 47(4): 129–56.

Lindio-McGovern, L. (2004) 'Alienation and labor export in the context of globalization', *Critical Asian Studies*, 36(2): 217–38.

Lindquist, J., Xiang, B., and Yeoh, B.S. (2012) 'Opening the black box of migration: Brokers, the organization of transnational mobility and the changing political economy in Asia', *Pacific Affairs*, 85(1): 7–19.

Lindstrom, D.P. (1996) 'Economic opportunity in Mexico and return migration from the United States', *Demography*, 33(3): 357–74.

Linebaugh, P. and Rediker, M. (2000) *The Many-Headed Hydra: Sailors, Slaves, Commoners, and the Hidden History of the Revolutionary Atlantic*, Boston, MA: Beacon Press.

Liu, W. and Dicken, P. (2006) 'Transnational corporations and "obligated embeddedness": foreign direct investment in China's automobile industry', *Environment and Planning A*, 38(7): 1229–47.

Liu-Farrer, G. and Yeoh, B.S. (eds) (2018) *Routledge Handbook of Asian Migrations*, London: Routledge.

Liu-Farrer, G., Yeoh, B.S., and Baas, M. (2021) 'Social construction of skill: an analytical approach toward the question of skill in cross-border labour mobilities', *Journal of Ethnic and Migration Studies*, 47(10): 2237–51.

Loess, K., Miller van, V., and Yoskowitz, D. (2008) 'Offshore employment practices: an empirical analysis of routines, wages and labour turnover', *International Labour Review*, 147(2–3): 249–73.

Lonergan, G. (2015) 'Migrant women and social reproduction under austerity', *Feminist Review*, 109(1): 124–45.

Lucas, K., Kang, D., and Li, Z. (2013) 'Workplace dignity in a total institution: examining the experiences of Foxconn's migrant workforce', *Journal of Business Ethics*, 114(1): 91–106.

Lucassen, J. and Bloch, Donald A. (1987) *Migrant Labour in Europe, 1600–1900. The Drift to the North Sea*, London: Routledge.

Lucassen, L. (2019) 'The rise of the European migration regime and its paradoxes (1945–2020)', *International Review of Social History*, 64(3): 515–31.

Lucassen, L. and van Voss, L.H. (2019) 'Introduction: flight as fight', in M. Rediker, T. Chakraborty, and M. van Rossum (eds) *A Global History of Runaways*, Berkeley, CA: University of California Press, pp 1–21.

Lutz, H. and Palenga-Möllenbeck, E. (2015) 'Global care chains', in A. Triandafyllidou (ed) *Routledge Handbook of Immigration and Refugee Studies*, London: Routledge, pp 139–44.

Lyons, L. (2009) 'Transcending the border: transnational imperatives in Singapore's migrant worker rights movement', *Critical Asian Studies*, 41(1): 89–112.

MacKenzie, R. and Forde, C. (2009) 'The rhetoric of the good worker' versus the realities of employers' use and the experiences of migrant workers', *Work, Employment and Society*, 23(1): 142–59.

MacKenzie, R. and Martínez Lucio, M. (2019) 'Regulation, migration and the implications for industrial relations', *Journal of Industrial Relations*, 61(2): 176–97.

MacKenzie, R., Forde, C., and Ciupijus, Z. (2012) 'Networks of support for new migrant communities: institutional goals versus substantive goals', *Urban Studies*, 49(3): 631–47.

Maldonado, M.M. (2009) ' "It is their nature to do menial labour": the racialization of "Latino/a workers" by agricultural employers', *Ethnic and Racial Studies*, 32(6): 1017–36.

Maloney, T.N. and Whatley, W.C. (1995) 'Making the effort: the contours of racial discrimination in Detroit's labor markets, 1920–1940', *Journal of Economic History*, 55(3): 465–93.

Manky, O. (2016) 'From towns to hotels: changes in mining accommodation regimes and their effects on labour union strategies', *British Journal of Industrial Relation*, 55(2): 295–320.

Mann, M. (1973) *Workers on the Move*, London: Cambridge University Press.

Mantu, S. and Guild, E. (2013) 'Acts of citizenship deprivation. Ruptures between citizen and state', in E.F. Isin and M. Saward (eds) *Enacting European Citizenship*, New York: Cambridge University Press, pp 111–31.

March, J. and Simon, H. (1958) *Organizations*, New York: Wiley.

Marino, S. (2012) 'Trade union inclusion of migrant and ethnic minority workers: comparing Italy and the Netherlands', *European Journal of Industrial Relations*, 18(1): 5–20.

Marino, S. (2015) 'Trade unions, special structures and the inclusion of migrant workers: on the role of union democracy', *Work, Employment and Society*, 29(5): 826–42.

Marino, S., Penninx, R., and Roosblad, J. (2017a) 'Introduction: how to study trade union action towards immigration and migrant workers?', in S. Marino, J. Roosblad and R. Penninx (eds) *Trade Unions and Migrant Workers: New Contexts and Challenges in Europe*, Cheltenham and Northampton, MA: Edward Elgar Publishing, pp 1–22.

Marino, S., Penninx, R., and Roosblad, J. (2017b) 'Comparing trade union attitudes and actions relating to immigration and migrant workers in 11 European countries', in S. Marino, J. Roosblad and R. Penninx (eds) *Trade Unions and Migrant Workers: New Contexts and Challenges in Europe*, Cheltenham and Northampton, MA: Edward Elgar Publishing, pp 353–88.

Martin, P. (2017) *Merchants of Labor: Recruiters and International Labor Migration*, Oxford: Oxford University Press.

Martínez Lucio, M. and Perrett, R. (2009) 'The diversity and politics of trade unions' responses to minority ethnic and migrant workers', *Economic and Industrial Democracy*, 3(30): 1–24.

Martínez Lucio, M. and Connolly, H. (2010) 'Contextualizing voice and stakeholders: researching employment relations, immigration and trade unions', *Journal of Business Ethics*, 97(1): 19–29.

Marx, K. (1967) *Capital. Volume III* [1867], New York: International Publishers.

Marx, K. (1993) *Capital: A Critique of Political Economy* [1893], *ii*, London: Penguin.

Mas Giralt, R. (2017) 'Onward migration as a coping strategy? Latin Americans moving from Spain to the UK post-2008', *Population, Space, and Place*, 23(3): 1–12.

Massey, D. (1983) 'Industrial restructuring as class restructuring: production decentralization and local uniqueness', *Regional Studies*, 17(2): 73–89.

Massey, D. (1984) *Spatial Divisions of Labour*, London: MacMillan.

Massey, D.S. (1990), 'Social structure, household strategies, and the cumulative causation of migration', *Population Index*, 56(1): 3–26.

Massey, D.S. and Taylor, J.E. (2004) *International Migration: Prospects and Policies in a Global Market*, Oxford: Oxford University Press.

Massey, D.S., Arango, J., Hugo, G., Kouaouci, A., Pellegrino, A., and Taylor, J.E. (1993) 'Theories of international migration: a review and appraisal', *Population and Development Review*, 19(3): 431–66.

Matsuda, M. (1991) 'Beside my sister, facing the enemy: legal theory out of coalition', *Stanford Law Review*, 43(6): 1183–92.

Mavrakis, T. (2015) *Migration and Temporary Agency Work in the EU Welfare, Tourist and Agricultural Sectors: Final Report for Marie Curie Actions, Intra-European Fellowships*. Brussels: European Commission

May, M. (1982) 'The historical problem of the family wage: the Ford Motor Company and the five dollar day', *Feminist Studies*, 8(2): 399–424.

Mazzacurati, C. (2005) 'Dal blat alla vendita del lavoro. Come sono cambiate colf e badanti ucraine e moldave a Padova', in T. Caponio and A. Colombo (eds) *Migrazioni globali, integrazioni locali*, Bologna: Il Mulino, pp 145–74.

McAdam, D. (1999) *Political Process and the Development of Black Insurgency, 1930–1970* [1982] (2nd edn), Chicago, IL: The University of Chicago Press.

McAlevey, J. (2016) *No Shortcuts: Organizing for Power in the New Gilded Age*, Oxford: Oxford University Press.

McCall, L. (2005) 'The complexity of intersectionality', *Signs: Journal of Women in Culture and Society*, 30(3): 1771–800.

McCollum, D. and Findlay, A. (2015) '"Flexible" workers for "flexible" jobs? The labour market function of A8 migrant labour in the UK', *Work, Employment and Society*, 29(3): 427–43.

McCallum, J. K. (2013) *Global Unions, Local Power: The New Spirit of Transnational Labor Organizing*, Cornell University Press.

McCollum, D. and Findlay, A. (2018) 'Oiling the wheels? Flexible labour markets and the migration industry', *Journal of Ethnic and Migration Studies*, 44(4): 558–74.

McDowell, L. (1999) *Gender, Identity and Place: Understanding Feminist Geographies*, Cambridge: Polity Press.

McDowell, L. (2008) 'Thinking through work: complex inequalities, constructions of difference and trans-national migrants', *Progress in Human Geography*, 32(4): 491–507.

McDowell, L. (2009) *Working Bodies: Interactive Service Employment and Workplace Identities*, Chichester: Wiley-Blackwell.

McDowell, L. and Massey, D. (1984) 'A woman's place', in D. Massey, and J. Allen (eds) *Geography Matters! A Reader*, Cambridge: Cambridge University Press, pp 128–47.

McDowell, L., Batnitzky, A., and Dyer, S. (2007) 'Division, segmentation, and interpellation: the embodied labors of migrant workers in a Greater London hotel', *Economic Geography*, 83(1): 1–25.

McDowell, L., Batnitzky, A., and Dyer, S. (2009) 'Precarious work and economic migration: emerging immigrant divisions of labour in Greater London's service sector', *International Journal of Urban and Regional Research*, 33(1): 3–25.

McGovern, P. (2007) 'Immigration, labour markets and employment relations: problems and prospects', *British Journal of Industrial Relations*, 45(2): 217–35.

McGovern, P. (2020) 'Long read: who are you calling unskilled?', London School of Economics, [online] 6 March, Available from: https://blogs. lse.ac.uk/brexit/2020/03/06/long-read-who-are-you-calling-unskilled/. Accessed 20 April 2020.

McGrath-Champ, S., Herod, A., and Rainnie, A. (eds) (2010) *Handbook of Employment and Society, Working Space*, Northampton, MA: Edward Elgar Publishing.

McKay, S.C. (2007) 'Filipino sea men: constructing masculinities in an ethnic labour niche', *Journal of Ethnic and Migration Studies*, 33(4): 617–33.

Meardi, G. (2007) 'More voice after more exit? Unstable industrial relations in Central Eastern Europe', *Industrial Relations Journal*, 38(6): 503–23.

Meardi, G. (2012a) *Social Failures of EU Enlargement*, London: Routledge.

Meardi, G. (2012b) 'Union immobility? Trade unions and the freedoms of movement in the enlarged EU', *British Journal of Industrial Relations*, 50(1): 99–120.

Meier, A. and Rudwick, E. (1979) 'Black violence: political impact of the 1960s riots', *The Journal of American History*, 66(2): 464–6.

Menezes, M.A., Silva, M.S., and Cover, M. (2012) 'Migrant workers in Sugarcen Mills: a study of social networks and recruitment intermediaries in Brazil', *Agrarian South: The Journal of Political Economy*, 1(2): 161–80.

Menz, G. (2013) 'The neoliberalized state and the growth of the migration industry', in T. Gammeltoft-Hansen and N.N. Sørensen (eds) *The Migration Industry and the Commercialization of International Migration*, London: Routledge, pp 126–45.

Meszmann, T. and Fedyuk, O. (2019) 'Snakes or ladders? Job quality assessment among temp workers from Ukraine in Hungarian electronics', *Central and Eastern European Migration Review*, 8(1): 75–93.

Meyer III, S. (1981) *The Five Dollar Day: Labor Management and Social Control in the Ford Motor Company, 1908–1921*, Albany, NY: State University of New York Press.

Mezzadra, S. (2004) 'The right to escape', *Ephemera*, 4(3): 267–75.

Mezzadra, S. (2011a) 'The gaze of autonomy: capitalism, migration and social struggles', in V. Squire (ed) *The Contested Politics of Mobility: Borderzones and Irregularity*, London: Routledge, pp 121–42.

Mezzadra, S. (2011b) 'How many histories of labour? Towards a theory of postcolonial capitalism', *Postcolonial Studies*, 14(2): 151–70.

Mezzadra, S. (2015) 'MLC 2015 Keynote: what's at stake in the mobility of labour? Borders, migration, contemporary capitalism', *Migration, Mobility, & Displacement*, 2(1): 30–43.

Mezzadra, S. and Neilson, B. (2013) *Border as Method, or, the Multiplication of Labor*, Durham, NC: Duke University Press.

Mezzadri, A. (2017) *The Sweatshop Regime: Labouring Bodies, Exploitation, and Garments Made in India,* Cambridge: Cambridge University Press.

Mezzadri, A. (2019) 'On the value of social reproduction: informal labour, the majority world and the need for inclusive theories and politics', *Radical Philosophy*, 2(4): 33–41.

Mezzadri, A. (2021) 'A value theory of inclusion: informal labour, the homeworker, and the social reproduction of value', *Antipode*, 53(4): 1186–205.

Mies, M. (1982) *The Lace Makers of Narsapur: Indian Housewives Produce for the World Market*, London: Zed.

Mies, M. (1986) *Patriarchy and Accumulation on a World Scale: Women in the International Division of Labour*, London: Zed.

Miles, L., Freeman, T., Wan Teng, L., Mat Yasin, S., and Ying, K. (2022) 'Empowerment as a pre-requisite to managing and influencing health in the workplace: the sexual and reproductive health needs of factory women migrant workers in Malaysia', *Economic and Industrial Democracy*, 43(4): 1676–98.

Migration Advisory Committee (2018) *EEA Migration in the UK: Final Report*, London: Migration Advisory Committee, Available from: https://assets.publishing.service.gov.uk/government/uploads/system/uploads/attachment_data/file/741926/Final_EEA_report.PDF. Accessed 21 May 2019.

Milberg, W. and Amengual, M. (2008) *Economic Development and Working Conditions in Export Processing Zones: A Survey of Trends*, Geneva: ILO.

Milkman, R. (ed) (1985) *Women, Work, and Protest: A Century of US Women's Labor History*, Boston, MA: Routledge & Kegan Paul.

Milkman, R. (2000) *Organizing Immigrants: The Challenge for Unions in Contemporary California*, Ithaca, NY and London: ILR Press.

Milkman, R. (2020) *Immigrant Labour and the New Precariat*, Cambridge: Polity Press.

Miller, J. (2013) 'Her fight is your fight: "guest worker" labor activism in the early 1970s West Germany', *International Labor and Working-Class History*, 84: 226–47.

Miller, M.J. and Castles, S. (2009) *The Age of Migration: International Population Movements in the Modern World*, Basingstoke: Palgrave Macmillan.

Millward, P. (2017) 'World Cup 2022 and Qatar's construction projects: relational power in networks and relational responsibilities to migrant workers', *Current Sociology*, 65(5): 756–76.

Mitchell, K., Marston, S.A., and Katz, C. (2003) 'Life's work: an introduction, review and critique', *Antipode*, 35(3): 415–42.

Mitchell, K., Marston, S.A. and Katz, C. (2004) 'Life's work: An introduction, review and critique', in K. Mitchell, S.A. Marston, and C. Katz (2012 eds) *Life's Work: Geographies of Social Reproduction*, John Wiley and Sons, pp 185–202.

Mitchell, T.R., Holtom, B.C., Lee, T.W., Sablynski, C.J., and Erez, M. (2001) 'Why people stay: using job embeddedness to predict voluntary turnover', *Academy of Management Journal*, 44(6): 1102–21.

Mobley, W.H. (1982) *Employee Turnover: Causes, Consequences and Control*, Reading, MA: Addison-Wesley.

Mohandesi, S. and Teitelman, E. (2017) 'Without reserves', in T. Bhattacharya (ed) Social Reproduction Theory: Remapping Class, Recentering Oppression, London: Pluto Press, pp 37–67.

Mometti, F. and Ricciardi, M. (2011) *La normale eccezione. Lotte migranti in Italia*, Roma: Alegre.

Monárrez Fragoso, J.E. (2018) 'Feminicide: impunity for the perpetrators and injustice for the victims', in K. Carrington, R. Hogg, J. Scott, and M. Sozzo (eds) *The Palgrave Handbook of Criminology and the Global South*, Cham: Palgrave Macmillan, pp 913–29.

Montgomery, D. (1979) *Workers' Control in America: Studies in the History of Work, Technology, and Labor Struggles*, Cambridge: Cambridge University Press.

Montgomery, D. (1987) *The Fall of the House of Labor*, Cambridge: Cambridge University Press.

Morad, M. and Sacchetto, D. (2020) 'Multiple migration and use of ties: Bangladeshis in Italy and beyond', *International Migration*, 58(4): 154–67.

Morad, M., Della Puppa, F., and Sacchetto, D. (2021) 'The dark side of onward migration: experiences and strategies of Italian-Bangladeshis in the UK at the time of the post-Brexit referendum', *British Journal of Sociology*, 72(5): 1311–24.

Morokvasic, M. (2004) 'Settled in mobility: engendering post-wall migration in Europe', *Feminist Review*, 77(1): 7–25.

Morrison, C., Sacchetto, D., and Cretu, O. (2013) 'International migration and labour turnover: workers' agency in the construction sector of Russia and Italy', *Studies of Transition States and Societies*, 5(2): 7–20.

Morrison, C., Sacchetto, D., and Croucher, R. (2020) 'Migration, ethnicity and solidarity: "multinational workers" in the former Soviet Union', *British Journal of Industrial Relations*, 58(4): 761–84.

Mosoetsa, S., Stillerman, J., and Tilly, C. (2016) 'Precarious labor, South and North: an introduction', *International Labor and Working Class History*, 89: 5–19.

Moulier-Boutang, Y.M. (1998) *De l'esclavage au salariat: économie historique du salariat bridé*, Paris: Puf.

Moyer-Lee, J. and Lopez, H. (2017) 'From invisible to invincible: the story of the 3 Cosas campaign', in: S. Lazar (ed) *Where Are the Unions?*, London: Zed Books, pp 231–50.

Mullings, B. (1999) 'Sides of the same coin?: coping and resistance among Jamaican data-entry operators', *Annals of the Association of American Geographers*, 89(2): 290–311.

Murphy, R. (2004) 'The impact of labor migration on the well-being and agency of rural Chinese women: cultural and economic contexts and the life course', in A. Gaetano and T. Jacka (eds) *On the Move*, New York: Columbia University Press, pp 243–76.

Nam, J.L. (1994) 'Women's role in export dependence and state control of labor unions in South Korea', *Women's Studies International Forum*, 17(1): 57–67.

Naufal, G. and Genc, I. (2012) *Expats and the Labour Force: The Story of the Gulf Cooperation Council Countries*, New York: Palgrave Macmillan.

Neergaard, A. and Woolfson, C. (2017) 'Sweden: A model in dissolution?', in S. Marino, J. Roosblad, and R. Penninx (eds) *Trade Unions and Migrant Workers: New Contexts and Challenges in Europe*, Cheltenham: Edward Elgar Publishing, pp 200–23.

Neilson, B. (2009) 'The world seen from a taxi: students-migrants-workers in the global multiplication of labour', *Subjectivity*, 29(1): 425–44.

Neilson, B. (2014) 'Zones: beyond the logic of exception?', *Concentric: Literary and Cultural Studies*, 40(2): 11–28.

Nesporova, A. (2002) *Why Unemployment Remains so High in Central and Eastern Europe: Employment Paper 2002/43*, Geneva: ILO.

Ness, I. (2011) *Guest workers and Resistance to US Corporate Despotism*, Chicago: University of Illinois Press.

Ness, I. (2014) *New Forms of Worker Organization: The Syndicalist and Autonomist Restoration of Class Struggle Unionism*, Oakland, CA: PM Press.

Neveling, P. (2015) 'Export processing zones and global class formation', in J.G. Carrier and D. Kalb (eds) *Anthropologies of Class*, Cambridge: Cambridge University Press, pp 164–82.

Newsome, K., Taylor, P., and Rainnie, A. (2015) *'Putting Labour in its Place': Labour Process Analysis and Global Value Chains*, London and New York: Palgrave Macmillan.

Nichols, T. and Beynon, H. (1977) *Living with Capitalism: Class relations and the modern factory*, London: Routledge & Kegan Paul.

Nickell, S. and Saleheen, J. (2015) *The Impact of Immigration on Occupational Wages: Evidence from Britain* Bank of England Staff Working Paper No. 574, London: Bank of England.

Nikolova, M. and Balhorn, L. (2020), 'The EU's seasonal farm workers are still forced to travel during the pandemic', *Jacobin*, [online] 5 November, Available from: https://www.jacobinmag.com/2020/05/migrant-work ers-strawberry-farms-england-bulgaria-eu-coronavirus. Accessed 11 December 2020

Nonini, D.M. (1993) 'On the outs on the rim: an ethnographic grounding of the "Asia Pacific Imaginary"', in A. Dirilik (ed) *What is in a Rim? Critical Perspective on the Pacific Region Idea*, Boulder, CO: Westview Press, pp 161–82.

Novitz, T. (2009) 'Workers' freedom of association', In J. Gross and L. Compa (eds) *Human Rights in Labor and Employment Relations: International and Domestic Perspectives*, Ithaca: Cornell University Press, pp 123–54.

Novitz, T. and Andrijasevic, R. (2020) 'Reform of the posting of workers regime – an assessment of the practical impact on unfree labour relations', *JCMS: Journal of Common Market Studies*, 58(5): 1325–41.

O'Brien, C. (2015) 'The pillory, the precipice and the slippery slope: the profound effects of the UK's legal reform programme targeting EU migrants', *Journal of Social Welfare and Family Law*, 37(1): 111–36.

OECD (1996) *Employment Outlook. Countering the Risks of Labour Market Exclusion*, Paris: OECD.

OECD (2018) *Employment Outlook 2018*, Paris: OECD.

OECD (2019) *International Migration Outlook. Labour Market Outcomes of Immigrants and Integration Policies in OECD Countries*, Paris: OECD.

OECD (2020a) *Labour Market Statistics: Employment by Job Tenure Intervals: Persons*, Paris: OECD.

OECD (2020b) *Employment Outlook 2020. Worker Security and the Covid-19 Crisis*, Paris: OECD.

Office for National Statistics (ONS) (2022) Half a million more people are out of the labour force because of long-term sickness. 10 November 2022. Available from https://www.ons.gov.uk/employmentandlabourmarket/ peoplenotinwork/economicinactivity/articles/halfamillionmorepeoplea reoutofthelabourforcebecauseoflongtermsickness/2022-11-10. Accessed 30 August 2023.

Olmos, D. (2019) 'Racialized im/migration and autonomy of migration perspectives: new directions and opportunities', *Sociology Compass*, 13(9): e12729.

Ong, A. (1997) *The Gender and Labor Politics of Postmodernity*, Durham, NC: Duke University Press.

Ong, A. (1999) *Flexible Citizenship: The Cultural Logics of Transnationality*, Durham, NC: Duke University Press.

Ong, A. (2006) *Neoliberalism as Exception: Mutations in Citizenship and Sovereignty*, Durham, NC: Duke University Press.

ONS (2019) 'Employee turnover levels and rates by industry section, UK, January 2017 to December 2018', Office for National Statistics, [online] 14 October, Available from: https://www.ons.gov.uk/employmentandlabou rmarket/peopleinwork/employmentandemployeetypes/adhocs/10685emp loyeeturnoverlevelsandratesbyindustrysectionukjanuary2017todecember2 018. Accessed 15 February 2020.

Organ, I. (2006) 'Do tax-free zones create employment? The case of Turkish free-trade zones', *South-East Europe Review for Labour and Social Affairs*, 4: 127–40.

Papadopoulos, D. and Tsianos, V.S. (2013) 'After citizenship: autonomy of migration, organisational ontology and mobile commons', *Citizenship Studies*, 17(2): 178–96.

Papadopoulos, D., Stephenson, N., and Tsianos, V. (2008) *Escape Routes: Control and Subversion in the Twenty-First Century*, London: Pluto Press.

Papastergiadis, N. (2000) *The Turbulence of Migration*, Cambridge: Polity Press.

Parreñas, R.S. (2022) *Unfree. Migrant Domestic Work in Arab States*, Stanford: Stanford University Press.

Parutis, V. (2014) ' "Economic migrants" or "middling transnationals"? East European migrants' experiences of work in the UK', *International Migration*, 52(1): 36–55.

Pattison, P., McIntyre, N., Mukhtar, I., Eapen, N., Bhuyan, O.U., Bhattarai, U., and Piyari, A. (2021) 'Revealed: 6,500 migrant workers have died in Qatar since World Cup awarded', *The Guardian*, [online] 23 February, Available from: https://www.theguardian.com/global-development/ 2021/feb/23/revealed-migrant-worker-deaths-qatar-fifa-world-cup-2022. Accessed 11 November 2022.

Paul, A.M. and Yeoh, B.S. (2021) 'Studying multinational migrations, speaking back to migration theory', *Global Networks*, 21(1): 3–17.

Paul, R. (2020) 'Europe's essential workers: Migration and pandemic politics in Central and Eastern Europe during COVID-19', *European Policy Analysis*, 6(2): 238–63.

Peano, I. (2017) 'Migrants' struggles? Rethinking citizenship, anti-racism and labour precarity through migration politics in Italy', in S. Lazar (ed) *Where Are the Unions? Workers and Social Movements in Latin America, the Middle East and Europe*, London: Zed Books, pp 85–102.

Pearson, R., Anitha, S., and McDowell, L. (2010) 'Striking issues: from labour process to industrial dispute at Grunwick and Gate Gourmet', *Industrial Relations Journal*, 41(5): 408–28.

Peck, J. (1989) 'Reconceptualizing the local labour market: space, segmentation and the state', *Progress in Human Geography* 13(1): 42–61.

Peck, J. (1996) *Work-Place: The Social Regulation of Labor Markets*, New York: Guilford Press.

Peck, J. (2003) 'Geography and public policy: mapping the penal state', *Progress in Human Geography*, 27(2): 222–32.

Peck, J. (2022) 'Modalities of labour: restructuring, regulation, regime', in E. Baglioni, L. Campling, N.M. Coe, A. Smith (eds) *Labour Regime and Global Production*, Newcastle: Agenda Publishing, pp 63–80.

Peck, J. and Theodore, N. (2007) 'Flexible recession: the temporary staffing industry and mediated work in the United States', *Cambridge Journal of Economics*, 31(2): 171–92.

Peck, J. and Theodore, N. (2010) 'Labor markets from the bottom up', in S. McGrath-Champ, A. Herod, and A. Rainnie (eds) *Handbook of Employment and Society: Working Space*, Cheltenham: Edward Elgar, pp 87–105.

Peña, D. (1997) *The Terror of the Machine: Technology, Work, Gender, and Ecology on the U.S.-Mexico Border*, Austin, TX: University of Texas, Center for Mexican American Studies.

Penninx, R. (2017) 'Migration and its regulation in an integrating Europe', in S. Marino, J. Roosblad, and R. Penninx (eds) *Trade Unions and Migrant Workers: New Contexts and Challenges in Europe*, Cheltenham and Northampton, MA: Edward Elgar Publishing, pp 43–65.

Penninx, R. and Roosblad, J. (eds) (2000) *Trade Unions, Immigration, and Immigrants in Europe, 1960–1993: A Comparative Study of the Attitudes and Actions of Trade Unions in Seven West European Countries*, New York and Oxford: Berghahn Books.

Pepper, S. (1988) 'China's special economic zones: the current rescue bid for a faltering experiment', *Bulletin of Concerned Asian Scholars*, 20(3): 2–21.

Pérez-López, Jorge and Diaz-Briquets, Sergio (1990) 'Labor migration and offshore assembly in the socialist world: the Cuban experience', *Population and Development Review*, 16(2): 273–99.

Però, D. (2014) 'Class politics and migrants: collective action among new migrant workers in Britain', *Sociology*, 48(6): 1156–72.

Però, D. (2020) 'Indie unions, organizing and labour renewal: learning from precarious migrant workers', *Work, Employment and Society*, 34(5): 900–18.

Perrotta, D. and Sacchetto, D. (2014) 'Migrant farmworkers in Southern Italy: ghettoes, caporalato and collective action', *Workers of the World: International Journal on Strikes and Social Conflicts*, 1(5): 75–98.

Perry, J. and Power, S. (2007) 'In Eastern Europe, low pay is driving workers away', *The Wall Street Journal Europe*, 10 July: 1(34).

Peters, M.E. (2015) 'Open trade, closed borders immigration in the era of globalization', *World Politics*, 67(1): 114–54.

Phillips, A. and Taylor, B. (1980) 'Sex and skill: notes towards a feminist economics', *FeministReview*, 6(1): 79–88.

Picchio, A. (1992) *Social Reproduction: The Political Economy of the Labour Market*, Cambridge: Cambridge University Press.

Piore, M.J. (1979) *Birds of Passage: Migrant Labour and Industrial Societies*, Cambridge: Cambridge University Press.

Piore, M.J. (1983) 'Labor market segmentation: to what paradigm does it belong?', *The American Economic Review*, 73(2): 249–53.

Piper, Nicola, and Uhlin, Anders (2002) 'Transnational advocacy networks and the issue of female labor migration and trafficking in East and Southeast Asia: A gendered analysis of opportunities and obstacles', *Asian and Pacific Migration Journal*, 11(2): 171–96.

Piper, N. and Yamanaka, K. (2008) 'Feminised migration in East and Southeast Asia and the securing of livelihoods', in N. Piper (ed) *New Perspectives on Gender and Migration: Livelihood, Rights and Entitlements*, New York: Routledge pp 159–88.

Piro, V. (2021) *Migrant Farmworkers in 'Plastic Factories': Investigating Work-Life Struggles*, Basingstoke: Palgrave Macmillan.

Piro, V. and Sacchetto, D. (2021) 'Subcontracted racial capitalism: the interrelationship of race and production in meat processing plants', *Work in the Global Economy*, 1(1–2): 33–53.

Polanyi, K. (1957) *The Great Transformation*, Boston: Beacon Press.

Poros, M.V. (2001) 'The role of migrant networks in linking local labor markets: the case of Asian Indian migration to New York and London', *Global Networks*, 1(3): 243–59.

Porpora, D.V., Lim, M.H., and Prommas, U.(1989) 'The role of women in the international division of labour: the case of Thailand', *Development and Change*, 20(2): 269–94.

Portes, A. (1997) 'Immigration theory for a new century: some problems and opportunities', *International Migration Review*, 31(4): 799–825.

Preibisch, K. and Binford, L. (2007) 'Interrogating racialized global labour supply: an exploration of the racial/national replacement of foreign agricultural workers', *The Canadian Review of Sociology and Anthropology/ La Revue Canadienne de Sociologie et d'Anthropologie*, 44(1): 5–36.

Price, J.L. (1977) *The Study of Turnover*, Ames, IA: Iowa State University Press.

Pugliese, E. (2000) *Rapporto immigrazione. Lavoro, sindacato e società*, Rome: Ediesse.

Pun, N. (2005) *Made in China: Women Factory Workers in a Global Workplace*, Durham, NC: Duke University Press.

Pun, N. (2007) 'Gendering the dormitory labor system: production, reproduction, and migrant labor in south China', *Feminist Economics*, 13(3–4): 239–58.

Pun, N. (2016) *Migrant Labor in Post-Socialist China*, New York, NY: Polity Press.

Pun, N. and Smith, C. (2007) 'Putting transnational labour process in its place: the dormitory labour regime in post-socialist China', *Work, Employment and Society*, 21(1): 27–45.

Pun, N. and Chan, J. (2013) 'The spatial politics of labor in China: life, labor, and a new generation of migrant workers', *South Atlantic Quarterly*, 112(1): 179–90.

Pun, N., Liu, A.Y., and Lu, H.L. (2015) *Labour Conditions and the Working Poor in China and India: The China Team's Final Report* [unpublished final report for the ESRC-DfID project 'Labour Conditions and the Working Poor in China and India'], London: Centre for Development Policy and Research, SOAS.

Qin, X., Hom, P.W., and Xu, M. (2019) 'Am I a peasant or a worker? An identity strain perspective on turnover among developing-world migrants', *Human Relations*, 72(4): 801–33.

Rabby, A.A. (2022) 'Labor Control Regime through Job contracts, Intermittent unemployment and Social reproduction among the Bangladeshi workers in Fincantieri, Italy', *40th ILPC Conference*, 21–23 April 2022, University of Padua.

Raghwan, S.M. (2000) *Report and Conclusions of the ILO Asia Pacific Trade Union Symposium on Migrant Workers*, Geneva: ILO Workers Activities.

Raj, J. and Axelby, R. (2019) 'From labour contractors to worker-agents: transformations in the recruitment of migrant labourers in India', *Contributions to Indian Sociology*, 53(2): 272–98.

Ramasamy, P. (1992) 'Labour control and labour resistance in the plantations of colonial Malaya', *The Journal of Peasant Studies*, 19(3–4): 87–105.

Rass, C. (2012) 'Temporary labour migration and state-run recruitment of foreign workers in Europe, 1919–1975: a new migration regime?', *International Review of Social History*, 57(S20): 191–224.

Rawick, G.P. (1972) *From Sundown to Sunup: The Making of the Black Community*, Westport, CT: Greenwood Publishing Co.

Raworth, K. and Kidder, T. (2009) 'Mimicking "Lean" in global value chains: it's the workers who get leaned on', in J. Bair (ed) *Frontiers of Commodity Chain Research*, Stanford, CA: Stanford University Press, pp 165–89.

Refslund, B. (2016) 'Intra-European labour migration and deteriorating employment relations in Danish cleaning and agriculture: industrial relations under pressure from EU8/2 labour inflows?', *Economic and Industrial Democracy*, 37(4): 597–621.

Refslund, B. and Sippola, M. (2022) 'Migrant workers trapped between individualism and collectivism: the formation of union-based workplace collectivism', *Economic and Industrial Democracy*, 43(3): 1004–27.

Reid-Musson, E. (2014) 'Historicizing precarity: a labour geography of 'transient' migrant workers in Ontario tobacco', *Geoforum*, 56: 161–71.

Reséndez A. (2016) *The Other Slavery*, New York: Houghton Mifflin Harcourt.

Rhoades, R.E. (1978) 'Foreign labor and German industrial capitalism, 1871–1978: the evolution of a migratory system', *American Ethnologist*, 5(3): 553–73.

Riccio, B. (2008) 'West African transnationalisms compared: Ghanaians and Senegalese in Italy', *Journal of Ethnic and Migration Studies*, 34(2): 217–34.

Rice, A.K., Hill, J.M.M., and Trist, E.L. (1950) 'The representation of labour turnover as a social process: studies in the social development of an industrial community', *Human Relations*, 3(4): 349–72.

Riedner, L. (2015) 'Justice for janitors? Marktbürgerschaft, Freizügigkeit und EU-Migrantinnen im Arbeitskampf. Einblicke in ein aktivistisches Forschungsprojekt', *Movements. Journal für kritische Migrations- und Grenzregimeforschung,* 1(2): 1–25.

Rigo, E. (2005) 'Citizenship at Europe's borders: some reflections on the post-colonial condition of Europe in the context of EU enlargement', *Citizenship Studies*, 9(1): 3–22.

Rinehart, J. (1999) 'The international motor vehicle program's lean production benchmark: A critique', *Monthly Review*, 50(8): 19–27.

Roca, B. and Martín-Díaz, E. (2017) 'Solidarity networks of Spanish migrants in the UK and Germany: the emergence of interstitial trade unionism', *Critical Sociology*, 43(7–8): 1197–212.

Rodriguez, N. (2004) ' "Workers Wanted" employer recruitment of immigrant labor', *Work and Occupations*, 31(4): 453–73.

Rodriguez, R.M. (2010) *Migrants for Export. How the Philippine State Brokers Labor to the World*, Minneapolis, MN: University of Minnesota Press.

Rodriguez, R.M. and Schwenken, H. (2013) 'Becoming a migrant at home: subjectivation processes in migrant-sending countries prior to departure', *Population, Space and Place*, 19(4): 375–88.

Roediger, D. (1991) *The Wages of Whiteness: Race and the Making of the American Working Class*, London: Verso.

Roediger, D.R. and Esch, E.D. (2012) *The Production of Difference: Race and the Management of Labor in US history*, Oxford: Oxford University Press.

Rogalewski, A. (2018) 'Organising and mobilising Central and Eastern European migrant women working in care', *Transfer: European Review of Labour and Research*, 24(4): 421–36.

Rogalewski, A. (2022) 'Trade unions challenges in organising Polish workers: a comparative case study of British and Swiss trade union strategies', *European Journal of Industrial Relations*, 28(4): 385–404.

Rogaly, B. (2009) 'Spaces of work and everyday life: labour geographies and the agency of unorganised temporary migrant workers', *Geography Compass*, 3(6): 1975–87.

Rogers, A. (2009) *Recession, Vulnerable Workers and Immigration: A Background Report*, Oxford: Centre on Migration, Policy and Society, University of Oxford.

Romens, A. (2022) *Deconstructing Essentialism. Migrant Women in Stratified Labour Markets*, Basingstoke: Palgrave Macmillan.

Roosblad, J. (2013) 'Trade unions and the representation of migrant and ethnic minority workers: challenges in deteriorating industrial relations', in A. van Heelsum and B. Garces-Mascarenas (eds) *Filling in Penninx's Heuristic Model*, Amsterdam: Amsterdam University Press, pp 35–49.

Rooth, T. (1993) *British Protectionism and the International Economy: Overseas Commercial Policy in the 1930s*, Cambridge: Cambridge University Press.

Roth, K.H. (1974) 'Le lotte operaie nella Germania Occidentale degli anni Sessanta', in A. Serafini (ed) *L'operaio multinazionale in Europa*, Milano: Feltrinelli, pp 109–48.

Ruhs, M. (2006a) *Greasing the Wheels of the Flexible Labour Market: East European Labour Immigration in the UK*, Working Paper 38, Oxford: Compas.

Ruhs, M. (2006b) 'The potential of temporary migration programmes in future international migration policy', *International Labour Review*, 145(1–2): 7–36.

Ruhs, M. (2013) *The Price of Rights*, Princeton: Princeton University Press.

Ruhs, M. and Martin, P. (2008) 'Numbers vs rights: trade-offs and guest worker programs', *International Migration Review*, 42(1): 249–65.

Ruhs, M. and Palme, J. (2018) 'Institutional contexts of political conflicts around free movement in the European Union: a theoretical analysis', *Journal of European Public Policy*, 25(10): 1481–500.

Ryan, L. (2008) '"I had a sister in England": family-led migration, social networks and Irish nurses', *Journal of Ethnic and Migration Studies*, 34(3): 453–70.

Ryan, L., Erel, U., and D'Angelo, A. (2015) 'Introduction understanding "Migrant Capital"', in L. Ryan, U. Erel, and A. D'Angelo (eds) *Migrant Capital: Networks, Identities and Strategies. Migration, Diasporas and Citizenship*, Basingstoke: Palgrave Macmillan, pp 3–17.

Rydzik, A. and Anitha, S. (2020) 'Conceptualising the agency of migrant women workers: resilience, reworking and resistance', *Work, Employment and Society*, 34(5): 883–99.

Sacchetto, D. and Vianello, F.A. (2015) Donne migranti e organizzazioni sindacali nella crisi, *Sociologia del lavoro* 140: 159–172.

Safa, H.I. (1981) 'Runaway shops and female employment: the search for cheap labor', *Signs: Journal of Women in Culture and Society*, 7(2): 418–33.

Salinas, C. (2018) *Managed Migrations: Growers, Farmworkers, and Border Enforcement in the Twentieth Century*, Austin, TX: University of Texas Press.

Salzinger, L. (2003) *Genders in Production: Making Workers in Mexico's Global Factories*, Berkeley, CA: University of California Press.

Samaluk, B. (2016) 'Migrant workers' engagement with labour market intermediaries in Europe: symbolic power guiding transnational exchange', *Work, Employment and Society*, 30(3): 455–71.

Sánchez, S. and Ravelo, P. (2010) 'Cultura obrera en las maquiladoras de Ciudad Juárez en tiempos catastróficos', *El Cotidiano*, 164: 19–25.

Sanders, J.M. and Nee, V. (1992) 'Problems in resolving the ethnic economy debate', *American Sociological Review*, 57(3): 415–18.

Sanders, J.M. and Nee, V. (1996) 'Immigrant self-employment: the family as social capital and the value of human capital', *American Sociological Review*, 61(2): 231–49.

Sanguinetti, A. (2016) 'Nuove migrazioni italiane in Germania. In fuga dalla crisi', *Mondi Migranti*, 3: 65–78.

Sanò, G. and Piro, V. (2017) 'Abitare (ne)i luoghi di lavoro: il caso dei braccianti rumeni nelle serre della provincia di Ragusa', *Sociologia del lavoro*, 146(2): 40–55.

Sargent, J. and Matthews, L. (2008) 'Capital intensity, technology intensity, and skill development in post China/WTO maquiladoras', *World Development*, 36(4): 541–59.

Sargent, J. and Matthews, L. (2009). China versus Mexico in the global EPZ industry: Maquiladoras, FDI quality, and plant mortality. *World Development*, 37(6): 1069–1082.

Sarkar, M. (ed) (2017) *Work out of Place*, Berlin: Walter de Gruyter.

Sassen, S. (1990) *The Mobility of Labor and Capital: A Study in International Investment and Labor Flow*, Cambridge: Cambridge University Press.

Sassen, S. (1996) *Losing Control? Sovereignty in the Age of Globalization*, New York: Columbia University Press.

Sayad, A. (2004) *The Suffering of the Immigrant*, Cambridge: Polity Press.

Scheel, S. (2013a) 'Autonomy of migration despite its securitisation? Facing the terms and conditions of biometric rebordering', *Millennium – Journal of International Studies*, 41(3): 575–600.

Scheel, S. (2013b) 'Studying embodied encounters: Autonomy of migration beyond its romanticization', *Postcolonial Studies*, 16(3): 279–88.

Schiek, D., Oliver, L., Forde, C., Alberti, G. (2015) *EU Social and Labour Rights and EU Internal Market Law*, Study for the EMPL Committee.

Schiller, N.G., Basch, L., and Blanc, C.S. (1995) 'From immigrant to transmigrant: Theorizing transnational migration', *Anthropological Quarterly*, 68(1): 48–63.

Schling, H. (2014) 'Gender, temporality, and the reproduction of labour power: women migrant workers in South China', *Sozial Geschichte Online* 14: 42–61.

Schmalz, S., Ludwig, C. and Webster, E. (2018) 'The power resources approach: developments and challenges', *Global Labour Journal*, 9(2): 113–34.

Schrover, M. (2018) 'Labour migration', in K. Hofmeester and M. van der Linden (eds) *Handbook: The Global History of Work*, Berlin: Oldenbourg De Gruyter, pp 433–68.

Schweitzer, R. (2015) 'A stratified right to family life? On the logic(s) and legitimacy of granting differential access to family reunification for third-country nationals living within the EU', *Journal of Ethnic and Migration Studies*, 41(13): 2130–48.

Scott, J.C. (1985) *Weapons of the Weak: Everyday Forms of Peasant Resistance*, New Haven, CT: Yale University Press.

Scott, J.W. (1988) *Gender and the Politics of History*, New York: Columbia University Press.

Scott, S. (2013) 'Labour, migration and the spatial fix: evidence from the UK food industry', *Antipode*, 45(5): 1090–109.

Seferiadis, A.A., Cummings, S., Zweekhorst, M.B., and Bunders, J.F. (2015) 'Producing social capital as a development strategy: implications at the micro-level', *Progress in Development Studies*, 15(2): 170–85.

Segato, R.L. (2008) 'La escritura en el cuerpo de las mujeres asesinadas en Ciudad Juárez: territorio, soberanía y crímenes de segundo estado', *Debate Feminista*, 37: 78–102.

Seifert, A.M. and Messing, K. (2006) 'Cleaning up after globalization: an ergonomic analysis of work activity of hotel cleaners', in L.L.M. Aguiar and A. Herod (eds) *The Dirty Work of Neoliberalism: Cleaners in the Global Economy*, Oxford: Blackwell, pp 129–49.

Selwyn, B. (2013) 'Social upgrading and labour in global production networks: a critique and an alternative conception', *Competition and Change*, 17(1): 75–90.

Seo, S. and Skelton, T. (2017) 'Regulatory migration regimes and the production of space: the case of Nepalese workers in South Korea', *Geoforum* 78: 159–68.

Serafini, A. (1974) 'L'operaio multinazionale in Europa', in A. Serafini (ed) *L'operaio multinazionale in Europa*, Milano: Feltrinelli, pp 9–17.

Sernett, M.C. (1997) *Bound for the Promised Land: African American Religion and the Great Black Migration*, Durham, NC: Duke University Press.

Shire, K. (2020) 'The social order of transnational migration markets', *Global Networks*, 20(3): 434–53.

Shor, F. (1992) 'Masculine power and virile syndicalism: a gendered analysis of the IWW in Australia', *Labour History*, 63: 83–99.

Silver, B.J. (2003) *Forces of Labor: Workers' Movements and Globalization since 1870*, Cambridge: Cambridge University Press.

Silverstein, P.A. (2005) 'Immigrant racialization and the new savage slot: race, migration, and immigration in the new Europe', *Annual Review of Anthropology*, 34: 363–84.

Simola, A. (2018) 'Lost in administration: (re)producing precarious citizenship for young highly skilled intra-EU migrants in Brussels', *Work, Employment and Society*, 32(3): 458–74.

Singa Boyenge, J.P. (2007) 'ILO database on export processing zones (Revised)', ILO Working Papers, International Labour Organization. Available at https://econpapers.repec.org/paper/iloilowps/993989593402676.htm. Accessed 1 September 2023.

Sivanandan, A. (1981) 'From resistance to rebellion: Asian and Afro-Caribbean struggles in Britain', *Race & Class*, XVIII(2/3): 111–51.

Sivanandan, A. (1990) *Communities of Resistance*, London: Verso Books.

Sklair, L. (1989) *Assembling for Development. The Maquila Industry in Mexico and the United States*, Boston, MA: Unwin Hyman.

Slichter, S. (1919) *The Turnover of Factory Labor*, New York: Appleton.

Smith, B.E. and Winders, J. (2008) ' "We're here to stay": economic restructuring, Latino migration and place-making in the US South', *Transactions of the Institute of British Geographers*, 33(1): 60–72.

Smith, B.E. and Winders, J. (2015) 'Whose lives, which work?: Class discrepancies in life's work', in K. Meehan and K. Strauss (eds) *Precarious Worlds: Contested Geographies of Social Reproduction*, Athens, GA: University of Georgia Press, pp 101–17.

Smith, C. (2003) 'Living at work: Management control and the dormitory labor system in China', *Asia Pacific Journal of Management*, 20(3): 333–58.

Smith, C. (2006) 'The double indeterminacy of labour power: labour effort and labour mobility', *Work, Employment and Society*, 20(2): 389–402.

Smith, C. (2010) 'Go with the flow: Labour power mobility and labour process theory', in P. Thompson and C. Smith (eds) *Working Life: Renewing Labour Process Analysis*, Basingstoke: Palgrave Macmillan, pp 269–96.

Smith, C. (2015) 'Continuity and change in labor process analysis forty years after labor and monopoly capita', *Labor Studies Journal*, 40(3): 222–42.

Smith, C. and Meiksins, P. (1995) 'System, society and dominance effects in cross-national organisational analysis', *Work Employment and Society*, 2(9): 241–67.

Smith, C. and Chan, J. (2015) 'Working for two bosses: student interns as constrained labour in China', *Human Relations*, 68(2): 305–26.

Smith, C. and Pun, N. (2018) 'Class and precarity: an unhappy coupling in the case of China's working class', *Work, Employment and Society*, 32(3): 599–615.

Smith, C., Daskalaki, M., Elger, T., and Brown, D. (2004) 'Labour turnover and management retention strategies in new manufacturing plants', *The International Journal of Human Resource Management*, 15(2): 371–96.

Smyth, R., Qian, X., Nielsen, I., and Kaempfer, I. (2013) 'Working hours in supply chain Chinese and Thai factories: evidence from the Fair Labor Association's "Soccer Project"', *British Journal of Industrial Relations*, 51(2): 382–408.

Sporton, D. (2013) '"They control my life": the role of local recruitment agencies in East European migration to the UK', *Population, Space and Place*, 19(5): 443–58.

Stalker, P. (2000) *Workers Without Frontiers: the Impact of Globalization on International Migration*, Geneva: International Labour Organization.

Stan, S. and Erne, R. (2016) 'Is migration from Central and Eastern Europe an opportunity for trade unions to demand higher wages? Evidence from the Romanian health sector', *European Journal of Industrial Relations*, 22(2): 167–83.

Statista (2023) Migrant Workers in China-statistics and facts Published by C. Textor, 9 June 2023. Available at https://www.statista.com/topics/1540/migrant-workers-in-china/#topicOverview. Accessed 30 August 2023.

Steinfeld, R.J. and Engerman, S.L. (1997) 'Labor – free or coerced? A historical reassessment of differences and similarities', in T. Brass and M. van der Linden (eds) *Free and Unfree Labour: The Debate Continues*, Bern: Peter Lang AG, pp 107–26.

Stewart, P., McBride, J., Greenwood, J., Stirling, J., Holgate, J., Tattersall, A., Stephenson, C. and Wray, D. (2009) 'Introduction', in J. McBride and I. Greenwood (eds) *Community Unionism*, Chippenham and Eastbourne: Palgrave Macmillan, pp 3–20.

Strauss, K. and Meehan, K. (2015) 'Introduction: new frontiers in life's work', in K. Meehan and K. Strauss (eds) *Precarious Worlds: Contested Geographies of Social Reproduction*, Athens, GA: University of Georgia Press, pp 1–24.

Strauss, K. and McGrath, S. (2017) 'Temporary migration, precarious employment and unfree labour relations: exploring the "continuum of exploitation" in Canada's Temporary Foreign Worker Program', *Geoforum*, 78: 199–208.

Streeck, W. (1992) *Social Institutions and Economic Performance: Studies of Industrial Relations in Advanced Capitalist Economies*, Newbury Park, CA: Sage.

Sun, S.H. (1987) 'Women, work and theology in Korea', *Journal of Feminist Studies in Religion*, 3(2): 125–34.

Swain, N. (2011) 'A post-socialist capitalism', *Europe-Asia Studies*, 63(9): 1671–95.

Swyngedouw, E. (1992) 'Territorial organization and the space/technology nexus', *Transactions of the Institute of British Geographers*, 17(4): 417–33.

Tagliacozzo, S., Pisacane, L., and Kilkey, M. (2021), 'The interplay between structural and systemic vulnerability during the COVID-19 pandemic: migrant agricultural workers in informal settlements in Southern Italy', *Journal of Ethnic and Migration Studies*, 47(9): 1903–21.

Tapia, M. (2013) 'Marching to different tunes: commitment and culture as mobilizing mechanisms of trade unions and community organizations', *British Journal of Industrial Relations*, 51(4): 666–88.

Tapia, M. and Turner, L. (2013) 'Union campaigns as countermovements: mobilizing immigrant workers in France and the United Kingdom', *British Journal of Industrial Relations*, 51(3): 601–22.

Tapia, M. and Alberti, G. (2019) 'Unpacking the category of migrant workers in trade union research: a multi-level approach to migrant intersectionalities', *Work, Employment and Society*, 33(2): 314–25.

Tarrius A. (1992) *Les fourmis d'Europe*, Paris: L'Harmattan.

Tattersall, A. (2018) 'How do we build power in coalition? Rethinking union-community coalition types 12 years on', *Labour & Industry: A Journal of the Social and Economic Relations of Work*, 28(1): 68–81.

Taylor, R. (2017) 'The interregnum: 11 years without free movement from 1962 to 1973', London School of Economics, [online] 25 May, Available from: https://blogs.lse.ac.uk/brexit/2017/05/25/the-interreg num-11-years-without-free-movement-from-1962-to-1973/. Accessed 2 May 2020.

Taylor, M. and Rioux, S. (2018) *Global Labour Studies*, Malen, MA: Polity.

Taylor, P. and Bain, P. (1999) '"An assembly line in the head": work and employee relations in the call centre', *Industrial Relations Journal*, 30(2): 101–17.

Teague, P. and Donaghey, J. (2018) 'Brexit: EU social policy and the UK employment model', *Industrial Relations Journal*, 49(5–6): 512–33.

Teeple Hopkins, C. (2017) 'Mostly work, little pay: social reproduction, migration and paid domestic work in Montreal', in T. Bhattacharya (ed) *Social Reproduction Theory: Remapping Class, Recentering Oppression*, London: Pluto Press, pp 131–47.

Tejani, S. (2011) 'The gender dimension of special economic zones', in T. Farole and G. Akinci (eds) *Special Economic Zones: Progress, Emerging Challenges, and Future Directions*, Washington, DC: The International Bank for Reconstruction and Development/The World Bank, pp 247–81.

The Tribune (2020) '4 crore migrant workers in India; 75 lakh return home so far: MHA', The Tribune (India), [online] 23 May, Available from: https://www.tribuneindia.com/news/nation/4-crore-migrant-workers-in-india-75-lakh-return-home-so-far-mha-88940. Accessed 14 January 2021.

Thelen, K.A. (2004) *How Institutions Evolve: The Political Economy of Skills in Germany, Britain, the United States, and Japan*, Cambridge: Cambridge University Press.

Thelen, K. (2014) *Varieties of Liberalization and the New Politics of Social Solidarity*, Cambridge: Cambridge University Press.

Theodossiou, I. (2002) 'Factors affecting the job-to-joblessness turnover and gender', *Labour*, 16(4): 729–46.

Theunissen, A., Zanoni, P., and Van Laer, K. (2022) 'Fragmented capital and (the loss of) control over posted workers: a case study in the Belgian meat industry', *Work, Employment and Society*, 37(4): 934–51.

Thomas, A. (2020) 'Cross-border labour markets and the role of trade unions in representing migrant workers' interests', *Journal of Industrial Relations*, 62(2): 235–55.

Thompson, E.P. (1963) *The Making of the English Working Class*, New York: Vintage.

Thompson, E.P. (1967) 'Time, work-discipline, and industrial capitalism', *Past and Present*, 38(1): 56–97.

Thompson, P. and Smith, C. (2001) 'Follow the redbrick road: reflections on pathways in and out of the labour process debate', *International Studies of Management and Organization*, 30(4): 40–67.

Thompson, P., Newsome, K., and Commander, J. (2013) ' "Good when they want to be": migrant workers in the supermarket supply chain', *Human Resource Management Journal*, 23(2): 129–43.

Thompson, P., Parker, R., and Cox, S. (2015) 'Labour and asymmetric power relations in global value chains: the digital entertainment industries and beyond', in K. Newsome, P. Taylor, and A. Rainnie (eds) *'Putting Labour in its Place': Labour Process Analysis and Global Value Chains*, London and New York: Palgrave Macmillan, pp 45–63.

Tiano, S. (1984) *Maquiladoras, Women's Work, and Unemployment in Northern Mexico* (No. 43), East Lansing, MI: Michigan State University.

Tilly, C. and Tilly C. (1998) *Work under Capitalism*, Boulder, CO: Westview Press.

Tören, T. (2018) *Documentation Report: Syrian Refugees in the Turkish Labour Market*, Working Paper No. 22, Kassel University Press.

Tosh, J. (2005) *Manliness and Masculinities in Nineteenth Century Britain*. Essays on Gender, *Family and Empire*, Harlow: Pearson Longman.

Towers, I., Duxbury, L., and Higgins, C. (2006) 'Time thieves and space invaders: technology, work, and organization', *Journal of Organizational Change Management*, 19(5): 593–618.

Trades Union Congress (2008) *Hard Work, Hidden Lives: The Short Report of the Commission on Vulnerable Employment*, Commission on Vulnerable Employment, [online], Available from: https://www.tuc.org.uk/online-shop/products/hard-work-hidden-lives. Accessed December 2013.

Trade Union Congress (2019) 'TUC submission to Migration Advisory Committee on points based system and salary thresholds', TUC, [online] 5 November, Available from: https://www.tuc.org.uk/research-analysis/reports/tuc-submission-migration-advisory-committee-points-based-system-and. Accessed December 2019.

Trappmann, V., Bessa, I., Joyce, S., Neumann, D., Stuart, M., and Umney, C. (2020) 'Global labour unrest on platforms', in *The Case of Food Delivery Workers,* Berlin: FES.

Tsing, A. (2009) 'Supply chains and the human condition', *Rethinking Marxism,* 21(2): 148–76.

Tsujimoto, T. (2016) 'Affective friendship that constructs globally spanning transnationalism: the onward migration of Filipino workers from South Korea to Canada', *Mobilities,* 11(2): 323–41.

Tsurumi, E.P. (1992) *Factory Girls: Women in the Thread Mills of Meiji Japan,* Princeton: Princeton University Press.

Turner, L. (2011) 'A future for the labor movement?', in G. Gall, R. Hurd, and A. Wilkinson (eds) *International Handbook on Labour Unions: Responses to Neo-Liberalism,* Northampton, MA: Edward Elgar, pp 311–28.

Tyner, J.A. (1998) 'Asian labor recruitment and the world wide web', *Professional Geographer,* 50(3): 331–44.

Tyner, J.A. (2002) 'Global cities and circuits of global labor: the case of Manila, Philippines', in F. Aguilar (ed) *Filipinos in Global Migrations: At Home in the World,* Quezon City, Philipines: Migration Research Network, and the Philippine Social Science Council, pp 60–85.

Ulman, L. (1965) 'Labor mobility and the industrial wage structure in the postwar United States', *The Quarterly Journal of Economics,* 79(1): 73–97.

UNCTAD (2019) *World Investment Report 2019. Special Economic Zones.* New York: UNCTAD.

Underthun, A. (2014). Stretching liminal spaces of work?: temporality, displacement and precariousness among transient hotel workers. In *A Hospitable World?*, Routledge, pp 27–38.

Underthun, A. and Jordhus-Lier, D.C. (2018) 'Liminality at work in Norwegian hotels', *Tourism Geographies,* 20(1): 11–28.

Ustubici, A. (2009) *Export-processing Zones and Gendering the Resistance: 'Women's Strike' in Antalya Free Zone in Turkey,* London: London School of Economics, Gender Institute.

Vandaele, K. (2018) *Will Trade Unions Survive in the Platform Economy? Emerging Patterns of Platform Workers' Collective Voice and Representation in Europe,* European Trade Union Institute for Research, Working Paper 2018.05.

van der Linden, M. (2008) *Workers of the World: Essays toward a Global Labor History,* Leiden: Brill.

van Doorn, N., Ferrari, F., and Graham, M. (2022) 'Migration and migrant labour in the gig economy: An intervention', *Work, Employment and Society,* 37(4): 1099–111.

van Rossum, M. (2018) 'Desertion', in K. Hofmeester and M. van der Linden (eds) *Handbook Global History of Work,* Berlin: Walter de Gruyter, pp 505–520.

van Rossum, M. and Kamp, J. (2016) (eds) *Desertion in the Early Modern World: A Comparative History*, London: Bloomsbury Publishing.

Varia, N. (2011) '"Sweeping changes?" A review of recent reforms on protections for migrant domestic workers in Asia and the Middle East', *Canadian Journal of Women and the Law*, 23(1): 265–87.

Vertovec, S. (2002) *Transnational Networks and Skilled Labour Migration*, Oxford: University of Oxford, Transnational Communities Programme.

Vertovec, S. (2009) *Transnationalism*, London: Routledge.

Vianello, F.A. (2009) *Migrando sole. Legami transnazionali tra Ucraina e Italia*, Milano: Angeli.

Vianello, F.A. (2014) 'Ukrainian migrant workers in Italy: coping with and reacting to downward mobility', *Central and Eastern European Migration Review*, 3(1): 85–98.

Vickers, T. (2020) *Borders, Migration and Class in an Age of Crisis: Producing Workers and Immigrants*, Bristol: Bristol University Press.

Virdee, S. (2014) *Racism, Class and the Racialized Outsider*, London: Bloomsbury Publishing.

Vosko, L.F. (ed) (2006) *Precarious Employment: Understanding Labour Market Insecurity in Canada*, Montreal: McGill-Queen's Press.

Vosko, L.F. (2010) *Managing the Margins: Gender, citizenship and the international regulation of precarious employment*, Oxford: Oxford University Press.

Wadauer, S., Buchner, T., and Mejstrik, A. (2012) 'The making of public labour intermediation: job search, job placement, and the state in Europe, 1880–1940', *International Review of Social History*, 57(S20): 161–89.

Wadsworth, J. (2017) *Immigration and the UK Economy*, General Election 2017 Economists Series, London: London School of Economics, Centre for Economic Performance.

Wagner, I. (2018) *Workers without Borders: Posted Work and Precarity in the EU*, Ithaca, NY: ILR Press.

Wagner, I. and Lillie, N. (2015) 'Subcontracting, insecurity and posted work: evidence from construction, meat processing and ship building', in J. Drahokoupil (ed) *The Outsourcing Challenge: Organizing Workers Across Fragmented Production Networks*, Brussels: ETUI, pp 157–74.

Waldinger, R. and Lichter, M.I. (2003) *How the Other Half Works: Immigration and the Social Organization of Labor*, Oakland: University of California Press.

Wang, B. and Gao, K. (2019) 'Forty years development of China's outward foreign direct investment: retrospect and the challenges ahead', *China and World Economy*, 27(3): 1–24.

Wang, F.L. (2004) 'Reformed migration control and new targeted people: China's hukou system in the 2000s', *The China Quarterly*, 177: 115–32.

Wang, X.R., Hui, E.C.M., Choguill, C., and Jia, S.H. (2015) 'The new urbanization policy in China: Which way forward?', *Habitat International*, 47: 279–84.

Ward, K. (2004) 'Going global? Internationalization and diversification in the temporary staffing industry', *Journal of Economic Geography*, 4(3): 251–73.

Weber, M. (1924) *Gesammelte Aufsätze zur Sozial- und Wirtschaftsgeschichte*, Tübingen: JCB Mohr.

Weghmann, V. (2022) 'Theorising practice: independent trade unions in the UK', *Work in the Global Economy*, 2(1): 132–47.

Wickramasekara, P. and Baruah, N. (2017) 'Fair recruitment for low-skilled migrant workers: issues and challenges', in ADBI, OECD, and ILO (eds) *Safeguarding the Rights of Asian Migrant Workers from Home to the Workplace*. Tokyo: Asian Development Bank Institute, the Organisation for Economic Co-operation and Development, and the International Labour Organisation, pp 23–38.

Wierzbicki, S. (2004) *Beyond the Immigrant Enclave: Network Change and Assimilation*, New York: LFB Scholarly Publishing.

Williams, E. and Passe-Smith, J. (1989) *Turnover and Recruitment in the Maquiladora Industry: Causes and Solutions*, Borderlands Research Monograph Series, No. 5, Las Cruces, NM: Joint Border Research Institute, New Mexico State University.

Wills, J. and Simms, M. (2004) 'Building reciprocal community unionism in the UK', *Capital & Class*, 28(1): 59–84.

Wills, J., Datta, K., Evans, Y., Herbert, J., May, J., and McIllwaine, C. (2009) *Global Cities at Work: New Migrant Division of Labour*, London: Pluto Press.

Wilson, K.L. and Portes, A. (1980) 'Immigrant enclaves: an analysis of the labor market experiences of Cubans in Miami', *American Journal of Sociology*, 86(2): 295–319.

Wimmer, A. and Glick-Schiller, N. (2003) 'Methodological nationalism, the social sciences, and the study of migration: an essay in historical epistemology', *International Migration Review*, 37(3): 576–610.

Winterton, J. (2004) 'A conceptual model of labour turnover and retention', *Human Resource Development International*, 7(3): 371–90.

Withers, C. (1991) 'Class, culture and migrant identity', in G. Keam and C. Withers (eds) *Urbanizing Britain. Essay on Class and Community in the Nineteenth Century*, Cambridge: Cambridge University Press, pp 55–79.

Wolkowitz, C. and Wahrhurst, C. (2010) 'Embodied labour', in P. Thompson, and C. Smith (eds) *Working Life: Renewing Labour Process Analysis*, Basingstoke: Palgrave MacMillan, pp 223–43.

Wong, D. (2006) 'The recruitment of foreign labour in Malaysia: from migration system to guest worker regime', in A. Kaur, and I. Metcalfe (eds) *Mobility, Labour Migration and Border Controls in Asia*, London: Palgrave Macmillan, pp 213–27.

Wood, A.J. and Lehdonvirta, V. (2021) 'Antagonism beyond employment: how the "subordinated agency" of labour platforms generates conflict in the remote gig economy', *Socio-Economic Review*, 19(4): 1369–96.

Woodward, P.N. (1988) *Oil and Labor in the Middle East*, New York: Praeger.

Woolfson, C., Fudge, J., and Thörnqvist, C. (2014) 'Migrant precarity and future challenges to labour standards in Sweden', *Economic and Industrial Democracy*, 35(4): 695–715.

Woolfson, C., Tho¨rnqvist, C., and Sommers, J. (2010) 'The Swedish model and the future of labour standards after Laval', *Industrial Relations Journal*, 41(4): 333–50.

World Bank Industry Development Division (1992) *Export Processing Zone*, Washington: The World Bank.

Wrench, J. (2004) 'Trade union responses to immigrants and ethnic inequality in Denmark and the UK: the context of consensus and conflict', *European Journal of Industrial Relations*, 10(1): 7–30.

Wright, C.F. (2012) 'Immigration policy and market institutions in liberal market economies', *Industrial Relations Journal*, 43(2): 110–36.

Wright, E.O. (2000) 'Working-class power, capitalist-class interests, and class compromise', *American Journal of Sociology*, 105(4): 957–1002.

Wright, M. (2006) *Disposable Women and Other Myths of Global Capitalism*, London: Routledge.

Wright, M.W. (2014) 'The gender, place and culture Jan Monk Distinguished Annual Lecture: gentrification, assassination and forgetting in Mexico: a feminist Marxist tale', *Gender, Place & Culture*, 21(1): 1–16.

Wright, S. (2002) *Storming Heavens: Class Composition and Struggle in Italian Autonomist Marxism,* London: Pluto Press.

Xiang, B. (2007) *Global 'Body Shopping': An Indian Labor System in the Information Technology Industry*, Princeton, NJ: Princeton University Press.

Xiang, B. (2012) 'Labor transplant: "Point-to-point" transnational labor migration in East Asia', *South Atlantic Quarterly*, 111(4): 721–41.

Xiang, B. (2020) 'The gyroscope-like economy: hypermobility, structural imbalance and pandemic governance in China', *Inter-Asia Cultural Studies*, 21(4): 521–32.

Xiang, B. and Lindquist, J. (2014) 'Migration infrastructure', *International Migration Review*, 48(supplement 1): 122–48.

Xue, H. (2008) 'Local strategies of labor control: a case study of three electronics factories in China', *International Labor and Working-Class History*, 73(1): 85–103.

Yea, S. and Chok, S. (2018) 'Unfreedom unbound: developing a cumulative approach to understanding unfree labour in Singapore', *Work, Employment and Society*, 32(5): 925–41.

Yeates, N. (2004) 'Global care chains', *International Feminist Journal of Politics*, 6(3): 369–91.

Yeo, C., Sigona, N., and Godin, M. (2022) *Parallels and Differences Between Ending Commonwealth and EU Citizen Free Movement*, Eurochildren Research Brief Series No. 4, [online] 3 May, Available from: https://ukandeu.ac.uk/partner-reports/parallels-and-differences-between-ending-commonwealth-and-eu-citizen-free-movement-rights/

Yuval-Davis, N. (2006) 'Intersectionality and feminist politics', *European Journal of Women's Studies*, 13(3): 193–209.

Yuval-Davis, N. (2013) *A Situated Intersectional Everyday Approach to the Study of Bordering*, Euroborderscapes Working Paper No. 2, European Commission.

Yuval-Davis, N., Wemyss, G., and Cassidy, K. (2019) *Bordering*, Cambridge: Polity Press.

Zatlin, J.R. (2007) 'Scarcity and resentment: economic sources of xenophobia in the GDR, 1971–1989', *Central European History*, 40(4): 683–720.

Zechner, M. and Hansen, B.R. (2015) 'Building power in a crisis of social reproduction', *Roar Magazine*, 1(0): 132–51.

Zontini, E. (2010) *Transnational Families, Migration and Gender: Moroccan and Filipino Women in Bologna and Barcelona*, New York: Berghahn Books.

Index

266

women, treatment of in 99–101, 102, 103
See also Enclaves of Differentiated
  Labour (EDL)

F

Faist, T. 128, 208n7
Fakiolas, R. 202n3
families
  bans on 124
  migration of 2, 125, 126, 133
  turnover and 141–3
  See also networks, migrant
FDIs *See* foreign direct investments (FDIs)
Federici, Silvia 121, 131
females *See* women
feminicidios (femicides) 101
FIFA World Cup (2022) 53, 204n3
Findlay, A. 35
Fishback, P.V. 157, 162
fly-in/fly-out (FI-FO) labour regimes 142–3
  See also regimes, migrant labour
Ford, Henry 115, 116, 117
Forde, C. 35, 75, 106
Forde, Michele 169
Ford Motor Company 5, 115–16, 117
foreign direct investments (FDIs) 9, 87, 100,
  103, 207n1
foundational mobility *See*
  mobility, foundational
Foxconn plant 83, 85, 105–6, 143, 187, 207n2
Franceschini, Ivan 141
Frank, Dana 160
Frankel, E. 22, 23–4
free zones *See* zones
'From Slavery to Wage Labour'
  (Moulier-Boutang) 57
Fudge, J. 16

G

Gambino, Ferruccio 140
gangmasters 65, 73, 74, 76, **81**, 198
Gastarbeiter system 70, 78, **81**, 124, 137,
  148–9, 197
gender
  -based employment 54–5
  dormitory labour regimes and 137, 138
  equal pay 33
  social networks 79–80
  See also women
genderization 94–5, 99–101, 103, 161
  See also social reproduction
Germany
  Gastarbeiter system 70, 78, **81**, 124,
    148–9, 197
  strikes 148–50
Glick Schiller, 10, 11, 61
global commodity (value) chains
  (GVCs) 85, 87
globalization 57, 61, 67, 89, 91, 129

global production networks (GPNs) 85, 87
Global Union Federation
  (GUF) 169, 210n17
Goldín, L.R. 135, 194
Gordon, Jennifer 170, 193, 213n13
Goss, J. 77
governance *See* states
governments *See* states
GPNs *See* global production networks (GPNs)
Granovetter, M. 154
Grappi, Giorgio 177
Gray, N. 49
Great Britain 8
Greer, I. 212n10
Groutsis, D. 74
Guatemala 135, 145
guest worker regimes 71, **81**, 82, 124, 125–6,
  146, 148–50, 164, 197, 205n22
  See also regimes, migrant labour
GUF *See* Global Union Federation (GUF)
Gulf *See* Persian Gulf
Gulf Cooperation Council (GCC) 53–4, 58,
  204n2, 206n30, 206n33
Gumbrell-McCormick, R. 211n19
Gutman, H.G. 158–9
GVCs *See* global commodity (value) chains
  (GVCs)

H

Hardt, M. 43
Harvey, D. 9, 201n11
Hernández-León, R. 77
hierarchization 7, 69–70, 89, 94–5, 118,
  121, 149
Hill, H. 159
Hirschman, A.O. 1, 37–8, 44, 65, 203n9
Hoang, L.A. 79
Hom, P.W. 26
homo economicus 35, 128
Hondagneu-Sotelo, P. 79
Hong Kong 169, 174–5
Hopkins, B. 154
HRM *See* human resource management (HRM)
hukou (residence system) 69, 84, 138
human resource management (HRM) 23,
  26, 157
Hyman, R. 211n19

I

ILO *See* International Labour Organization
  (ILO)
Imboden, N. 33
indentured labour
  as migrant labour regime 54, 55, 57, 68–9,
    73, **81**
  power and 7–8, 14, 201n9, 205n14–15
India
  IT workers from 65
  return migrations, forced 2

Printed and bound by CPI Group (UK) Ltd, Croydon, CR0 4YY

24/04/2025

14661357-0001